THE DAWNING OF THE APOCALYPSE

THE DAWNING of THE APOCALYPSE

the roots of slavery, white supremacy, settler colonialism, and capitalism in the long sixteenth century

 GERALD HORNE

MONTHLY REVIEW PRESS
New York

Library of Congress Cataloging-in-Publication Data
available from the publisher

ISBN 978-1-58367-872-5 pbk
ISBN 978-1-58367-873-2 cloth

Typeset in Eldorado

Monthly Review Press, New York
monthlyreview.org

5 4 3 2 1

Contents

Introduction

It should not have been deemed surprising when in 1977 Washington's ambassador to the United Nations—Andrew Young, a former chief aide to Dr. Martin Luther King, Jr.— asserted audaciously that London "invented" racism. Instead, the pastor-cum-diplomat was pelted ferociously in a hailstorm of invective,[1] as he backpedaled rapidly. Actually, London had a point it did not articulate: if anything, its bastard offspring in Washington, in the government the envoy represented, was probably more culpable for the continuation of this pestilence,[2] as it lurched into incipient being in the 1580s in what is now North Carolina and gravitated toward a model of development that diverged from those spurred by the Ottomans and Madrid, then rebelled in 1776 to ensure this putridness would endure.[3] How and why this deadly process unfolded in its earliest stage rests near the heart of this book.

Still, Ambassador Young, an ordained Protestant minister, would have better served historical understanding (besides providing useful instruction to predominantly Protestant London) if he had reflected on the point that the rise of this once dissident and besieged sect in the North American settlements led to the supplanting of religion as an animating factor of society with "race,"[4] a major theme to be explored in the pages that follow.[5] Certainly "whiteness"—effectively, Pan-Europeanism—provided a broader base for colonialism than even the Catholicism that drove Madrid. Historian Donald Matthews has observed that white supremacy in any case—a ruling ethos in London's settlements, then the North American Republic— had a religious cast, indicative of its tangled roots, with lynchings of Negroes emerging as a kind of sacrament.[6]

Ambassador Young would also have better served understanding if he had had the foresight to reflect the penetrating view of the eminent scholar Geraldine Heng, who has argued that at least by the thirteenth century, England had become "The First Racial State in the West," referring to the pervasive anti-Judaism that then prevailed. And just as it became easier to impose an expansionist foreign policy that propelled colonialism, given the experience with the Crusades, likewise it became easier to impose the racism that underpinned settler colonialism and slavery, once anti-Judaism became official policy in London. As U.S. Negroes were to be treated, the Jewish community in England was said to emit a "special fetid stench," while bearing "horns and tails" and engaging in "cannibalism." Religion was deployed "socio-culturally" and "bio-politically" to "racialize a human group" in England in a manner eerily similar to what was to unfold in North America. Certainly, there are differences that distinguish anti-Judaism from anti-Negro bias. The persecuted in England were "unable to own land in agricultural Europe," but in response, "Jews famously established themselves as financiers," a status generally unavailable to Negroes, though the ban on landowning was. Interestingly, though this murderous bigotry is understandably associated with Madrid, which dramatically expelled the Jewish community in the hinge year that was 1492, it was London that was the first European country to "stigmatize Jews" as "criminals"—another parallel to U.S. Negroes—and the "first to administer the badge" this community was forced to wear. England was the first to initiate "state-sponsored efforts at conversion" and, more to the point vis-à-vis Spain: "the first to expel Jews from its national territory." Then it was the prevailing religion, says Heng, that "supplied the theory

and the state and populace supplied the praxis" of bigotry, analogous
to the deployment of the "Curse of Ham" and racism targeting U.S.
Negroes. Fear of "interracial sexual relations" was then the praxis in
London, just like it was subsequently in Washington.[7] Ironically and
perversely, London's earlier bigotry positioned England to capitalize upon Madrid's later version, by appealing to Sephardim and the
Jewish community more broadly that had been perniciously targeted
by the Spanish Inquisition.

THIS IS A BOOK ABOUT the predicates of the rise of England,
moving from the periphery to the center (and inferentially, this is a
story about their revolting spawn in North America post-1776). This
is also a book about the seeds of the apocalypse, which led to the
foregoing—slavery, white supremacy, and settler colonialism (and
the precursors of capitalism)—planted in the long sixteenth century
(roughly 1492 to 1607),[8] which eventuated in what is euphemistically termed "modernity," a process that reached its apogee in North
America, the essential locus of this work. In these pages I seek to
explain the global forces that created this catastrophe—notably for
Africans and the indigenous of the Americas—and how the minor
European archipelago on the fringes of the continent (the British
isles) was poised to come from behind, surge ahead, and maneuver adeptly in the potent slipstream created by Spain, Portugal, the
Ottomans, even the Dutch and the French, as this long century
lurched to a turning point in Jamestown. Although, as noted, I posit
that 1492 is the hinge moment in the rise of Western Europe, I also
argue in these pages that it is important to sketch the years before this
turning point, especially since it was 1453—the Ottoman Turks seizing Constantinople (today's Istanbul)—that played a critical role in
spurring Columbus's voyage and, of course, there were other trends
that led to 1453, and so on, as we march backward in time.[9]

In brief, and as shall be outlined, the Ottomans enslaved Africans
and Europeans, among others, as contemporary Albania and Bosnia
suggest. The Spanish, the other sixteenth-century titan, created an
escape hatch by spurring the creation of a "Free African" population,

which could be armed. Moreover, for 150 years until the late seventeenth century, thousands of Filipinos were enslaved by Spaniards in Mexico,[10] suggesting an alternative to a bonded labor force comprised of Africans or even indigenes. That is, the substantial reliance on enslaved African labor in North America honed by London was hardly inevitable.

Florida's first slaves came from southern Spain, though admittedly an African population existed in that part of Europe and wound up in North America. Yet at this early juncture, sixteenth-century Spanish law and custom afforded the enslaved rights not systematically enjoyed in what was to become Dixie. Moreover, Spain's shortage of soldiers and laborers, exacerbated by a fanatical Catholicism that often barred other Europeans under the guise of religiosity—a gambit London did not indulge to the same extent—provided Africans with leverage.[11]

However, as time passed, it was London's model, then accelerated by Washington, that prevailed,: focusing enslavement tightly on Africans and those of even partial African ancestry, then seeking to expel "Free Negroes" to Sierra Leone and Liberia. London and Washington created a broader base for settler colonialism by way of a "white" population, based in the first instance on once warring, then migrant English, Irish, Scots, and Welsh; then expanding to include other European immigrants mobilized to confront the immense challenge delivered by rambunctious and rebellious indigenous Americans and enslaved Africans. This approach over time also allowed Washington to have allies in important nations and even colonies, providing enormous political leverage.[12]

This approach also had the added "advantage" of dulling class antagonism among settlers, who, perhaps understandably, were concerned less about the cutthroat competition delivered by an enslaved labor force and more with the real prospect of having their throats cut in the middle of the night by those very same slaves. Among the diverse settlers—Protestant and Jewish; English and Irish et al.—there was a perverse mitosis at play as these fragments cohered into a formidable whole of "whiteness," then white supremacy, which involved class collaboration of the rankest sort between and among the wealthy and those not so endowed.

In a sense, as the Ottomans pressed westward, Madrid and Lisbon began to cross the Atlantic as a countermove by way of retreat or even as a way to gain leverage.[13] But with the "discovery" of the Americas, leading to the ravages of the African slave trade, the Iberians, especially Spain, accumulated sufficient wealth and resources to confront their Islamic foes more effectively. [14]

The toxicity of settler colonialism combined with white supremacy not only dulled class antagonism in the colonies. It also solved a domestic problem with the exporting of real and imagined dissidents. In 1549 England was rocked to its foundations by "Kett's Revolt," where land was at issue and warehouses were put to the torch and harbors destroyed. A result of this disorienting upheaval, according to one analysis, was to convince the yeomanry to ally with the gentry,[15] a class collaborationist ethos then exported to the settlements. Assuredly, this rebellion shook England to its foundations, forcing the ruling elite to consider alternatives to the status quo, facilitating the thrust across the Atlantic. It is evident that land enclosure in England was tumultuous, making land three times more profitable, as it created disaster for the poorest, providing an incentive for them to try their luck abroad. A plot of land that once employed one or two hundred persons would—after enclosure—serve only the owner and a few shepherds.[16]

This vociferation was unbridled as the unsustainability of the status quo became conspicuous. Palace intrigue, a dizzying array of wars, with allies becoming enemies in a blink of an eye, the sapping spread of diseases, mass death as a veritable norm, bloodthirstiness as a way of life—all this and worse became habitual. This convinced many that taking a gamble on pioneering in the Americas was the "least bad" alternative to the status quo. Indeed, the discrediting of the status quo that was feudalism provided favorable conditions for the rise of a new system: capitalism.

As I write in 2019, there is much discussion about the purported 400th anniversary of the arrival of Africans in what is now the United

States, though Africans enslaved and otherwise were present in northern Florida as early as 1565 or the area due north as early as 1526. As the following paragraphs suggest, this 1619 date is notional at best or, alternatively, seeks to understand the man without understanding the child. In my book on the seventeenth century, noted above, I wrote of the mass enslavement and genocidal impulse that ravaged Africans and indigenous Americans. That book detailed the arrival in full force of the apocalypse; the one at hand limns the precursor: the dawning of this annihilation. The sixteenth century meant the takeoff of the apocalypse, while the following century embodied the boost phase. In brief, this apocalypse spelled the devastation of multiple continents: the Americas, Australia,[17] and Africa not least, all for the ultimate benefit of a relatively tiny elite in London, then Washington.

Thus, for reasons that become clearer below, the enslavement of Africans got off to a relatively "slow" start. From 1501 to 1650, a period during which Portuguese elites, at least until about 1620, and then their Dutch peers, held a dominant position in delivering transatlantic imports of captives: 726,000 Africans were dragged to the Americas, essentially to Spanish settlements and Brazil. By way of contrast, from 1650 to 1775, during London's and Paris's ascendancy and the concomitant accelerated development of sugar and tobacco, about 4.8 million Africans were brought to the Americas. Then, for the next century or so, until 1866, almost 5.1 million manacled Africans were brought to the region, at a time when the republicans in North America played a preeminent role in this dirty business. Similarly, at the time of the European invasion of the Americas, there were many millions of inhabitants of these continents, but between 1520 and 1620 the Aztecs and Incas, two of the major indigenous groupings, lost about 90 percent of their populations. In short, the late seventeenth century marked the ascendancy of the apocalypse, and the late sixteenth century marked the time when apocalypse was approaching in seven-league boots.[18] Yet the holocaust did not conclude in the seventeenth century, as ghastly as it was. The writer Eduardo Galeano argues that in three centuries, beginning in the 1500s, the "Cerro Rico" alone, one region in South America, "consumed eight million lives."[19] Thus, due north in California, the indigenous population was about 150,000 in 1846 at the onset of the U.S. occupation, but it was a mere 16,000 by 1890,[20] a direct result of a policy that one scholar has termed "genocide."[21]

IN LATE 1526 IN WHAT is now South Carolina, perhaps closer to what is now Sapelo Island, Georgia, in what was to be the case for centuries to come, enslaved Africans were on the warpath, along with their indigenous comrades. The Africans had escaped from a Spanish settlement, which had endured for a scant three months before the uprising, and set it aflame, as they fled into the waiting arms of similarly rebellious indigenes—Guale—and put paid to Madrid's attempt to extend their tenuous remit beyond the territory to the south they had named Florida.[22] In a sense, this was not a first for a territory later to labor under the Stars and Stripes, for in 1514 scores of enslaved Africans revolted in Puerto Rico in what one scholar has described as "the first African uprising known to have taken place anywhere in the Indies."[23]

Evidently, Madrid's minions envisioned turning the southeast quadrant of North America into a feudal empire staffed by indigenous workers and enslaved Africans, but the latter's joint revolt buried yet another exploiter's dream. In the resultant chaos, even some Europeans appeared to join the victors and deserted to the Native American side.[24] Actually, if alert Spaniards had been paying closer attention, they would not have been overly surprised by this uprising and what it portended, for in 1527 in the region stretching southward from Panama an African escaped from a colonizer's vessel, swam ashore, and ensconced himself among the indigenes, who he then proceeded to organize and lead so thoroughly that this community became a continuing thorn in the flesh of the would-be European usurpers.[25]

Madrid was dimly aware of the dilemma it had created for itself. Enslaved Africans were being imported to the Americas by 1503, in part premised on the idea that—perhaps because of the disorientation delivered by dumping aliens in a foreign land—the labor of one of these imported workers was equal to or surpassed by that of four "Indians."[26] But as early as 1505, reconsideration was occurring, as there was a suspension, albeit temporary, of the importation of slaves into Hispaniola, as quite ominously, this would-be chattel had been fleeing and setting up outlaw settlements of their own in the mountains and forests and from there executing violent raids on Spanish towns and haciendas. Thus, by 1522, the first large-scale uprising of the enslaved occurred during the Christmas holiday (which was to become a prime time in following centuries to attack dulled and inebriated settlers), as a sugar mill belonging quite appropriately to the son of Columbus was victimized, with a number of his comrades slaughtered. That same year an enslaved man named Miguel led an army of 800 former chattel that forced the closing of profitable mines and delivered horror to the homes of settlers due south. By 1529, four years after being built, Santa Marta on the northern coast of South America was razed by rebellious Africans. In Mexico, there were slave insurrections in 1523, 1537, and 1546. Puerto Rico experienced severe trouble of this type in 1527, and by the 1540s it was again Hispaniola's turn as settlers were terrorized by maroons or cimarrones.[27] Slave revolts hit Cuba in 1530, not to mention the capital along the coast of today's Colombia that same year, which was destroyed. Africans fled to today's Ecuador and formed an independent polity that Madrid was compelled to recognize in 1598.[28]

This earlier North American revolt of 1526 made it possible for Londoners, many decades later, to make their own claim to this vast territory, which was then inherited by their preening settler colony, now known as the United States of America. In other words, those who triumphed in what is now the United States had a kind of "second mover's advantage," advancing in the wake of Spanish retreat and, as shall be seen, learning lessons from this competitor's defeat that proved to be devastating to Africans particularly.

Today's Dixie is well aware of the debt owed to Madrid: the conquistador Hernando de Soto nowadays is venerated as the "first white hero" of the region; towns and cities annually hold parades, barbeques, and pageants in his honor, downplaying his conspicuous role as an enslaver and his catastrophic impact on indigenes, while pooh-poohing the massive evidence that depicts his savage quest as the handiwork of a psychopathic killer.[29]

Though often neglected, the contemporary United States remains ensconced in the shadow of the original colonizers. Before the arrival of Spanish conquistadors in the 1500s, the population of the Caddo people in the southeastern quadrant of what is now the United States was an estimated 200,000, but by the eighteenth century, as the new nation was being launched, their population had shrunk reportedly to about 1,400, making the final ouster of indigenes more likely.[30] By the nineteenth century, the northern reaches of Mexico, soon to be incorporated into the United States, was regarded widely as the "land of war," indicative of how indigenous resistance had not only been long-standing but also had been weakening the original inhabitants of the land.[31] The genocide that was visited upon the indigenous of North America was a rolling process, with the republican knockout blow facilitated mightily by the preceding blows inflicted by Madrid.[32]

Thus, it was in the twentieth century that enraged settlers in the newly minted republican state New Mexico remained furious about the indigenous challenge to their alleged right to the land. The settler delegate returned to a 1551 decree by Charles V for justification supposedly sketching "separation of races" that was said to castigate "'Negroes, Mulattos and Mixed Bloods" who were said to "teach . . . evil ways" to indigenes. Then the rationalizer returned to Spanish law of 1513 for justification for what would have been deemed "Anglo" occupation of the land.[33]

Washington was even able to co-opt, to a degree, settlers dispatched by Spain. Recently, for example, the *New York Times* reported the story of Patricia Aragon Luczo, a retired flight attendant from New Mexico, who traced her Sephardic legacy to Juan de Vitoria Carvajal, a member of the Spanish expedition that sought to seize the area surrounding Santa Fe in 1598.[34]

TODAY A SELF-DESCRIBED "New Conquest History" has arisen that stresses the sixteenth-century presence of African maroons whose very existence called into question the purported control of Spain, even in Hispaniola, to the point where the notion of "maroons as conquerors" has to be taken seriously.[35] As events in 1526 in what is now South Carolina indicate, there was a kind of advantage of the latecomer, the tardy, enjoyed by London, which could profit as Africans and indigenes, on the one hand, pounded would-be conquistadors and, on the other hand, allowed Englishmen to administer knockout blows to the exhausted survivors in succeeding decades.

Debilitating blows were also unleashed by the initial invaders too. For the land upon which Dixie was built still groans from the excruciating dread delivered by the likes of de Soto and his comrades, groans that continue to resound in the form of dispossessed indigenes and severely oppressed Africans. These conquerors bulled their way into indigenous settlements, murdering all they encountered, including small children, old men, pregnant women—especially pregnant women. They hacked them mercilessly, slicing open their bulging bellies with their sharpened swords with macabre intensity. They grabbed suckling infants by the feet, ripping them from their mothers' breasts, dashing them headlong against the ground.[36] There were "Holocaustic levels of slaughter and enslavement,"[37] asserts scholar Matthew Restall with accuracy, speaking of Mexico in words that are hardly unique to this territory.

The deadliness of the resultant apocalypse commenced virtually from the day Columbus reached terra firma in October 1492.[38] In the decades immediately following, an estimated 650,000 indigenes were enslaved and by 1580, in Algiers, enslaved indigenes from the Americas were to be found.[39] In other words, it was not just European microbes that devastated indigenes, it was also a conscious strategy of naked profiteering from enslaving combined with a maniacal desire to remove the existing population, with enslaved Africans then arriving to develop the land. Thus, by 1530, 69 percent of the enslaved in Puerto Rico—now a U.S. "possession"—were African.[40] Simultaneously, a market in Europe quickly developed involving indigenous American women and children deployed as domestic or household slaves.[41]

For as early as 1514, a few decades after the epochal voyage of Christopher Columbus, Madrid was frightened by the rapid increase in the number of enslaved Africans in Hispaniola, their initial foothold, and as one twentieth-century observer put it, "By 1560 the natural increase of that prolific race," meaning Africans, "coupled with the constant inflow brought by the slave traders"—intoxicated by the maddening scent of profit—"had created a most alarming preponderance in their number" compared to the colonizers.[42]

As early as 1570, Africans in the Caribbean exceeded the number of Europeans and, after bloodily targeted violence, probably that of indigenes too; that year, there were an estimated 10 million indigenes, 250,000 Africans—"mulattos" or "mestizos"—and 140,000 "Europeans" in Iberian America. That first figure fell sharply in succeeding years, while that of Africans continued to rise relative to that of Europeans. By 1576 there were reportedly more Africans than colonizers in the important node that was Mexico City. Part of Madrid's problem was overweening ambition; more Spaniards reached Manila in 1580 than any other year of the sixteenth century, and it was near then that the grasping power began dreamily to contemplate an invasion of China, to then be followed by thrusts into India, Cochin China (or Vietnam), Siam, the Moluccas, Borneo, and Sumatra. Still, by 1600, Madrid controlled the largest collection of territories the world had seen since the fall of the Roman Empire and the heyday of Genghis Khan, as it also dominated Italy, southern Netherlands (the ancestor of modern Belgium), a good deal of the Americas, and its pioneering neighbor, Portugal. Yes, it was a Pan-European project, albeit with a Catholic tinge from the start; after all, Columbus's roots were in Genoa; there were Basques, of course, and Florentines and Frenchmen (Magellan was Portuguese), Greeks and Cordobans.[43] Yet, as the following pages suggest, it was also a religious project, as signaled by the vanguard role played by Jesuits.[44]

Spain's vaulting ambition, according to one assayer, led to the commencement of the dominating process known as "globalization," in that in 1571 Manila was founded as a crucial entrepot linking the Americas and Asia in the trading of silver bullion between China and

Spain, with knock-on effects worldwide, including in Africa, increasingly the favored source of labor supply. Silver traded for Chinese silk, tea, and porcelain fueled the rise of Madrid, facilitating the precipitous decline of indigenous Americans and their replacement by enslaved Africans.[45] After 1571, Chinese fabrics were arriving in substantial quantities in South America, as a result of the Manila galleon trade. This form of "globalization" is in a sense a euphemism for the roots of capitalism.[46]

By 1500, China accounted for an estimated 25 percent of the world's output of goods and services and England for about 1 percent, but by 1900 as an outgrowth of slavery and rapacious colonialism, those numbers had been virtually reversed.[47]

We continue to reside in the shadow of this important century—the sixteenth—as globalization accelerated and the state was strengthened. Not accidentally, it was then that John Harrington, described recently as the "cynic-in-residence" in Queen Elizabeth's court, opined: "Treason doth never prosper: what's the reason? Why, if it prosper, none dare call it treason,"[48] a statement that also reflected the overthrow and weakening of various unsustainable polities in the name of the new force created by "globalization."

STILL, DESPITE THE ONRUSH of the global, the ruler in Madrid was not known as "His Catholic Majesty" by accident, for religion, or more precisely, Catholicism, was privileged. "Religious adherence was more important as a test of loyalty than ethnicity"—or race—according to an analysis of the Spanish settlement in St. Augustine, Florida: "Slaves, therefore, received different treatment here than in English or even other Spanish colonies" in part because protecting the wealth of Cuba and Mexico was the primary goal,[49] not least by dint of slave-constructed fortifications and in part because religion was overdetermined.

This telescoped disquisition about Florida brings into sharp relief major themes of this book: the firm implantation of settler colonialism in what is now the United States—including the enslavement of Africans—originated in today's "Sunshine State" and, as shall be seen, in New Mexico, the "Land of Enchantment." The history of Virginia and New England, which wrongly deems either or both to be the seedbed of settler colonialism in what is now the United States—and, in the long run, the United States itself has to be adjudged with this point firmly in mind. Thus, armed Africans in Spanish Florida played an expansive role, in a way that would have been difficult in Virginia or Massachusetts, for example.[50] London, the "second" colonizer and their republican successors, grappled assiduously with the formidable problem of how to defang embattled and armed Africans in Florida, leading to ruinous nineteenth-century wars.

Thus, the armed Africans of northern Florida were an obvious counterpoint to the enslaved Africans languishing across the border in what became London's settlements in Georgia and South Carolina, forcing Britain to expend blood and treasure to extirpate this "threat," which it did by about 1763, which was then followed by the rebellious settlers intervening more forcefully in Florida over the next half-century or more, until the matter was resolved by the creation of the "Sunshine State" in the slaveholders' republic. London, then Washington, decided not to build on the "St. Augustine exception" created by Madrid but to strangle it instead. It was left to London, then Washington, to leapfrog Madrid altogether by developing a sturdier axis of colonialism, namely "whiteness," the privileging of "race" over religion, a process (again) extended by Britain's erstwhile stepchild in 1776, allowing for the incorporation more readily and easily of a growing number of European immigrants, with little room to compromise with a "Free Negro" population.[51]

THERE WAS A CONTRADICTORY APPROACH to Africans by Spanish colonizers. There were so-called Black Conquistadors, for example, Juan Garrido, instrumental in the creation of "New Spain" or Mexico, and Sebastian Toral, who obtained his freedom because of his role in the siege of Yucatan, and Juan Valiente, who helped to conquer Guatemala, then settled in Chile. On the other hand, there was a history congruent with subsequent slave revolts within the slaveholders' republic, for example, that of Miguel in 1553 in the gold-rich region of Venezuela; similar rebellions erupted in like gold mining regions in today's Colombia in the late sixteenth century. It is possible that thousands of the enslaved murdered their masters and foremen and hid in the mountains and forests, constructing palenques and various forms of marronage that proved difficult to eradicate. Near that same time, in Cuzco in Peru, enslaved Africans and indigenes—in contrast to the Black Conquistadors—formed a rebellious contingent led by an indigene, Francisco Chichima. Due north in Vera Cruz, a citadel was formed in the 1580s by Nanga (Yanga), possibly of Akan or West African origin. About three decades later, the settlers effectuated a kind of entente with these rebels. Perhaps as a partial result, legislation enacted by the monarchs in Madrid and Lisbon were more demanding of masters and more humane toward the enslaved than their peers in London, Paris, The Hague, and especially Washington.[52]

In a sense, Madrid took religion too seriously, seemingly oblivious to the rising notion that settler colonialism required "race" more than religion. Madrid assumed that it could both enslave and empower Africans, whereas the ultimately victorious republicans begged to differ. I argue that this difference between Madrid and London is to be found in religion, not necessarily because Catholicism was more "progressive" than Protestantism,[53] but more so because the former was a more centralized faith, better able to enact and enforce edicts, as opposed to the fissiparous latter. Decentralized Protestantism was a better fit than rigid Catholicism, perhaps by virtue of the fabled "absence of mind" in forging a settlement project that relied more heavily on a construction of "whiteness" or the ingathering of various and disparate European ethnicities. Similarly, the heralded "religious liberty" that characterized the republican secession in the late eighteenth century coincidentally allowed for a Pan-European mobilization to crush rebellious Africans and indigenes alike.

AS THE TIME APPROACHED TO colonize what became St. Augustine in 1565, the monarch in Madrid was told that "there are many Negroes, mulattoes and people of evil inclination in the islands of Santo Domingo, Puerto Rico, Cuba, and others nearby. In each of these islands," said conquistador Pedro Menendez de Aviles disconsolately, "there are more than thirty of them to each Christian. It is a land where this generation multiplies rapidly," and, besides, "in possession of the French" most notably, "all of these slaves will be set free," since "to enjoy this freedom, the Negroes will help them against their own masters and rulers, for them to take over the land. It will be a very easy thing to do with the help of the Negroes."[54] This was perceptive, and combined with Madrid's self-defeating religious sectarianism, which hindered the necessity to build, à la London, a "whiteness" project, crossing theological borders, left few alternatives beyond seeking to co-opt Africans, creating a "Free African" population that could be armed, an endangering process that certain settlers may have deemed to be a cure worse than the illness.

This was part and parcel of the elongated process whereby religion was supplanted by "race" as the animating axis of society, which reached its zenith in the Americas, especially Protestant-dominated North America. For as the late doyen of historians Herbert Bolton once averred, "In the English colonies the only good Indians were dead Indians."[55] But this induced morbidity did not occur to a similar degree in, for example, French settlements in North America. After all, London coveted the land of indigenes for settlement, while Paris was more intrigued by the trade in furs and a military alliance with the indigenes against other European powers such as London. Thus, says the scholar W. J. Eccles, Perfidious Albion "had to displace—that is destroy—the Indians" and France was more interested in seeking to "preserve them, in order to achieve their aims."[56] Furthermore, as a nineteenth century California leader put it, "the success of Britian as a colonizing power was ascribable to its strict policy of racial separation and that the failures of France and Spain"—and Portugal too, it might have been added—"were due to the absence of such a policy. . . ." [57] And the hateful Jim Crow policy installed in the revolting spawn of London in Washington further bolstered this malignant analysis.

Paris was the wild card in terms of European powers, willing to work with indigenes—and Africans too—against their competitors. On 10 July 1555, Jacques de Sores (at times known as Soria), described as "the most heretic Lutheran," attacked Havana, which was defended in turn by a force of 355, including 220 indigenes, 80 Africans, and only 35 Spaniards, the numbers a hint as to how dependent the colonizers were at fraught moments. This "heretic Lutheran" was a kind of John Brown of the Pan-Caribbean, threatening slave revolts in order to attain his sweeping goals,[58] and providing untold leverage to Africans and lessons for them too, in terms of aligning with one power against another. The Frenchman and his hearty crew of a mere 53 men had leveraged African disgruntlement when he freed the enslaved in attacking Margarita, Cabo de la Vela, La Burburata, Santa Maria, Cartagena, Santiago de Cuba, and Havana—and, for a while, captured all of these enriched sites.[59]

TO BE SURE, EVEN IF London were to surpass Madrid or Paris, it would not guarantee European supremacy, setting aside the ultimate goal of global dominance. For in the sixteenth century, in some ways the most fearsome of them all was the Ottoman Empire. The potency of the Ottomans was signaled when Christians, sensing the directions of the prevailing winds, began defecting to the Ottoman side.[60] Yes, some of these "defections" were coerced, but many were not. In any event, the formidable Ottoman fleet was a microcosm of the Ottoman Empire. Commanders tended to be Turks, but the oarsmen were Greeks and Bulgarians, and the specialists emerged from the heart of Christian Europe: Genoese, Catalans, Sicilians, Provençals, Venetians.[61]

So bolstered, as Madrid was seeking to repress Africans, Constantinople captured Belgrade in 1521, conquered Rhodes in 1522, destroyed the Hungarian army at Mohacs in 1526, and besieged Vienna with a massive army of 400,000 in 1529. On the western Mediterranean front, the Turks seized Tripoli from the Knights of Malta in 1551, destroyed a Spanish armada at the island of Djerba in 1560, and besieged Malta in 1561.[62] The Ottomans seemed to be soaring from strength to strength in the early sixteenth century, not only bombarding Serbia and Buda but more generally besieging eastern Europe too. Syria and Palestine were subjugated, along with Baghdad, Basra, Aden, and Cairo. Bases were established in Ethiopia and Algeria. In the prelude to 1492, the Ottomans were seeking to bolster their fellow Muslims in Andalusia. Ironically, as the Habsburgs, as well as Spain, expanded into the Americas, this made it easier for the Ottomans to expand into Europe and nearby regions. Ultimately, however, the wealth accumulated by Spaniards and other Western Europeans in the Americas allowed Madrid and their immediate neighbors to reverse what appeared to be insuperable advantages enjoyed by the Ottomans.[63]

Yet, as matters evolved, 1516–17 was a critical time, not only because of the ascendancy of Martin Luther[64] and the expansion of the Ottomans into North Africa and beyond, but also because of the consolidation of Spain and the Habsburgs. The split among Christians appeared at first glance to provide an immense opportunity for the Ottomans, but instead, in the longer term it boosted Luther's heirs.

Western Europe's contestation with the Ottomans was a precondition of the rise of plundering of the Americas and Africa. The Iberians pirouetted deftly from the directive of Pope Nicholas V in 1452 sanctifying Lisbon's praxis of selling into slavery all "heathens" and "'Foes of Christ'"—principally Moslems—to the broader application in the Americas.[65] This fifteenth-century edict was an extension of the Crusades.[66] That is, a Pan-European Christian campaign against Islam extended to a campaign against non-European/non-Christians (especially in the Americas and Africa); arguably, this Pan-European initiative was a prelude to the rise of the similarly devastating "whiteness" project. Thus, in fifteenth-century Valencia, Spain, captors sought to misrepresent what amounted to Senegalese and Gambians (West Africans) as Moors (North Africans)—religious-cum-political antagonists—so as to enslave them consistent with theological mores.[67]

As suggested earlier, with the taking of Constantinople in 1453, Christian Europe endured an existential crisis, a calamity that was seen as almost unprecedented in history. Unshackled ire was not caged when Ottomans began gifting Hungarian slaves to their North African allies.[68] Defeated Christians were forced into slavery, contributing to a growing sense of "Europe" against "Asia," a confrontation that was fungible and easily transferable to "America" and "Africa." The explosive charge was made that the 1453 setback meant "virgins prostituted, boys made to submit as women," garnished with the repeated use of the term "inhuman race" affixed to victorious Turks. By 1530 the eminent Dutch Christian philosopher Erasmus continued to charge that even God would sanction war against the Turks, this "race of barbarians," a fury then being transferred to Africans and "Americans" too.[69] "We are far inferior to the Turks unless Christian Kings should unite their forces," said Pope Pius II in 1462,[70] a putative precondition for the racial vehemence—white supremacy, in other words—that was to be unleashed in the sixteenth century in the Atlantic corridor.

This was an era of an enslaving free-for-all in any case, one that ensnared others besides Africans; the Turks and those in their vicinity were preeminent in this regard but part of the diabolical "genius" of settler colonialism, notably as it matured in North America, was that those who had once been victimized by enslavers instead were invited to become enslavers themselves—or perfidious discriminators—in the new guise of "whiteness." About 2,000 Slavs yearly were enslaved by Crimean Tartars and sold to the Ottomans in the fourteenth century, with that figure rising in the fifteenth century; slave raiding into Muscovy reached crisis proportions after 1475 when the Ottomans took over the Black Sea trade from the Genoese, as the Crimeans were instigating industrial-scale enslaving, especially between 1514 and 1654.[71]

Indeed, it is easy to surmise that the impetus impelling Europeans westward—particularly the Spaniards who had endured the most bracing experience with Islam, arriving at a terminal point (ironically) in 1492—was the continued push westward of Islam, veritably chasing the Iberians in that direction too. Periodic defeats at the gates of Vienna failed to squelch fears altogether of being overrun, especially given that Islam long since had established a beachhead in North Africa, visible from Gibraltar. Algiers alone—whose very name sent frissons of nervousness coursing down the spines of

Western Europeans—was said to have an enslaved population of at least 25,000 Christians by the late sixteenth century, many of whom were Spanish, Portuguese: and English.[72] These latter nations, particularly London, "won out" in the sixteenth century, replacing West Asia and Turkey as the core of the world system,[73] argues contemporary analyst, Bruno Macaes, though he could have added that this was done by way of imposing apocalyptic conditions on Africans and indigenes of the Americas.

Thus, a telling indicator is that from the sixteenth to the mid-seventeenth century, Russia's trade with the East was more profitable than European trade, but then, as the impact of slavery and settler colonialism in the Americas began to assert itself, this commerce with the Ottomans, Safavid Persia, Mughal India, and China began to decline,[74] then reawakened in the twenty-first century.

Yes, the Ottoman Turks also enslaved Africans: each year from the sixteenth century through the late nineteenth century thousands of slaves from Ethiopia, Nubia, and Southern Sudan arrived in the slave markets of Cairo—seized by the Ottomans in 1517, as post-1492 competition with the Habsburgs and Spain accelerated—then hundreds of these manacled workers made their way to Istanbul and provincial capitals of the empire alike. Ironically, as embodied in the power and influence wielded by the eunuchs of African descent,[75] the Ottomans' designation of Africans differed from that created by London, then Washington, with the latter waiting until the twentieth century to create a virtual equivalent of the "Black Eunuch." Moreover, unlike the "whiteness" project captained by the slaveholders' republic that led to the creation of a powerful capitalist economy, the Ottomans deigned to enslave Europeans too.

There were a number of signposts on the road to Ottoman decline, a power that by the mid-sixteenth century seemed to be an unstoppable juggernaut with their equal-opportunity enslaving. But surely one of these emblazonments was their defeat at Lepanto in 1571 when the Christian, principally Catholic, powers ganged up and administered a withering setback on their foe to the east. No, the Ottomans did not sink into precipitous decline thereafter, but as the nineteenth-century historian Leopold Ranke put it succinctly, "The Turks lost all their old confidence after the Battle of Lepanto."[76]

A predicate to the rise of London was the deal that it brokered with the Ottomans, then the Moroccans, against Spain, not altogether unlike the deal brokered by China in the late twentieth century with those thought to be its capitalist antagonists, which has left this Asian giant in the passing lane.

London, in other words, which had been buying an alliance with the Ottomans to blunt its mutual Catholic antagonist in Madrid, could now calculate that this policy was less of a necessity after Lepanto and could then begin to turn its attention to weakening Spain at the source of its then immense wealth: the Americas. More to the point, all this set the stage for the eclipse of the Ottomans' equal-opportunity enslaving policy and the rise of London's—then Washington's—single-minded focus on bonding Africans and indigenes. A by-product of this lengthy process was the formation of today's "Latin America," characterized on this side of the border in a decidedly racialized manner,[77] a legacy of the continuing and defining stain of white supremacy in the North American republic.

Thus, a few years after Lepanto, the officially authorized pirate Francis Drake set sail and landed in what was said to be Spanish territory—California—where "New Albion" was declared, making the so-called Golden State, appropriately enough, the "founding site for the overseas British Empire," according to scholar Robert H. Power,[78] and today's citadel of republican and capitalist hegemony.

IT IS CRUCIAL TO ACKNOWLEDGE that not only did Western European nations, especially England, rise on the backs of enslaved Africans and dispossessed indigenes, but that this too arrested development on a continental scale.[79] The story of Mali's Mansa Musa is now well known, not least the immense wealth that obtained in his golden realm, where Islam prevailed. Actually, most of the gold then circulating in what amounted to global markets and providing currency for the silk and spice roads in antiquity and the Middle Ages came from West Africa, soon to decline vertiginously, as Western

Europe rose at its expense.[80] The "fame" Musa and his polity generated, especially the gold there, "inundated the fourteenth century," says one leading scholar. This "left a deep impression," says François Xavier Fauvelle, to the point that "people were still talking about it half a century later."[81] For millennia, gold has been a means of exchange and a store of value,[82] making it hardly coincidental that a great swathe of Africa was pillaged to obtain this mineral.

Ironically, this religious inflected battle with Islam was accompanied by yet another bitterly sectarian conflict, that between Catholics and Protestants (with both having difficulty in overcoming deeply rooted anti-Semitism). This was not simply a theological difference. The Iberians' "first mover advantage" in looting the Americas, then sanctified by the Vatican in the Treaty of Tordesillas, dividing the world between Madrid and Portugal, provided London with disincentive to continue adherence to the One True Faith. When Henry VIII broke bonds with Catholicism, ostensibly because of differences over his divorce, this also meant the dissolution of monasteries, an act that filled royal coffers and released timber, stone, and bronze for national defense projects—precisely to challenge Spain. Also empowered were ascending lawyers and merchants who became influential stakeholders in the newer system, an aristocracy that stood to lose all in a return to the old faith and old relationships.[83]

The abject terror of the horrendous Protestant-Catholic conflict in Europe was in a sense a dress rehearsal and precedent for what was visited upon indigenes in the Americas and their African counterparts. As late as the twentieth century, the lapsed populist turned demagogue Tom Watson of Jim Crow Georgia continued to wallow in the rampant religiosity run amok of the epoch-making St. Bartholomew's Massacre of 1570s France, when thousands of Protestants were liquidated by genocidal Catholics. This bloodthirstiness was employed as a rationale for the anti-Catholicism of a resurgent Ku Klux Klan, illustrating once more the continuing potency of the sixteenth century.[84] The soon-to-be Senator Watson apparently did not realize that a kind of reconciliation between once warring Protestants and Catholics on a common altar of "whiteness" and white supremacy was the essential epoxy that bound together those in his own former slaveholders' republic, a principle enunciated solemnly in the First Amendment to the U.S. Constitution that this attorney knew well.

Catholic Spain's military prowess was honed in a centuries-long battle with Arabs and Muslims, which was then exercised brutally not just against Protestants but indigenes in the Americas and Africans there too.

Protestant England evolved similarly. The costs of war were immense, exacting a heavy cost in lives and taxes alike. London's ill-fated French campaign of 1513–14 alone consumed a million pounds, equivalent to ten years' worth of ordinary revenue. Military expenses between 1539 and 1552 came to about 3.5 million pounds, a million of which was spent on campaigns in Scotland and keeping Boulogne. The 1513 initiative witnessed an English army of 28,000 men joined in France by around 7,000 German and Dutch mercenaries. Simultaneously, a force of more than 26,000 marched speedily to meet King James IV's army in Northumberland for the slaughter of Flodden. Campaigning on a similar scale took place in 1522, 1544, and 1545. Even the stupendous gain delivered by the liquidation of monasteries was insufficient to cover the expense of warmongering: more taxes were imposed. Thus, England contained a precursor of a military-industrial complex, as towns and parishes stored armor and weapons and coastal works—bulwarks, beacons, and bastions— were constructed for defense. As early as 1468 Southampton had a gun of about 1,000 pounds in weight. Landowners were expected to maintain an armory of sorts. The monarch had no standing army, but every able-bodied man was expected to fight, again making a venture into the wilderness of the Americas seem tame by comparison, a speculation reflected in the high level of desertion and mutiny. Certainly, military experience in Europe proved to be quite useful for London on the battlefields of the Caribbean, Africa, and North America.

London, during the tumultuous reign of Henry VIII in the sixteenth century, endured a much higher proportion of Englishmen than French or Spaniards serving as soldiers at some point during his reign. With regard to Paris alone, there were wars in 1475, 1489–1492, 1512–1514, 1522–1525, 1542–1546, 1549–1550, 1557–1559, 1562–1564, etc. In yet another sixteenth-century idea that has yet to dissipate, per Machiavelli, was that foreign wars defuse domestic conflict. In any case, European elites often sought to depend on mercenaries rather than domestic forces to suppress domestic dissent, with the resultant benefit flowing to these guns-for-hire, serving as yet another boost for a Pan-European identity that could easily morph into "whiteness"— a militarized identity politics, in other words. In any event, London had its hands full seeking to contain Wales, Ireland, and Scotland during the sixteenth century (and before) with settlements and wars in the Americas emerging as not only a safety valve relieving pressure on London but allowing often disgruntled "minorities," especially Catholics, to stake a claim on the fruits of Empire, thus diverting their anger away from England.[85]

Necessity is not only the mother of invention but the crucible of warfare is as well. The "discovery" of the Americas raised the stakes for sovereignty with Madrid's wealth and firepower seemingly threatening the existence of London itself. Coincidentally, post-1500 there was a much ballyhooed "Military Revolution," which transformed warfare on the old continent, and had the added "benefit" of destabilizing Africa and the Americas. The invention, then proliferation, of gunpowder meant that old medieval city walls could no longer offer adequate protection. New fortifications also meant that wars became longer with many sieges lasting more than a year. The rise of firearms translated into a need to train soldiers. Armies became increasingly professionalized, evolving from bands of mercenaries. Armies expanded in size, meaning more men under arms and militarized societies, as well as militarized thinking, suitable for conquest abroad. Along with dispatching domestic foes to far-flung settlements as disposable colonizers, armies also facilitated the liquidation (or quieting) of domestic opponents. Government debt also rose coincidentally in the sixteenth century, enhancing the power of the state. Spain was an initial beneficiary here as their legendary ruler, Philip II, was at war in every single year of his long sixteenth-century reign.[86] But, again,

London—then Washington—surpassed Madrid in virtually every
one of these important categories.

The repeated attempted invasions of England by Spain—the late
sixteenth century notwithstanding—culminated in the game-chang-
ing defeat of the Armada in 1588, with London maneuvering adroitly
in the slipstream created by Madrid's propulsion. Certainly 1588 was a
true sign of things to come. Historian Geoffrey Parker has argued that
the failure of the Armada "laid the American continent open to invasion and colonization by northern Europeans and thus made possible
the creation of the United States." The future, he asserts, "pivoted on
a single evening—August 7, 1588," as "Spain began a slow decline
and a new world order [began] its gradual ascendancy."[87]

Of course, alert Spaniards would have been wise to pay attention to Londoners within their ambit, prior to invading. There were
English merchants resident in Andalusia from 1480 to 1532, a number
of whom were slaveholders actively engaged in the transatlantic
slave trade. One scholar argues, contrary to previous assessments,
that 1489 marks the starting point in the English history of African
slaveholding. "Englishmen of all social classes from low class to high
class, and even to royalty . . . emerge[d] as slaveowners," asserts
historian Gustav Ungerer, a trend that waxed and waned over the
centuries but continued to carry sufficient strength to shed light on
the prolonged existence of alliances across class lines among those
defined as "white" that exerted itself most recently in the former
slaveholders' republic in November 2016. There was also a goodly
number of slaveholders who were Englishwomen too, which may
shed light on their descendants' twenty-first-century voting habits in
North America as well.[88]

YET ANOTHER CONDITION PRECEDENT for the rise of London
and the simultaneous decline of Africa and the Americas took place a
few years after the failed Armada, in 1591. The site was north central
Africa. Morocco, yet another predominantly Islamic nation courted
by London, had invaded with England's assistance the once mighty
Songhay Empire. This proved to be a double disaster, with both

victor and vanquished emerging weaker, a boon to an ascending "Christian"—if not Protestant—Europe. By destroying the strongest centralized state in sub-Saharan Africa, the Moroccan conquest did irreparable harm to the trans-Saharan routes that had enriched both Morocco and West Africa, and this instability radiated to the aptly (and unfortunately) named Gold and Slave Coasts of Africa, indicative of what was soon to be plundered excessively on the beset continent.[89] Morocco's force of 5,000 was bolstered by Moriscos (Muslims expelled from Spain) and mercenaries, as they proceeded to Gao on the Niger River. Over 80,000 fighters with mere lances and javelins were mowed down systematically by weapons, an outgrowth of the aforementioned "Military Revolution." In a sad coda to a bygone era—and the commencement of a newer one—they reportedly cried, as they fell, "We are Muslims, we are your brothers in religion,"[90] apparently unaware that this newer era was in the long run to sideline religion in favor of conquest and commerce and capitalism. Moroccans had been armed with English muskets in return for saltpeter for ammunition, then soon wielded in what was to be called Virginia in the early seventeenth century. The Moroccan envoy in London was quite close to Anthony Radcliffe, residing at his home for six months at one point; the latter's daughter, Anne, was a benefactor of what became Harvard University, which once housed a women's college named in her honor, continuing the resonances from the sixteenth century.[91] Relations between England and Morocco were so close—perhaps a key to understanding Shakespeare's *Othello*, for example—that less than a decade after the transformative 1591 vanquishing of the Songhay Empire, the two powers were huddling and discussing a joint invasion of their mutual foe, Spain, then followed by a joint ouster of the Spaniards from the Caribbean.[92]

The Moroccan-English collaboration was not the only factor contributing to the subjugation of Africa and the Americas. By 1420, Europe counted barely more than a third of the people it contained one hundred years before as a result of the disease known as the Black Death. Predictably, the Jewish minority was blamed, leading to terrible violence against them; thus, early in 1348 the rumor arose that

this minority in northern Spain and southern France were poison-
ing Christian wells and thus disseminating the plague.[93] This served
to lead to the mass expulsion of this minority from Spain in 1492,
and, in the longer run, their being incorporated with untoward consequences for Madrid in the Netherlands, Turkey, and, to a degree,
in England too. In the shorter term, their diaspora networks proved
to be essential to the new era that was arising, purportedly investing
in Columbus's voyage and—perhaps absconding from inquisitorial
Madrid—fleeing on his vessels. Some from this Iberian minority
were present when São Tomé in West Africa was being subjected
to enslavement and sugar production, a pestiferous process then
exported to Brazil with devastating consequences for Africans and
indigenous Americans both.[94] Other "New Christians," that is, those
from the minority subject to an inauthentic conversion, wound up in
Cape Verde and Congo with untoward consequences for Africans.[95]

   Still, it was not just a more forthcoming approach to the Jewish
community and Islam that served ultimately to catapult London
into the first rank of nations. Protestants and their often bewilder-
ing array of sects and tendencies—Arminian, Calvinist, Lutherans,
Presbyterians, Anabaptists, Antinomian, Socinian, Society of Friends
(Quakers) et al.—jutted out of Europe, undermining existing beliefs
and preparing the ground for a new kind of thinking: capitalism, white
supremacy, and anti-Catholicism too, destabilizing the One True
Faith—and "His Catholic Majesty" in the bargain, as a previously
mighty Gulliver was tied down by an ant-like army of Lilliputians.[96]

   In undermining existing beliefs, Protestants set the stage for the
rise of others: racism, not least, a point that Ambassador Young
could have mentioned in 1977. In short, the radical decentraliza-
tion of Protestantism, as opposed to the hierarchical centralization
of Catholicism, provided fertile soil for the rise of racism and other
"faiths." Besides, as besieged underdogs in the midst of religious wars,
Protestants were poised to make overtures to the Jewish community
and Islam alike, as a matter of survival if nothing else but contrary
to past praxis,[97] and, ultimately, Protestants and Catholics, then the
Jewish, were rebranded as "white" republicans, curbing murderous

interreligious conflict and ushering in an era of racialized conflict, vic-
timizing Africans and indigenes alike.

Ambassador Young also could have noted that the evolution of
settler colonialism in his homeland involved a religious compromise
between Protestants and Catholics, then a transition to "race" as
they were rebranded as "white" in North America, easing the path
for racialized slavery and uprooting of indigenes, which in turn was
disrupted by the Haitian Revolution,[98] which then gave rise to an
emphasis on class as the animating axis of society with the rise of
socialism and working-class movements.[99] He could have mentioned
that English, Irish, and Scots warred against each other but then
united as "white" in the colonies to fight "others." This book is about
the earliest stage of this centuries-long process.

CHAPTER 1

Approaching 1492 | Approaching Apocalypse

D id anti-African racism emerge from the Arab world and enslavement of Africans in the Islamic world? Is contemporary racism a function of this encounter with forces eastward, just as today the norm is to use Arab—not Roman—numerals? As far back as the eighth century, this racializing process was unfolding—or so it is said—though, as noted, enslavement in that part of the world did not only encompass Africans. One historian has contrasted the way in which "white mamluks" (*European* might be a more apt term to affix to this exploited humanity) were treated versus their darker brethren, though the substantial Christian ransom of the former might account for any difference.[1] And, in any case, comparing the legacy of racism centuries later in North America, including lynchings and immolations, with what unfolded in what is now Iraq centuries earlier, seems once again to be an extended effort to exonerate perpetrators in London, then Washington: that is, "the Arabs made them do it." Perhaps English anti-Semitism (or even the German variant) should be laid at the doorstep of Pontius Pilate or post-Constantine Rome, again exculpating London elites. Or, is attenuation or even the chain of causation disrupted in this instance?[2]

Whatever the case, the fact remains that enslavement of Africans reached a high point under the aegis of London and its descendants, not least because it was turbo-charged with emerging notions of "race" (a term with hazy roots at best in the mire of 1,300 years ago) and the shift from religion as the axis of society, which characterized the post-1492 dispensation.[3] For in examining fifteenth-century Valencia, on a peninsula deeply influenced by Muslims for hundreds of years, the scholar Debra Blumenthal argues—correctly, I think—that it is "misleading to label what we see here . . . as 'racism' or even 'protoracism.'"[4]

Because the Iberian Peninsula played such an instrumental role in the story of conquest, it is a focus in these pages. Thus, from the eighth to eleventh centuries, neighboring France was a center of selling of Irish and Flemish slaves, while in the ninth century the Vikings sold tens of thousands of Europeans to the Arabs of Spain.[5]

Moreover, during the seventh and eighth centuries, predominantly Muslim regions commanded the mightiest gold reserves in the world, not least because of their tie to Africa where this precious metal proliferated. Buoyed by this wealth, these forces ruled in Iberia, the southern Mediterranean, and due east from there. The gravity of the situation was signaled when a subsequent analyst announced gravely that back then "an Iron Curtain now divided the Mediterranean"[6]—featuring Muslims not Communists—which provoked a kind of angst that rivaled the sentiments of recent history when this poisonously marbled phrase was first enunciated. This difficult moment for the Western Europeans tended to provoke the kind of imprecations toward Muslims, including inventing racism, that had been thought to be peculiar to twentieth-century Moscow.

Nonetheless, the conflict on the Iberian Peninsula between Arabs and those we now call Spaniards[7] was a critical factor contributing to the post-1492 apocalypse, since the invaders were constructed as "black" when there was a long medieval tradition of associating blackness with devils and of seeing dark-skinned Muslims as quasi-diabolical creatures. Eerily, in pre-1492 Christian-dominated areas on the Peninsula, there was often an attempt to bar sexual relations with "Saracens" or Muslims and other non-Christians (for example, those of the Jewish community), just as anti-miscegenation statutes were a fixture in the United States, at least until 1967.[8] Moreover, at times during the ninth-century reign of Alfonso III on the Peninsula, the descriptors "Moor" and "Negro" were used interchangeably,[9] which did not bode well for what was to become the beleaguered continent, namely Africa.

The plundered riches of Africa notwithstanding, the Iberian Peninsula too was a target-rich environment. Sparsely defended churches and monasteries were repositories for gold, silver, and bejeweled items of all types, all poised for plucking. The bounty could also include crops, livestock, and people that could be transported eastward and southward to North Africa. Slaves were a valuable commodity and foreign women seemed to be particular prizes.[10]

Likewise, slavery was not unknown on the Peninsula pre-1492. In Andalusia, for example, slaves were in great demand and there was an abundant supply as a result, with many taken in raids on the Christian North or "pagans" seized in eastern Europe and imported by merchants described as being Frankish and Jewish, notably those among the latter described as "Radhanites."[11] Jewish merchants were accused of providing the ships that carried Muslim troops to the European shore and, subsequently, Muslim chroniclers alleged that this same group collaborated in the conquest and rule of the Peninsula, volunteering to serve in the garrisons of towns. Basque women were sold as slaves to Medina, and Berbers were recruited to cross the Mediterranean to protect the regime, which in turn drew Europeans into African events more closely. The ubiquity of the enslaved and their influence within the regime was pervasive. The royal court employed them by the thousands, as did the estates of the Umayyad royalty. Some slaves acquired great influence, unlike those who were to languish in North America, while, à la the Ottomans, some became eunuchs. This Almoravid imperium established an empire on the Peninsula and northern Africa in the eleventh century, which then extended its tentacles deeper into Africa, where the flow of gold (and slaves) from the Niger delta served as a precursor of the post-1492 debacle.[12] Southern Spain was propelled economically as an entry point for trade with an Africa that had yet to be devastated.[13]

SNIFFING WEALTH, ENGLISHMEN were flocking to Iberia too,[14] which brought them into closer contact with Africa and the fortunes to be made there. As early as the eighth century and continuing thereafter, Muslims, pre-1492 rulers of a good deal of Iberia, commanded the mightiest gold reserves within thousands of miles, with Africa often being the source, which then provided strength in the Mediterranean, the Peninsula, and what has been called the "Near East."[15] As more African gold began to pour into Europe via the Peninsula, increased trade resulted continentally to the point that by the early 1100s the Bay of Biscay was termed the "Sea of English," and English pirates were detained in Galicia.[16]

It was in 1290 that the Jewish community was ostensibly expelled from England, though some never left. It was ironic that Oliver Cromwell's mid-seventeenth-century embrace of this community helped London surpass the Spanish Empire in many respects. Interestingly, England was then besieged by savage anti-Jewish pogroms, leading to property seizures and expropriation of those perceived as akin to them, for example, Cahorsins, who were involved with banking; with roots in southwest France they too were associated with alleged usury,[17] with some refugees alighting on the European mainland, perhaps making their way to a more welcoming Muslim-dominated Iberia.

Coincidentally, the first recorded commercial treaty between Portugal and England was signed in 1294, binding London to the Peninsula and allowing England not only to capitalize upon Lisbon's subsequent perambulations but also to counter Madrid's thrust into Ireland by backing the Portuguese against the Spaniards. Of course, Portugal and Spain often backed different sides during the frequent conflicts between England and France, a crucial shaper of the balance of power continentally, with lethal implications for Africa and the Americas. For as this thirteenth-century trend began to assert itself, several of the West African coastal peoples had quite advanced civilizations, though their trade connections were with the interior, not the ocean, that evolved subsequently. East Africa long had been linked to a wider world, via the maritime superhighway known as the Indian Ocean.[18]

ENGLISH PIRATES WERE PERCEIVED regionally as a menace as early as the 1300s in the German Hanse.[19] Their depredations were to prove essential to the rise of London, as the otherwise dismal archipelago leveraged its sea-bound locale. The same could be said about trade with the Iberians, which was waxing as early as the fourteenth century, and which may have brought London in touch with North Africans.[20]

In a continuation of a lengthy trend, Lisbon's tensions with Castile deepened an ongoing alliance between Portugal and England. By 1380, London had dispatched an army of 3,000 lancers and archers to their ally, allowing them to confront more effectively their Iberian foe. As peace emerged, Portugal then accrued the "advantage" of having experienced fighters with time on their hands, which led to the seizing of Ceuta on the African continent by 1415, a signpost en route to this continent's subjugation. It was also in the early fifteenth century that Madeira was settled by Portuguese, whose sugar plantations were worked by enslaved Africans, providing a model for Brazil in the following century.[21]

AS THIS RAMPAGING WAS occurring, there was a gnawing fear in Europe that the fate of the Muslim-dominated Peninsula would soon be theirs, which by 1095 led the Crusades to seize Jerusalem, to make the Muslims play defense, in other words. There is also evidence to suggest that from 1095, Western Europeans had Turks in the crosshairs, suggesting the existential fear that arose in 1453 when Constantinople was taken.[22] This was a Pan-European Christian crusade, which was galvanizing continentally and which imbricated a fungible religious intensity that could be transferred into the succeeding epoch of white supremacy and conquest. In any case, the conflict between Islam and the Iberians in Spain had long been placed in terms of a crusade. By the late eleventh century, the Pope encouraged French knights to aid Castilians and Aragonese against Muslims,[23] a project that also carried the seeds of Pan-Europeanism, "whiteness," and the borderless essence of what became capitalism and imperialism.

The Crusades also fueled transport generally and the concomitant imperative to gain wealth and influence in the face of the "Islamic Threat," so by 1291 the Vivaldi brothers of Genoa were seeking to reach India by sailing southward. The thought had dawned that the fabled lure of "Muslim Gold" could be reached by heading in a like direction.[24] In a sense, this was a rehearsal for 1492, because when the Crusades failed in Acre, it threatened Christian overland routes via Mespotamia to the east and the spices, silks, and riches to be accrued.[25]

The eminent warrior Sultan Saladin had won Jerusalem (though losing the aforementioned Acre on the battlefield in a seesaw of victory and defeat). Saluted since that time at the end of the twelfth century, he has also been blamed for blunting the intellectual growth of Islamic societies and has not been viewed benignly by non-Sunnis. Even the praise of him in Western Europe may have been a function of Christians seeking an excuse for losing to a man and his troops characterized as being larger than life.[26]

In a sense, these were journeys of desperation, since by 1300 it seemed to many that Christianity generally and Christian Europe specifically were in terminal decline and the future rested with a triumphantly ascendant Islam. This desperation served to compose a "convert or perish" ethos among sectors of European Christendom, in contrast to what was perceived as a more tolerant Islam.[27] The hysteria and revenge-seeking that was gripping European Christendom was manifested in 1250 when the Moors were expelled from Portugal.[28] The collective depression was so profound that some within Western European Christendom hailed the mindboggling sack of Baghdad in 1258 by the then rising Mongols on the premise that a new putative ally would aid in destroying Islam and arrest the rampant idea that God was on Islam's side, given that it generally seemed to be prevailing, fomenting a widespread and destabilizing theological crisis.[29]

The very compactness and contiguity of Western Europe, combined with the overlapping and often borderless warfare that
eventuated, served to contribute to advancements in warfare and
weaponry that ultimately leveled then destroyed cultures and polities in the Americas and Africa. By 1350 cannons were common in
Europe.[30] According to one account, the first mention of a handgun
in England occurred on 7 November 1388, with the earliest breech-
loading handguns emerging, not coincidentally, during the century
of conquest, in 1537.[31] In Sheffield since the time of Chaucer from the
middle to the end of the fourteenth century, sharp blades had been
made, propelled by the ruthless Earl of Shrewsbury. He imported
French craftsmen to upgrade forges, coincidentally accelerating Pan-
Europeanism, a trend that proved crucial to conquest in the Americas.
He was also a precursor of the robber barons, a phenomenon also
essential to conquest.[32]

The scholar Priya Satia asserts: "The first European firearms were
late fourteenth-century 'hand cannons,' essentially tubes mounted on
a pole. Shoulder arms, such as muskets, rifles and shotguns followed.
Pistols could be fired with one hand," unleashing unrivaled firepower
in aid of conquest. Birmingham had been a center of metalwork since
the fourteenth century, and by the pivotal sixteenth century its workers had supplied bridle bits and horseshoes for the army of Henry
VIII and nails for Hampton Court and Nonsuch Palace in Surrey.
Gunmakers, straining to keep up with demand, were also proliferating. Eventually, the gun trade was critical to Birmingham's—and
Britain's—rise, and the entire existence of this ugly commerce
depended on the African market, as the beset continent absorbed
otherwise worthless unserviceable arms in return for immense value,
thereby facilitating war, dislocation, prisoners, and slavery to fuel the
gargantuan wealth of plantation slavery.[33]

These malignant trends were hardly unique to England. By 1470
in France there was an effective matchlock musket: the harquebus
was developed, preceded a decade earlier by the hexagonal nation's
reputation for having high-quality guns. By 1494 France had developed the high-wheeled gun carriage with its long tail, complemented

by plentiful supplies of saltpeter for gunpowder. Like other Western European powers, Paris, despite this firepower, had difficulty competing in the Mediterranean with the Ottomans and North Africans and, almost by necessity, had to utilize strength in the Atlantic, especially the Americas and Africa. By the late fifteenth century, France had what has been described as the "first modern army," integrating cavalry, infantry, and artillery, which, combined with the gritty ability to absorb heavy casualties, guaranteed a premier role at the top table of enslavement and colonialism.[34]

Advances in making weapons were also generated by conflicts between, for example, the English and Scots, with the latter often assisted by France,[35] a manifestation of the once mighty "Auld Alliance" that was to be somewhat blunted as Edinburgh was invited to feast alongside their erstwhile foes at the colonial and enslaving banquet. Edward I's attempt to crush Scotland in the late thirteenth and early fourteenth centuries led to two centuries of conflict that the lucrative diversion into the Americas and Africa served to divert.[36] Similarly, when Wales revolted against England in the fourteenth century, France was blamed, just as when King João I in Portugal defeated Castile in a protracted conflict from 1385 to 1433, English aid was essential.[37] When Wales revolted again in the early fifteenth century, again France was fingered as a collaborator, an easy conclusion to reach given the presence on Welsh soil of French troops, inducing London to get further involved in France's internal affairs.[38] In one of the decisive elements of the sixteenth century, much collaboration emerged between Catholic Scots and Irish—not to mention English Catholics—with Spain and other so-called Catholic powers.[39] In the long run, this bellicosity honed the fighting machines of Western Europeans, contributing to their conquests in the Americas and Africa.

THE ASCENDANCY OF DEADLY martial tools also was useful in coercing religious minorities. Writing in 1750, a Londoner observed that "Jews are very numerous at Algiers," and "the greatest number are those who have been banished out of Europe. As from Italy in 1342, from the Netherlands in 1350, from France in 1403, from England in 1422 [and earlier] and from Spain in 1462 [and later]."[40]

More to the point, in the wake of the hysteria created by the Black Death and scapegoating of the Jewish minority pogroms, befell their precincts on the Peninsula in 1391,[41] igniting their dispersal deeper into Africa. Thus, by 1350 in Iberia, mortality rates in certain areas reached an eye-popping 90 percent, which was bound to induce hysteria in the reigning atmosphere of obscurantism. Of course, such bigotry was nothing new in Europe.[42]

Even as this fourteenth-century trend was unwinding, events in Europe were already emerging with dire implications for Africa and the Americas. More than a century and a half before Columbus headed westward, a Tartar army besieged his own Genoa, then the Black Death arrived and the defense observed happily as the marauders began dying. But then joy became horror as the attackers began catapulting their dead combatants over the city walls, intentionally creating an epidemic inside. The Genoese fled and the Tartars advanced, with the former spreading the disease in the sites where they arrived. This comprehension of the potency of infectious disease was to be unleashed in the Americas particularly.[43]

Nonetheless, perhaps because it implicated Christians and Muslims too, the ferocity of anti-Semitism appeared to be especially intense in Aragon, with hundreds—perhaps thousands—slaughtered in a matter of months.[44] Ironically, just as anti-blackness tended to solidify an emerging "white" identity in the settler colonialism of North America in the seventeenth century,[45] and just as in the twentieth century in central and eastern Europe, the very vulnerability of the Jewish community reassured non-Jews that they were relatively safe, thus stabilizing society,[46] it is possible that anti-Semitism played a similar role in the fourteenth century, bracing and uniting Christians for the final push against the Muslims, which culminated in 1492 with their ouster.

In sum, 1391 was a crossroads. It led in part to the acceleration of the Inquisition, initiated formally decades earlier and assuming warp speed post-1492. Certainly, it allowed for the looting of more affluent Sephardim, which in turn allowed for war against Moors and Muslims and plundering of the Americas too.[47]

THE ACCELERATION OF THE AFRICAN Slave Trade occurred as Western Europe was wracked with pressure from the Ottomans, disease, rancorous discrimination, and economic unease. Forced religious conversions followed these bloody riots,[48] creating "New Christians" who were to play an instrumental role post-1492.[49] In a way, the tremendous depopulation of the Black Death also drove the enslaving of Moors on the Peninsula and the compulsion for labor, especially in Valencia.[50]

The historian Toby Green declares that this 1391 tumult sent these erstwhile Iberians fleeing to West Africa, where they became involved in various aspects of trade and commerce, which was to accelerate post-Columbus. Thus, he says, "In the fifteenth century when European ships first arrived on the West African coast to procure slaves, the economic difference between Africa and Europe was not vast; yet by the nineteenth century there was no denying the gulf,"[51] as conquest and mass enslavement ensued.

It was also in the fourteenth century that cartographers in Majorca, described as Jewish, produced several useful maps of Africa containing information about the interior that proved to be a revelation to many. Their source for this information was apparently their co-religionists, chased there as a result of anti-Semitism. The presence of gold in Africa, which these informants helped to reveal, set pulses racing in Europe, a continent that continued to be dazzled by the wealth displayed earlier by Mansa Musa.[52] Like others they had been attracted by the legend—and reality—of the fabled gold that was thought to rest in Africa.[53]

For the kingdoms of Aragon and Castile (Spain in brief), as they were waging the Reconquista, had designs on the Maghreb since the thirteenth century, a process that was not deterred when agreements were inked allowing Christian merchants (Iberians and Italians) to

settle in North Africa.[54] This was followed by the "Disputation of
Tortosa," yet another anti-Semitic marker that became linked with
the emerging bludgeoning of Africa.[55]

Thus, it was not only free labor but the presence of gold that helped
to propel Africa on its downward slide, serving to exacerbate the "economic difference" between this continent and its continental neighbor
due north. For as early as 1290, there was a mutually beneficial commercial treaty between Genoa and Ethiopia, and a Dominican monk
who visited Alexandria in 1322 spoke of "warehouses . . . maintained"
by merchants of Venice, Marseilles, and Genoa.[56]

"The Africa of this period," says French historian François Xavier
Fauvelle, "was home to powerful and prosperous states" that were
"integrated . . . into some of the great currents of global exchange.
. . . The continent enjoyed a considerable reputation from Europe
to China, a reputation exemplified by the celebrity that Musa, King
of Mali . . . achieved in the Islamic world and Christian Europe."
Thus, in the mid-thirteenth century, King James, the Conqueror of
Aragon, invited Solomon ben Ammar, a prominent member of the
Jewish community of Sijilmasa at the northern edge of the Sahara, to
come along with his co-religionists to settle Majorca and Catalonia;
at that juncture, besieged as they were by Arabs, many Aragonese
sought fervently to attract those with knowledge of these important
African commercial networks, to the detriment of the Maghreb competition. Indeed, a good deal of the intelligence relating to Mali's
Musa was due to the Jewish communities established along these
vital African routes that reached the western Mediterranean vicinity.
As early as the fifteenth century, Portugal was snatching up to about
1,000 Africans from Arguin to be enslaved, with gold following soon
thereafter, if not simultaneously. Eastward in Tuat in today's Algeria,
a gold trade erupted and, ironically, those that had fled anti-Jewish
pogroms became critical to this commerce, given their refuge there
and the existence of a diaspora network.[57]

There was a perversity in the process that drove an ever-larger
Jewish community, fleeing persecution into Africa, where they could
then play a role in a similarly dastardly process that was emerging: the

African Slave Trade. It was also in 1391 that murderous pogroms, of a kind that would become common in the Americas, erupted in Sevilla and Andalusia, eventuating in the devastation of members of the Jewish community, along with forced conversions. It happened again in Toledo in 1449, followed in 1478 by a Castilian Inquisition. The sequence of dates suggests the momentum of onrushing events: by 2 January 1492 Granada had been captured by the Christians, ending 800 years of the still potent shards of Islamic hegemony. By 31 March an edict was rendered to expel the Jewish community and some may have been alongside Columbus on 2 August.[58]

Yet, as Africa went into decline, so did other regions disrupted by this radical change in the status quo. Quite logically declining was also Venice—then a major power—that has been adjudged to possess an "armed . . . navy since the early fourteenth century, the first state to do so,"[59] in order to enforce its diktat in the event of disputes, commercial or otherwise. Yet when Vasco da Gama "discovered" a new route to the east in 1498 via Africa, Venice was headed toward eclipse, yet another milestone in the rise of London in its stead.[60]

ANOTHER REVEALING SIGN EMERGED in 1437 with Portugal's successful attack on Tangiers, employing arms developed by craftsmen from Flanders and points north and east, yet another Pan-European project that carried the germ of an arriving "whiteness."[61] At least by the 1440s Lisbon was involved in enslaving Africans with the utterly cynical rationalization of converting them to Christianity as justification. (Of course, it was a capital offense for a Moor or one who was Jewish to own Christian slaves.) Simultaneously, Pope Eugenius IV provided his blessings to this enterprise.[62]

Enslaving Africans in what is now Sierra Leone had begun as early as the 1440s, with interpreters aboard slave ships who often were "New Christians," that is, those from the Jewish community who had "converted" and often had dispersed precisely to Africa.[63] Historians subsequently have seen the 1440s as a turning point in the rise of the Atlantic slave trade,[64] priming the pump for the post-1492 surge. Thus, in the century following the 1440s, Lisbon alone had an

African population of 10,000 out of 100,000 with a similar percentage throughout Iberian cities. By the 1550s, enslaved Africans were a reputed 10 percent of Spain's population.[65]

In sum, even before the post-1492 devastation, the Iberians were enmeshed deeply in the horror of enslavement. As Portugal moved more intently into Africa in the 1400s, more gold poured into Europe, along with African pepper for Antwerp, a city that was to evolve as a prime partner of England.[66]

Though Prince Ferdinand was taken prisoner earlier in North Africa—quite disastrous for Lisbon—the important city that was Tangiers was taken by 1471, yet another stepping-stone to a brutalizing penetration of Africa. The Portuguese also harmed the competition when they eliminated a pirate base on the present site of Casablanca and forced the chieftains of Safi and Azemmour to pay tribute.[67] Also, by the 1470s Portuguese adventurers had arrived in the region that came to be known as Calabar, to the detriment of the Ibibio and the Ijaw.[68]

The fragmentation of Christianity, following the rise of Martin Luther in 1517, was matched in an opposing devolutionary direction by the political fragmentation of the Maghreb, induced in no small measure by the Iberians. This latter trend accelerated post-1415, and Morocco, quite noticeably, was disrupted by the influx of those fleeing anti-Semitism, not to mention Muslim refugees escaping Iberia. The response in the receiving region of the Maghreb was the fomenting of religious fundamentalism, which was arguably not conducive to socioeconomic progress, as Western Europe began to take off post-1492. By 1444, Portugal was bringing enslaved Africans to Europe. From the early 1440s to 1521 an estimated 156,000 Africans arrived in Spain, Portugal, and the Atlantic islands, mostly from today's Guinea-Bissau, Guinea-Conakry, Senegal, the Gambia, and parts of Mali and Burkina Faso.[69] (In 2019 the German Historical Museum in Berlin agreed to return to Namibia the Stone Cross of Cape Cross, an 11-foot-tall, 1.1-ton cross placed on the coast of southwestern Africa by Portuguese explorers, years before Columbus's journey westward.)[70]

By 1446, Senegal and Cape Verde had been reached by Portugal and by 1474 Benin and Biafra, along with Fernando Po and São Tomé. Fernando Po was larger, but São Tomé was favored since it was farther from the African shoreline, at times in an uproar about the presence of uninvited visitors. Again, ironically, colonization often was driven by those fleeing inquisitorial Lisbon, though generally, as in Upper Guinea, the invaders included Castilians, French, and Genoese, as a synthetic "whiteness" began to take shape, given the exigencies of colonizing, along with various exiles, convicts, and adventurers who provided the rough-and-tumble necessary for oppression.[71]

Portugal, whose contemporary population is a mere 9 million, exemplified this Pan-Europeanism or what morphed into "whiteness" in that as early as the 1460s Lisbon granted concessions to Flemish captains in the Azores, which had been seized in 1431,[72] and by 1475 Flemish ships were trading on the Gold Coast.[73]

EVENTUALLY, A NINETEENTH-century scholar concluded that a "Frenchman, a Briton, a Dane and a Saxon make an Englishman," as full-blown "whiteness" had emerged. What had occurred beginning in the sixteenth century is that Protestants flocked—often fled—to London from various European sites, bringing their ingenuity and capital, enhancing England, then Britain, and germinating "whiteness."[74] There was another essential element involved in this Pan-Europeanism. It is also worthy of reiteration that as the Portuguese reached what is now Sierra Leone by 1446 and began enslaving Africans, aboard ship were translators of African languages. These were "New Christians" or forced converts to Christianity, who had been chased southward.[75] In other words, the religious persecution endemic in late feudalism prepared the stage for the racism that was so crucial to the rise of capitalism, and settler colonialism in particular.

By 1471 the Portuguese had reached as far as the River Volta in Africa and by the 1480s were trafficking in the enslaved in Benin.[76] Even as Portugal and Queen Isabel were crossing swords, boldly she announced that she and her subjects "always enjoyed the right of the

conquest of parts of the Africa and Guinea," as if she were asserting that feasting on the continent to the south served to curb often
fatal conflicts in Europe. And even before her reign, Andalusians
frequently sailed to the African coast and snatched and enslaved the
unlucky, adding them to an already burgeoning slave population in
Sevilla.[77] By 1475 in eastern Iberia, the authorities were devising provisos concerning Africans.[78]

Yet, despite the pillaging of this portion of Africa, by 1428 Yeshaq I,
emperor of today's Ethiopia—across the sprawling continent—was
proposing to the royal court of Aragon an alliance via marriage targeting Islam, and by 1487, Lisbon was proposing something similar to
Addis Ababa,[79] suggesting that it would be an error to assume without nuance a transhistorical version of the subsequent anti-blackness
in full force in the late eighteenth century.

THE DELIRIUM INSTIGATED BY 1453 and the ascendancy of
the Ottoman Turks was reflected in the continuing resonance of the
legend of Prester John of East Africa,[80] who would supposedly aid
Christians in defeating Islam. Thus, in December 1456 Pope Calistus
III contacted the "King of Ethiopia" requesting an envoy in a desperate ploy to defeat the Ottomans, a repetitive plea. Apparently, the
idea still reigned that Africans could be helpful in making Christian
domination of Jerusalem permanent, a replay of the Crusades in other
words.[81] After all, Christianity had been weakened by the internal
revolt embodied by John Huss and the "Hussites," a century before
the rise of Martin Luther, making the search for allies (even African
allies) imperative with Islam looming menacingly.[82]

The mid-fifteenth century also featured certain influential
Christians castigating Egypt as "our enemy," linking Cairo with the
Ottomans, with both allegedly "aiming at the downfall of Christianity,"
underscoring the importance of Ethiopia as the guardian of the Nile,
Egypt's lifeblood.[83] The Ottomans were such a fearsome foe that it is
possible to frame the Crusades, not least in the latter phases, as targeting a formidable "Race" that had yet to supplant Religion as an axis
of society.[84] It is fair to say that simple notions of "White Over Black"

had yet to take hold,[85] and would only take hold not just with the rise of colonialism but, more specifically, the rise of settler colonialism, when the oppressor and oppressed resided side-by-side and a mechanism was needed to demonize enslaved Africans and indigenes alike.

THE HYSTERIA ABOUT ISLAM WAS occurring as a chaotic free-for-all of enslavement gathered speed. As the fifteenth century approached, Valencia's captives included Moors, Tatars, Circassians, Russians, Greeks, Canary Islanders—and Africans from the north and farther south. It is also true that as this century rushed to a bruising conclusion, almost 40 percent of the enslaved were African,[86] though given what was to occur in North America this percentage seems paltry. The diversity of the enslaved in pre-1492 Spain was extraordinary, ensnaring Circassians, Bosnians, Poles, Russians, and Muslims of various ethnicities.[87] As of 1492 in Spain, there was a startlingly eclectic array of the enslaved, including Moorish, "Turkish" (actually Egyptians, Syrians, and Lebanese); "white" Christians, including Sardinians, Greeks, Russians; Canary Islanders (Guanches); Jews; and those described as "Black Africans."[88]

Converting captives to slaves was standard operating procedure for the invading Mongols, steadily moving westward, especially in the midst of the earthshaking uprisings in 1262 of northeastern Russian towns. Eastern Europe generally, from the Caucasus to Poland-Lithuania, was, according to scholar Christopher Witzenrath, second only in numbers to sub-Saharan Africa as a source of the enslaved. Between 1475 and 1694 this beleaguered territory provided an estimated 1.25 million slaves. Crimean Tartars captured about 1.75 million Ukrainians, Poles, and Russians from 1469 to 1694. Post-1453 and the seizing of Constantinople not only meant hampering access to the riches of Persia, India, and China, it also blocked Venice's eastward slave trade, helping to topple this once would-be superpower into enervating desuetude. As in points westward, the Black Death was impactful too, as it complicated the evolution of the slave trade.[89]

That is, post-1453 there was a drop in the number of Slavic and other European slaves in the Mediterranean, and, concomitantly, an increasing number of Africans, which was to grow spectacularly in coming centuries as a direct result.[90]

The immediate island neighbors of the Iberians, including the Canary Islands, were the immediate victims of these Europeans' rapacity. Revealingly, joining the looting were Genoese, Flemish, and French merchants, yet another Pan-European project pointing to the artificial identity of "whiteness." Genoese, well established in Andalusia in any case, participated actively in the trade in slaves, an ugly trait that was to characterize the most notorious of their many compatriots: Columbus. Blocked in their Mediterranean trade by Ottomans and Muslims and Italian rivals, they flocked westward in order to take advantage of the ascendant post-1492 new order. Sugar and slaves were the death-dealing duo that was to wreak so much havoc in the Caribbean, Brazil, and North America as well, and the Canary Islands provided a kind of mortal blueprint.[91]

Post-1453, the Ottomans were the best bet to become the world's preeminent power. By 1487, they were aiding the Moors in Andalusia, and the success of this venture would have undermined the other competitors. In coming decades, the Turks were to take Syria and Palestine in 1516 and establish bases in Ethiopia and Algeria by 1517. They captured Belgrade in 1521; Buda in 1526; besieged Vienna in 1529; Baghdad, Basra, Aden, and Southern Yemen by the 1530s. Indeed, as Spain expanded into the Americas, this allowed the Ottomans to expand. Madrid was moving westward precisely because the competition to the east and south was so stiff.[92]

A cause and result of this state of affairs was the reality that the Ottoman field army was probably superior to any other in the world, and it also possessed a superior logistical organization. It was likely that the ban on alcohol was yet another advantage they held over their often inebriated opponents with their clouded thinking. They certainly were experienced, for during the long sixteenth century, from 1453 to 1606, they were continuously at war.[93] Moreover, the Ottomans had raw materials for both gunpowder and guns, unlike many of their rivals.[94]

Similarly, just before Columbus's voyage, dozens if not hundreds of English merchants were operating in Andalusia, a major depot of the enslaved. The Treaty of Medina del Campo concluded between Catholic monarchs and in 1489 their London counterpart granted Englishmen the right to trade in Spanish dominions, the Canary Islands included, the latter then being decimated by the rising era of slavery and the slave trade that was tugging at the outskirts of Africa.[95] A few years before this date, two Englishmen were equipping an expedition with the aim of becoming involved in trade to West Africa; the London monarch requested permission to do so from the Vatican but was ignored, a possible prelude to the Protestant breakaway under Henry VIII.[96] In these halcyon days—in contrast to what the next century was to deliver—this Anglo-Spanish treaty envisioned a merger of the royal families of the two powers.[97]

Facilitating these new developments was the ascendancy of new technologies. By the early 1400s, the Portuguese—a maritime nation, facing the Atlantic—had made advances in shipbuilding, including the caravel, making it easier to reach Africa. Spain had made advances in artillery and cannon during the same time. As this was occurring, a merger of the interests of the Crown and merchants was taking place, an evident precondition for the emergence of capitalism, that is, capital backed by the state. This also meant that West Africa was lured away from trade in the interior and north and instead toward where the Iberians were arriving along the shoreline, just as the Iberians were lured away from North Africa (where Ottoman and Islamic strength did not seem to be declining) toward the easier pickings of the Americas.[98]

Nevertheless, Portugal's increasing mastery of the dual potency of the caravel and the cannon, not to mention artillery, did not allow for superiority of the Ottomans, though it did allow for superiority in Africa.[99] Portuguese navigators mastered Greek and Arab maritime science, connecting the outskirts of Europe to the Atlantic world and in the process shaping Europe's global vision. Portugal pioneered the oceanic sailing ship, building large vessels for Asian trade and, not coincidentally, made advances in naval warfare as well.[100] Meanwhile, at this juncture, though similarly facing the sea, England lagged behind Iberian mariners and many of their works on navigation were translations from Spanish and Portuguese. [101]

Europeans were seeking the source of the famed gold of Guinea, from which the English coin of the same name was minted, and when by 1482 Lisbon erected its largest castle in Africa, São Jorge de Mina, it was not just slaves but gold that was contemplated.[102] Indeed, the gold trade in Africa proved more valuable to Lisbon than the slave trade until about 1650, revealingly, when this latter odious commerce took off under London's aegis.[103]

This imposing edifice—this castle—complemented what was seen as their first outpost, south of the Sahara: El Mina in 1469. A Portuguese explorer had arrived farther south in the Kongo (Congo) by 1483.[104] The resultant conversion of the African elite there to Catholicism did not save the Congolese from mass enslavement but most likely facilitated it as this vast land became one of the first victims of the new epoch featuring "race" replacing religion as a marker.[105]

In some ways, the smaller Portugal, despite its grand pretensions, was to serve as an advance guard for England. London allied with Lisbon early on as a counterweight to a rising Madrid. As was the pattern, this was reflected in marital patterns as the fabled "Henry the Navigator" of Portugal had an English mother (this too undergirded the coming "whiteness" project). Feeding into this project as well was Lisbon's heavy reliance on "New Christians" in Africa, which was eroding religion as an axis of society and propelling the rising identity that was "race."[106]

Despite this early reliance on Lisbon, London, according to scholar Andrew Lambert, "carefully obscured Portuguese input," though even such pioneers as Walter Raleigh worked closely with Iberian seafarers. The Dutch too exploited Portuguese expertise, then in turn were plucked by Englishmen. On the other hand, the advent of movable type printing gave the English access to the intellectual and cultural riches of sea-power precursors.[107]

Thus, in the prelude to 1492, enslavement was an established fact in Europe and Europeans had been enslaving Africans—and others—for decades. With 1492, this heinous process was extended to the Americas and deepened in Africa. However, the Spanish, the first movers, and taking religious seriously, made the fateful decision (admittedly under pressure) to develop a Free Negro population in the Americas, not even taking the precaution of depriving them of arms. Like an adroit chess grandmaster, London countered eventually by seeking to tighten the enslavement noose around the necks of Africans, while incorporating other Europeans into the favored category of "whiteness," or Pan-Europeanism—up to and including, admittedly with bumpiness, the persecuted Jewish minority—which proved to be the winning ticket in the valuable sweepstakes of settler colonialism.

CHAPTER 2

Apocalypse Nearer

U pon arriving in the Americas in October 1492, Columbus compared the palm trees he saw to those of "Guinea," West Africa, a land where he had sojourned earlier. "I have travelled to Guinea," he confessed, though his experience there put him on guard, as he set out to enslave Tainos, Arawaks, and the indigenes of the Americas. "When men have been brought from Guinea to Portugal to learn the language," he said a few weeks after landing in the "New World," Lisbon was traduced when "they returned and the Portuguese thought that they could make use of them in their own country, because of the good treatment and the gifts they gave them," but "when they got to land they ... [dis]appeared."[1] Early on Columbus rounded up about 1,200 indigenous prisoners-of-war and selected five hundred for sale in Spain. This was not an extraordinary event in that it was the Crown that had enslaved the entire population of Malaga in 1487 and sold enslaved Muslims throughout the Mediterranean. Still, the Americas' main crop seemed to be the enslaved.[2]

Columbus's crew had been trained and disciplined in earlier voyages to Guinea, which hardly predisposed them to humanitarianism in the Caribbean. That is, there had been Castilian voyages to Guinea as early as 1453, but as these would-be conquistadors encountered stiff opposition there, they were impelled to sail westward, bulked up on the wealth of the Americas, and then returned post-1492 with a vengeance, as the zeal of the crusader was replaced, if not supplemented, by the zeal (and greed) of the merchant.[3]

Columbus, the Genoan, had a Portuguese spouse, a precursor of the Pan-Europeanism that was to take flight subsequently. Although the countries were neighbors, Portugal and Castile/Aragon often were at odds; as early as the thirteenth century they were jousting over the bounty that was the Canary Islands. Papal bulls backed one side, then the other, until the Treaty of Alcacovas in 1479 seemed to disfavor Lisbon.[4] It was also in 1479 that Aragon and Castile united, and the resultant monarchy also controlled parts of what became Italy, all of which meant being well positioned for the final push against Islamic rule on the Peninsula. As these opponents were subdued, those remaining were ordered to convert, inflaming sentiment in North Africa, which London was to leverage against the Peninsula in due time. Muslims of Portugal were also being quietly expelled.[5]

Simultaneously, there was an attempt by Lisbon to delimit the ability of Madrid to help London sail southward to Africa, indicating that as early as this pivotal moment, England was being eyed, though on the fringes of the continent and continental power.[6] This was understandable since the Italian navigator John Cabot, under London's aegis, in the late fifteenth century found himself off the coast of North America.[7] Revealingly, as Cabot was preparing to sail from Bristol, rebellions were rocking Cornwall and did not cease simply because the seaman crossed the Atlantic and made landfall close to what is now called Cape Breton, near Nova Scotia and Newfoundland. Soon Breton and Norman fishermen would be found in the same waters.[8] Similarly, as the end of the fifteenth century approached, a trade that was growing in West Africa was often an offshoot of Anglo-Iberian commerce.[9]

As a Genoan and cosmopolitan, Columbus probably knew that those from his hometown, as well as Pisa—along with those of Provence and Catalonia—fetched leather, wool, and gold from the ports of North Africa. Trade in gold was also part of the mix, with the metal coming from deeper in Africa's interior, Sudan, and the valley of the Senegal River, all providing a hint of the immense wealth—and talent—to be seized on this continent.[10] As for talent, it is probable that there was an African pilot alongside Columbus during his 1492 voyage.[11]

Columbus, in any case, was well suited for this 1492 venture.[12] Slavery was common in Genoa and Venice from about 1000 to 1350, and by the fifteenth century the enslaved were about 5 percent of Genoa's population. Post-1453, slaves became more expensive in Genoa, given the disruptive capture of Constantinople, though sub-Saharan slaves were quite rare in Genoa during this pivotal century. Unsurprisingly, early on and writing from Hispaniola, Columbus pointed out that this island could export thousands of slaves annually, which would boost the market in Europe, as it drove down prices.[13]

So schooled, the Caribbean interlopers perceived that harsher methods would be needed to entrap these latest victims of exploitation. When Columbus's band of outlaws routed Tainos in what has been billed as the "first major contest between Europeans and Native Americans," their prevailing was vouchsafed with the use of what has been called "hand cannon." Though advancement in the art and science of killing served to guarantee European conquest, Mayans in Yucatan shortly thereafter repulsed the enslavers in the face of cannon fire. Just in case, as early as 1501 an arms embargo was imposed upon indigenes that, despite leakiness in coming centuries, was generally effective.[14]

(Tellingly, there was an etymological similarity between pistol and the coin referred to as "pistole," a Spanish gold piece, at the beginning of the sixteenth century.[15] Appropriately so, given how "pistols" were deployed to extract wealth.)

Soon, Columbus's brigands had rounded up 1,200 captives and selected 500 for sale in Spain. Although gold was a lure, as it was in West Africa, it was evident that for the conquistadors, slaves would soon become the main bounty of the region.[16] "I took by force in the first island that I discovered some of these natives," he boasted, adding crudely, "They have been very serviceable to us." Perhaps averring to foul play in West Africa, he mentioned, "Nor are they black, as in Guinea."[17]

It did not take long for the newly arrived exploiters to say of the Caribbean islands that "there is much gold in this land, but few slaves to get it out," since a considerable number "hanged themselves because of the harsh treatment received in the mines from Christians." Indigenes were also fleeing in all directions, attacking the invaders too,[18] necessitating a shift to a newer labor force if the entire colonial project were to survive. For Iberians and other continental neighbors were discovering that escape by European slaves was made easier by the fact that slaves carried no special sign, wore no distinctive clothing, and besides were aided in rescue by fellow Christians,[19] all of which contributed to the escalation of enslavement by epidermis, the hallmark of what befell Africans in the Americas. Early on in the Spanish colonies, the enslaved were purchased in the Balearic Islands—or Majorca (Mallorca)—and Sardinia, many of whom were either Moorish or Muslim converts or even those of partial Jewish ancestry. Over time, however. there was a shift to others, especially as the "Negro trade" became a large and regular source of income.[20] For from about 700 to 1500, enslaved sub-Saharan Africans that flowed from south to north and west to east, ranged from 1,000 to 6,000 annually, rather small in comparison to the millions that were to be captured.[21]

Predictably, other potential victims of enslavement chose the path of homicide, not suicide. One of the early heroes of resistance was Hatuey, a Taino with roots in Hispaniola who fled to Cuba and waged war against the usurpers, but in early 1512 he was tied to a stake and burned alive. Earlier, indigenous comrades in Puerto Rico rebelled, perhaps seeking to forestall what had befallen their compatriots in St. Croix where Ponce de León captured indigenes with malign purposes in mind. For by the early 1520s in the vicinity, there was a thriving slave trade in indigenes.[22] As early as 1513, Ponce de León traveled from Puerto Rico to Florida, planning to enslave indigenes, this after the Bahamas had been virtually depopulated as a result of the same impulse.[23]

Actually, the purported seeker of the "Fountain of Youth" had fought Moors in Granada before accompanying Columbus on his second voyage in 1493. He was as a result well positioned to fight Caribs, who were fighting invaders furiously to the point that there was a possibility that Puerto Rico would be abandoned. By 1514, King Ferdinand ordered three vessels, well armed and staffed, to sail from Sevilla to the Caribbean with the aim of reversing this seemingly dire fate. Ponce de León was put in charge. Yet by 1515, on what is now Guadeloupe, Caribs continued to rampage, leaving the would-be conquerors depressed, humbled, mortified.[24]

Ponce de León, supposedly in search of a youthful elixir, found its antipode in 1521 when he sought to form a colony in what is now Florida, and was attacked by combative indigenes and wounded mortally. The continuing attempt to create slaves to create wealth by compelling them to toil ignominiously in mines and on sugar plantations and cattle ranches was encountering a fierce reaction, engendering fiercer still violence and then a shift to enslaved African labor. As early as 1514, this cruel search for free labor had brought con-quistadors to what is now South Carolina, where some were snared and deposited in Iberia.[25] Yet, in the long run, both Spaniards and the indigenous weakened each other in repetitive rounds of battling, allowing both to be ousted eventually by London, then Washington.

Also wandering into today's Carolinas was a Florentine seafarer in the pay of France. Giovanni da Verrazano, in what was becoming the parasitic norm for those who wished to weaken Spain, attacked the latter's commerce in 1523 as he and his crew crossed the Atlantic in futile search of a route to Cathay. The next year he reached the vicin-ity of today's Carolinas, then sailed northward for hundreds of miles. He spoke of seeing individuals whose "complexion . . . is black, not much different from that of the Ethiopians; their hair is black and thick," who could have been escaped and once enslaved Africans or, alternatively,[26] Africans who had crossed the Atlantic without European escorts, riding escalator-like currents.

SURELY AS EARLY AS 1503, enslaved Africans were arriving in the Caribbean, and as the Spaniards busily exterminated indigenes, they felt compelled to increase the number by 1511, as indigenous resistance mounted, with an assumption afloat that African labor was worth more effectively than that of the indigenous.[27]

As early as 1514, however, the rapid increase in the number of enslaved Africans in Santo Domingo already had become a source of nervousness besetting the colonizers.[28] In 1521, Spaniards were heading northward from their base in Santo Domingo to seize and enslave indigenes on the North American mainland, before being massacred in response by the would-be captives, a bloody process repeated in 1524,[29] establishing a trend that was to continue in the early history of the resultant United States until 1865. It was precisely in the early 1520s that the Spaniards, with enslaved Africans in tow, built what amounted to the first settlement of colonizers in what is now the United States. Quite appropriately, given the subsequent history that unfolded on this territory, these Africans were also implicated in the uprising that destroyed this settlement, then fled into the embrace of indigenes.[30] It was there that they bonded with the Guale in one of many unions of Africans and indigenes, a process that was to characterize northern Florida as a whole.[31]

It was understandable why the conquistadors would stray from the Caribbean northward since in December 1521 a major revolt of the enslaved rocked Hispaniola, reportedly executed by Jolof (or Wolof), who came from a powerful state that ruled parts of Senegal from 1350 to 1549; and by 1532 the shaken Europeans passed a law seeking to bar this ethnicity from the Americas.[32] It was in 1521 that, quite appropriately, a sugar mill owned by Columbus's greedy son was rocked by revolt. This was viewed worriedly as an attempt by the enslaved Africans and their indigenous comrades to seize control of the island, an eventuation that emerged finally by 1804. Arguably, this tumult motivated the move to the North American mainland, today's South Carolina, a few years later.[33]

In Hispaniola the Wolof were blamed when in 1522 about twenty Spaniards were killed in the midst of five days of furious fighting.[34] Still, the continuing resistance of indigenes and Africans repelled Madrid, creating an opening for London in the following century, which was then bequeathed to Washington. In a sense, the unrest

in the Caribbean compelled Madrid to seek other sites of exploitation, dispersing their forces and perhaps weakening them overall.
At the other end of the continent, in what is now Massachusetts,
Miguel Corte-Real's ill-fated 1502 expedition arrived.[35] Less than two
decades later, Europeans had reached Texas, inaugurating centuries
of enhanced conflict.[36]

Stymied by the strength of the Ottomans in raiding the usual sites
for slaves in the eastern Mediterranean and North Africa, the Western
European invaders turned to West Africa. Indeed, it was in 1463 that
an analyst warned, "The Turk, not content with what he has, is making
eager preparation to subjugate the entire world, starting with Italy,"
which could easily be interpreted as a threat to the Vatican itself.[37]
The Catholic Church provided "indulgences" to those so bold as to
fight the Ottomans, while Turks figured as an object of terror to many
a European state to the west.[38]

As the sixteenth century unwound, Spain, England, France, the
Netherlands, Sweden, and Denmark, among others, all constructed
sites in Africa where they traded for slaves and a range of goods.[39]
Driven by the proverbial pot of gold at the end of the rainbow,
gunpowder weapons were honed and then deployed promiscu-
ously for conquest, which then stimulated the development of the
modern state.[40] While the invention of the cannon came earlier, in
the thirteenth century, the so-called Military Revolution, a critically
important factor in propelling colonialism, also arrived in the sixteenth century at a time of population increase and even what was
thought to be overpopulation, which technological advances in the
ability to kill brutally addressed.[41]

Yet, even as Spain began its vertiginous rise post-1492, there already
were troubling openings that competitors, especially London, could
well exploit. For 1492 also meant the final expulsion of Muslim rule
from the Peninsula and their subsequent expulsion altogether and, as
well, the acceleration of the Inquisition that proved to be catastrophic
for the Jewish community. As early as 1501, those preparing to set sail
for Hispaniola were instructed that "no Jews, Moors, reconciled heretics or recent converts from Mohammadanism [sic] . . . allowed."

This proved to be self-defeating, not least since it served to create an embittered class bent on revenge. Moreover, Spain deprived itself of the diaspora networks of the Jewish community that it had helped to create by periodic expulsions, in 1391, for example, paving the way for exploitation of Africa. "New Christians" or "Crypto-Jews" often comprised the very group most apt to control the capital needed to develop colonial trade.[42]

The foregoing notwithstanding, it is possible that Inquisitorial targets may have had an incentive to flee the Peninsula for the Americas, where the colonizers were desperately in need of forces to confront often rambunctious indigenes, creating "whiteness" by subterfuge in other words. Thus, despite the official ban on their presence, there were reports of Moors and Jews in the Caribbean as early as 1508; their exile to Africa has been noted already.[43] Purportedly, there were at least six Jews accompanying Columbus in 1492, and they may have found less overt anti-Semitism upon arrival,[44] not necessarily because colonialism was more enlightened than the metropole but because colonizers and settlers needed all the help they could get, including the disfavored back home. Supposedly, "New Christians"—or those who may have been Jewish originally—invested in Columbus's initial voyage.[45] On the other hand, Madrid may have placed itself at a disadvantage in the eventual competition with London by pursuing inquisitorial policies.

Given the Lisbon-London tie, England may have been the beneficiary when Portugal post-1492 allowed certain Jews to arrive— forking over a hefty fee, of course—with about 100,000 accepting this deal. However, some wound up against their will in São Tomé, where the attempt to establish slavery off the west coast of Africa, as we shall see, was thwarted by repetitive rebellions, with the crowning glory spearheaded by the heroic Amador.[46] Nonetheless, this African dumping ground had the advantage for these forced exiles in that it was more conducive to being integrated into a cohesive Portuguese identity with their Christian counterparts than in the Peninsula itself. These "Christian" trespassers were more concerned about being overrun by malcontented Africans, [47] and had less fear of what befell their peers in Lisbon in 1506—bloodthirsty massacres of "New Christians."[48]

It would have been understandable if this beset community decided that the anti-Semitism of London was tolerable compared to what they had endured to this point. Assuredly, it is now well known that "New Christians" of Portugal and their Sephardic relatives dispersed to Holland, England, France, and the Baltic region, playing a salient role in the colonization process that commenced in the early sixteenth century. In fact, the sugar they helped to capitalize propelled their fortunes and the new order generally.[49]

London was then lagging in comparison to its European peers; still, English vessels may have reached what became Newfoundland as early as the 1480s and areas to the south soon after but found that to claim the territory, boots on the ground were needed, which opened the door for expulsion of dissidents and the attracting of adventurers, all for the aim of settlement. And this in turn led to a newer identity: "whiteness." Though the area south of what became Florida was the major site, not far from Newfoundland in what became Maine, a Portuguese freebooter—less than a decade after Columbus's initial arrival in the hemisphere—abducted about four-dozen indigenes for trafficking purposes.[50] Soon, Breton and Norman fishermen were found off the coast of Newfoundland, as the scavenger hunt was on.[51] By 1521, the peripatetic Portuguese had landed at what is now Cape Breton, Canada, but as so often happened, were chased away.[52]

Enslavement had always been an exceedingly ugly process but seemed to reach new depths of decimation when combined with the untold wealth introduced by plundering the Americas. By January 1499, Vasco da Gama was sailing past Mogadishu on the Indian Ocean coast of Africa; it "belonged to the Moors," meaning Muslims. And as casually as flicking dandruff from his shoulder, he observed, "As we passed before it" and "nearly upon it we fired off many bombards." Africa was being targeted in part because it represented the path of least resistance for plunderers, as evidenced by a lucrative slave trade then emerging in Congo and the "bombards" aimed at Mozambique, south of Mogadishu.[53] The fact that *"degradados"*—the degraded, the *lumpen*—were often exiled to Africa, including to da Gama's vessel, facilitated the utilizing of degraded methods of subjugation.[54] And these degraded elements with their degraded methods were essential as Cape Verde, off the coast of western Africa, became a depot for the slave trade by the early 1500s.[55] By 1524, exploitative Portuguese had established a foothold in Mombasa, north of Mozambique, which was to become one of the strongest and most important fortresses along the East African coast, complementing the influence they had initiated in the fortified town of Qasr al-Saghir, Morocco, as early as 1458.[56]

Thus, as the Iberians were bombarding eastern and southern Africa, by 1505 corsairs from Mers-el-Kebir in North Africa were launching a series of devastating raids against the Iberian coast, leading to years of internecine conflict. There were thousands of casualties, leading to the inference that as the Iberians were losing population at home, this fed the felt need to compensate by seizing bonded labor abroad. Iberians were not solely victims either, because from about 1492 and thereafter Christian knights and inhabitants of Granada frequently banded together to launch an annual raid against the Barbary Coast.[57]

This Mediterranean conflict was nothing new. During the summer of 1397, North African pirates attacked the Valencian port of Torralba, burning it down and seizing the inhabitants as slaves. Arguably, the "threat" from Islam had helped to unite Castile and Aragon and, possibly, a good deal of Europe itself in a Pan-European enterprise, a predicate to "whiteness" and the transition from religion to "race," a condition precedent for mass enslavement of Africans and dispossession of indigenes in the "New World." In response, by 1492 Swiss and Germans joined in the final push in Granada to oust the Muslims. Not to be left behind, King Edward IV of England opportunistically dispatched a top admiral to Lisbon, then Cordoba, where the monarch garlanded this seafarer with gifts.[58]

Decades earlier, in 1437, the Portuguese were subjected to a punishing defeat in Algiers, leading to a virtual cessation of the supply of captives fueling Europe, a trend hastened with 1453. This also led to Castilians and Portuguese bumping up against each other in the

Canary Islands, as they hunted for Guanches to enslave, although
there were hardly enough to satisfy their seemingly unquench-
able hunger for slaves, a hunger that was to be somewhat sated in
coming decades when West Africa was targeted. In the half century
preceding 1492, one estimate concludes that Portugal seized 80,000
captives from sub-Saharan Africa while ports from Sevilla to Valencia
witnessed an increase in the number of enslaved sent from Lisbon,
especially after 1480.[59]

The number of enslaved Africans brought to Iberia and the
Caribbean beginning in the sixteenth century and continuing thereafter was astounding by any measure. On the Peninsula itself, including
Portugal, there were perhaps 100,000 enslaved of various origins by
1600. Sugar plantations in Valencia and the Canary Islands and salt
mines under Madrid's jurisdiction relied on enslaved labor. At the
same time, according to scholar Antonio Feros, Spaniards "feared
Africans" yet "tended to see Africans as more useful and superior to
Indians," an awkward combination that guaranteed combustibil-
ity.[60] This reliance contributed to the aforementioned role of Africans
in St. Augustine, Florida, a city that was to bedevil English settlements to the north for some time to come, before the successor state
in Washington finally moved to swallow this citadel and impose their
rigid racialism in return in the nineteenth century.[61]

Hence, in nearly all the territories invaded by Spain—sadly
enough—Africans and those defined as "mulatto," often enslaved but
with a modicum of the "free" also, accompanied the first arrivals and
played a military role that was not insignificant. Some hailed from
Angola or thereabouts,[62] a nation whose martial traditions continued
to flourish in the twentieth century.[63]

Spain continued to expand its jurisdiction, reaching to the River
Plate, or Rio de la Plata, in today's Argentina and Uruguay, by 1516,[64]
with Africans crossing the South Atlantic in greater numbers thereafter. Sebastian Cabot arrived in what is now Paraguay as a result of his
1526–29 journey, but his attempted settlement was squashed by those
they had invaded.[65]

Indicative of the estimated strength of prevailing winds is that this younger Cabot was sailing on behalf of Spain from 1533 to 1547, departing in the latter year for England, indicative of the borderlessness that was to fall intentionally on the rest of the planet. His alleged betrayal was said to surprise Madrid, especially when he became "Chief Pilot" of London. The ever-entrepreneurial Cabot also had sought Venice to fund his voyage to Cathay, as he claimed not without justification that it was he, and not the elder Cabot, who was the great navigator and explorer. This younger Genoan also visited Jiddah. He was in London when Columbus's voyages were "much discussed."[66]

Madrid should not have been surprised by the footloose Cabot, since by the early sixteenth century, King Ferdinand accorded to English and other foreigners who had been residing in Andalusia for the space of fifteen or twenty years and possessed real estate and a family the right to exploit the new overseas trade opportunities opened up in the "New World." Nicholas Arnold can claim to be the first English merchant-settler and factor to have been authorized to do business in the Caribbean.[67]

THE ASCENT OF MARTIN LUTHER in 1517 was of monumental significance for the evolution of the apocalyptic events then emerging in the Americas and Africa. On the surface it seemed that Christian unity in the face of the Ottoman challenge had been torn asunder, allowing the Turks to play off one religious faction against the other, and it did seem initially that predominantly Catholic France and soon-to-be Protestant England were more than willing to consort with the Turks against perennial foes. It appeared as well that religious wars would erupt between Protestants and Catholics, a suspicion reinforced when in 1521 the Edict of Worms called for complete suppression of Luther's teachings.[68] In the short term, Luther's initiative may have fueled the flames of anti-Semitism, spurring more migration across the Atlantic in order to escape an increasingly bigoted Europe. Contemporary writers, for example, have cited Luther as an inspiration for the diabolical anti-Jewish schemes of Nazi Germany.[69]

Though the acidulous anti-Semitism of Protestantism was to dissipate over time, the dehumanizing nature of this bigotry may help to explain why the Reformation became so closely associated with enslavement. It was Luther who demanded the destruction of synagogues, books, schools, and homes of the Jewish community and insisted upon barring rabbis from preaching and that their congregants' property should be seized. He recommended that this minority have no legal rights and argued for their deployment as forced labor or banished altogether; of course there was no sin involved in liquidating them altogether, he said. Over time, this astonishing bias began to shrivel, but it was then directed against Africans, as Protestants made a peace of sorts with the Jewish community in the face of a stubborn Catholic challenge.[70] Still, this ersatz peace, as later centuries were to reveal, was hardly sincere and heartfelt.

The unperceptive observer in the 1530s could have easily concluded that because London was enmeshed in internecine crisis as Spaniards began to approach the vast and golden territory they called California,[71] leaving mayhem in their midst and weakening the indigenes as they had to confront a surging republic by 1848, that all this meant England was forever doomed.

Yet, for an ambitious Henry VIII in London, breaking with the Catholic Church made sense, the need for divorce and remarriage aside. The portly monarch reportedly had a gambling addiction—and seceding from Rome was no minor matter in lining his pockets for further mercantile adventure. Besides, he needed financing to bolster the apparatus of the state, not to mention funds to confront an ever-expanding array of internal and external foes. The Catholic Church in his jurisdiction was too lush a target to ignore.[72] Assuredly, he did not hesitate to employ murderous tactics against foes. Those unwilling to accept his diktat were executed. In 1535, several prominent Carthusians, a Catholic religious order, were dragged (Negro-style) across London from the Tower to Tyburn, now Marble Arch, where they were half-hanged, disemboweled, quartered, and beheaded. In nationalist London, the hegemonic line was to reject the "Bishop of Rome" but, as well, to despise the words of the "heretic" Martin Luther.[73]

The One True Faith had sided with the Iberians in divvying up the planet, which facilitated the Vatican's role as a major landowner and enterpriser, not least in London's backyard. Already this had led to much conflict between the monarch and his ostensible Church. The Vatican was slow to realize that the very nature of the Crusades, mandating sacrifice and trading indulgences, leading to wealthy clerics and rampant corruption, was made-to-order for schismatic reform. As matters evolved, the resultant conflict between Catholics and Protestants compelled the latter—as scrappy underdog—to jettison Luther's initial virulent anti-Jewish fervor in favor of an entente with a beleaguered Jewish community. Likewise Protestant England was to seek entente with Moors and Turks to outflank Catholic Spain and this too helped to propel London into the ionosphere of nations.[74] In retrospect, it is apparent that these profound maneuvers were driven more by life-or-death calculation, pragmatic maneuvering as philosophy driving strategy.

The Protestant Reformation was not simply a top-down coup. The seeds of Puritanism were planted perhaps as early as the fourteenth century with the rise of the Lollards and John Wycliffe and the notion that the Church should aid folk to live a life of evangelical poverty and emulate Jesus Christ. Their example shaped John Huss (or Jan Hus) who in turn influenced Martin Luther. By 1526, William Tyndale was inspiring growing numbers of the English in a way that would give impetus to Henry VIII.[75]

The English monarch's break with the Vatican also served to buy him favor with the Turks. For, as the Ottomans sought to advance to Persia, more munitions were needed and crafty Englishmen would deliver to them the scrap metal resulting from the upheavals of the Reformation—for example, dismantling of monasteries and other Church property. Lead from the roofs of ecclesiastical buildings, old bells and broken metal statuary, all sailed eastward on flotillas bringing Turkish gratitude.[76] During the 1530s virtually all the monasteries in the kingdom were liquidated and their expansive property empire was transferred to others, especially Cambridge colleges (yes, Massachusetts can also be referenced). Colleges plundered countless buildings made empty for stone and tiles, or even lead. Suddenly, monks and friars and their distinctive dress disappeared, as in a fantasy.[77] In a sweepingly draconian manner, made all the more remarkable in light of today's blather about "totalitarianism," Catholic literature was repressed systematically.[78] Likewise, dissident and radical Protestants too were suppressed; in a notorious example, a Wiltshire farmer was burned at the stake for reading Tyndale's Bible.[79]

As could have been envisioned, Ottoman Turks were an early beneficiary of the split in Christendom. For even the seemingly all-powerful Turks had to proceed cautiously given their proximity to Russia and its feisty neighbors. By 1501, Crimean Tatars had seized 50,000 Lithuanians, doomed to an uncertain fate as captives, and as this was occurring, Russia itself was steamrolling eastward into Siberia and into some Cossack areas as well, with both trends opening the door to mutually advantageous business with London.[80]

The Ottomans could not be reassured by trends due west in Spain: in Valencia, Muslims were being forced to convert at swords' point. Madrid had been unsettled by a revolt in 1501 in the Aplujarras, blamed on Muslims, that was crushed bloodily. By 1526, all Muslims were being ordered to convert or depart, a prelude to their total expulsion by the beginning of the seventeenth century. The ostensible reason was yet another Muslim revolt, where these believers were accused of assaulting and killings of Christians and despoiling their places of worship. Soon thereafter, Ottoman comrades in Algiers dispatched a clandestine flotilla to evacuate tens of thousands of newly minted refugees, which served to reinforce—if not create—yet another base to target Spain. The coerced Muslims were being accused of conspiring with the Ottomans against the Habsburgs. Muslims in Spain were boxed in, with even concessions to them boomeranging. "Much like has happened with African Americans in the aftermath of the Civil Rights Movement," says scholar Brian Catlos, "the theoretical removal of Muslims' subordinate status provoked a hostile reaction among those non-noble Christians who saw Moriscos [Muslims] as economic competitors and who no longer enjoyed an advantage over them as a consequence of Christian religious and legal superiority."[81]

A central and non-trivial difference is that by the late sixteenth century, Algiers barely contained a purported enslaved Christian population of 25,000 of what were termed "valuable possessions,"[82] some of whom were English and many of whom could easily be described as "white." As slavery evolved and as London and republicanism rose, African and enslaved became coterminous.

However, indicative of the constellation of forces then, Paris saw the ascendancy of the Habsburgs as a central threat, and as early as 1500 sought a treaty with the Ottomans to that effect, which led the latter to attack Vienna a few decades later.[83] London also served as supplicant when engaging the Ottomans. The Ottoman conquest of Syria, Palestine, the Hijaz, and Egypt in 1516–17, ultimately may have been as weighty historically as Martin Luther's demarche as the preeminent Islamic Empire rose; these new conquests compelled the Turks to improve their navy, leading to conflict with the Habsburgs, along with increased influence in Algiers and Tunis, which was to bedevil Western Europeans sailing southward to the riches of Africa.[84] By 1519, after at least seven years of warfare on the Barbary Coast, Khayr al-Din Barbarossa and his comrades in the western Mediterranean sought aid from the Ottomans and against the Spaniards. The bolstered Ottomans proceeded to augment their holdings in the Balkans and as far west in what is now Romania.[85]

A problem for the Ottomans in their contest with the Spaniards was the latter's geographic reach,[86] arriving in what became Micronesia and the Philippines in the first few decades of the sixteenth century, providing Madrid with seemingly limitless sources of free labor and stolen resources. The explorer known to some simply as Magellan was aided by the indigenes of the Pacific, who gave him and his crew food and water, which was countered by burning homes, destroying water vessels, and killing men. Ferdinand Magellan himself died at the hands of indigenes in what is now the Philippines in 1521,[87] but not before establishing a toehold that was to bring Madrid untold wealth.

Tunis was the site of a ferocious conflict between the two giants, the Habsburgs and the Ottomans, by 1534. This ostensible religious

war between the two had erupted in earnest as early as 1521 and cli-
maxed fifty years later with the Turks back on their heels, though far
from being defeated wholly; yet this setback did open the door for
yet another showdown between Catholics and their growingly potent
rivals, English Protestants,[88] who were to benefit by the incessant
focus on Islam.

Coincidentally, pirates of various sorts began to sprout, not just
in Tunis but also in Morocco, Algiers, and Tripoli, all of which to
a greater or lesser extent was fed by the Ottomans, along with com-
plementary trends in Western Europe. Pirates pillaged the coasts of
Spain and due east continually, weakening Madrid as London began
to rise. Mercenaries, the comrades of the pirates, began to grow, and
London employed disaffected Spaniards and "Germans" too in this
parasitic role, which could be seen as another stage in the evolution of
what was becoming "whiteness."[89]

Part of what was occurring was what appeared to be not just a
degrading of Catholicism but religion itself. "People learned to
devalue sacred properties and objects," says Dan O'Sullivan, facilitating the shipping of so much materiel to Ottoman Turkey. "The
livery men whose cushions were made of altar cloths," he says, and
the "woman whose crystal perfume bottle once held the finger bone
of a saint, the carpenter who made his living making and dismantling sacred objects, the yeoman whose doorstep had been an altar,
and all the families whose fortunes were improved by the dissolutions
had lost their fear of the sacred," which did not bode well for religion generally, not just Catholicism, a trend that spurred the rise of a
kind of neo-religion: capitalism. Catholicism at the pinnacle, in any
case, was seen as a repository of wealth, rather than religious comfort,
which helped to create a void then filled by settler colonialism driven
by the emerging "race" construction and the devaluing and revaluing
of Africans, and attendant commerce.

Catholicism could both absorb and administer blows. It was not
just the Lutherans, it was also the Calvinist Protestants, who often
disdained monarchs—and monks—who were thought worthy of
liquidation. Certain Catholics were starting to believe that unless

Calvinists were liquidated, there could be no peace, especially in France. This was at odds with the opposing idea that real security meant the utter devastation of the Vatican.[90]

THE OTTOMANS AND THEIR FOES were also jousting in East Africa, involved in what has been described as a "proxy war" with Lisbon as early as the 1520s, as the Portuguese crept up the Indian Ocean coast from Mozambique. Here the Ottomans were aided immeasurably—including in Goa—by understandably embittered members of the exiled Jewish community, still angry about their persecution. By 1538, there was a massive Ottoman expedition to India, possibly the largest flotilla in that region since Zheng He's Chinese-sponsored journey about a century earlier. Thus unwound what has been described as "history's first world war," between the Portuguese and the Ottomans with the Horn of Africa as a major site of contention.[91]

During the wars against the Ottoman Turks in the 1520s, their Spanish and what could be described as Italian antagonists lost far more than they gained, an indicator that the strongest horse was to the east.[92] The wider point being that it was not easy for Spain and the Habsburgs to sense the rise of England when the Ottomans were so formidable.

In any case, Spanish colonizers were encountering a hailstorm of unrest in the Caribbean and the Americas. For it was also in 1538— and previously in 1533—that revolts of the enslaved shook Cuba with indigenous from there and the Yucatan as well fighting alongside the bonded laborers of varying ancestries.[93] A few decades earlier, a voyage from Cuba to the Yucatan was punctuated upon arrival by a punishing encounter with indigenes. Hernán Cortes thought he was sly when he induced one group of indigenes to work against another in the Yucatan. He felt compelled to tell the emperor that "the Indians had attacked the garrison on all sides, and set fire to it in many places. . . . Our people were in extreme distress and begged me to come to their aid with the greatest possible haste." This bruising reality did not prevent the would-be conquistador from alleging that the "people are rational and well disposed and altogether greatly superior to the most civilized African nations," a high compliment indeed.[94]

They moved on at the instigation of these "civilized" indigenes, scurrying to their vessels bearing heavy losses. Then it was on to Florida, and a captain who had visited there earlier with Ponce de León cautioned his comrades to be vigilant in light of the inhospitality of indigenes, who rather promptly and, like their peers in Yucatan, caused a scurried flight back to vessels. Yet they did return with gold, serving to justify the loss of life, spurring a journey to what is now Mexico.[95]

Understandably, France, which bordered Spain, looked on nervously as Madrid swelled with the loot plundered from the Americas and Africa and the Asia-Pacific, but preexisting tensions with London meant confronting a two-headed antagonist, an untenable position that should have become clear by 1525 and the defeat at Pavia and the capture of the French king by the Habsburgs.[96] London was not displeased by this French misfortune and contributed to it by earlier declaring war on Paris, a decision punctuated in May 1522 when Charles V of the Habsburgs arrived in England for an extended six-week visit.[97]

France was not without weapons in confronting the antagonist across the Channel, allying with Scotland, placing enormous pressure on London, and forcing the kingdom to seek to gain more strength, particularly by colonial conquest, in order to stymie this alliance.[98] Another by-product of this alliance was a growing French presence in Scotland, placing considerable pressure on London to reverse this threat to sovereignty.[99] This "auld alliance" at least reached 1295 when the two parties inked a pact targeting their mutual target in London.[100] There was also Catholic collaboration that included not just Scotland and France but Ireland too.

Likewise, there were a growing number of Irish in Spain, including soldiers, seafarers, and, looming above all, co-religionists. Many were noblemen forced to flee their estates, though departing with political wherewithal capable of being wielded against London. Ireland had been conquered by England effectively as early as the twelfth century, but the rise of Protestantism inflamed what appeared to be a burning religious conflict.[101] The ties between Ireland and Spain were as long-standing as the winds from the southwest and concomitant trade. A lingering query is this: Did London's subjugation of Ireland act as a precursor for the rise of sixteenth-century colonialism, or did London merely see Spain's conquest of the Americas as a model to impose on Ireland (or both)?[102]

The intensifying conflict between and among England, Scotland, and Ireland stimulated the growth of an arms industry,[103] which then proved to be quite useful in subjugating Africans and the Americas alike. Indeed, according to one analyst, "The colonists in America were the greatest weapon-using people of that epoch in the world." But it was not just weapons—or technological determinism—that led to the massive defeats of indigenes; after all, by 1514 Mayans in the Yucatan repulsed the Spanish invaders in the face of cannon fire. However, what occurred was the would-be conquerors learning from their setbacks because some years later the matchlock arque-bus, despite poor and often unreliable performance, supplanted the crossbow at the point of attack, not least because of its enhanced deadliness. By 1535 Spain had successfully standardized the martial matchlock arquebus and its ball to permit interchangeability, advantaging Madrid vis-à-vis its wide array of enemies.[104] By 1537, as the arms race proceeded, the earliest breech-loading handguns had arisen in the vicinity of England, complementing the first mention of a hand-gun there, many decades earlier.[105]

These militarizing trends also proved essential in yet another development that marked the surge of London: the defenestra-tion of Ireland, which at the beginning of the sixteenth century was essentially medieval and feudal but by century's end was yet another appendage of the Crown in London,[106] albeit after devastation that drove many of Eire's finest sons and daughters across the Atlantic. Then there were the direct descendants of the Scots who colonized the north of Ireland during the reign of Henry VIII and to the time of William II, who wound up settling again, this time in Virginia, where they wreaked much havoc, a praxis honed decades earlier. Ulster, a byword for murderous conflict in the twentieth century, was their haven before descending upon North America.[107] Conversely, the Reformation guaranteed that Catholic Spain and heavily Catholic Ireland would align against Protestant London, instigating immense conflict for years to come.[108]

There were good reasons to flee London in the sixteenth century. Many infants died because of the insalubriousness of urban life; if an indigene from North America had visited a typical town across the Atlantic, he or she would have been stunned by the proliferation of pollutants and the dearth of personal hygiene. Actually, the search for perfumes in Asia to deodorize this nostril-wrinkling problem led directly to navigation feats and colonialism itself. Dysentery, smallpox, cholera, plague—and worse—were generally diseases unknown in the precincts invaded by the English and their allies in the Americas, along with the horrid unsanitariness that rampaged in crowded cities on the northeast bank of the Atlantic. This stinking stew of rankness along with an unbalanced diet would have been a step backward if experienced by indigenes of the Americas. Families were suffering from famine, especially when the price of basic foodstuffs rose. Flight from the countryside generated a tidal wave of vagabonds in the cities. High rates of mortality curbed the ability of parents to show "undue" affection to children, to avoid the psychological backlash of early death of infants. The stratified nature of land ownership and the yawning chasm between rich and poor would have alienated many an indigene from North America, though this was precisely the system that was imposed in the "New World," albeit on a racist basis.[109]

Given the ugly travails of Africans in the Americas, many of them, given the subsequent trajectory of white supremacy, would have been shocked by the underdevelopment of Western Europe. Certainly, given the prohibition of miscegenation that characterized the subsequent history of the United States, even today there are those who are taken aback by the existence of the "Black Prince of Florence," Alessandro de' Medici, who in 1532 with the backing of the Vatican and the Holy Roman Empire became the Duke of Florence at the tender age of nineteen. Of course, by 1537 he was murdered by his cousin, but even this was par for the course in terms of the customary palace intrigue that characterized royal life throughout the continent. During the sixteenth and seventeenth centuries, about 1.5 percent of the population of what is now Italy were enslaved—which was not precisely coterminous with being African—although Sicily had a high percentage of enslaved Africans resident. The tawny "Black Prince" was the son of a dark-skinned mother and, consistent with the power dynamic of the era, at times dressed as a Turk, the meaning of which was unclear.[110]

What *was* clear then was the potency of the Turks, which at once kept Spain occupied and England in a state of pandering toward them. Ottomans battling Spaniards allowed Englishmen to prevail.

CHAPTER 3

Liquidation of Indigenes | Reliance on Africans | Tensions in London

B y the 1540s, it had been almost a half century since the beginning of European invasions in the Americas. What was
called the "Mixton War" took place in what was called New
Galicia, in the heart of today's Mexico—the states of Aguascalientes,
Guananjuato, Colima, Jalisco, Nayarit, and Zacatecas—in a conflict
that had thrown up sparks as early as 1524. Later, due north in what
is now New Mexico, *conversos*, those who were Jewish "passing"
as Christian, were blamed for fomenting slave raids, but "Mixton"
was said to have a similar purpose. Because of the spectacular losses
imposed on indigenes, in the war's aftermath more enslaved Africans
were delivered, which simply substituted one problem for another
from the colonizer's viewpoint.[1]

For our purposes here, note that the rampant bloodshed in this
section of North America ill prepared indigenes for the siege warfare
that culminated in their mass ouster in what is now New Mexico in
the nineteenth century. And Spain's detrimental reliance upon armed
Africans was a partial product of privileging religious affiliation, which
could at once attract Africans and repel non-Catholic Europeans,
a trend that fell victim to the onrushing trend of "whiteness"

construction, notably in North America, as perpetrated by London and their republican successors.

IN THE EARLY YEARS OF the 1500s, Spain authorized delivering enslaved Africans in the Americas, though it was not long thereafter that limitations were placed upon the arrival of Spanish-speaking Africans since they seemed to have a proclivity to flee and influence indigenes. However, the monarch cancelled this initiative because many of the enslaved were good workers. So by 1510 the Spanish authorities authorized the arrival of non-Christian enslaved Africans from Guinea, and by 1518 the continuing slaughter of indigenes seemed to admit no alternative to admitting more Africans. Certainly, the deployment of Africans as footmen and warriors alike created numerous problems for the colonizer. Ultimately, the slaveholder was seeking to entice Africans to enforce his will on other Spaniards, the prospect of which, arising in London's settlements in the 1770s, contributed mightily to the successful republican revolt, animated by a "whiteness" that served to disrupt the possibility of alliances across increasingly rigid racial lines.[2]

By 1532, the elite in Santo Domingo complained to the Crown that rogues and rebels among Africans belonging to the clergy had committed grave crimes, with some fleeing to monasteries on the island where the believers hid and defended them from molestation of any sort. Earlier the Africans demonstrated that they were not eternally bound to the Spaniards when a rebellion of the indigenes spearheaded by the *cacique* Enrique on the island was joined by Africans who fled the plantation to join them. These were the reputed Wolof rebels from today's Senegal, who induced an equal number to join them on one of the earliest revolts of the enslaved in the hemisphere, a rebellion that may have lasted until 1533. Then, as already noted, there was the revolt with the Guale in the southeast quadrant of the North American mainland, which was followed by yet another trend that served to set "whiteness" in motion: by 1539, Frenchmen, working closely with African maroons in Cuba, attacked and burned Havana and attempted to seize neighboring Santiago. Interestingly, John

Brown was emulating these adventurers by 1859, with similar impassioned response in both instances.

In what is now the U.S. Southwest, Spanish conquerors were clearing the ground for the eventual arrival of republicans by waging a brutal war against *chichimecas*, a generic term of contempt, a dehumanization of indigenes to the level of "uncivilized dogs," a prerequisite for liquidation. Indigenes were left with unappetizing choices of enslavement or annihilation.[3] Nevertheless, there was a real danger to settlers in Mexico in what were described as "chichimeca" raids, often augmented by allied Africans escaped from servitude, notably in the areas stretching from Guadalajara and Zacatecas to Guanajuato. Official complaints about this can be tracked from the 1540s in Nueva Galicia, and raids by Africans were invariably linked to official reports to the "chichimeca" marauders.[4]

Across the Caribbean, African rebels had plagued the government of "Cartagena de Indias" for nine years by 1545, a repetitive tendency. Madrid again sought to exclude African Ladinos, those most acquainted with Spaniards, just as another futile attempt was made to exclude Wolofs and Muslims generally and Berbers too. Yet by the 1540s, as one acute observer put it, Santo Domingo resembled Ethiopia. Then the count was maybe 30,000 Africans and 1,200 Spaniards, with perhaps 6,000 that could be defined as "white" if dependents were included. The slavocracy of the island included a goodly number of what the late scholar France Scholes of New Mexico described as "Spanish Jews who managed to run the island as it suited them by holding a majority of offices in the Cabildo or administration as late as 1554." Like others, they were in the hot seat when thousands of Africans compelled some slaveholders to sue for peace. By 1546 war had been declared upon these insurgents, as Africans, said Scholes, "threatened to become masters of the island." Their holy cause was symbolized by Sebastian Lemba, one of a number of remarkable African insurgents in the Americas—Guinean in his case—in the conflicted century. His courage was echoed across the water in Panama, where religious ceremonies that spurred on Africans were said to have originated in the Sudan, and also resembled what was then occurring in the land of Yorubas.

The beset colonizers were in the untenable position of bringing more enslaved Africans to the hemisphere, just as free labor of indigenes was being impacted by the genocidal lust of the conquerors.[5] As the midpoint of the sixteenth century passed, Africans outnumbered significantly the number of Spaniards in the colonies. Spain was overstretched as early as midcentury with financing dependent upon Lombardy since—again—religious sectarianism meant exclusion of Moors and those from the Jewish community, a now archaic principle incongruent with the rise of the new system that was capitalism.[6]

Unfortunately, among the Africans joining the Spaniards in fighting indigenes were the famed conquistadors Juan Garrido and Juan Valiente. There was much work to be done in this regard since indigenous and enslaved rebellions (at times combined) were becoming regularized: Santo Domingo in 1522, New Spain in 1523; as noted, today's Carolina by 1526; Cuba in 1530 and what is now Colombia by 1530 when the five-year-old capital was destroyed by slave rebellions; restiveness in what is today's Ecuador was so severe that by the end of the century an independent polity had been formed, recognized partially by the Crown.[7] Given Spain's religious sectarianism, which narrowed the base of colonialism, the Crown was left with the unappetizing prospect of empowering Africans. Thus, in the second half of the sixteenth century in Chile, there was continual warfare between the colonizers and indigenes, leaving few appetizing alternatives. Due north, in the Yucatan, indigenes rose in 1546 as one and were squashed by the colonizers, who enslaved those they captured and sold them in the Caribbean islands. Nonetheless, a few years later there were enslaved Mozambicans in that vast region, meaning the Crown was relying upon one group of Africans not to ally with another.[8]

Thus, Africans were aboard Magellan's fleet as early as 1519. Understandably, one Spaniard was cited for the proposition that "we cannot live without black people; it is they who are the labourers and no Spanish person will work here," meaning the Americas, but increasingly, Africans were toiling in Europe too. By 1550 Africans comprised a reported 7.5 percent of the population of Sevilla and later the city was described as a "giant chessboard containing an equal number of white and black chessmen," a reputed inflation that conveyed an accurate point. England was not so marked, at least not to the same degree, and that may help explain why Africans probably fared better there than in Iberia for a good deal of the sixteenth century. And after Iberia, the largest African populations in Europe were in Milan—continuously the subject of bicker between "Frenchmen" and Milanese—Naples, and Sicily (all ruled from Madrid after 1535).[9]

Moreover, Spaniards were enduring revolts by thousands of organized indigenes in Darien, a province of Panama.[10] Predictably, in 1537 Africans revolted in the heart of New Spain, as their numbers were at a level that gave them confidence that they could succeed, and then they rebelled again in 1612.[11] Tristan de Luna y Arrellano, who reached today's Pensacola by 1559, sharpened his skill in combating indigenes in Oaxaca by 1548.[12]

Moreover, in the first half of the sixteenth century, there was an acute shortage of Spanish women in many of the hemispheric colonies, yet as the inevitable occurred and the number of mestizos grew, the Crown fretted that this would simply fuel dreams of secession.[13] The situation cried out for a "whiteness" project, curbing religious sectarianism and inviting settlers from various European polities irrespective of confessional preferences, but it would take the scrappy underdogs who were the Protestants to embark on this pragmatic route. Assuredly, rampaging indigenes were not sitting around waiting for the Crown to sort out its demographic problems but, instead, were attacking on virtually every front.[14] Enslaving indigenes and Africans was complicated when in 1550 the Crown hampered the ability to acquire slaves from the eastern Mediterranean—similar grounds hindered acquiring Wolofs, that is, their being largely Muslim, not to mention rebellious; in the long run, this would mean more enslaving of non-Muslim Africans and indigenes.[15]

Not accidentally, the mass liquidation of indigenes increased the odds of Spanish colonialism prevailing. But working against Madrid was its intensifying rule of the Netherlands, dominated by the Crown for decades, which drove numerous refugees into England. This flow increased beginning in about 1550 and continued for decades and contributed to the tens of thousands who made England their new home—and also, coincidentally, contributed to an incipient "whiteness." Tellingly, Antwerp, a nearby site of Spanish influence, had one of the largest populations of Africans in Europe.[16] In short, Spain's religious sectarianism was at odds with the needs of colonialism, meaning, for example, that Havana's resident European population generally did not grow in the 1540s and 1550s, which would mean more reliance upon Africans.[17]

This reliance was understandable since the liquidation of indigenes since 1492 had been nothing less than breathtaking. The objection of the colonist Bartolomé de las Casas is now well known, as indigenous numbers fell precipitously from approximately two million in 1492 to less than 15,000 a few decades later.[18] The enraged cleric lamented that "there is no language, no art or science, that can avail to recite the abominable and bloody actions committed by these human monsters. Neither is it possible to exaggerate their detestable deeds" for "to all these horrible scenes, I was an eye-witness." He cried that the conquerors sought to "blind their eyes with red hot irons, sear their tongues from their mouths," and "drop molten lead on their bare flesh."[19] Thus, alert to the demographic debacle, when Charles V authorized the importation of more Africans into the Americas, the license for delivering 17,000 unfortunate souls was said to be for "philanthropic motives," that is, "to preserve the Indians," an exercise in the rankest cynicism.[20]

His protestations notwithstanding, las Casas was not wholly innocent. He was present in Sevilla in 1493 when Columbus after his first voyage exhibited indigenes in the streets, and his father was on the seafarer's second voyage. Las Casas was said to have been gifted a slave during his student days at the University of Salamanca, and he traveled to the Americas in 1502 where he was said to have bought slaves that toiled in the mines. By 1512, it was reported that he was involved in the conquest of Cuba and received land and slaves in return.[21]

In response to his outcry, the Crown sought to curb indigenous slavery but something had to give, since free labor was seen as mandatory. So, ultimately the Crown had to pirouette and enslave more Africans, but this only entangled contradictions like a bowl of spaghetti.[22]

Whatever the case, las Casas's intervention proved to be beneficial to London, contributing to anti-Spanish and anti-Catholic sentiment and the rise of the "Black Legend," which proved to be useful in befouling the already besmirched reputation of Spain. Though torture was hardly unknown in London, one would have thought that Madrid was the expert in this dark art; the gathering conflict between Spain and the Netherlands also served to undergird this ideological offensive.[23] As the Dutch came under pressure from the Habsburgs and Madrid, Las Casas's explosive words were translated and touted as to what would befall the Dutch themselves if they did not stoutly resist this foreign takeover.[24]

Even as las Casas was beginning to protest, shifts were in motion: as early as 1525 there was evidence to suggest a shift from Taino labor to that of enslaved Africans in the Caribbean.[25] Further south in Peru, Spanish soldiers and settlers were bogged down during this same time in guerrilla warfare.[26] Yet, symptomatic of the importance of Madrid's variegated conquest, is that it was also in the 1540s that Spain was enjoying the free labor of enslaved African blacksmiths in South America. Enslaved Africans were an essential aspect of the enriching Andean economy and society, which was likewise the case in Bogotá and Quito, which facilitated Spanish conquest more generally.[27]

Spain's reach was exceeding its grasp, for it was also in the 1540s that colonizers were sent to what is now Arizona and New Mexico; unbeknownst to Madrid they were simply preparing the ground for the ultimate arrival of republicans. The contradictions that ensnared this early attempt at colonialism were exposed when a twentieth-century scholar archly asserted that "the first 'white man' to set foot within the confines of the State of Arizona was a jet-black Negro from the north of Africa, one Estevan or Estevanico." He was from the west coast of Morocco, said Merrill P. Freeman, and was enslaved, making it ironic when he and those that accompanied him encountered those heading north from the heart of New Spain on a slave-hunting expedition with indigenes as targets. "Estevan" made it to what is now the northwest corner of New Mexico, near the Arizona border, where he was reportedly "put to death" by angry indigenes. [28]

Despite this tragic engagement, says contemporary scholar Robert Goodwin, Estevan—or Esteban—was treated, if not equally, better than Negroes would be treated subsequently in North America. This perception is understandable since the subsequent devolution of racist ideologies, especially anti-African thinking, was hardly formed fully in the sixteenth century. Contrary to Freeman, Goodwin contends that "Indians revered Esteban . . . he spoke their language."[29]

APPARENTLY, INDIGENES DID REACT negatively to tales of torture and worse inflicted upon them by invading conquistadors.[30] Seizure and rape of indigenous women was a hallmark of the invasion spearheaded by Francisco Coronado, who led a bloody expedition from today's Mexico to today's Kansas.[31] Like other invaders, Coronado seemed to find Turks thousands of miles from their homeland.[32] Ominously, the intruders encountered an indigene they termed "the Turk" because of his apparent resemblance to those within Ottoman rule, which was hardly reassuring given religious enmity.[33] Possibly, it was the fierce resistance of indigenes that reminded the invaders of 1453, for chastened Spaniards then stayed away from this region for decades.[34]

Perhaps understandably, Spaniards found Ottomans in the deserts of North America, for it was around then that a Venetian diplomat, representing a region in vertiginous decline, asserted that the Ottomans were seeking to become rulers of the world, including Africa, Asia— and Europe too. In the prelude to the pivotal decade of the 1540s, the Ottomans had launched a "German" offensive and besieged Persia as well (capturing Baghdad in the process), in addition to quashing a revolt in Egypt. The treasury of the Ottomans was expanding because of slavery, and the dealers in human flesh were diverse, including

Greeks, Armenians, some "Italians", and a number of non-Muslims, including members of the Jewish community. In fact, Istanbul may have been the single largest market for the buying and selling of slaves, and the appetite for this odious commerce showed few signs of slackening in the sixteenth century. This was a turnabout because in late medieval times much of the Black Sea trade had been controlled by the aforementioned Venice and Columbus's Genoa. Hence, since the late fifteenth century Ruthenia was among the regions drained by slave raids. Moldova felt the sting of the Ottomans in the 1530s and the latter's agent, Barbarossa, from his perch in Tunis was seeking to repel Genoa's Andrea Doria, the celebrated anti-Ottoman seafarer. An Ottoman fleet of seventy-two ships proved essential in seizing Aden and making Yemen yet another province, just as a Portuguese fortress on the Indian Ocean coast was battered. By 1541 there was a decisive Ottoman victory in Hungary. Mosques were proliferating, and not just in Istanbul. Vienna was able to resist, though the stream of gold ducats heading from there to Istanbul appeared to be a form of tribute.[35]

As a result of Ottoman advance,[36] the number of Spanish settlers in the colonies—a rich source of wealth and thus armaments—required augmentation but, contrarily, Madrid honed an obsession with Lutheranism, designated as the "great enemy of Spanish society." And if the era from 1480 to 1520 was the "Judaizante" phase of the Spanish Inquisition, thereafter it was a Protestant phase. Embarking from the peninsula for the settlements were persons vetted to ensure that they were of unquestioned orthodoxy. There was a brief period from 1526 to 1549 when Charles V permitted his "German" and Flemish subjects into the colonies legally, but this was hardly the norm during the century. Generally, there was a prohibition on the dispatch westward from Sevilla of members of the Jewish community or even—at least theoretically—New Christians or conversos, Moors, and the like. Of course, so-called heretic migration continued by devious and illegal means.[37] But ultimately this was self-defeating, given the Ottomans' unquestioned potency and the ascendance of Protestants in Europe.

Whatever the formal provisos suggested, there were Basques well represented when New Spain was invaded and indigenous rule was overthrown; Andalusians were also present, along with Portuguese and Flemish.[38] The embryo of "whiteness" was also reflected in the fact that Queen Isabel herself, says German Arciniegas, "had English blood in her veins," and "some Germans were delegated to govern Venezuela, while others were put in charge of Chile as far as the Equator."[39] Near this time, the only engineer in Poland was a Venetian; the Grand Prince of Moscow had his castle built by a man from a region nearby this engineer's, whereas the Spanish and Italians were knit tightly by religious commonalities. The Castilian poets adopted the forms of the Tuscan masters, while the martial attainments of the latter's comrades were won in Spanish campaigns.[40] The conquistadors of various stripes in New Spain also brought enslaved indigenes to Spain itself, further complicating bloodlines.[41]

The overriding point was that Madrid's religious sectarianism was inappropriate for a new era of conquest that mandated building a broader coalition for the liquidation of indigenes and mass enslavement of Africans. Yet, even before the formal proclamation of the Inquisition in New Spain, an Englishman there was asked peremptorily if he had any ties to Judaism or Islam or "any other sect condemned by the Church."[42]

Just as feasting at the colonial banquet helped to calm—somewhat—irredentist and secessionist trends in Edinburgh, non-Castilians, albeit Catholics, played an essential role in Madrid's colonial quest, as suggested above. (And, coincidentally, with the demise of colonialism in the twentieth century, secessionist impulses began to percolate in both Edinburgh and Barcelona.) The Jesuits were established in this pivotal century by a Basque, Ignatius Loyola, and wound up being shock troops of colonialism, and by 1557 were sited in Macao. Basques were also essential to the subduing of the archipelago to be named after the monarch, the Philippines.[43]

Consequently, and as noted, non-Castilians were likely to be Catholic, and this religious category as a vector of colonialism was bound to fall to the competing, and much broader, category of "whiteness." Perhaps because of an absence of mind, there were more free Africans in Mexico in the latter part of the seventeenth century than enslaved—a trend that was becoming evident as early as 1540—which was a recipe for instability, as English comrades then settling into the vast Atlantic seaboard could have attested.[44] By one account, there were more "Crypto-Jews" than Catholics in Mexico City, an untenable position that maladroit settler colonialism had created.[45]

HERNANDO DE SOTO WAS RENOWNED for leading a murderous expedition into territory that now comprises the vast region stretching from Florida through Georgia, Alabama, Mississippi, and across the Mississippi River. As ever, gold was the object, along with a passage to Asia, but enslavement inevitably was an accoutrement, with some exploited laborers committing suicide because of the harshness, including gross sexual abuse, that was inflicted upon them.[46] De Soto was yet another conquistador whose crimes ultimately benefited republicans. One of the largest battles ever fought between North American indigenes and Europeans occurred in 1540 in what is now Alabama, with the epic battle reduced in essence to the two principals: de Soto versus Chief Tuskaloosa. Thousands were killed. The Spaniard was aided immeasurably by the estimated four hundred African and indigenous enslaved that he held and the terror he imposed by dint of mass rape.[47]

By 1542, fellow conquistador Juan Cabrillo landed in California, encountering four indigenes who wisely fled upon sighting him and his entourage. Like de Soto, Cabrillo also did not survive his journey and was replaced by a man reportedly with roots in the Levant.[48] According to one writer, "In the early modern period Japan was once very near to endangering Spain's hold on her Pacific colonies," hastening Cabrillo's arrival and demise. A powerful, warm ocean current, argues Charles Chapman, "called the Black Stream or Japan Current," propelled some from Asia to the east bank of the Pacific. Even in the twentieth century, he declares, "among the Indians" there were "many traditions of recognizably Chinese origin and also linguistic affinities, notably so in the Puget Sound." Further, "Aztecs, Mayas and Incas show a marked similarity to . . . the Chinese." Thus, "In the course of excavations ancient Chinese implements and coins have been found" as "regular trade existed between China and California in the first century of the Christian era." In contrast, by 1542 Portuguese had arrived in Japan, leading to a concerted effort to repel these invaders, leading ultimately to barring such foreigners until the United States shattered the barriers in the 1850s.[49]

The Portuguese were truly on the move. By 1553 they had reached the Mono River in today's Benin, an arrival that one scholar said "signified something radically new" in terms of penetration of the continent.[50] Yet, like the Netherlands, Portugal's historic role was to be a stalking horse for England, then Britain, an advance guard for London, clearing the underbrush for the arrival of a new era.

As Iberians and Ottomans were rampaging overseas, back in London 1 in 12 men were in arms in 1512, and 1 in 6 by 1545, a direct response to a deteriorating environment across the Channel and internally. Inexorably, this meant more crippling taxes and disruption of trade as income was diverted to the Exchequer, followed by local government struggles and churches feeling compelled to buy armor in response to religious conflict.[51] London's laws targeting the Pope and Catholics were an essential part of the landscape in the 1530s, as property continued to be appropriated willy-nilly. By 1536 there was a serious uprising in Lincolnshire generated by these deeds—and misdeeds—perhaps the most significant revolt of the entire Tudor era, as some were unwilling to accept the ditching of the old-time religion. Nonetheless, the monarch continued to sell Church property in order to construct more effective coastal defenses, as conflict with the "auld alliance" of France and Scotland threatened. When the Treaty of Toledo was signed between Paris and the Habsburgs, with explicit anti-London aims in mind, England seemed terribly isolated diplomatically, especially because Paris had worked out an entente with the other major power: the Ottomans. The threat of annihilation concentrated the mind wonderfully, however, in London, forcing initiatives and actions that were to flourish by the beginning of the seventeenth century.[52]

The crude euphemism "rough wooing" was the term ascribed to England's relationship to Scotland, still viewed suspiciously as a kind of mass agent of Paris. The pitched battle between the two, denoted as the Battle of Pinkie Cleugh in September 1547, culminating in London's victory, did not squelch Scotland's reluctance to reside under the thumb of England: it would require a bountiful invitation to the banquet of colonialism, which would be extended in the seventeenth century, to assuage many Scots.[53]

The complex and ever-shifting ties between England and Scotland made it difficult for London to adopt and pursue a consistent line, generating erratic blunders on both sides. For during the high tide of the Reformation, roughly 1534 to 1561, the two were variously enemies, allies, co-belligerents, friends, though it would be unwise to forget that perhaps the overriding factor was the "auld alliance" with France, which in turn was shadowed by Protestant-Catholic conflict in the hexagonal nation.[54]

The city of London grew from about 40,000 in 1500 to 120,000 by 1550, an indication of unrest, as refugees headed for this urban node, including those fleeing religious persecution. Beginning in 1531, there was also more outreach to Africa, in what soon would become a staple; there were sixteen trips leading up to 1567 either to West Africa or to that coast en route to the Americas, with crews and passengers dodging enslavement themselves as they sailed by Algiers.[55] This overseas venture was virtually mandated, since by 1549 because of the drain of conflict with Scotland, not least, England was almost bankrupt. This led to the old reliable: renewed plunder of Catholics, engendering more conflict and more need to spend on defense (and offense) and more prospect of bankruptcy. The poor continued to be driven off the land, inducing more upheaval.[56]

As for religious persecution, the Vatican's initiation of the Council of Trent in 1545[57] marked the escalation of the Counter-Reformation, a fierce fightback against Protestants, a decision leading directly to a heightening of conflict.

Urban anonymity was one way to hide from religious and other kinds of persecution. By 1545 Henry VIII approved the use of enforced servitude as a criminal penalty when he ordered that vagabonds, alleged ruffians, and "evil disposed persons" be sent to the galleys, then propelling water-bound vessels so important for the new era. By 1547, London had passed a statute that imposed slavery as a punishment for vagrants who refused to work, a dress rehearsal for what was to befall Africans. Simultaneously, Englishmen were being detained and enslaved off the coast of North Africa, just as London was enslaving Irish and Scots.[58] The monarch's maneuvers were influenced by what happened during the summer of 1545 when England was under attack by thirty-five ships bearing 30,000 from the hexagonal nation across the Channel during the Battle of Solent.[59] At a certain point, poorer subjects realized that it made more sense to take one's chances in the wilds of the Americas, and perhaps become a slaveholder, rather than run the risk of being a slave in Europe.

The historian Gustav Ungerer asserts that Londoners intentionally suppressed the ignominious English record of enslaving Africans, even in the first few decades of the sixteenth century. Africans as enslaved domestic workers was not just a seventeenth-century phenomenon. he says: "Among the foreign merchants residing in England [were] the Portuguese New Christians or *conversos*," a number of whom "had been accustomed to keeping and handling slaves before they took refuge in England in the 1540s." He goes on, "They enjoyed the privilege of keeping up their old lifestyle, practicing their Jewish rites on the sly and developing their commercial networks with their old *converso* partners in Amsterdam, Antwerp, and Constantinople," central financial sites all.[60]

London, in short, was influenced deeply by the anti-Jewish turn in Lisbon by the 1540s and an acceleration of an Inquisition that was said to be "crueler" than Spain's. This was a reversal of sorts in that in 1495 the monarch had moved to ease anti-Jewish fervor, but he wanted to marry Spanish royalty who insisted on a different course. The latter trend was complemented in 1521 by the ascension of militant bigotry in Lisbon. The Madrid-Lisbon condominium was extended to Jamaica and, correspondingly, the Jewish community of Portugal began to decamp there as early as 1530.[61]

As early as 1526 there was English trade with the Canary Islands, the traditional jumping-off point for explorations into Africa and the Americas alike. Before then, England's Thomas Tyson had reached the Caribbean, where London was to plant its flag more than a century later. By 1530, William Hawkins—father of the enslaver John—had reached Brazil.[62] Actually, he made three voyages between 1530 and 1540, bringing an indigenous leader to present to Henry VIII. Other Englishmen eventually became involved in trading of enslaved indigenes.[63]

The grandfather of the man who was to become Governor Winthrop of Massachusetts in the seventeenth century was born in 1498 and jailed by 1543 after supposedly negotiating with foreigners contrary to the King of England—an anticipation of republicanism. This was happening at a time when nerves were frazzled because of the external threat from Paris and Madrid and internal ruckuses engineered by those then being tossed off the land. It was likely, says biographer Lawrence Shaw Mayo, that the elder Winthrop was "buying or selling cloth without sufficient regard for England's protection of her wool trade," a kind of self-interest that proved essential to the subsequent triumph of republicanism. London in an uproar found it useful to reconcile with him, since by 1544 he was buying a manor in Groton, appropriated by the monarch when he dissolved monasteries. He expired in 1562, but earlier his son, the future governor's father, born in 1546, moved on to Ireland, at that time being wrenched by like-minded expropriations. By 1588 the future governor was born,[64] just as London was about to take off after repelling the Spanish Armada, a true turning point in world history.

Ironically stimulating London was the decline of Antwerp, with whom England had conducted a mutually profitable cloth trade. This led England to seek a "Northwest [or Northeast] Passage" by sailing north via Norway to Russia; and, complementarily, sailing as well southward to Africa for riches. Seed capital for these ventures often emerged from the looting of Catholic properties. The increase in the number of demobilized soldiers, stemming from repetitive conflicts with Paris and Scotland most notably, provided staffing for those accustomed to "rough wooing." Soon these men were buying Africans in territories influenced or controlled by longtime ally Portugal, then selling same in the Americas. Ultimately the Spanish crackdown on Antwerp sped up these devastating trends.[65]

As Antwerp declined, London rose, as embodied in the controversial figure Thomas Gresham, government banker to three English monarchs, initiator of two of England's most important institutions: Gresham College and the Royal Exchange. Today he is associated with "Gresham's Law," that is, "bad money drives out good money," a sturdy principle of an emerging capitalism that continues to resonate. His father, Richard Gresham, was a manipulator for King Henry VIII, especially as a merchant of death, or arms procurer. When the elder expired in 1549, he was widely regarded as one of the most despised men in London, not only as a bringer of death but in his added role as a debaser of currency and inducer of misery, not to mention as a "welsher"—a curious word that—on adhesion loans extracted from European banking families, which too boosted the Crown. The younger Gresham earned his spurs in Antwerp, where he pioneered in double-entry bookkeeping, yet another staple of an emerging capitalism, and sidelined as a smuggler, a similar staple. Finagling with exchange rates and arbitrage between and among currencies was another specialty of his, paving the path for today's George Soros. His mastery of the magic of the marketplace—legerdemain often performed in Antwerp—meant that he played an outsized role in funding London's seemingly incessant wars, by dint as well of, yes, smuggling military materièl and money too (often using beer barrels) in a labyrinth difficult for outsiders to comprehend. The Royal Exchange, England's first stock exchange—yet another signpost on the road to capitalism's rise—was predictably patterned after Antwerp's Bourse. He was a precursor of today's world in which national sovereignty is shaped if not dictated by the magic of the marketplace.[66]

As Lisbon accumulated wealth from the crimes of colonialism, it too saw its tie to Antwerp decline; the same held true for its relationship to Venice, a now fading power, joined growingly, and ironically, by Genoa.[67] Englishmen could easily conclude that the wave of the future was emulating Lisbon and Madrid, not Venice and Genoa. By the 1550s, William Towerson, merchant and investor—epigone of the rising class—financed three expeditions to West Africa. His first was the most successful, as he traded cloth and other commodities and returned to England with about 50 ivory tusks and 127 pounds of gold. Then there was Thomas Lok, a founding member of the Muscovy Company, bent on exploiting trade to the north; he was a co-investor, along with Sir George Barne (a financier and politician, foreshadowing the rise of state monopoly capitalism) and Sir John Yorke, in yet another expedition to West Africa that was captained by John Lok, member of a family that bequeathed the Locke family. Martin Frobisher, a future explorer of note, as a teenager was part of these African forays, surviving his first voyage to Guinea, even though most of the crew, including the captain, died. Frobisher was detained for about nine months.[68]

Not detained or deterred was the growth of English cities, fattening on the profit of trade: in 1500 Liverpool was a one-horse town, but by the end of the century this city, soon to grow larger on the wealth of the African Slave Trade, was a seven-street town at least.[69] Revealingly, Englishmen made fewer than 50 voyages to Guinea before 1600 and 150 by 1650.[70]

England seemed to be soaring as a top wool-producing nation, critical as temperatures dropped, but it was being squeezed by Spain, particularly as wealth poured into Madrid's coffers from the Americas and elsewhere. By the 1550s, however, supply seemed to outstrip demand, forcing merchants into other businesses, a quest that ultimately led to the trade in Africans. By 1551 Thomas Wyndham, scion of a premier war-fighting family, visited Morocco, which was becoming a key ally of London, in search of sugar and saltpeter, the latter important for ammunition needed to subdue Africans. Even the loss of Calais in 1558, a real setback, somehow became something else when this current French territory helped to transform the Channel from a highway into a formidable moat. On the other hand, the Treaty of Cateau-Cambresis of 1559 resolved a lengthy contentious struggle between Paris and Madrid for control of what amounted to

Italy, leaving the Habsburgs dominant for the next 150 years, thereby strengthening Madrid further, to London's detriment.[71] This pact had emerged after a combined French-Ottoman fleet landed in Corsica and seized it from Genoa, Charles V's ally.[72]

By 1555, there was a new monarch in Paris—Henry II—and he too turned east to the Ottomans, requesting a force be sent to the Mediterranean to aid in further war against Spain. That same year, almost on cue, the Pasha of Algiers—Salah Rais—laid siege to Bougie, a Spanish possession since 1510, a defeat for Madrid in North Africa.[73] Scotland was still split down the middle between Catholics and Protestants, and as long as the former retained strength, London itself could be threatened but soon the One True Faith would be on the defensive in Holyrood.[74]

By 1558, there was a new monarch in London too—Queen Elizabeth—who presided over her nation's ascendancy until her passing from the scene in 1603. A predecessor, Henry VIII, anticipated her mastery of foreign affairs. He had been receiving arms from Flanders, but in 1543 he induced the Flemings Peter Bawd and Peter Van Collen to settle in London as gun and ordnance makers, yet another example of Pan-Europeanism, a potent trend stimulated by contiguity. During her reign, this deadly business increased in sync with conquest until there were 37 accredited gun makers in that part of London called the Minories, not to mention in other precincts.[75]

Speaking of foreign affairs, England's Russian ties also expanded, at least for a while. The Muscovy Company was founded in 1555 in the midst of the sorties by Towerson, Lok et al.—at times by the same parties—but while Londoners were seeking to traverse the often chilly waters northward,[76] the Iberians were encountering warmer seas off the coast of Africa and sending settlers to Brazil by the 1530s. By 1600, this investment had paid off when Brazil was regarded widely as the most prolific producer of sugar in the world.[77]

Opportunistic Paris, soon to be marked by bestial conflict between Catholics and Protestants alike, chose to ally with what seemed to be the rising power, the Ottomans, which could at least blunt the possibility that London would outflank them by doing the same.[78]

Actually, a Franco-Turkish alliance had materialized as early as 1520, when Paris was seeking a powerful partner to menace what today is Italy and deflect attention from hexagonal attempts to conquer or reconquer the region surrounding Milan. The Turks were not exactly passive partners since they had not forsworn conquering the whole of this elongated peninsula, down to the toe of the boot and including the Vatican. The Sultan had vowed to take Rome and oust the Pope, just as Constantinople had been seized most dramatically in 1453.

From 1484 to 1530, France was unusually free of rebellion and unrest, allowing Paris to gear up for further confrontation with England. But then, Paris had the misfortune of crossing swords with Charles V and that draining conflict along with bad harvests generated popular unrest, particularly in urban areas, already notorious for the extraordinary aggressiveness that marked such sites. This helped to facilitate judicial torture, which was normalized. The cleverly sly Parisian elite managed to have relations with the Ottomans and the Vatican and "German" Lutherans too. Since the monarch in London thought of himself as the monarch of a good deal of what amounted to France, especially Calais, diplomatic flexibility was a must in order to confront England. Correspondingly, London sought to leverage Charles V against Paris, which did allow him to gain Paris's approval of the annulment of his marriage to Catherine of Aragon. But the monarch in Paris won no applause in London when his daughter married James V of Scotland, seemingly solidifying this important alliance. Predictably, by 1543 London and Paris were again at war,[79] a godsend to Madrid then being hounded in the Americas.

Soon thereafter a proposal was made that "there shall be an inviolable friendship and confederacy between France and Scotland for ever."[80] But just as the death of Copernicus in 1543 signaled that what seemed to be eternal verities were open to challenge, the alliance between France and Scotland, which was seen as threatening in London, seemed to disintegrate as Edinburgh was invited to participate in the colonial feast.[81]

By 1544, Turkish ally Barbarossa was actually accompanied by French soldiers and galleys when he led pillaging of the Catalonian coast and sacked the ports. Frenchmen and Turks were shoulder-to-shoulder as they broke down doors of homes with sharpened axes and burst inside with mayhem in mind. Tunis and its Moorish king continued to object to this powerful alliance as succor was sought in Spain though it seemed that they were bucking history.[82] Alas, the Inca treasure pouring into Spain from Peru not only financed the conquest of Tunis but also financed the building of St. Peter's Basilica.[83]

Galley slavery of the Mediterranean degraded labor generally, or at least wherever the principals of this praxis, such as the Iberians, alighted, as in Africa and the Americas. "If there be a hell in this world," was the common plaint then, "it is in the galleys"—and increasingly on another vessel: slave ships, then plantations and mines of the Americas. Still, the worst prison on shore seemed preferable to the galley's roofless dungeon, where flogging, drowning, and being shot were common. Cervantes wrote movingly of this hell on earth, and the impression left to history was that the Inquisition itself was preferable to the lash of the boatswain.

Many Christians believed that they were persecuted by Muslims aboard Algerian vessels, flogged from daylight to night—in the best case, as this was preferable to having one's eyes gouged out and ears and noses bitten off by benighted Moors. Muslims had their own gripes, as they smarted when in the early 1500s they were forced to set aside robes and turbans and adopt the increasingly hated hats and breeches of their oppressors. Then they had to keep the doors of their homes open on Fridays, Saturdays, and other Christian designated days. They had to speak Castilian too, and get rid of their Arabic names. Many thought that such strictures were directed heavily against wealthy Moors, weakening the overall community. By 1560 the Crown made the extraordinary step of barring Moriscos (or Muslims under Spain's rule) from holding enslaved Africans. Christians had their own complaints, including seeing women and children being taken to the markets of Tunis and northern Morocco, snatched from Granada.[84]

Muslims in Valencia were being forced to convert coercively. Moriscos were accused of collaborating with the Ottomans, making them a peculiar danger to national security. Soon Morisco dance and music were circumscribed.[85]

Reportedly, the Ottomans despised the Iberians, including the Portuguese, who were accused of aiding the Persians in the use of firearms and cannon, at a time when they were under siege. Dragut likely was of Greek origin and was seen as being as deadly competent as Barbarossa as he and his crew ravaged the coasts of Sicily, Italy, and even Spain. Tunis was a principal haunt, which brought Christian retaliation,[86] leading to apprehension about the latter's incursion into the prize that was Egypt.

Unfortunately for him, the arms race and rivalry with the Ottomans was quite draining for Charles V, arguably fomenting more adventurism on his part. Seeking to take Algiers in 1541 proved to be notably disastrous.[87]

To the southeast, the son of the late Vasco da Gama thought he could emulate the depredations of his father when he reached Abyssinia in 1541; instead, like de Soto, Cabrillo, and Coronado, he lost his life in the bloody process.[88]

AFRICANS, IN SHORT, WERE a major shaper of this new era inaugurated in 1492, not just as slaves but soldiers—at times combining and blurring these roles; for example, in 1555 a number from this group joined French attackers in sieging Havana. At the tip of the spear was a Protestant—or Huguenot—named Jacques de Sores (or Soria), whose comrades were implicated when neighboring Santiago was sacked in 1554; yet another corsair plundered Havana in 1538, a pattern eased since defense of Cuban cities depended heavily upon Africans and indigenes.[89] Until at least 1865, slaveholders feared that those akin to Sores—like John Brown—would organize to free the enslaved, which is precisely what occurred in the 1550s when Huguenot corsairs attacked throughout the circum-Caribbean where a mere 53 men captured these sites with the aid of the enslaved, who were then freed.[90]

In other words, post-1492, Spain was on the march but exposed a glaring weakness when it at times allowed religious sectarianism to trump racist solidarity. England filled the breach when it turned this paradigm on its head and did not allow the conversion of Africans to Protestantism to prevent their being enslaved, and eventually invited the presumed Catholic foe to join the brutal colonizing of what became Maryland, which, quite appropriately, then retroceded land to provide the republican capital of Washington, D.C.

CHAPTER 4

Florida Invaded

As the 1550s were shuddering to a close, Protestantism was on the march in France, embodied by the continuing influence of the Huguenots.[1] Increasingly, they were seeking refuge in England, which was creating a perceived security threat for Paris while bearing the seeds of an incipient "whiteness" as well.[2] Between 1521 and 1559, Spain and France were, seemingly perpetually, in a state of war,[3] draining coffers of both. Madrid, however, had the advantage of accumulated wealth from Peru and New Spain, which did not bode well for Paris, as events in Florida were shortly to expose.[4]

What became Italy, however, seemed safe from neighboring French incursions, since it was during that decade that a kind of fortification, called the Italian trace, had become popular. It involved low, thick walls with triangular bastions at regular intervals. This was important because the vast properties of the Catholic Church, headquartered in Rome, were quite tempting to their growing list of adversaries. Internally, the Vatican remained challenged by Protestantism, symbolized by the number of noblewomen who were highly visible in their support of Church reform and, at times, converted their families to their cause. By 1560, there was a well-organized and powerful Huguenot party that was cooperating with London, creating

apprehension among some in Paris. An inflow of gold and silver from
the Americas arriving in Spain had an inflationary impact hardly lim-
ited to Spain, creeping continentally, including across the border to
the hexagonal kingdom. Needless to say, this growing wealth was not
shared equitably, leading to a growing legion of vagabonds, beggars,
and highwaymen, contributing to an impulse to ship them and their
ways to the Americas.[5]

It was then that William Cecil, a chief adviser to Queen Elizabeth,
was informed morosely that the monarch was "poor, the realm
exhausted, the nobility poor and decayed. Want of good captains
and soldiers. The people out of order. Justice not executed. All things
dear . . . divisions among ourselves. Wars with France and Scotland.
The French king bestriding the realm, having one foot in Calais and
the other in Scotland. Steadfast enmity but not steadfast friendship
abroad." Early Elizabethan England was vulnerably weak, particularly in its frequent standoffs with Paris and Holyrood.[6]

This decay contributed to one of the most pressing problems of
that conflicted era: what to do about "surplus" population, with a
prime remedy being shipping them westward for purposes of colonization. War too absorbed the "surplus,"[7] as did piracy, which
became a major source of wealth for London. All this was occurring
in the context—again—of the simmering Dutch revolt against Spain,
the decline of Antwerp as a result, hammering the cloth market in
England, and inducing a search for other sources of wealth, which
led to Africa. There eventually enslaved Africans were purchased
in territories ostensibly controlled by the long-term ally that was
Portugal, then sold in the Spanish Caribbean.[8] Correspondingly and
not coincidentally, it was during the sixteenth century when George
Best, a sea captain, extended the Curse of Ham—a purported bibli-
cal injunction mandating degradation of Africans—to all of Ham's
descendants, which served to rationalize enslavement and brutalization of Africans.[9] This facilitated their enslavement even when they
capitulated to Protestantism. Another telling indicator of what was
to befall Africans arrived in 1555, when the term "Negro" was used to
describe them, the first recorded use of the word during that fraught

century, according to one analyst.[10] Arguably, the change in nomenclature facilitated a change in status and a shift toward more overt dehumanization.

Another first occurred when Englishmen were detected in New Spain in a surprisingly short time after the conquest. Some had traveled to Spain to learn the language and then sped westward, where some ran afoul of the Inquisition. Some remained in Spain, right through the middle of the sixteenth century and the onset of the reign of Elizabeth; her merchants flourished there, especially in Sevilla.[11]

BY THE EARLY 1560s, as invaders landed in what they called Florida, John Hawkins hijacked a Portuguese slave ship and sold the unfortunate Africans in the Caribbean. This launched his profitable career, blazing a trail for others involved in the odious commerce. But by 1567, also indicative of what was to befall those so audacious as to enter this business, Hawkins and his confederates were attacked by Africans in Cabo (Cape) Verde as they tried to carry away scores to be enslaved.[12] Hawkins himself was not greeted warmly as he reached African soil, wounded in Cape Verde as he was trying to capture and enslave Africans and forced to use clove and garlic to salve his wound.[13]

Hawkins encountered fierce resistance in Africa: he and his crew were attacked with poisoned arrows, a fusillade that created wounds with a distinct resemblance to lockjaw.[14] In 1567 Hawkins hired the now better known Francis Drake, soon to be knighted, for an enslaving venture off the Gold Coast; they managed to load five hundred Africans into an atrociously small space, then sailed toward Vera Cruz, where they came under attack.[15] During that same time, Hawkins's brigands intervened in local conflicts in the vast region encompassing Guinea and Sierra Leone, exacerbating tensions to the detriment of Africans; Hawkins's pirates actually assaulted one group of Africans on behalf of another, leading to the seizing of hundreds who wound up in the Caribbean basin.[16] The wily Hawkins was buttressed by the fact that Queen Elizabeth herself invested in slave trading, a commerce that was rapidly buoying considerable wealth.[17]

Hawkins was keen to keep Her Majesty apprised of his deviltry. In 1567 he told her that the "Portuguese who were to have directed [us] in their enterprize have fled," leaving him little choice but to "undertake it himself," meaning to load "Negroes in [Guinea] and sell them in the West [Indies]," along with "gold . . . perles and esmeraldes [*sic*]."[18] Yet for centuries to come, England was to pay a steep price when ships were sent southward. It was also in 1567 that the authorities in London were beseeched to "make a collection for ransom of certain Englishmen, captives of Algeria."[19]

Hawkins was not singular in his hunger to entrap and enslave Africans. By 1561, Sir William Chester was about to receive four ships for the purpose of making a voyage to the increasingly beleaguered coast of Africa.[20] West Africa was hardly supine then, a state that was to accelerate in 1591 with the subjugation of the Songhay Empire. It was in the middle of the sixteenth century that the potent Akan Kingdom of what was to become Denkyira, due north of El Mina in the forested hills south of Kumasi—in the vicinity of today's Ghana—attained liftoff (though the apex of their military and political power was not to arrive until the 1660s). Jolof (or Wolof) envoys from Senegambia continued to reside in Portugal, alongside those from the Kingdom of Benin. Borno continued to enjoy diplomatic ties to the Ottomans.[21]

In Congo (or Kongo), resistance to enslavement continued to soar. By 1568, there was an upsurge from below generated by the proliferating violence and destabilization that accompanied the rise of the commerce in captives. Ripples spread across West and West Central Africa. This complicated mightily the ambitious plans to convert this part of Africa into a simple warren for the ensnaring of Africans.[22]

Africa was not the only site of fierce contestation. For a variety of reasons, including ferocious resistance by indigenes, the conquest of what became Costa Rica came relatively late. It was not until the 1560s that the Spanish invaders subdued the Central Valley. Still, by 1600 the population of this resisting population had plummeted precipitously and in this process the colonizers began to import more enslaved Africans. All the while, the Spanish Empire was being weakened as it was advancing, to the ultimate benefit of London. Thus, there were an estimated 400,000 indigenes in this region and less than 70,000 by 1569, about 8,000 by 1611, a catastrophic pattern replicated in the hemisphere.[23] The angry resistance of indigenes was a factor contributing to the Spanish decision to liquidate this population.[24]

HAWKINS'S ADVENTURES WERE OF A piece with London's growing interests in Africa, especially Morocco. These interests were aided mightily by the presence of Dr. Hector Nunes (Nunez) an eminent *converso*—an expellee of Iberian Jewish descent—a prominent merchant, shipowner, marine insurance broker, banker, and pioneer in forging ties in the Mediterranean, including Morocco's sugar and molasses, often traded via Antwerp. He also managed to invest in voyages southward for enslaved Africans.[25] There was an increase in the number of enslaved Africans in New Spain—or Mexico—in the 1550s, despite the abject danger provided by their presence. Many had roots in São Tomé, Angola, Mozambique, and Cape Verde, areas where Portuguese were influential and English were encroaching.[26]

It was also during the 1560s that the busy Hawkins managed to investigate the coast of Florida, as events and the scent of misbegotten wealth had lured London into more overt competition with Madrid.[27] Overreach ultimately was to undermine Turkey and Spain, but during this time, it could easily apply to Hawkins, as some of his men were snared off the eastern coast of New Spain in San Juan de Ulúa, though Hawkins himself and his soon to be knighted cousin, Francis Drake, managed to escape. The captives were then subjected to the frightening Inquisition.[28] These Englishmen had been seeking to sell enslaved Africans there before becoming captives themselves. David Ingram, one of these men, felt abandoned by Hawkins but somehow he allegedly made it all the way to today's Maine in escape.[29]

This encounter in New Spain was a stunning and embarrassing setback for London and left a deep impression on the man who was soon to be known as Sir Francis Drake. Low in stature and rather thickset, ruddy with a beard and with a distinguishing arrow wound in his right cheek, the versatile pirate was also adept in painting. This skill did not allow him to whitewash the small fortune he lost as a result of this misadventure, leaving him thirsting for revenge.[30]

In any case, New Spain was tempting fate by relying upon African soldiers and slaves alike. A few years before the untimely arrival of Hawkins and Drake, officialdom in New Spain was complaining about a revolt of the Indios—"Salineros" in this instance—which included "Negritos."[31] As ever, those in northern New Spain were embroiled in what was referred to as yet another "chicimec uprising."[32]

The presence of Englishmen in the vicinity was not altogether unusual. They were in Mexico City as early as 1555.[33] Hawkins and his cutthroats were bent on selling Africans in relatively close Cartagena.[34]

Madrid did not welcome London into the hemisphere, a reality governed by both geopolitical and religious considerations. This was mutual antipathy. As late as 1924, when anti-Catholic sentiment had yet to be extirpated in the United States, a Virginia-based writer was stupefied in recalling that "the length to which the Roman Catholics carried their persecution of the Protestants staggers the imagination. The height of frenzy was reached," wrote Conway Whittle Sams, "when, on February 16th, 1568 the 'Holy Inquisition' condemned to death as heretics, the whole population of the Netherlands with the exception of a few persons specially named." Before long, the Netherlands became a prime religious battlefield, with Protestants emerging triumphant, who then went on to make their mark globally in the Caribbean and even, for a while, in Angola and Brazil.[35]

Just before then, Madrid dispatched the Duke of Alva to the Netherlands; he had fought the Ottomans in North Africa and quickly adopted the scorched earth tactics there to include mass executions and book burnings.[36] Soon Pope Pius V issued a bull of excommunication targeting Queen Elizabeth as a "servant of wickedness" who had the temerity to have "suppressed the embracers of the Catholic faith."[37] A Florentine banker, Roberto Ridolfi, conspired alongside His Holiness, the woman known as Mary, Queen of Scots, and others on an invasion that was designed to topple Elizabeth.[38]

Many Catholics felt they had no choice but to disobey London's monarch, which in turn led to a new scale of surveillance of them by the state, featuring fear of Catholics at home and abroad.[39] Soon London formulated laws that criminalized every aspect of Catholic life. Those who professed the disfavored faith had to attend parish churches on pain of a fine, and it was treason for a priest to enter England or to convert someone to Catholicism. Ultimately, this barrier did not travel well across the Atlantic and had to yield in the face of the requirements of "whiteness"—or the need for enhanced numbers to confront angry indigenes and rebellious Africans.[40]

England had another advantage: Portugal often sought succor in London in order to wrongfoot Spain, which was to occupy its neighbor for decades. Even as Florida was being invaded in 1565, European occupation created an opening for London, as the small Lisbon monarchy was forced to confront a major revolt of indigenes in Pernambuco in the 1560s.[41]

Being surrounded by choppy waters, literally and figuratively, proved to be an ironic advantage for England, necessitating the launching of skilled seafarers, navies, and commercial vessels, all indispensable in the era that was rapidly arriving: the heyday of settler colonialism, the slave trade, and the shoots of capitalism. Actually, English privateers—or pirates—were preying on foreign shipping off the Barbary Coast as early as 1546, an offshoot of London's ongoing commerce with Morocco.[42]

Sharpened religious conflict continued to flourish. It was not overly unusual when a pregnant woman in the Channel Isles who gave birth at the stake had her newborn flung back into the flames. This was a reflection of a larger conflict embodied by a French army attacking the Netherlands followed by Paris's support for yet another rebellion in England—albeit involving a deployment of thousands in arms, mostly Englishmen—payback for London's support of Huguenots. The snatching of Calais, the ultimate result of this venture, was a humiliation for England, which had held this territory for two centuries. However, London was down but not out, as the Treaty of Berwick of 1560 showed, and by which Queen Elizabeth took Scotland under her protection and pledged to expel the French. Paris responded by the "Massacre of Vassy" of 1562, a prelude to the epochal and more foreboding Massacre of St. Bartholomew's a decade later, yet another setback for Protestants.[43] During this era, Scotland and England were alternately antagonists and allies, with France intermittently comprising a threesome.[44] By 1569 there was yet another rebellion in the north of England and Spain sought to land troops in solidarity with the rebels. Meanwhile, Ireland remained troublesome to London, as Catholics, Scots, and Spaniards were also active—often overlapping.[45]

Arguably an incessant cycle of religious conflict was interrupted by the felt need to participate in the looting of the Americas and Africa, as sectarian combatants came together as "whites," especially under the Union Jack. London, the underdog, had to be more innovative, as it was largely on the defensive, as indicated by the fact that the Spanish envoy there was allowed to celebrate the Catholic Mass, but the Protestant favor was unreturned in Madrid.[46]

In Spain itself, this sectarian turmoil was contemplated more by the continuing presence of Moriscos—Muslims—who, it was thought, were not reconciled to Catholic rule and eager to collaborate with their co-religionists in Ottoman Turkey.[47]

Spain believed that presumed Turkish allies in Algiers as well as Moors were backing a revolt in Granada with arms, ammunition, and men, creating momentum for war and/or expulsion of Muslims from the Peninsula altogether.[48] In response, Granada passed laws barring Morisco dance and music and the ownership of the enslaved, though enslaved Guineans were allowed to perform their songs and dances. Yet an armed insurrection in Alpujarras was augmented by Ottoman troops and volunteers from North Africa, and the Moriscos were accused of working alongside them and collaborating with Protestants.[49] When Christian women and children were taken from southern Spain to an uncertain fate in North Africa in the markets of Tunis and Tetuan, Moriscos often were blamed. Similar accusations arose when churches were attacked.[50] In sum, southern Spain was rocked by 1568, and this continued for months on end. The rebels were seen as also maintaining contact with Paris and London, magnifying the perceived threat to Spain.[51]

An exasperated Madrid was moving steadily toward radical remedies, the likes of which both reflected and induced similar ongoing trends in the Americas, including attempting the total extinction of Moriscos, by way of drowning and forced sterilization, along with deportation to faraway lands and confiscation of their property. Finally, in 1609, in a fateful decision as fraught with self-harm as the expulsion of the Jewish community in 1492, 320,000 Moriscos were expelled from the Peninsula.[52]

As it peered over the horizon, Madrid had reason to be worried. The Ottoman Turks captured Tripoli in 1551, destroyed the Spanish Armada at the island of Djerba in 1560, and attacked Malta in 1565; then, seemingly unstoppable, seized Cyprus, the most distant relative of a now fading Venice, in 1571.[53] But even before their soon to come setbacks, it was apparent that the Ottomans, like their prime competitor in Madrid, were overreaching, as they were simultaneously attacking to the east in Persia.[54]

Just as conquistadors in the middle of North America had thought they had espied Turks, headquarters in Madrid and Sevilla were also espying Ottomans under every bed. In 1566 Madrid was urging the dispatching of vessels to the Azores to warn a fleet groaning with wealth from the Caribbean that Turkish men-of-war were in the vicinity.[55]

Spain was a paranoid that confronted real enemies. Besides feisty indigenes and Africans, raising searching questions about the future of settlements in the Americas, not to mention the supposed subversive nature of Moriscos, Madrid faced threats from neighbors, including France and Turkey, along with a brewing Protestant revolt in the Netherlands.[56]

Spain was also under siege in the Americas. It was in 1561 that a large uprising of what were termed contemptuously the "chichimecas"—organized indigenes—erupted and disrupted the tenuous lines of communication in the mining frontier of New Spain in territory that was to be bequeathed to the victorious United States.[57] Vessels groaning with wealth from Peru and Mexico often sailed by Cuba en route to Iberia, where French corsairs threatened, particularly because of their penchant for making overtures to Africans. To reach Spain from Cuba, Spanish vessels grouped together for safety, then sailed north along the coast of Florida riding the Gulf Stream and prevailing winds. But here they were subjected to another kind of unsafety, namely, exposure to natural hazards: the waters were dangerous, the weather was variably erratic, and the storms regular and overturning, providing a potential bounty for pirates. A way-station in Florida was thus seen as a way to guard the wealth from the Americas generally.[58] Moreover, to sail from the Americas to Spain, the money route underpinning empire, with vessels heavily weighted with riches extracted from Peru and New Spain particularly, stopping by Cuba, close by what became the Florida Keys was seen as a must. The waters were choppily perilous, the climate varied wildly, and hurricanes were not infrequent, all of which made these moneyed vessels vulnerable to English and French privateers. Forming St. Augustine was the defensive response.[59] The currents encircling the Bahamas headed northward were one of the most dangerous passages globally, resting frontally in the path of frequent hurricanes, accompanied by lost ships on the Bermuda reefs; a settlement in Florida was the reaction to nature's revenge.[60]

Indeed, Madrid's formation of a settlement in Florida was in essence a defensive maneuver, driven by fear that Paris or London were on the verge of doing the same. Menendez de Aviles, founding father of settler colonialism in what is now the United States, reflected anxieties that were to manifest repeatedly in coming centuries: "Considering the proximity of the islands of Santo Domingo, Puerto Rico and Cuba," he said anxiously, "where there are such vast numbers of Negroes and mulattoes of bad disposition, there being in each of these islands more than thirty Negroes to each Christian. And it is a land in which this generation multiplies with great rapidity." More to the point, it was "in the power of the French and English" to make sure "all these slaves would be freed and to enjoy their freedom would help them even against their own masters and lords and there would be an uprising in the land and with the help of Negroes it would be easy to capture us." He recalled once again with a shudder, the John Brown of the sixteenth century: "Take Jacques de Soria [Sores]," he recollected, the Frenchmen who "in the year fifty-three with one boat of a hundred tons and eighty men, by simply freeing the Negroes took and plundered the islands of Margarite and Saint Martha and burned Cartagena, plundered Santiago de Cuba and Havana, although at times there were two hundred Spaniards there. They took the fort with all it contained and twelve pieces of bronze artillery," besides and "carried them off." A sturdy defense had to be constructed in Florida given the "danger of an uprising as there are so many cunning and sagacious ones who desire this liberty."[61]

The alert Menendez may have been unsettled when he settled St. Augustine in 1565 and reportedly encountered Africans remaining in the peninsula, products presumably of prior European expeditions, or travelers along the escalator like currents that blew from Africa westward. Soon he endured what was to befall Florida for centuries to come: enslaved Africans fleeing his settlement, necessitating the importation of even more, as knowledge of Florida's swampy interior as a refuge began to spread.[62]

Moreover, Spain knew that if only to block ravenous rivals it was necessary to establish a position on the vast territory stretching north from Florida, which was to be occupied within decades by London, then inherited by the Republic post-1776. In 1561, a Spanish vessel in what became the Chesapeake seized—as was the pattern—an indigene, who was renamed Don Luis Velasco and became a Spanish speaker who traveled to Spain, Mexico City, Cuba, then Florida. But he enticed his alleged Spanish comrades to take him back to his original homeland, and his past captors complied, doubtlessly and mesmerizingly with dreams of untold wealth in mind. But they found to their dismay that they had been lured into a trap: they were murdered, a sobering experience reminding of the perils of colonialism and, in a sense, a roadblock that facilitated the coming arrival of English settlers. This was not the first time that such a daunting experience occurred. Earlier, the indigene known as Francisco de Chicora was seized and taken to Santo Domingo, learning Spanish and becoming an apparent Christian. He traveled to Spain where he wove elaborate tales of the wealth of the Catawbas of today's Carolinas. He returned with his erstwhile Spanish comrades—then fled. He provided a role model for enslaved Africans often dragged from Santo Domingo to the same region—who also fled.[63] Again, a deterrent to Spanish expansion was created by crafty indigenes.

Finally, seeking to beat Madrid to the punch, French Protestants sought to establish a foothold in Florida: this was seen comprehensibly as a looming threat to Spanish colonialism. Subsequently, Huguenots were termed derisively as "probably our first Communists" because of their tendency to seize and expropriate this troublesome property, known as enslaved Africans. By the early 1560s, Jean Ribault (also spelled Ribaut), a Huguenot navigator, finding the ongoing turmoil in France not to his liking, crossed the Channel into London where he was accused of collaborating with the monarch—the often besieged Queen Elizabeth—a prelude to his arrival in what was thought to be Spanish territory, what is now South Carolina and Florida.[64] He was said to have collaborated with London in his failed enterprise with the ultimate object of taking Havana, freeing the Negroes, then doing the same in Hispaniola and Puerto Rico.[65]

Madrid was increasingly hysterical about the prospect of the arrival of French—Protestants at that—in their neighborhood, given the strategic importance of nearby Cuba. Weeks before the founding of St. Augustine in 1565, Spanish officials in Santo Domingo were repelling a French attack on the north side of the island while reporting that 5,000 French were building a fort in Florida, a seemingly inflated number in retrospect but indicative of the size of the concern.[66]

In short, prior to Ribaut's demarche, there was good reason for Spain to be concerned about encroachment. There were Huguenots who in the early 1560s supplied John Hawkins and his band of cutthroats with water, wine, and bread—and pairs of shoes—when they limped into port.[67] Their presence was an indicator of the slow but steady involvement of the English in Florida. Some had been captured by Spaniards before being released, while traveling from the Caribbean.[68]

In the twentieth century, the writer Emma Rochelle Williams boasted that the Huguenot incursion was "the first colonization of the white race in the vast country from Mexico to the Polar Seas and from the Atlantic to the Pacific at the end of 50 years from the landing of Ponce de León." Yes, she exclaimed, "Forty-three years before the first settlement of the English at Jamestown" and "one year before [Pedro] Menendez," given credit for founding St. Augustine in 1565, exiling Huguenots were planting the flag.[69]

Ribaut was quite a finagler. He settled in territory that is now part of South Carolina. He had worked with the notorious Thomas Stukeley, an unscrupulous Catholic double-dealing between London and Madrid and who may have been a double agent—or a triple agent. The Treaty of Amboise of 1563 implicated Madrid and Paris certainly facilitated targeting of the mutual foe in London.[70] Stukeley was accused of stirring the pot of unrest in Ireland in league with the Vatican and Madrid, and Mary, Queen of Scots.[71] The devious Stukeley won protection from Madrid as a supposed victim of anti-Catholic bias and was accused in turn of championing a Catholic invasion of England or Ireland. When London jailed Spanish merchants in 1569, proselytizing them with Protestant preaching, Stukeley's presumed value to Spain increased.[72]

Stukeley, who hailed from a gentry family in Devon, in June 1563 told the queen and others that he intended to establish a colony in Florida (he also hedged by telling Spain too). Instead, he proceeded to Ireland where, like other Englishmen, he set up a base for piracy, looting, among others, those who had formed colonies, and consequently attained notoriety throughout Europe.[73]

Stukeley had reason to double-cross London. For it was not just plunder of rivals that provided London with the primitive accumulation of capital. The ongoing looting of Catholics continued apace, propelled in 1563 by the infamous anti-Vatican philippic, the *Book of Martyrs* by John Foxe, by some accounts the most widely read book in England during that time after the Holy Bible.[74]

It was understandable why braggadocio about the settling of Florida continued to soar. Earlier attempts beginning with Ponce de León decades earlier had ended in defeat at the hands of fearsome indigenes. Then Frenchmen intervened, seeking an entente with the original inhabitants: "Their evil sect," complained Spaniard Gonzalo Solis de Meras, "is very close to that of the Indians." There was a related worry that there were "many black men and women, mestizos and mulattoes in the ports that have been settled in the Indies, islands and mainlands of the ocean sea" similarly capable of wooing the original Floridians. "Most of them are unruly people with bad tendencies, too restless with an angry disposition. In that land, the black women give birth often and this race and kind grows greatly in number because of their birth rate. Since the land is hot as in Guinea, few of them who are born [to them] die, while of those borne by Spanish women, those who survive are few. . . . That is why black men and women get on well there, and live long and healthy lives. . . . In all those parts there are thirty or forty black men and women for every Spaniard."[75]

In other words, Africans and indigenes on the peninsula fought repeated incursions by invaders but in turn were weakened, which then made it easier for Englishmen to seek a toehold due north in what became Carolina.

A CHALLENGED SPAIN PEREMPTORILY massacred the Huguenots, shortly after their arrival,[76] a reiteration of Madrid's edict that French seafarers should be executed summarily.[77] "I do this not to the Frenchmen," was the inscription implanted on the victims, "but to Lutherans," making religious sectarianism explicit.[78] Nonetheless, Ribaut was liquidated mercilessly, his beard and skin sent to His Catholic Majesty, and his head split into quarters.[79] Retaliating in massacring Spaniards, Frenchmen inscribed, "I do this not as unto Spaniards, nor as unto seamen but unto traitors, robbers and murderers."[80] Therein was the ultimate divide in the oncoming epoch: the wider issue was not whether victims of massacres were being slaughtered for religious or non-religious purposes but rather that they were being sacrificed in the long run for what were to become larger goals: settler colonialism, then capitalism.

Under threat, Spain decided to beef up its presence on the North American peninsula, authorizing a settlement in what was to become St. Augustine.[81] Actually, this 1565 decision was not entirely new. Indicative of how indigenes had foiled Madrid repeatedly, giving London and its republican descendants breathing space, was the fact that the original inhabitants of North America had beaten back potential Spanish settlers led by Ponce de León in 1512–13 and 1521 and another set of invaders in 1519, yet another in 1526, another in 1528, de Soto during his 1539–43 reign of terror, yet another in 1543, and another in 1559–61. It did seem, however, that the prospect of a successful French Protestant settlement in Florida focused the mind of Madrid, especially since it was announced tremblingly that "their evil sect is very close to that of the Indians." Demography was another preoccupation of the Spanish, though they did not move with the alacrity of London—and the republicans particularly—in retreating from the constriction of religion to the capaciousness of "race" as the wave of the future.

"Most of them are unruly people with bad tendencies," which was true from their narrow perspective: such was the Spanish edict about those they encountered in Florida, including Africans. Perhaps worse was that this handed an advantage to Paris since "those people could not be slaves in France, because everyone lives in freedom there." Only recently, "The French decided to go from Florida with the fleet to all parts of the Indies to free the black people, who would rise up rebellion and take the land, killing their masters. The French would then establish their fortresses and their governing bodies, letting the black people, mulattoes and mestizos live in their Lutheran freedom and not be slaves." They knew this after seizing a "coffer of documents" devised by the Huguenots, which included an "instruction from the Admiral of France"; all this turmoil was raging as "New Spain had begun to rise up [in] rebellion" against His Catholic Majesty, raising the stakes and increasing the headaches for him too.[82]

The founding documents for Spanish St. Augustine, soon to follow, allowed for the arrival of 500 enslaved Africans but none from the Jewish community, or Moors either, as religious sectarianism continued to characterize what was becoming a flailing colonialism. As early as 1514, the rapid increase in the number of enslaved Africans in Santo Domingo already had become a source of fear for settlers, an apprehension unassuaged by the manic energy of slave traders, who continued to import potential gravediggers of a rickety system. Pedro Menendez de Aviles, given the burdensome task of establishing a settlement on the northeast coast of Florida in order to provide cover for colonies due south, warned Madrid that "in the island of Puerto Rico there are above 15,000 Negroes and less than 500 Spaniards and in all of the island of Hispaniola there may be 2,000 Spaniards and there are over 30,000 Negroes. . . . The same is the case in the island of Cuba and in Vera Cruz, Puerto de Cavallos, which is in Honduras, and in Nombre de Dios, Cartagena, Santa Maria and the coast of Venezuela, where there are twenty Negroes to one white man and with the lapse of time they will increase to a great many more. . . . In France, no Negro is a slave," he claimed, and "neither can he become one by law of the realm. Were France to arm three or four thousand men they would be masters of all these islands and ports," he warned ominously in 1562, in anticipation of an all-out assault on the Huguenots then encamped in Florida. For these presumed interlopers were bent on "seizing Havana, freeing the Negroes and subsequently those of Hispaniola, Puerto Rico and tierra firme." St. Augustine was the response.[83]

The small population of settlers notwithstanding, Florida soon became a significant market for Havana—by some measures, second only to Mexico—and, therefore,[84] a critical link in the chain of colonialism that Madrid had formed.

Despite the admonition of Menendez, there was a gnawing feeling in Santo Domingo that forming a settlement in Florida was a diversion of resources better expended elsewhere. This perception only grew as the settlement endured teething problems. It was from what became the Dominican Republic that Hernán Pérez informed Madrid that Florida was largely overrated, that Havana and Santo Domingo were actually the key to control of the Caribbean; more exploration of the

Florida coast was warranted, he said, but spending on a settlement there was a diversion from truer interests.[85]

Madrid was walking a slippery tightrope, empowering "Black Conquistadors" on the one hand and presumably expecting their class (and religious) interests to bar any residual sympathy these conquerors might have for fellow enslaved Africans. From the beginning it was clear that these "500 slaves" expected to be delivered to the settlement, that is, "Negro slaves from Spain, Portugal, Cape Verde Islands or Guinea" would—conveniently—be "free from royal duties," facilitating their imminent arrival. "A third at least shall be females," raising the prospect of population increase. "License will be forfeited if the slaves are taken to a place other than Florida," was the conclusion, underlining their importance on this peninsula. These forced laborers were critical "for the more expeditious building of towns, cultivation of the land, planting of sugar cane and building of sugar mills" and were grouped inauspiciously and inhumanely alongside "100 horses and mares, 200 calves, 400 hogs. . . ."[86]

Spain was tempting fate, in other words. By early 1566 her forces were detaining unregistered Africans, which was understandable given their political unreliability generally when not accorded the status of "Conquistador"; yet the simultaneous confiscating of so-called heretic texts, likely Protestant literature, was a continuing sign that Madrid was trapped by religious sectarianism.[87] Anxiety did not cease in April 1566 when an English slave ship with a Portuguese captain was sighted in the Caribbean, an indicator of two rising rivals.[88]

Before sailing under Spanish colors, Menendez had been in touch with Lisbon, seeking backing for his various ventures.[89] Yet by 1562, Philip II was providing strict religious instructions to him for his impending journey—no "blasphemy or execration" of course, "and if anyone should say it you shall castigate him in conformity to what the offense merits." There were also geopolitical considerations in that the monarch knew that some "corsair ships, French as well as English and Scotch are traveling on the route to the Indies, trying to rob those which go to and come from those parts, which is a disservice to God our Lord"—inevitably—"and to us and contrary to the peace agreed to between us and the Princes of those kingdoms." Hence, "such corsairs by law deserve to hanged as robbers." The conquistador was further constrained: he was forbidden to not accept as crew "a man of less than twenty years or one above fifty," not to mention "none lame, one handed or useless"—ditto "for the navigators."[90]

Even then Menendez fretted that Englishmen were headed to the peninsula to "settle" because "five very large English galleons, heavily artilleried" were on their way to the area north of Cuba. Naturally, he had plans to "sack them and rive them from the land" for it might not be "possible to do it afterward because of the friendship they will have established with the natives," a tacit admission of Madrid's missteps and misdeeds.[91]

Menendez de Aviles was not alone in being dispatched to the peninsula. After a riot in Mexico City involving a fracas between the chief of police, his assistant and their Negro servitors versus soldiers, one of the participants, Tristan de Luna, was sent to Florida near the time that Ribault was considering his journey there. His mission was to secure the territory against competitors, to gain wealth and, allegedly, to save souls.[92]

This latter claim has been viewed skeptically with some assurance since it was near this same time that an indigenous leader in Chile, Caupolicán, was captured and was about to be executed when he expressed a desire to be baptized and become a Christian. His wish was granted, at which point the colonizers made him sit on a sharp stake and then shot him to death with arrows. Presumably the chieftain's soul had been saved, and, consequently, it was unnecessary to save his life, exposing the rigid formalism of a certain religious expression.[93]

Thus, predictably, His Catholic Majesty was informed worriedly after the arrival in Florida in 1565 of Menendez and his band that these "French have many Indians for friends"; in fact, said Menendez, "It is a thing to marvel at, to see how these Lutherans have enchanted this poor savage people." Thus, he said, Ribaut was an "enemy" and thus, he and his men would wage "war upon them with fire and blood, for their being Lutherans." Among them, there was none of his faith: "I did not find one," he said,[94] suggestive of the potency of the religious imperative in early colonizing in North America, an imperative that then shifted decisively to "race."

These religious snares continued to beleaguer Spanish colonialism. Even the founder's religious origins were questioned: Menendez was vetted, and it was found that on his "father's side as well as on the mother's" that they were "Old Christians and are or were not touched by lineage of Jew or Moor."[95]

Typically, members of the Jewish community were formally excluded from those dispatched to Florida in 1565 but as so often happened, it was possible that they were aboard when vessels docked, as was the case potentially with Columbus and Ponce de León.[96] There was evidence of the presence of Jewish merchants in Panama as early as 1550.[97] As early as 1528, Hernando Alsono was depicted as the "first Jew burned at the stake in the North American continent," Mexico City in this instance. By 1783 Madrid sought "not to imprison Jews or to sequester their property," but by then it was probably too late to reverse the import of the Inquisition which as early as 1502, if not before, sought to "prohibit the entry of Moors or Jews into the New World."[98]

New Spain was enduring an Inquisition shortly thereafter, but a turning point arrived in 1569 when instead of being shipped across the Atlantic to be tried, the accused were tried instead in the Americas, an indicator of colonizers settling into their new environment.[99]

Meanwhile, upon arrival in Florida, the invaders encountered a shipwrecked man identified as a "mulatto" by the name of "Luis," who was among the fiercely resistant Ais nation of that vicinity. The man's knowledge of their language had saved other shipwrecked victims, an African woman among them. Since European labor was in short supply and the indigenes were deemed inadequate for the task, particularly because of their adamant resistance, this placed a premium on the labor of Africans.[100]

It was unclear how "Luis" had arrived. At some point between the late summer of 1514 and December 1516, the first documented voyage to the Atlantic coast following Ponce de León took place. Pedro de Salazar, an enslaver representing interests in Santo Domingo, probably reached the middle latitudes of what is now the southeast United States with 500 enslaved and two-thirds perishing en route. By 1521 Pedro de Quijo and Francisco Gordillo were on a slaving expedition near the mouth of what is now the Santee River in South Carolina. In other words, there were a number of opportunities for Africans to defect and then merge with indigenes in North America.[101]

Understandably, the sight of "Luis" was unsettling. In the prelude to Menendez's arrival, he was warning not about de Sores, the feared John Brown of the sixteenth century, but "Pedro Brasques, a French pirate" who with "only one ship of a hundred tons and eighty men in it . . . took and robbed the island of Margarita, the Cape of Vela, Barbuda and Santa Marta; burned Cartagena and burned and robbed Santiago de Cuba and Havana. Although there were two hundred Spaniards there," he said wondrously, "he took the fortress with twelve pieces of artillery." The reason was clear: "This matter of Negroes," he said euphemistically was "very inconvenient." This was a clear and present danger since "if the French or English are settled in Florida, which is so near" to the strategically sited Havana, "this alone will be enough, without any help from the French or English, for them to rise; because there are many crafty ones among them," speaking of Africans, "who desire freedom."[102]

Shortly after the founding of St. Augustine, Menendez was in Matanzas, Cuba, still complaining about Frenchmen. He warned that they desired to "give freedom to all the Negroes in the Indies. This is the way they think to be rulers of the land, without making war and without any labor or cost." This was no chimera, he advised, since "many French and English corsairs were traveling about Puerto Rico, Hispaniola and this island of Cuba, to rob and to trade Negroes and linen goods for gold, pearls, sugar and hides"—besides, there were "many Portuguese ships which do the same." Still, de Sores— or as he was at times called, Jacques Soria—who "took Havana and burned the fortress"—was the prime worry.[103] By December 1565, Menendez de Aviles, writing from Matanzas, Cuba, told Madrid that the "Frenchman Jacques de Soria is rumored to return" to this dangerous neighborhood, teeming with unsettled Africans.[104]

That was not Madrid's only worry. A few years later His Catholic Majesty was told that there were many pirates swarming about Florida and the Caribbean including "Master Hawkins, the English corsair . . . with a great armada. If this is so," fretted Menendez, "he will do much harm in Havana and Florida and may be able to take possession of these places."[105]

In short, the disproportionate number of Africans in the Caribbean basin and thereabouts presented a clear and present danger to the trajectory of settler colonialism, which minimally mandated an increase in the number of Europeans to countervail their forbidding presence. In a sense, the ultimate victory of republicanism arose not least from the point that it could offer a palette of benefits often not as prevalent in Europe, including vast tracts of land seized brutally from indigenes and even "rights" that emerged post-1688 in the wake of the "Glorious Revolution" in England. This was "combat pay" akin to the extra payments offered to soldiers willing to go to war. But this colonial predicament also undergirded fear and loathing of Africans, perceived widely as antagonists—the "internal enemy"—willing to ally with foreign invaders in missions designed precisely to overthrow settler colonialism.

That is not all. Though Spain was reaping untold riches from its exploitation of Peru and New Spain particularly, shortly after arriving in Florida scores of soldiers were revolting in the midst of indigenes not enthusiastic about the overall invasion and presumed lurking Huguenots still, all of which was jeopardizing the infant settlement.[106] It appeared that those who were wary of forming a settlement in Florida in the first place were being vindicated when Madrid continued to receive alarming reports about their soldiers in St. Augustine starving (the upside might be they were too weakened to revolt), which led to mutterings about the presumed untrustworthiness of Spanish seafarers, thereby egging on European rivals to challenge Spain in the neighborhood.[107] Other soldiers were requesting back pay.[108] Worryingly, Lisbon seemed to be collaborating with London against Madrid—five English vessels had just sailed from Iberia with a Portuguese pilot, a rising trend. Africans were being brought in illegally to the Caribbean and bound to be in ill humor; a couple were sent to Havana, which was just exporting a problem.[109] Yet heedlessly, there were continued requests to import more enslaved Africans to Havana, which was unwise given the penchant of Huguenots to ally with them against Spaniards.[110] The number of slave ships to Spanish America from African ports leapt to eleven in 1562 from a mere handful previously, and the upward trend was evident.[111]

Perhaps most worrisome of all to Spain was the frequent raids by Frenchmen on Spanish ports in the Caribbean, with the express aim of allying with, if not liberating Africans. Moreover, in Havana particularly, there had been a sizeable community of free Africans and those defined as mulatto; by 1565, as St. Augustine was being settled, these two groups were almost 15 percent of the town's free population. They had their own company in the militias, under the command of an African officer; they were small owners of land, businesses, and houses and soon they were able to sustain two impressive religious cum social organizations.[112] This was contrary to the model that was to develop due north in what became initially a London colony, then the United States, as Cuba provided a troublesome example exerting a gravitational pull upsetting English settlers and motivating "their" Africans too.

Understandably, Spain was viewing these events through a religious lens. Both the French and English that were of concern in the Florida Straits were Protestant, and by the 1560s London was backing the Huguenots in France and the Calvinist rebels in the Low Countries.[113] There was a contemporaneous revolt of Protestants in Scotland, not displeasing in London.[114]

Her Majesty, Queen Elizabeth, never ceased to provide aid to European Protestants, particularly Huguenots and those in the Netherlands, which was a kind of self-defense on London's part. Driving Catholic France out of neighboring Scotland was a priority. Yet during the whole of her reign, Catholic Ireland had been a burden not as easy to resolve as the problem in Scotland. Indeed, it was in Ireland that the combined forces of the Vatican, Spain, and dissident Scots were increasingly active.[115] Only later in the century

did Spain eclipse France as an ally of Catholic Ireland,[116] indicative
of the dilemma faced by London and indicative of why it had to
become bolder and more adventurous—including sailing westward
for wealth and leverage—as a matter of survival. Simultaneously, the
difficulties London encountered in Ireland well prepared the Crown
for the roughhouse that was the Americas. In Ireland, England had
met resistance with total war, slaughtering men, women, and children alike. Sir Humphrey Gilbert, who would later sail westward
to the Americas, had been a military governor in Munster, a province of Ireland in 1569 where he became notorious for decapitating
the defeated and posting their severed heads along the path to his
abode.[117] Unsurprisingly, along with Gilbert, Drake, and Walter
Raleigh—pioneers in subduing indigenes in the Americas—all were
implicated in atrocities in Ireland.[118] At this juncture, religious and
nationalist biases were diverging to the point that Spanish Catholics
even threatened English Catholics who sought to move to Florida:
ultimately, the latter bias would continue to rise, while the former
would recede.[119]

A revived London during Queen Elizabeth's reign, propelled by
the looting of Catholics, trade with Morocco, the peregrinations of
Hawkins and Drake, was now poking into Florida waters, with an
English ship captured there by October 1565 by the Spaniards.[120] This
was a presentiment of what was to unfold in coming decades and
centuries.

CHAPTER 5

Turning Point

A number of turning points on the road to the rise of London appeared in the 1570s. The Turks suffered a stunning setback in Lepanto; the man soon to be known as Sir Francis Drake harassed and hounded the other power—Spain—exposing its weaknesses while delivering immense wealth to London, which could then be translated into a bigger fleet that deployed colonizers westward, laying the foundation ultimately for the ascendancy of capitalism. Reputedly, in a 1577 voyage Drake and his backers spent the equivalent of 2 million pounds and returned with 2.5 billion, supposedly enough to retire England's national debt. This was not a moment too soon, for indicative of the fluidity of global power was the report that his comrade, Hawkins, had stood ready to defect to Madrid.[1] This was hardly minor since Queen Elizabeth came to the throne with a huge national debt.[2]

In the prelude to this pivotal decade, it would have been difficult to imagine that London was in the passing lane, slated to surpass Madrid and Constantinople both. The Exchequer seemed on the verge of bankruptcy, which meant further plundering of Catholic wealth at home, which was bound to worsen relations with the mighty Catholic powers, including the Vatican. The poor continued to be driven from the land, though this created momentum for exporting this problem, giving liftoff to settler colonialism, even in Ireland, which too would worsen relations with an important neighbor. In Scotland, Protestants were being burned at the stake, and the authorities were confident since there were several thousand French troops to vouchsafe their decisions. But deft diplomacy and rough tactics convinced Edinburgh to stray from this course. Catholic targeting of Queen Elizabeth in jujitsu-like fashion was used to generate further antipathy to the religious foe. London's backing of Dutch rebels was paying off in a manner unforeseeable at the time,[3] that is, generating a powerful Rotterdam/Amsterdam that would challenge and weaken the Iberians for decades to come, thereby allowing London to advance in the slipstream. Lepanto added to this pleasing scenario insofar as it weakened a formidable power creating room at the top for an English competitor, but this too was hardly foreseeable in the 1570s.[4] When the Pope sought to excommunicate Queen Elizabeth during this decade, it backfired spectacularly, providing further reason for London to continue the policy of trading with Muslims, be they in Constantinople or Rabat, a policy which as much as any other helped to propel England to the front rank of nations.[5]

In the prelude to Lepanto, it did not seem that the Ottomans were in decline. Not only did they have real and imagined allies in Spain in terms of the much reviled Moriscos, but across the Mediterranean they had taken back Tunis in 1569.[6]

The Habsburgs for some time had sought to maintain a fleet minimally equal to that of the Turks, a lesson reinforced by their disastrous campaign in Algiers in 1541, a decided blow to Spain's maritime power too, at a time when it could hardly afford this setback. The continental wars that soon followed absorbed resources that could have been more fruitfully deployed due eastward: slaughtering Ottoman Turks.[7] The Turkish fleet was probably the largest on the seas in 1570—the apogee of Ottoman power—and their frightful Janissaries were probably less addicted to enervating habits and vices than any other fighting force globally.

Still, Madrid retained the disadvantage that inhered in the fact that French ports were routinely open to Ottoman vessels where commanders could also secure provisions, even munitions, shortening supply lines and conveying a distinct logistical advantage. Mutual antipathy toward the Habsburgs and those allied with them united Paris and Constantinople in a marriage of convenience.[8] Simultaneously, Madrid was justifiably wary about the reach of the Ottomans, whose influence in North Africa was further firing their ambitions.[9]

Spain's nervousness extended to the neighborhood, including the Azores, for it was near this same time that Madrid granted permission to send one hundred farmers from there to struggling Florida, to bolster that faltering settlement,[10] even though this could have jeopardized Spain by denuding this nearby neighbor. By 1570, there were unrelated reports on French and English pirate activity near the Canary Islands, as Madrid's antagonists seemed to be approaching closer and closer to the heart of the empire.[11] This resort to the Azores, followed by anxiety in the Canaries, may have been a reflection of a kind of "imperial overstretch"; that is, Spain had bitten off more than it could chew in grabbing sprawling lands in the Americas and having insufficient forces to subdue them altogether in the face of indigenous resistance, African rebelliousness, and tests of religious piety to qualify settlers.

But by 1571 things were seemingly on the upswing for Spain, enthusiasm propelled by apparent success in suppressing the revolts of the Moriscos that had just occurred.[12] This rebellion had inflamed Madrid's ire particularly since these perceived religious dissidents were seen over the years as not only appearing to collaborate with the Ottomans but with London and Paris too.

Catholic Spain was at the tip of the spear in combating Muslims, at a time when Protestants in London were seemingly capable of cutting deals with this ostensible religious opponent. The pretentiously named "Holy League," a kind of Spanish front group, was tellingly inaugurated at the Vatican itself on 25 May 1571 and was slated to target not only the Ottomans but also the deadly trio of Algiers, Tunis, and Tripoli.[13]

Still, Madrid, perceived as the rising power and the chief beneficiary of the looting of the Americas, was not as quick as Protestant
England, the feisty long shot, in pouring more revenue into science,
including astronomy, natural history, mathematics, medicine, and
shipbuilding,[14] yet another reason for Madrid's decline which, like
a seesaw, propelled England upward. At the same time, London
proved to be adroit in ransacking Iberian knowledge; that is, many
of the most important books in English on the all-important field of
navigation were translations from the Spanish and Portuguese.[15]

This upward swing was not evident in 1571 when Spain spearheaded a stunning defeat of the Ottomans—in a sense halting the
momentum that post-1453 seemed unstoppable—providing more
confidence to Western European Christian elites as they continued
their surge westward. Miguel de Cervantes, who was present at this
creation of a unique moment in history termed this victory—perhaps
excessively—as "the greatest event witnessed by ages past, present
and to come." Evidently his departing with a permanently maimed
left hand did not disenthrall him. His enthusiasm was a microcosm
of what was occurring in Christian Europe, emboldening them and
binding them at once in what could be seen retrospectively as generating a newer identity of "whiteness": Lepanto fever was also detected
in Protestant London and Lutheran Stockholm. After 1453, war
between continental Christians and Muslims had waxed and waned,
erupting in earnest in 1521 as Catholic Europe was buoyed by colonial
exploitation. By 1534, the two combatants squared off in Tunis, and
opportunist France sided with the Ottomans against Spain by 1543;
Christian Europe got a taste of what was soon to be imposed heavily
on Africans, as the vanquished often found themselves enslaved by the
victors. Near that same time, the Habsburgs failed to take Algiers and
it continued—if not heightened—its role as a slave market for them.
Cervantes was held there for five years before managing to depart. In
the prelude to Lepanto, Madrid was embroiled in a seemingly end-
less cycle of conflicts with rebellious indigenes in the colonies, along
with Africans rebelling against enslavement and a Protestant revolt
among the Dutch, which was to lead to an even more formidable

rival, buoyed by London. This was akin to England fattening this sheep for slaughter, as was glimpsed in 1664 when Manhattan was taken. The Sultan too had his own problems facing down revolts in Basra and Yemen. In a sense, all of these conflicts were intertwined as the two powers—Spain and the Ottomans—felt forced to generate more wealth to fight each other, which then placed pressure on their actual and would-be colonial appendages, weakening both to London's long-term advantage. Concurrently, the power of the previous era—Venice—was fading into the sunset,[16] with its historic policy of aligning with the Ottomans fading with it.

Thus for Spain, Lepanto was akin to a parachute drop where one is seemingly heading upward, when actually one is headed downward. For the Ottomans had prepared steadfastly for this battle of the titans, assembling a formidable armada. As far back as 1453, the Ottoman Turks had incorporated into their chants of victory a new battle whoop: "To Rome, to Rome," to seize and pillage the purported capital of the Christians. There was a collective sigh of relief after Lepanto as a result, with scores of songs celebrating this victory providing evidence of the significance. That London could seem to cut deals with Muslims while upstanding fellow Christians were under threat underscored the gathering reputation of Perfidious Albion, thereby heightening the mortal tensions between Catholics and Protestants. The anti-Ottoman forces recruited widely. Spanish galleys were drawn from Naples, Sicily, Venice, the Papal States, Malta, Savona, and Genoa. Spanish and Italians alike had been living on edge for decades, tremulously experiencing their villages being sacked and their men, women, and children kidnapped and sold into slavery. Those of Corsica and Sardinia and the boot-heel of Italy—even Rome itself—suspected that the Ottomans were straining to subdue them, conquer them, enslave them, that is, foist upon them what many Spaniards were then foisting upon the indigenes of the Americas. Churches would become mosques, as Christians would be compelled to become Muslims. Lepanto, at least for the immediate future, put paid to these ambitions, providing breathing space for Western European Christians, especially Iberian Catholics, to turn with renewed vigor to enslaving

Africans, for example. But even here the news for London was not all bad. For the self-described Holy League that bested the Ottomans at Lepanto began to split apart post-1571, as Madrid wanted to turn on North Africa (for example, London's ally in Morocco), while some Venetians, in closer proximity to the Vatican, wanted to turn eastward, bolstering firewalls that would hamper further Ottoman lancing attacks. And even those who wanted to attack North Africa were split; should the target be Morocco or Tunis or Algiers? No other port on the coast had the maritime infrastructure of the latter city, all of which was bolstered by bonded labor, virtually all enslaved Christians. Galley slaves, whether Christian or Muslim, endured a reprehensible fate, often chained to their oars and commanded by those who would rather see these unfortunates drown than swim away somehow. Of course, placing Christian slaves at the oars presumably meant that their opponents would not make full use of their guns for fear their co-religionists would be the first to be victimized.[17]

Algiers notwithstanding, it was March 1573 to February 1574 that a successful expedition to Tunis occurred. This unnerved Paris and London both since this conquest gave Spain one more base from which to launch sallies into Europe, up to and including Rotterdam, then reeling despite aid from fellow Protestants.[18]

Having galley slaves could not explain the Ottoman advantage,[19] propaganda to the contrary notwithstanding. Their field army was likely superior to that of any potential foe and complemented nicely its evident superiority in logistics. Besides, the ban on alcohol likely gave them a decided advantage over rivals, often intoxicated and thereby, ineffective. Too much can be made of military advantage, however, in determining victors; thus, Lisbon mastered caravels and cannon and yet fell victim to Morocco, then Spain.[20] Nonetheless, Catholic Europe felt it had dodged a sharpened projectile aimed for its heart when the results of Lepanto were tallied.

In a sense, what occurred post-Lepanto was that the momentum deployed to combat Muslims was transferred with added intensification to Africa and the Americas with apocalyptic results. The development of the wheel lock in the late 1570s facilitated the development of deploying mounted soldiers with firearms, a formidable advance for colonialism.[21] Yet signifying the "success" of Spain's policy of incorporating African conquistadors if they were religiously correct, is the point that the Spanish poet of African descent Juan Latino celebrated Lepanto, untoward consequences notwithstanding: the emergence and advance of the "whiteness" project would serve to erode such effusions subsequently.[22]

Post-1453, the Ottomans were advancing westward and, almost defensively, Western European Christians began to move westward in response both in retreat from the perceived "Green Menace" and advance on the Americas, but as wealth from the latter continents began to fill coffers in Madrid, the Ottomans received a comeuppance in 1571. However, this was not a Turkish fiasco in that the Ottomans were hardly defeated for all time; however, Lepanto did open the Mediterranean for incursions by other forces that, yes, included London. The excommunication of Queen Elizabeth in 1571, a virtual declaration of war, was not as potent as it appeared since England could flout this bar by trading with Muslims.[23] This proved to be an adept training ground for London, as the Mediterranean was in a sense the cockpit of the emerging region, with enslavement being a premier reason. By 1574, London was considering "reasons offered to the Queen for the establishing of an exclusive trade with the Barbary States."[24] By 1579, under consideration in London was "a treatise on the intentions of Spain and how the plans of the Kings of Spain"— and France too—"may be frustrated by forming a league with the King of Barbary."[25]

Lepanto was also a setback for Africa. In 1575 Lisbon sunk its claws further into Angola with the official founding of Luanda in 1575–76, which rapidly became a major slave trading port and, once more, a booster for London as England parlayed its long-term alliance with Portugal into yet another victory. Soon neighboring leaders in nearby Congo were complaining that Europeans were fomenting conflicts in order to generate even more captives to be shipped westward,[26] a trend that was to gain jet-propulsion in coming centuries, devastating a continent.

Even as Lepanto was being mounted, Africans were under assault, as if victorious Europeans were contemplating the need for an expansion of their all-important enslaved labor supply. In 1570, Akan warriors in West Africa ambushed and killed more than three hundred Portuguese huddling in El Mina in anticipation of ensnaring more Africans. The Portuguese attempt to pacify today's Luanda, Angola, accelerated in 1575 nonetheless, which ignited conflicts among Africans making them more easily victimized by enslavers. From the 1570s until 1592, Portuguese enslavers shipped 52,000 bonded laborers to Brazil—or Portuguese America, as it was sometimes called—facilitating the expansion of sugar plantations and enabling the development of Lisbon and Oporto.[27]

MEANWHILE, RELIGIOUS CONFLICT continued unabated when Catholics massacred Protestants by the thousands in France, though the lure of riches to be gained in the Americas by massacring indigenes and enslaving Africans ultimately restrained this religious fanaticism in the interest of "whiteness." Still, these bloody religious conflicts, which were also inter-royal conflicts, served to liquidate a number of royal families, lubricating the path for other ennobled families, merchants principally, whose purses were bulging as a result of the enhanced prosperity delivered by slavery and colonialism.

Thus, when in 1572 Catholics fell upon Protestants in France, eliminating at one fell swoop thousands, it was not only an expression of gory sectarianism,[28] it was also an expression of a brutally enforced political-cum-economic rule. How many were slaughtered? Estimates vary. One source states 25,000, then a few pages later raises the number to 40,000.[29] Yet another source says 30,000, but whatever the estimate, the religious sectarianism was obvious, with priests encouraging an orgy of bloodletting. Violence against women was pronounced, as if the idea was to stem Protestant childbirth: pregnant women had their wombs ripped out and baskets of small children were tossed randomly into the Seine. His Catholic Majesty in Madrid was said literally to have danced for joy when he heard the news.[30]

But things were somehow going London's way, since in coming decades beset French Huguenots began to enrich England's settlements,[31] while the Treaty of Blois in 1572 meant that London and Paris backed down from their historic rivalry and sought to unite against Madrid.[32] By 1582, London was greedily considering a "plan for the employment of the French refugees in the manufacture of cloth and the erection of a staple for wool in London," in what was to become the signature British industry and a launching pad for capitalism itself.[33] The shock waves emitted from France traumatized a good deal of the continent, influencing alliances that led to the rise of London. The shock waves continued to roil three centuries after the massacre.[34]

Given the often raw tensions that flowed effortlessly across the Channel, London kept a close eye on trends in France. As early as 1568, officialdom in London was apprised that Protestants of the coast of Normandy departed from their houses, armed and furnished in a warlike manner, and likewise those of Brittany were "leaving their wives and children behind and advising the Papists to use them as they will answer at their peril."[35] Yes, it was confided, there was more than an "appearance of troubles in France." Weeks later, Sir Hugh Paulet was told that "Protestants of France" had been "put to flight" and the "French King's army . . . pursued them."[36]

It is difficult to overestimate the ire and fear that suffused London in the wake of this 1572 massacre, the monitoring of France's tensions notwithstanding. Catholics, as some Englishmen saw things, were viewed in the way that Nazis were viewed in the 1930s—or how Communists were seen in Washington and on Wall Street in the 1950s. Protestant clergy who suspected—probably correctly— that they would be the first to walk the plank if Catholicism were to make a comeback in London, were a kind of ideological, perhaps theological, vanguard, whipping up anti-Vatican sentiment and seeking to compel the nation to see things their way. Richard Hakluyt, described as "preacher and imperialist"—the rising union of the epoch—was a central figure here. He had spent time in France and was profoundly influenced by the massacre and the Huguenots alike and became a primary promoter of English colonization[37]—a project that seemed mandatory in order to confront effectively Catholics (and Spain).

Unsurprisingly, veterans of the religious wars were also pioneers in colonizing the Americas. The man who became Sir Humphrey Gilbert was virulently anti-Madrid and in the pivotal year of 1572 as sectarian conflict boiled over, led a force that warred on Spanish forces in Antwerp and the Low Countries. (This source argues that 13,000 were slaughtered in France during the St. Bartholomew bloodshed in France, a time when, it is said, the French word *massacre* brusquely entered the English language.) Gilbert's intervention did not prevent the 1577 looting and plundering of Antwerp by Spanish forces, a site where England conducted much of its valuable cloth trade, necessitating a further search for more sources of wealth. This Spanish escapade was denoted subsequently as the "Spanish Fury."[38]

Antwerp was not just important to London,[39] it was a key node for Iberians generally and was to become a transmission point for the Dutch to funnel investment into Brazil. The problem here was that like the Spaniards in Florida, the Portuguese were reluctant to admit entry for non-Catholics. Protestant Dutch were quick to see that this was not a firm basis for colonialism, nor an emergent capitalism for that matter; what evolved was a kind of "whiteness," or a Pan-European project in which the Dutch were a pioneer (as the rise of apartheid was to demonstrate) and the English were a major beneficiary.[40]

England itself was being pressed on the religious front because of Ireland, London's unsteady back door, made more unhinged by the continuing attempt to Anglicize this neighbor. Scotland remained restive, not least because of poverty, houses—hovels, more precisely—where animals and their ostensible human masters shared the same accommodations. Soon a flood of wealth from slavery and colonialism, and inviting Scots and Irish to sample the filthy lucre by dint of "whiteness," served to resolve this knotty problem.[41]

Ireland—and the Irish—were in an anomalous position, victimized by colonialism while eventually enticed to join in the fray abroad. For the English, this too was a dress rehearsal for a grander exploitation across the Atlantic, involving as it did those who thought they could either climb the class ladder via colonialism or grasp firmer their already higher rung by subduing Ireland. Essex Colony in Ireland was to be thoroughly military in character and organized along feudal lines besides, though the wealth generated was transmuted down the road into a nascent capitalism. But to begin with, there were forts and castles, incorporated towns, and—especially—the ability to wage war sanctified by what was cavalierly called law.[42] Thus, Ireland had few choices beyond allying with Spain, with which it had been linked for some time.[43]

Thus, there was an ongoing Irish migration to Spain during this era and thereafter, as His Catholic Majesty saw himself as the protector of these dissident subjects of the Queen. They provided sinew to Madrid's muscle, becoming doctors, musicians, poets, as well as soldiers and intelligence agents. Yet, flexible Spain allied with England to beat France by 1557 in the Battle of San Quentin, reflective of how relations were shaped by geography and not just religion. This short-lived alliance did not quell the hope in Ireland that Spain would rise to their defense during the 1569–73 conflict known as Desmond's Rebellion, and, responsively, in 1571 Spain contemplated an invasion of England.[44]

During that same tumultuous decade, Lord Burghley was informed tremblingly that that "which was often advertised but never believed is now come to pass. Spain and France are joined together," the equivalent of a Moscow-Beijing or Beijing-Tokyo duopoly facing Washington in the twenty-first century. "Ireland will first be invaded," perhaps as a result of Catholic unity and Protestant weakening in Paris, while "Scotland is to be entertained with marriage, men and money, England stored for a rebellion and the Scottish Queen delivered and made sovereign," pleasing Catholics in Edinburgh besides. Moreover, "Our friends in the Low Countries"—Antwerp and Rotterdam/Amsterdam—"of the same religion to be overthrown; plots raised against the Queen's person, as against the late Queen of Navarre," all of which meant a plot to "exterminate us by fire and sword." Thus, "The King of Spain, fearing nothing so much as intelligence between England and Barbary, has drawn the present King of Barbary to a covenant with him against the Turks. I offer myself," said this emissary to London, "to undertake this negotiation with Barbary," further cementing a relationship, especially with Morocco, that was to place London in the passing lane.[45]

London had good reason to be concerned about what appeared to be a perpetual problem: restiveness in the neighborhood, especially Scotland. Even before the alarm was sounded, Lord Wharton was told that "great numbers of French daily repair to Scotland and . . . the border fortresses are in a weak state."[46] Then the Earl of Shrewsbury was informed that "the French being in arms at home, daily send great number of men into Scotland . . . all armed with shot and weapon."[47]

Thus, as memories of religious terror were still fresh in 1574, Pedro Menendez, erstwhile of Florida, was heading away from Santander, Spain, but he knew that "when the armada encounters a storm I can take refuge . . . in Ireland," and because "we have peace with England they cannot prevent it," a status overdue for alteration. Ambitiously, this conquistador thought it might "be necessary to go to Flanders to join with the force which may be there" amassed to "destroy the enemy," meaning Protestants of various stripes. Boastfully, perhaps guilelessly, he asserted: "Our armada can cut off trade and commerce of all the Kingdom of England," not least because of the tie to Ireland "and of Normandy and of Flanders, Holland, Zeeland and Germany" too, suggestive of Dublin's strategic importance. This kind of hubris led directly to the 1588 disaster to overthrow Her Majesty, but then what was occupying Menendez's imagination was that his presence nearby in Ireland "will make them [England] refrain from going out to rob as they are doing until now."[48]

YET ANOTHER PIVOTAL MOMENT arrived in 1578 at the Battle of Alcazar, fought in northern Morocco and pitting a faction of North Africans allied with Portugal against other Moroccans, who emerged triumphant. The Portuguese monarch was vanquished notwithstanding an army that included slaves, Africans, and those described as "mulatto," with many of these defeated sold into slavery, fueling further Moroccan thirst for degradation of other Africans. The humiliation of Portugal in the wake of Alcazar was so profound that some historians have argued that the nation never recovered, whittling downward another power and making more room at the top for England.[49] The humiliation was so startling that it created fertile ground—as such events often do—for the rise of myth: In 1599 one Englishman instructed another breathlessly, "I hear that Sebastian, King of Portugal, said to be killed in battle at Barbary is at Venice, and has so persuaded the Venetians of his identity that they maintain 80 persons about him. He tells how he, with 14 others, escaped from the battle and got into the mountains . . . till he came to Ethiopia or Prester John's land"[50]—as one myth merged with another.

The defeat of Portugal led directly to the takeover of this small European nation by its larger neighbor, Spain, which provided access to Lisbon's seemingly inexhaustible supply of enslaved Africans, especially from Angola, for colonies in the Americas.[51] The defeat of Portugal also made more Portuguese susceptible to the blandishments of London, especially in devising anti-Madrid plots and giving Englishmen access to the coin of the realm: enslaved Africans, for example, from Angola.

Just before then, Sir William Cecil was informed about something that he probably already knew: "The King of Portugal was not the first discoverer of Guinea," epicenter of the commerce in enslaved Africans, yet this pushy monarch "was the first that built there a fort as big as a dove house" and "challenges the whole land of Africa to be his, which is . . . I suppose almost the fourth part of the earth. In all his fortifications there, he has no great number of Portuguese"[52]— perhaps a reflection of the relatively small population of Lisbon and Oporto. Hence, the defeat of Portugal in North Africa, though it was in the short term a boost for a rapacious Madrid, did serve to weaken yet another competitor for the untold wealth of Africa.

In the short term, Alcazar bolstered His Catholic Majesty, perhaps to the point of debilitating hubris, impelling the failed 1588 attempt to overthrow Queen Elizabeth at the same moment that Madrid was stymied in yet another failed attempt, this time to establish a firmer foothold in China. These failures placed gusts in London's sails.

Spain's fishing fleet was large, twice as large as England's, and that was the good news for Madrid; on the other hand, London's ships carried more weaponry. This virtual standoff likely influenced the 1574 Treaty of Bristol, whereby the embargo on English goods came to an end and trade relations were restored. That is, both parties paused before reloading.[53]

Yet problems were rising on the Iberian Peninsula. The Portuguese shellacking in North Africa also signaled that Morocco was a force to contend with, not least because of its continuing ties to London, and it likewise signaled that Africa was hardly supine—a state that could fairly be said to have been inaugurated in 1591 when Morocco (again) defeated the forces of the Songhay Empire, due south (again) with the assistance of London.

During this era and before, the majority of Portuguese merchants who were involved in overseas expansion were so-called New Christians, that is, shrouded members of a once vibrant Jewish community; assuredly this community had good reason to believe that with the Spanish takeover of Portugal, their lives—if not their beliefs—were now jeopardized. Thus, many of these New Christians began to flock to Amsterdam where they were instrumental in constructing a "Golden Age" for the Netherlands, where, for a time, this small European nation seemed to be headed toward global domination, though as matters evolved, the Dutch became a kind of stalking horse for the English.[54] The "conversos" were so potent that the charge arose that they had infiltrated the Jesuits, vanguard of Spanish (and Catholic) colonialism.[55]

Alcazar also witnessed the killing of Thomas Stukeley, the sly and slippery Englishman—and Catholic—who fought in France, Ireland, even Lepanto and, thus, was a symbol of an entire era. His killing was further good news for London and indicative of the fact that the ties to Morocco were returning dividends. He had won protection from Madrid because of his being victimized on religious grounds by London, but his death suggested that England's aggressiveness, which included jailing Spanish merchants and proselytizing them with Protestant cant was a worthwhile investment.[56] One British analyst wrote of Stukeley contemptuously as a "ruffian, a riotous spendthrift and a notable vapourer," or pompous twit, who "offered his services to the Pope, promising to drive the English out of Ireland" and wound up being "put in command of some eight hundred Italian soldiers"—all before being struck down in North Africa.[57] The demise of Stukeley also was a message to Paris and Edinburgh that their joint planning against London was likely to run aground.[58] Stukeley's passing was also a message that betting on Madrid's continued ascension was a wrongheaded wager.[59] A problem here was that the Catholics themselves were split, as Paris often conflicted with Madrid, which made it easier for London to isolate and crush Catholic dissidents in both Dublin and Edinburgh.[60]

IT WAS NOT JUST INTER-EUROPEAN tensions that were bedeviling Madrid. In 1576—precisely two centuries before the iconic year of 1776, for which it prefigured—there was a major uprising of indigenes in Florida,[61] a frequent occurrence in coming decades, until finally a republican surge suppressed such. In the prelude to this tumult, the colony was enduring a basketful of problems. Understandably, the settlers sought to stir up animosity toward interloping European rivals, but stoking anti-European sentiment among the indigenes might create blowback, helping to induce indigenes to oppose Europeans generally, including Spaniards. Thus, even as St. Augustine was being established in 1565, Francisco Lopez de Mendoza conferred with what he termed "two Indian chiefs who are great enemies of the French," a sentiment he did not seek to allay or suppress. These were religious foes too, he warned, "two clerics who preach the Lutherans have enchanted this poor savage people"; these presumed panderers had "their bodies tattooed like some of the natives." Unlike priests, some of these clerics were "married," he said wondrously. "Their armada arrived not twenty days before ours," he advised, though he was able to report that "a great many Lutheran books were found," along with "many packs of playing cards," a sign of frivolity. These interlopers were bent on "ridiculing and scandalizing the things of the Church," he concluded.[62] Even after it seemed that the French had been squashed in Florida, a Spanish seafarer departed from Pensacola en route to St. Augustine and encountered, he said, a French vessel with "three Negroes and about five hundred hides" aboard: "I sold the hides and the caravel," he said happily and "took the Negroes with me."[63]

Despite the wealth pouring into Spain from pillaging the Americas and then the ostentatiously named Philippines, soldiers in St. Augustine complained repeatedly about not being paid, a trend that could easily threaten stability.[64] Even sailors were at times left unpaid, which was no way to run an ocean-bound colony.[65] As the overall climate in Florida was deteriorating precipitously in the 1570s, the Spanish authorities made the fateful decision to compensate grousing soldiers by providing them with licenses to import enslaved Africans,[66] a decision made repeatedly.[67] This made sense to a degree, but given the tendency of disgruntled Africans to ally with indigenes and Frenchmen alike, this was akin to arranging the arrival of more gravediggers for an unsteady Florida. In any case, this maneuver was made even more questionable when the authorities complemented this questionable decision with another: sending undesirables generally from Havana to an uncertain exile in Florida, where the prospect of making mischief was even more likely.[68]

By November 1570, complaints about the flimsy nature of St. Augustine continued to proliferate. If "two hundred French or English" arrived, it was said warningly, defenders "could not prevent . . . injury because the forts already are no defense, being made of sand and wood"; hence, if "enemy corsairs" arrived, the "soldiers who remained" to fight "would run much risk," it was concluded understatedly.[69]

Paris and Madrid remained at odds, complicating mightily attempts to mount religious-cum-political challenges to England and the Ottomans alike. Ordering the liquidation of Frenchmen encountered in certain American precincts did not improve bilateral relations, a policy that did not prevent Cartagena from temporarily falling into French hands.[70]

Frenchmen and the much-feared Soria were Public Enemy Number 1, as far as Spaniards in Florida were concerned. After all,

Frenchmen were to be found in profusion in the neighboring isles; for example, Rene Laudonnierre, a Frenchman who had toiled as a consultant in London in the 1540s and in the next decade was in Scotland. His fellow Frenchman Ribaut, an early mover in Florida, had fought Catholics alongside Protestants in Dieppe, France, then sought sanctuary in England. Ladonnierre had initiated a fort nearby today's Jacksonville, which, according to one observer of today, ranks him alongside Menendez: "Thus began," wrote U.S. Congressman Charles Bennett, who represented this metropolis, "the permanent settlement by Europeans within the present day limits of the United States." By 1565, the English sea dog John Hawkins, stopped nearby, raising Spanish suspicions further. But like the Spanish settlement that emerged in St. Augustine, this one too suffered discord and mutiny of besieged settlers, forced to drink their own urine and engage in cannibalism, leaving them vulnerable to attack. Certainly, indigenes were displeased with their presence—Spaniards too—though these original inhabitants may have been pleased in the short term by the presence of Europeans who brought quantities of gold and silver then plucked from the many shipwrecks and capable of being traded for other goods.[71]

Even in Santo Domingo, which had witnessed a ferocious French attack on the north side of the island, weeks before Menendez's arrival in Florida in 1565, the authorities detected a complement of an astonishing 5,000 Frenchmen building fortifications on the peninsula.[72] Even as Menendez was arriving in Florida, he continued to fret about the French Huguenots amassing among indigenes, a force that could not be confronted effectively given that his own soldiers were in a continual uproar about inadequate pay and the like.[73] Increasingly, English-speakers—the next level of conquerors—were found in the waters of Florida too, evident as early as October 1565, forcing Madrid to dispatch vessels that could only weaken Spain's overall strategic posture.[74] By mid-1571 the authorities suspected that Englishmen were preparing to attack Havana, a more formidable target than Florida, thus jeopardizing this latter settlement.[75] By late 1572 the cry was emitted for more corn to be shipped to Cuba for the

maintenance of enslaved Africans working on fortifications, so necessary to block the thrusts of Englishmen and Frenchmen.[76]

Besieged by indigenes, Africans, and European competitors,
Spain was akin to a beleaguered police force in a crime-ridden neighborhood, racing futilely from hotspot to hotspot. Months after the
establishment of St. Augustine, officialdom in Puerto Rico detected
offshore an increasingly common combination: an English slave ship
with a Portuguese captain.[77] Thus, it was not just Frenchmen and
Englishmen that were causing conniptions in Havana and Madrid:
by 1568, Menendez thought he had detected a Portuguese settlement
in Florida, this at a time when his own soldiers were complaining of
starving and many of his seamen were seen as untrustworthy.[78] By
October 1569, more reports emerged of English ships disembark-
ing from Cadiz with Portuguese pilots; in the same report, the other
fear of Spaniards was reflected: Africans being brought into Santo
Domingo illegally, with no evidence of their provenance—or allies.[79]

Though taking Florida was seen by Spain as a way to shield against
increasingly frisky Frenchmen and Englishmen, elites in Santo
Domingo were beginning to disagree.[80] Corroboration was received
when stories of needy and besieged settlers proliferated, with some
seeking a hasty departure, casting a cloud over the prospect of a successful Florida colony.[81]

Despite the destructive blows inflicted on Frenchmen in Florida,
by January 1566 Menendez was warily eyeing a fort these assumed
interlopers were building alongside indigenes, Guale in this case.
Frenchmen were then pursuing a model of development—per
Soria—that presented a mortal danger to Spanish settlements, including allying with Africans and indigenes, as opposed to the ultimately
prevalent option honed by Englishmen and their progeny: mass
enslavement and liquidation.[82] Days earlier, writing from Matanzas,
Cuba, Menendez informed His Catholic Majesty that "it is rumored"
that the "Frenchman Jacques de Soria . . . will return."[83] Weeks later,
Governor Francisco Bahamon in Puerto Rico was detaining a suspect vessel with unregistered Negroes and heretical books aboard,
presumptive evidence of Protestant interlopers.[84]

Still, this French settlement was not long for this peninsula, but for
a while the same appeared to be true of the Spanish counterpart. By
early December 1570, Menendez's complaints escalated. French corsairs were marauding nearby, including the much-feared Soria, who
in Havana "cut the throats of thirty of [the] most principal people
with his own hands." He was said to have acted similarly in Brazil and
Madeira: "He cut the throats of more than five hundred persons," it
was said, and "left only six boys alive," though he conceded that "he
is a corsair of great valor." Absent immediate remedies, he advised
pessimistically, "I greatly fear that this corsair will make himself ruler
of Havana and Florida." Menendez requested with a gasp of desperation more settlers and soldiers alongside them, since many there
residing were "very naked, hungry and discontented."[85] Weeks later,
the predictable occurred: faced with an attack by French corsairs,
Spanish deserters fled into the wilderness.[86]

But could soldiers or settlers surmount religious hurdles, in any
case? Certainly, the emerging London solution of "whiteness" or
welcoming settlers and soldiers irrespective of religious heritage, then
cloaking this colonizing tactic in a gauze of "liberty," appeared to be
sufficient to bamboozle credulous analysts for centuries to come.

Sensing this dilemma, Menendez, then in Sevilla, saw "many
Flemings, Levantines and Portuguese" who were worthy potential settlers and, presumably, religiously correct, especially since "no others
could be found for such short pay and so few payments." So, he said
with command, "I am giving them the same salary Your Majesty gives
me, that is, one ducat each month to each one above the three ducats
which Your Majesty gives." Yes, he knew that it was "very unsuitable
that foreigners go in a royal armada like this" since "little faith can
be placed in them." Yes, it made more sense to "discharge foreigners
and enlist natives" of Spain, "even if they are less skillful," conced-
ing that the ethnic-cum-religious status quo was unsustainable. He
should have screamed from the rooftops, "Move toward Whiteness,"
but alas, this was apparently beyond his ken. Certainly, he realized
from the other end of the spectrum that "three hundred Negroes"
were needed right away "who must go to work on the fortifications of

Havana." He also knew that if Soria or his like—"enemies" in sum—
were to "attack . . . there are many Indians, Negroes and mulattoes
in the neighboring islands who will obey them," seemingly vitiating
his cry for more "Negroes." He knew that "because the Negroes and
mulattoes" were "slaves in our power" they "will see themselves free"
if lured by the French, especially French Protestants, and "their evil
sect and customs." So, he was considering "selling of slaves" in "New
Spain or in Honduras or in Campeche or in some other port where it
is known that their value is greater"[87]—exporting his problem to other
settlements, in other words.

But would that not simply denude his settlement of the kind of
manpower it needed to develop? Or was the threat of their very presence so formidable that few viable options remained? Such was the
dilemma of Spanish Florida, which in the long run was to compel
their relinquishing this land to colonizers able to capitalize on "whiteness." As noted, as early as 1565 Menendez had a charter that allowed
him to import five hundred enslaved Africans but, possibly wary
of their destabilizing, even revolutionary, impact, only about fifty
arrived, hampering development (but possibly preserving order)[88]
and ensuring that His Catholic Majesty would be expressing satisfac-
tion at how things were going in Florida by May 1566.[89] Nonetheless,
when he set sail from Cadiz for Florida on 29 June 1565 in pursuit of
implanting settler colonialism in what became the United States and
weakening Huguenots in the neighborhood besides, he was accompanied by enslaved Africans.[90]

For with the arrival of more Africans, the threat that intimate
knowledge of the enslaved of St. Augustine and its immediate
vicinity, critically important intelligence for restive indigenes and
scheming Frenchmen alike,[91] would be delivered to eager foes. It was
also in the 1560s that a new fort was under construction in Havana—
mostly by enslaved African labor—though contradictorily the order
was uttered that no Negro was to be allowed in the garrison of said
fort on the premise that this would only hand Frenchmen an opportunity to incite these oppressed and jeopardize the all-important
Bahama Channel.[92]

By 1571 Menendez was back on the North American mainland but his anxieties hardly had eased for it was then that he spotted more corsairs on a vessel "loaded with Negroes and merchandise too." "Indians," he said sagely, "in general are more friendly to the French, who let them live in liberty," than they were "to me or the Theatines," a Catholic religious order then entrenching. "We straighten their lives," he added wobbling, though he knew the "Frenchmen can do more with them in a day than I can in a year."[93]

By 1573 Menendez was granted a royal license to bring fifty Asturian families to Florida though evidently they could not be a "Moor, a Jew or of those newly converted who have been penalized by the Holy Office of the Inquisition and the identifying features of his person."[94] Yet this raiding of Asturias may have been debilitating the homeland at a time when challenges from the Ottomans, France, and England had yet to be extirpated. This concern was not extinguished when that same year permission was granted to send settlers to Florida not only from the Canary Islands but the heartland: Sevilla and Cadiz.[95]

Menendez, the Founding Father of settler colonialism in what became the United States, was dogged by problems large and small. By 1574 what was nagging him was the insecurity of the mail, which was subject to being purloined, conveying useful intelligence to corsairs—not to mention facilitating the increasingly ambitious plans of Africans.[96]

By 1574, optimism reigned as far as Menendez was concerned. "The war in Flanders is going much better," he chortled and the Ottomans, though still with "great power," had been brought down a peg or two. "I have no doubt that this winter will find the war in Flanders ended," he said, a tad unrealistically, at which point he would return to Florida. "I have ready a great crowd of farmers in our native country," he told his nephew, "as well as Portuguese," reliably Catholic, "from the river of Mino," poised to "embark," including "craftsmen, stonecutters and carpenters," the "best there are in these realms and most suitable for the settlements we at present have in Florida."[97]

These settlers would be needed, for it was in 1576 that what has been described as "the true conquest of Florida" began. The settlement authorities, armed with a royal mandate, launched a pulverizing war against indigenes, along with a companion attempt to clear the coasts of corsairs. Indigenes were ordered—as a precondition of peace—to turn their backs on their French comrades.[98] Anxious orders were sent with the aim of punishing the Tocobaga, a chiefdom near today's Tampa Bay; the idea was to either ship survivors to the Caribbean or redistribute them to other pacified settlements.[99] Muskets for Florida were requested—rather tardily in retrospect—and artillery too. Africans with unclear intentions had wandered into the zone of conflict as well, which was untimely since a French vessel had just chased a ship from New Spain into the vicinity.[100]

Indigenes were also dishing out multiple blows of their own,[101] with the Guale and Orista in the vanguard.[102] The first phase of the Spanish occupation in what is now the United States, in a region designated as "Santa Elena," ended in essence in July 1576 when the aforementioned indigenes were joined by others, compelling a helter-skelter retreat. By March 1577 the Spanish authorities were considering abandonment of the fort at Santa Elena because of indigenous counterattacks.[103] By April 1577 worrisome reports were made concerning a joint attack on St. Augustine by indigenes allied with Frenchmen.[104] The response by June 1577 was to send hurriedly to northern Florida arms, servants, the enslaved, and jewels to rescue the beleaguered, which simultaneously was weakening the settlement from which this booty was taken.[105] Pouring kerosene on the flames was the 1578 decision to send indigenes from Florida to labor as mine workers in Cuba; predictably the same report requested more artillery for the peninsula.[106]

Yet with all these problems—marauding indigenes, angry Africans, scheming Frenchmen, lurking Englishmen—one of the most significant issues encountered by Spaniards was the weather in 1578: a considerable amount of silver and gold was lost in the Florida Keys—and many men too—a direct result of choppy seas.[107]

However, it was easier to combat human foes. A counterattack by the colonizers—described accurately as "wars of fire and blood"—lasted in its insistent phase until 1583 and then continued thereafter, further clearing the ground for the eventual arrival of republicans.[108]

Inexorably, Spanish settlers and leaders sought a "divide and conquer" stratagem, seeking to pit one group of indigenes against another, creating tensions that paved the way for their decline. For example, there was an all-out war between indigenous allies of the French and their indigenous opponents.[109] In a sense, this was just a continuation of business as usual since there had been slaving expeditions along the coast heading north from St. Augustine from as early as 1515. Still, a 1570s edict was still chilling as prisoners of war were directed to be sold as slaves in Cuba, Puerto Rico, and Santo Domingo, so as to ensure the land was "clean and depopulated," another indirect blow for inheriting republicans, spared the expense.[110]

At that point it seemed that St. Augustine was surrounded by antagonists of various stripes, a reality that led directly to massacres of indigenes, clearing the land for a takeover, centuries hence, by republicans.[111]

UNFORTUNATELY, IT WAS NOT JUST the indigenes of Florida who were being pummeled. The colonizers had been hounded for years by those called cimarrones—or maroons—a kind of African-indigene axis that roamed throughout the chokepoint now known as the Isthmus of Panama. This was strategic territory, linking the Atlantic and Pacific oceans and thereby a bridge leading to immense wealth in both directions. For example, the staggering riches of Peru often had to be transported overland via this territory, creating sniping and marauding opportunities for Madrid's many foes, especially the army of the cimarrones, said to number about 1,200 men and women. By 1574, His Catholic Majesty's own cosmographer conceded that "many black cimarrones live in [Panama]. . . . They number 3,000 and . . . they freely live and operate there without any means available to overpower them due to the conditions of the land." To Madrid's dismay, when the Queen's emissary, Sir Francis Drake, arrived in the vicinity, he coordinated his profitable activities with those described as Free Negroes.[112] These Africans were said to have provided intelligence to the arriving Englishman about their mutual Spanish foe as they continued to smart from what was termed the "many wrongs and injuries received from the Spanish nation."[113] Panama was at the mercy of pirates often aided objectively by raids by African maroons. Europeans were heavily outnumbered by the 3,700 Africans, many of whom spoke their African languages; there were fewer indigenes, not least because of European depredations.[114]

It was not just Drake. As early as 1574, the authorities in faraway Havana were fretting about accused thievery by Lutheran pirates who had made friends with runaway Africans in Panama—Nombre de Dios in this instance—which could boost French interests in the region overall.[115] Ongoing indigenous resistance in Florida complicated Spanish ambitions further.[116]

As if this were not enough, in northern New Spain—the southern fringes of today's southwestern United States—the indigenes referred to contemptuously as chichimecas were on the warpath, raiding furiously and delimiting the implantation of settlements to the ultimate advantage of republicans. By the 1570s, it was not evident that even this small Spanish presence could long survive in such hostile territory.[117] When Drake skirted New Spain's shores, the authorities diverted troops from fighting these rowdy indigenes to guard against his expected depredations, suggesting the objective alliance between and among Madrid's many foes.

Peru, along with New Spain, may have been the epicenter of Spain's newfound wealth. But Madrid's men were also under siege in this South American territory. Responding with unrelenting and merciless force, in 1571 the heroic Tupac Amaru was executed in the vast square of Cuzco, an atrocious crime that hardly arrested ongoing revolts of the Incas, again putting enormous pressure on the Spaniards, who had yet to find a solution to their colonial problem of relying unduly on religion as a key marker of society. The wave of the future was bending and embracing religious outliers in the name of the new religion that was "whiteness," while planting the seeds of capitalism.[118]

CHAPTER 6

1588: Origins of the U.S.A.?

The failure of the Spanish Armada in 1588[1] and Madrid's desperate attempt at regime change in London was when this Iberian power was unequivocally weakened, opening the way for London's own invasion of North America, which was a condition precedent to the formation of the current (linguistic and otherwise) configuration of the United States of America. More to the point, the future pivoted on a single evening—7 August 1588—when Spain began a slow decline and a new world order began to take shape, which crystallized in 1898 when the ascendant United States delivered a devastating knockout blow to the tottering Spanish Empire.[2] And, as the previous chapter limned, inhospitable indigenes, angry Africans, and scheming Frenchmen had compromised the ability of Spaniards to move northward from St. Augustine, creating an opening for Englishmen to arrive in today's North Carolina by the 1580s. In sum, London had a "second mover's advantage": as Madrid absorbed arrows in its chest in the Americas England stood aside or participated in the drain of Spain, then swept into territories that this potent empire could hardly defend.

Assuredly, envisioning this optimistic post-1588 scenario was hardly on offer. Beginning in 1582 Spain had ejected with relative ease

France, England, and rebel Portuguese from the Azores, the back door to Iberia and the front door to the Americas. This provided confidence for an onslaught on England, given presumed support from co-religionists in Ireland and Scotland, not to mention the assembling of the largest naval force ever marshaled to that point. Lepanto meant that Madrid could spend more time battling religious foes, perhaps stirring the pot of unrest in Ireland and Scotland.[3] As late as 1585 there was moaning at the highest level in London, as Sir George Carey reported that he was "sorry to learn" of the "outward overthrow of the Protestants in France." This made even more imperative the "necessity of sending assistance to the Low Countries."[4] To state the obvious, the Protestant revolt decades earlier had proven to be a game-changer, allowing Spain to enlist Ireland as an ally, threatening the existence of England. [5]

For it should not be forgotten that this was a ruthless struggle for material advantage often cloaked in religious cant. Thus, in 1587 Queen Elizabeth gave Catholic priests twenty days to vacate Ireland and ruled that any such cleric subsequently spotted there was to be hanged, cut down while yet alive, disemboweled, then—in the pièce de resistance—burned. She outlawed Catholic religious services and, most important, confiscated 200,000 acres of Catholic-owned land and distributed it to her co-religionists, English noblemen,[6] solidifying their allegiance and adding impetus to the settler colonialism that soon was to bloom across the Atlantic.

England had no standing army for a good deal of the sixteenth century, whereas even France had one of the most powerful militaries on the continent. This led to conscription, which did provide flexibility but potentially could create more dissidents who either could threaten the regime—or be shipped westward to settlements. It also led to bolstering the strategically significant harbor city that was Portsmouth, which the French had sacked four times during the fourteenth century alone, underscoring the importance of the Treaty of Blois which had brought a truce of sorts with Paris. Yet this key node had been flooded with French refugees fleeing massacres of Protestants and related unrest, giving rise to the fear that there were sleeper agents among them.[7] London could hardly fall asleep on this prospect since with Spain swallowing Portugal, His Catholic Majesty had become by some measure the most powerful man in history, at least to that point. In the prelude to 1588, London passed a law authorizing a fine of 20 pounds per month—a royal ransom, in effect—on those who refused to attend the established Church of the authorized faith, which targeted Catholics and provided a potent debating point for republicans to come who could then shroud the real point that religious liberty was also a motivating force for broadening the base of settler colonialism by dint of redefining European Protestants and Christians as "white." Moreover, such punitive measures and other draconian acts meant that prisons were "full to bursting," according to London's prime propagandist, Richard Hakluyt, making them ripe to be cannon fodder for settlements abroad.[8]

(In one of those strange twists of history, Martin De Arguelles, who is said to be the first European born in what is now the United States—St. Augustine in 1566—also was with the losers in 1588, when the fate of his birthplace was sealed.)[9]

With 1588, London's path to seizing the North American mainland was lubricated. These settlements would not only be a receptacle for dissidents but would provide profit for London that, in turn, would counter Cuba and Mexico, thereby clipping Spain's wings. London remained angered by the massacre of Huguenots in Florida, and Paris as well, a fury fueled by the growing presence of this religious minority in England itself. Survivors of these massacres were consulted by the men who became Sir Walter Raleigh (for whom the capital of today's North Carolina is named) and Sir Humphrey Gilbert too.[10] Reportedly, on 18 August 1587 Virginia Dare was born, said to be the first child defined as "white" born in North America under the Union Jack, a date that continued to be marked, appropriately enough, by white supremacists (the vanguard of settler colonialism) for centuries on end.[11]

Soon a lengthy list of all the possible commodities produced in North America was produced while it was noted licentiously that indigenous women were "of reasonable good proportion" and, to

consolidate the point in a manner that has yet to cease, they were por-
trayed bare-breasted, a status generally spared European women.[12]

As the soon-to-disappear Roanoke colony of the 1580s suggested,
in the prelude to 1588, London was flexing its muscles in New Spain's
backyard, as the complaint was made that the "Spanish authorities refused to deliver up any English subjects they had in prison in
exchange for Spanish prisoners, whom they had therefore determined
to sell to the Moors." Tweaking Madrid, reference was made to the
"many combats with the Spaniards," meaning the seizure of "forts,
ships, barks, carvels and divers other vessels."[13] But this muscle flexing could hardly obscure the true balance of forces. English Catholic
exiles festooned Paris and plotted ceaselessly against Queen Elizabeth,
who was burned in effigy there in 1588.[14]

As is evident, women were at the core of this geostrategic dispute.
Apparently His Catholic Majesty was miffed when Queen Elizabeth
rebuffed his intimate entreaties, and she was displeased when the
Vatican sought to undermine her, nor was she happy about Stukeley
purportedly fomenting unrest in Ireland in league with her religious adversaries. Mary Queen of Scots was reputedly part of this
far-reaching scheme and was liquidated as a result. Revealingly, the
1588 attempted conquest featured scores of Jesuits and monks providing divine blessings. Evidently these men of the cloth did not object
strenuously at the repeated plots to assassinate or poison the Queen:
"Never perhaps in the history of the world," sniffed one Londoner
subsequently, "was a sovereign delivered from more conspiracies
than Queen Elizabeth." Also subsequently, in an echo of today's religious plotting, conspirators falling in battle were told that they would
go "directly to heaven," while "heretics to hell" was their doomed fate.
Since from about 1075 to 1570 pontiffs repeatedly had deposed sover-
eigns and since the weighty St. Bartholomew's Massacre of 1572 was
said to be applauded at the Vatican, murderers had good reason to
commit foul deeds.[15]

In retrospect, it is difficult to exaggerate the influence of this
bloodletting, as killers went about their business not in ill humor
but smirking and cackling instead. Corpses were sliced like cuts of

beef, then slung through the streets. Hence, when scores of seminary priests were found in England by 1586, it seemed to be overly cautious to execute 33, jail 50, and banish or arrest 60.[16]

London continued to be haunted by the tie between France and Scotland, the beheading of Mary Queen of Scots notwithstanding. Again, it was the fervent religionists who were in the vanguard, with Jesuits landing in England in 1580 and the Pope Himself bruiting the idea of an invasion of the sceptered isle in 1582,[17] with bloodshed on the agenda.

Even without an invasion, blood was flowing like wine on the west bank of the English Channel. "Reivers" was the name ascribed to ruffians along the border between Scotland and England, a region that bequeathed to North America a band of cutthroats suitable for settler colonialism with such surnames as Armstrong, Maxwell, Johnston, Graham, Bell, Scott, Nixon, Kerr, Crozier, and Robson. Visiting their new homeland in North Carolina centuries later, a perceptive writer "had begun to notice Billy Grahams, Lyndon Johnsons and Richard Nixons sitting on benches, sweeping the streets and smoking outside." But a bishop in 1578 did not see these purported ancestors of the U.S. elite as worthy of embrace: "They think the art of plundering is very lawful," he huffed about those accused of creating a "kleptocratic system" since "for the ancient Celts too cattle raiding had been a vital tradition. . . . The Gauls had honored Hercules the cattle thief as a founder of their race. . . . Rustling was associated with the heroic deeds of a demi-god" in an "early Irish epic." Thus, even during the London liftoff earlier in the century, these maneuverers planned to distract the monarch from his proposed attack on northern France in accordance with the "auld alliance" between Paris and Scotland. The result was the Battle of Flodden of 1513, in which thousands of Scottish soldiers lost their lives, embittering thousands more. By 1550, the French elite were urging their Scottish counterparts not to cede any ground to England—though the 1551 accord between Edinburgh and London was a milestone on the road to a United Kingdom, which existed on the border decades before the Union of the Crowns in 1603—yet another boost phase of Britain's rise. Even the bad news had a silver lining, for by the late sixteenth-century clan spats, land seizures, roughhousing expeditions, marauding of all sorts, interventions, and counter-interventions were all creating sizeable numbers of internally displaced persons suitable for export to emerging settlements; for example, those that emerged by 1587, then 1607 in North America. These scalawags included Walter Scott, the Laird of Buccleuch; his descendant, the current Duke, is the biggest private landowner in the UK, but as early as 1591 this estate was already gigantic and then grew larger. Preparing for genocide in North America, the Laird of Buccleuch was a reiver who intentionally killed his victims, for along with hunting and horse racing, killing was a favored sport of his, as the infamous Tynedale Massacre indicated. In the "debatable" land between Scotland and England, soldiers burned down every dwelling along a four mile stretch, well preparing both perpetrators and victims for the horrors of settler colonialism in North America.[18] Nearby, in Gaelic society, cattle raids and burnings were a routine method for imposing dominance over others.[19]

It is intriguing to consider if Roanoke was a model for Ireland, even portions of Scotland—in terms of devastation—or vice versa. As noted, when the Spaniard de Ayllon was chased out of this neighborhood in the 1520s because of an uprising by Africans and their allies, he was considering converting this southeast quadrant of North America into a feudal empire staffed in part by bonded indigenes and enslaved Africans, that is, yet another model of exploitation. Thomas More followed in these horrendous footsteps when his Utopia envisioned dispossessing indigenes, just as Irish were being looted. Still, in Roanoke in the 1580s, London had allies reflective of the current correlation of forces: the pilot of the incoming vessel was Portuguese, born in the Azores in 1538, an emblem of the point that this island chain and Bristol were tightly linked. Wisely, this pilot converted from Catholicism before embarking.[20]

The fate of Ireland thus was critical to the rise of England, as well as Spain's decline. For Madrid's investment there did not pay great dividends, while London's subjugation of Dublin eroded a security concern that could have curtailed England's lucrative buccaneering abroad. At the beginning of the sixteenth century, Ireland was medieval and feudal to the core and a potential compliant tool in the hands of those unwilling to accept the rise of Protestantism. By the end of the century, after more than "rough wooing"—more like bloody bludgeoning—Ireland endured the authority of London, perhaps absolutely so. This unpleasantness was asserting itself as early as 1587 when London was fretting about the coming Spanish invasion, especially since what was described as the "Catholic Party" remained strong.[21]

It is likewise intriguing to consider that, as ever, Madrid prepared the path for republicans centuries hence with its ill-considered 1572 punitive expedition against indigenes in what is now Virginia.[22] Possibly the fierce resistance encountered by His Catholic Majesty's forces caused Madrid to turn away from today's Chesapeake, allowing London—then a bottom-feeder—to pounce soon thereafter.[23]

Almost ritualistically, Spanish invaders in North America had been tricked by indigenes who purported to defect to the side of the enemy before wreaking revenge. London was victimized similarly in the 1580s by an indigene, Wachese, who aided an Englishman in learning the Algonquian language, before he abandoned the doomed colony and helped launch attacks against it, again providing entry for subsequent republican conquest.[24]

DESPITE THE SETBACKS, LONDON continued to enjoy advantages. Even the "auld alliance" could be interpreted as a long-term boon for London as it provided practice in waging war on multiple fronts and exercising diplomatic muscles simultaneously. Hence, it made strategic sense for London to pressure Madrid in the Americas, the source for its great leap forward in the century, just as it made sense for Spain to counterattack, as happened quite famously in August 1588. By July 1588, one Englishman observed with dismay that "Spaniards had been sighted" in the "Channel. . . . As far as the eye could see it was nothing but ships, ships, ships! Huge galleons, towering two decks above any England could show, big vessels that were up in the hundreds of tons," and "one hundred fourteen sail in that mighty fleet!"[25]—the direct fruit of mass plunder.

This was a terrifying moment. The revolt of the Dutch had petrified Madrid, contributing to the decision to dispatch an armada of what a later analyst counted as 140 ships and 30,000 men to threaten England, the presumed source of the Protestant sedition. Madrid was not mollified when Walter Raleigh and his hearty band set sail westward on 15 April 1584, reaching what is now North Carolina, then returning with what was described as "two of the natives," who they sought to "impress . . . with the greatness of England." Then a year later Raleigh's cousin, Sir Richard Grenville, sailed to the same land, as the English invasion of North America gathered momentum.[26]

As Englishmen set foot in North America in the 1580s, Madrid envisioned few alternatives except squelching this threat at the source: England itself. There was a real fear in London that Catholics would join the invaders, which accentuated the reason why it was necessary to establish a base due north of St. Augustine and Havana from which Spain could be debilitated. Nevertheless, Madrid was confident that this religious alliance with English Catholics would spell victory—along with the thousands of galley slaves dragooned for His Catholic Majesty's military.[27]

Panic was ascending in London as August 1588 was arriving. Spain had had enough with this cantankerous foe. In 1574, in pursuit of better ties with London, Madrid had expelled hundreds of Catholic refugees with roots in the Isles, which called into question the de facto alliance with Ireland. Even bracing for an expected invasion was costly for England, underlining the importance of Sir Francis Drake's looting, which was also a reason for Spain's inflamed ire as it was a principal victim of his brigandage.[28]

Drake, saluted later as the "Father of the British Navy," sailed into headlines when he looted Spanish gold and silver by the hundredweight, scooping up jewels and pearls by the chest, along with Chinese silks and porcelain.[29] According to one source, his raid in Panama alone, aided revealingly by anti-Madrid Africans, deposited more funds into the Queen's treasury than all the taxes collected in her domain that year.[30] Between 1575 and 1630, what was euphemistically termed "privateering"—piracy in sum—meant England invested far

more here than in any trading company (usually given credit for capitalism's vertiginous ascent): 4.4 million pounds versus 2.9 in the East
India Company, with the former also delivering enslaved labor in the
bargain.[31]

The wily Drake—the paragon of this departure—not only seized
gold and silver and jewels, he captured Spanish and Portuguese vessels, and their pilots and charts too. He sated Queen Elizabeth's
growing appetite for enslavement, which he had stoked earlier with
his journeys with John Hawkins.[32] Drake's adventure was one of the
most profitable enterprises in the history of seafaring. When his vessel
arrived in Plymouth harbor, it was laden above the watermark with
Spanish coins, precious stones (possibly emeralds from Cartagena),
bars of gold and silver, and rare spices (some, gram for gram, more
valuable than gold). Elated shareholders divided among themselves
hundreds of thousands of pounds, amounting in modern terms to tens
of millions of pounds. Comprehensibly, the envoy in London of his
principal victim—meaning Madrid—termed him "the master thief of
the unknown world," while his compatriots celebrated him in song
and story and even today his surname continues to resonate.[33]

Individually essential to advance was Sir Francis Drake. It was
he who arrived in the Netherlands, site of what amounted to Spain's
version of Vietnam, just as Madrid was contemplating overthrow-
ing Her Majesty. He was lionized in London after delivering three
years of plunder to the monarch, allowing a continued hounding of
Spain for years to come and reanimating the animal spirits of the
merchant adventurers who sponsored him; they received a reported
"forty-seven pounds sterling" for "every pound" invested, a level
of profit that even the African Slave Trade at its peak had difficulty
matching.[34]

Drake was away from home from roughly 1577 to 1580, but it was
not just sating homesickness that induced the monarch to summon
him within a week of his return and spend six hours of quality time
with him. (It is likely that the recent merger of the thrones of Portugal
and Spain and the strategic implications of same was a point of
conversation.)[35]

Drake accomplished what previous explorers had not—including, tellingly, Magellan—in one lucrative voyage arriving home safely, carrying Spanish treasure he had captured. He was present at the creation of the transition from cold war to hot war afflicting London and Madrid.[36] London was a latecomer to the colonial party and even to the era of heightened trade across complex borders, which it was said to enter in the 1550s with the formation of the Muscovy Company. But England caught up and then surpassed with a vengeance, thanks to proto-gangsters like Drake.[37] His piratical maneuvers ignited Spain's fervent desire to execute regime change in London in 1588.

In a sense England's island status allowed Spain to more easily pummel Protestant Holland, complicating the ability to supply Amsterdam directly: another advantage accrued by London in its climb to the apex. When the Earl of Leicester arrived in Holland on 19 December 1585, this was in a sense an inspection tour of a firewall. An astute weaker party, London, because of its secondary status had an eye and ear pressed against virtually every keyhole in Europe, an intrusiveness that left England in good stead as it embarked on the long march to global supremacy.[38] Thus, in 1588 a priest confided to Her Majesty's top aide, Francis Walshingham, that "all last year Irishmen came to Bilbao, St. Sebastian's and Groyne with French and Scottish ships, laden with wheat. Likewise some from Waterford with hides; they are all against Her Majesty and speak villainous words respecting her." London knew of "William Snow, another English rebel" who began to spy for Madrid, and London was aware that Spain was "full of Irish prelates" and "they still increase. They come from France by way of Nantes and so to Bilbao."[39] Walsingham, who spoke French and Italian, was well positioned to absorb the import of diverse missives. He also was invested in the Muscovy Company, which provided him with a material basis for staying au courant on European affairs.[40]

An aide to the monarch in London was convinced that there was less peril in hearing too much than too little, as "spiery" or counterespionage was taken to new heights, providing London with yet another advantage. Walsingham deployed thievery, bribes, blackmail, entrapment, even torture and worse as he built a matrix of contacts that crossed borders. (Since His Holiness in the Vatican was not above encouraging murder, including the extirpation of the monarch in London, this was not as unusual as it seemed.) A besieged London thought it had little choice but to make sure that unscrupulousness was an indispensable device of the state,[41] making today's misdeeds appear to be almost mundane by comparison.[42] Perhaps not coincidentally, in 1588 a special edition of the writings of Machiavelli was published,[43] as the reputation of "Perfidious Albion" was solidified, a relatively small island monarchy that managed to construct an empire on which the sun never set.

Of course, Madrid had its own intelligence networks, alerted when an English flotilla rounded southern Portugal low on both food and water, making an attack on Santander unlikely.[44] Not to be ignored were the numerous Irish exiles in Spain, including soldiers, seafarers, clerics, students, and noblemen forced from their estates, all with an interest in sharing intelligence with Madrid about their erstwhile homeland. Ireland may have been subdued by London as early as the twelfth century, but it did seem that the Protestant-Catholic cleavage during the reign of Queen Elizabeth turbo-charged this conflict.[45] Thus, Spain was overly confident in 1579 when it landed a motley force of soldiers in Ireland, near Dingle, under the command of a renegade Irishman, James Fitzmaurice—and was rebuffed, though it remained optimistic about a turnabout in 1588.[46]

Like so many English pirates and soldiers-of-fortune, Drake had earned his spurs in quashing the Irish, in league with the Earl of Essex in his case. His importance was indicated when in 1914 at the apogee of the British Empire—just before its precipitous decline—a London propagandist rhapsodized that "the present occupation of the North American continent by the Anglo-Saxon race is, after all, but a realization of what may be called Drake's Dream," an opinion garnished by late sixteenth-century Spain ironically concurring.[47]

There was also Madrid's hubris, contemplating invading China at the time that the Armada disembarked.[48] In the narrowest sense, this scheme made sense in that this Asian giant was beginning to drain

Spain and her settlements of silver in return for silks, chinaware, beeswax, spices, perfumes, jewelry, and the like. This was networking Manila closer to the Asian mainland and in turn connecting Acapulco to both, with the latter containing a sizeable population of Africans and Chinese. Conquering China would have provided more Spanish control over this opulent network. But at what cost?[49]

Hubristically, Madrid, at least by 1587 was seeking to enslave Japanese and, said one astonished nineteenth-century observer, "carry them away . . . to the Indies."[50] Spain was compelled to pull back from Japan, which may have allowed for further advance in California, where, reportedly, Chinese had sojourned a millennium before Columbus. But as Europeans advanced, made fat on the plunder of Africa and the Americas, they arrived in Japan—leading Japan to expel their advance guard, the Jesuits, then wall itself off from such visitors for two centuries until the door was pried open (appropriately enough) by the ultimate beneficiary of colonialism: the United States.[51]

Thus Madrid had reason to be confident in the prelude to the 1588 debacle. Despite tensions between the two, there was a confluence between Spanish and Moorish taste and design in the all-important realm of firearms, in which both were advancing. In the late sixteenth century—circa 1585, though possibly earlier—the snaphaunce lock, the forerunner of the true flintlock, was invented. The earlier snaphaunces of the late sixteenth century are very much like the snaphaunces that were made by Moorish craftsmen.[52] During that same decade, a contemporaneous report suggested that the key to a Portuguese defeat of Angolans on the battlefield of Africa was the Europeans' armaments.[53]

No better example of Spain's hubris was what occurred after August 1588. Refusing to draw the appropriate lesson, months later Madrid sought a replay of this failed invasion—and failed again.[54] The humbling and bumbling of Spain itself proceeded when, just after the 1588 defeat, a Spanish mariner informed His Catholic Majesty that he and his adventurous crew sailed from Lisbon only to have his and other vessels wrecked off the coast of Ireland. Some men drowned.

Others swam ashore and were promptly liquidated by Englishmen. Unsurprisingly, he found to his dismay that "the land and beach were full of enemies who were going about skipping and dancing for joy at our misfortune, whenever any of our men reached land two hundred savages and other enemies rushed upon them and stripped them of everything they wore, leaving them stark naked and without any pity beat them and ill used them. . . . They were assisted by over two thousand savages and Englishmen," the former an apparent reference to putative Irish comrades. These alleged traitors performed dispiritedly, though "they hear mass and follow the usages of the Catholic Church." This perfidy occurred though "almost all their churches, monasteries and hermitages have been destroyed by the soldiers from the English garrison." Still, a saving grace was that there were other "savages" who "liked us very much for they knew that we were great enemies to the heretics and had it not been for them not one would now be alive."[55]

Emboldened by Spain's 1588 fiasco, months later a confident London was "ready to sail to Cadiz or Barbary to revictual or else to return by the Spanish coast." Fortunately in Lisbon there was to be found "biscuit and corn . . . sufficient for 40,000 men for one year" and various "stores," which would doubtlessly wrongfoot the King of Spain, who "had intended to have fitted out a new fleet for England." Instead, "with 12,000 footmen and 100 lancers Her Majesty might march through Spain and Portugal and dictate terms of peace." This would not necessarily mean restoring the authority of the Portuguese comrades, who—Sir Francis Walsingham was told—"are the greatest cowards ever seen."[56]

London had potentially attractive options. Al-Mansur in Morocco wanted London's aid against Spain, while Portuguese wanted their throne restored as against Madrid, and perhaps seizing Andalusia in the bargain. Drake's privateering was helping to resolve the problem of paying for these ventures, and from this cogitation emerged the idea of a joint-stock company—the entity that was to deliver gargantuan wealth in coming centuries—with Dutch Calvinists, who pioneered in both capitalism and republicanism, the twin bedevilments of

Africans in the immediate future, as paymasters supplying troops, ships, and supplies.[57]

Like the Netherlands, Morocco too was no cipher, an important waystation en route to African gold—and enslaved African labor—along with a counterweight against Ottomans and Spaniards alike, and as Alcazar demonstrated, a formidable military power capable of taking on European military powers, as Lisbon could well attest.[58] Serendipitously for London, the Antwerp crisis of 1550 led London to increase trade with Morocco and by 1553 Africa farther south, both of which proved to be crucial to the rise of England.[59]

ALERT OBSERVERS MAY HAVE NOTICED that the ascension of His Catholic Majesty was flawed fundamentally. For example, with the takeover of Portugal, those in the Jewish community that had not fled began to do so, and were welcomed with open arms in Amsterdam and Constantinople and even London—ironic in that England had been in the vanguard of expelling this minority in the first instance, bulwarking Madrid's present and coming foes, allowing them to take advantage of "diaspora networks" built so assiduously by this minority.[60] The Spanish swallowing of Portugal also allowed London to revivify its lengthy alliance with Lisbon; Londoners as early as 1580 were requesting "authority to assist Don Antonio, King of Portugal, against any of his enemies," and in the same missive, quite tellingly, a commission was granted for a "fleet of ships to be employed on a voyage of discovery on the coasts of Africa and America,"[61] a devastating signal to inhabitants of both continents. Lisbon had reason to be grateful when in 1589, keeping Spain off balance, a flotilla from London set sail for Portugal with the aim of ousting Spanish rule.[62]

A subdued Lisbon, nonetheless, was on a steady march to decline, destined to gloat for centuries on end about its past glories and willing to overlook the reality that London, its newest patron, was in league with Morocco, which had ruled that portion of Iberia in the thirteenth century and seemingly was headed again for that pole position as of 4 August 1578 and the epochal Alcazar.[63]

Attentive spectators with acute hindsight may have noticed after Alcazar that the freebooter John Smith, soon to make his mark in North America, arrived in Morocco shortly after this turning point in world history. Like other Englishmen, the scent of gold in Africa was stimulating his and others' more devious aspirations. Already, the idea was in the ether that England and Morocco should unite further, this time to oust Spain from the Americas. Already, English trade with Morocco and Guinea was outraging Lisbon, which had thought it had a stranglehold on this misbegotten wealth. Already, Queen Elizabeth herself was said to have the "black teeth" that character-ized those with undue fondness for sugar, a commodity that was to propel waves of Africans across the Atlantic with Morocco receiving lances and pikes in return, easing the conquest of Africa due south and facilitating this odious commerce. Again, Portugal, driven out of Agadir in 1541—a setback blamed on London and Paris— could only watch in dismay as the tides of time left Lisbon in the lurch.[64]

Part of Lisbon's problem was the antagonism with Morocco, sealed, perhaps irrevocably, as early as 1415 with Portuguese seizure of Ceuta, launching Portugal on a round-robin of conquest. London, on the other hand, cut deals with Morocco, a wiser course in ret-rospect. By 1576, English trade with this North African nation was worth twice as much as trade with Portugal, which liked to think of itself as one of England's oldest allies. Lisbon's Vatican allies issued a Papal Nuncio—a fatwa in essence—that blamed the fiasco of Alcazar on Queen Elizabeth, making her worthy of slaying.[65]

Indeed, the ripples from Alcazar were so encompassing that histo-rian Karen Ordahl Kupperman strode a step further and argued that this event "changed the course of European, North African and even American history," not least since it inspired the Vatican to step up its attempt to depose the London regime, leading directly to the Spanish disaster of 1588.[66]

Post-Lepanto, the Franco-Turkish relationship continued, facili-tating England's attempt to woo both, since the relationship was in aid of destabilizing Spain, which was London's goal too. However, the 1571 Turkish defeat made this tie less relevant and, thereby, was another boost for London. But another kind of sleeper was the fascination in Paris with all things Turkish, which shaped Parisian cultural life for years to come. Other Catholics were not as taken with Constantinople, especially the Vatican, where in 1581 His Holiness was organizing the buying back of Christian slaves ensnared by Muslims. Corsairs continued to roam the Mediterranean, leaving a deep imprint on the exceedingly important science of seamanship; the state was obliged to become involved since one merchant was insufficient to carry this weight, as these entrepreneurs found their actions increasingly governed by official intervention and regulation, including the need for maritime insurance, all of which planted more seeds that sprouted in capitalism.[67] As the shoots of this new system began to break through the concrete of the preexisting order, the energy that had driven enslavement in the Mediterranean and North Africa began to be diverted more and more southward down the western coast of Africa.

Intriguingly, just as "Communist" China leapfrogged the pack in the late twentieth and early twenty-first centuries by cutting deals with presumed antagonists in Washington and Brussels,[68] England acted similarly in the latter part of the sixteenth century with its eagerness to forge ties with predominantly Muslim nations, thought by many (especially in Spain) to be little more than heretics and enemies. London was ever in need of gold from Morocco—much of it scooped up from the latter's neighbors—and saltpeter too, useful for making ammunition, which helped fuel colonial conquest in Ireland and the Americas. Morocco had to be convinced of London's goodwill since at Alcazar in 1578, the beginning of a slow decline for Portugal (akin to 1588 for Spain), England, true to history, had sided with Lisbon in this battle to the death. But Morocco had few options, since like so many nations it was nervous when glimpsing the unassailable strength of the Ottomans nearby in North Africa, and the fact that London was snuggling closer to Constantinople was not worth ignoring. Besides, both Morocco and England had mutual interests in conquering Africa to the south—which led to a cataclysmic defeat for this theretofore wealthy region in 1591, a dawning of the apocalypse for Africans—and grabbing the gold there. This provided financial wherewithal for the conquerors, while converting Lisbon and its vast holdings in Brazil, Angola, Cape Verde, and Mozambique into a satrap and slave supplier to the Americas for London's benefit.[69] (Portugal's role in Macao also was to provide a steppingstone when centuries later, London saw fit to seize Hong Kong, creating the possibility of taking the greatest prize for colonialism of all: the Chinese mainland).[70]

From the time of Spain's takeover of Portugal, upward of 90 percent of the enslaved Africans dragged to the Americas had roots in Angola.[71] Certainly, the 1580s witnessed London paying more attention to North Africa, as one Londoner wandered into Algiers and Tripoli and was quick to describe the weapons men carried.[72] In 1582, London was informed happily that "merchants" were "trading to Barbary."[73] Spain, as was its wont, was a recruiter accidentally for London. Madrid won few favors in North Africa when as late as the seventeenth and eighteenth centuries, Moors and Berbers from that important region—and Turks as well—were a sizeable portion of the enslaved population of Cadiz and other cities in Andalusia, as if Spain was wreaking religious revenge.[74]

Morocco was not the only African nation imbued with ambition. Arriving at the strategic Straits of Malacca in the early sixteenth century, an observer found Abyssinians trading there, along with Cairenes.[75] At this juncture, London's two-faced policy of courting Africans and enslaving Africans was a rational response to the reality that the continent as a whole had yet to fall into the torpor that was to be its sad fate in succeeding centuries. As historian Toby Green asserts, "Gold Coast armies were formidable in the late [fifteenth] century" and "until perhaps in the 1680s and 1690s"—that is, the period of takeoff of the new system of capitalism goosed by the slave trade—"all the cards were held by the Gold Coast Kingdom."[76]

Nevertheless, the Ottomans, presumed patron of Muslims, had weaknesses all their own that Lepanto highlighted, if not exposed. The looting of Africa and the Americas was so handsome for Western Europeans that it provided impetus for the latter to surge ahead indefinitely, virtually nullifying whatever gains the Ottomans accrued in the Arab lands and beyond.[77] On the other hand, the Ottoman interest in the Mediterranean and points east made them a suitable ally for London, which did not discourage their real and imagined threats against the Vatican and Madrid alike. Of the more than sixty theatrical plays in London between 1576 and 1603 featuring Turks, Persians, and Moors, forty were staged between 1588 and 1599. Since Constantinople did not view London as a serious power, this was truly a marriage of convenience. The commercial intermediaries of the Turks were often Sephardim, who also had an interest in undermining Madrid and bolstering the antagonists of His Catholic Majesty. So developed a three-way trade among English merchants, Muslim rulers, and Jewish intermediaries, which proved to be mutually beneficial. Moreover, there were those in the Jewish community of North Africa who proved to be quite useful to London in that they often controlled the trade in both sugar and Christian captives.[78]

Speaking of Africa, London was hardly a bystander or passive beneficiary of Portuguese depredations. On 4 November 1586, a group of armed English voyagers financed by George Clifford, third Earl of Cumberland, invaded a town in today's Sierra Leone, scattering its residents and eyeing ravenously its attributes—before torching it and creating a heap of ashes and embers. Beforehand, the invaders were struck by the cleanliness of the town, unsurprising since many villages in the British Isles featured animals and humans living cheek by jowl. Of course, looting occurred, rice in this case, and about 6,000 pounds of related merchandise was then carted back home, an emblem of how Europe not only underdeveloped Africa but benefited from its plundering. The Clifford enterprise was the fourth recorded group of Englishmen to descend upon Sierra Leone in the late sixteenth century and the second since the slaving voyages of John Hawkins in the 1560s, all of which violently uprooted Africans. The captain of Clifford's ship, Robert Widdrington, then headed to Brazil, which was also scheduled for pillaging. Hawkins notwithstanding, 1586 signaled an acceleration of London's unprovoked aggression in West Africa, a portent of what was soon to come.

Thus, along with Widdrington and his curiously named vessel, the *Red Dragon*, there arrived William Cavendish in the same vicinity in 1586; he too uprooted Africans, drove them from their homes, which were then sacked, and he too torched their abodes. Then again, shortly thereafter more homes were subjected to arson because of upset with the unwillingness of Africans to accept one-sided bargains with those described as "Christian"—not "white," as they were to be termed subsequently.[79]

Theology was busily adapting to the renewed order of conquest, in that ransacking and laying waste was seen as executing the will of God, not unlike "Israelies [*sic*] entering Canaan."[80] As suggested earlier, the maunderings of Machiavelli attained a reenergized popularity in London in the 1580s.[81]

As the tumult in what became Sierra Leone indicated, this ideological turn arrived at a propitious moment. Recall that in 1567 Hawkins had hired the man to be known as Sir Francis Drake for their slaving venture in West Africa, a foretaste of what coming centuries was to deliver. They headed for the appropriately named Gold Coast, where they loaded about five hundred unwilling Africans into the squalid holds of their vessels, then sailed westward to Vera Cruz where they came under attack. This experience doubtlessly steeled Drake for further escapades, including reaching the Moluccas where he agreed to support indigenes fighting Iberians. By 1585, Drake was a terror of the high seas; torching, despoiling, and pillaging Spanish settlements was his specialty as he roamed in swashbuckling mode from Cartagena to Santo Domingo and Cuba, before reaching St. Augustine in 1586, which too was devastated and left Madrid vulnerable when London sent settlers due north to what was called Roanoke. Agreeing to migrate to the unknown territory in what was to be called Carolina were artisans, small landowners, lesser merchants, and lumpen of various sorts,[82] along with small businessmen, tailors, lawyers, goldsmiths, and adventurous teachers.[83] That is, from its inception, settler colonialism, English style, was an exemplar of class collaboration, as investors picked up the tab while those beneath them on the class totem pole were deployed into veritable battle zones.

In the Caribbean in the 1580s Drake was reported to have taken "much wealth," simultaneously bolstering London and debilitating Madrid. In Santo Domingo, in some ways, the key settlement, Drake left a smoking ruin in his wake. Two friars were hanged and two were immolated in the church, a reflection of the St. Bartholomew Massacre. The enslaved were freed, and jailed Frenchmen likewise were released. A number of African and Moorish galley slaves appeared to have accompanied the Englishmen when they departed.[84] Ottoman Turks too were part of this dragooned crew, as a reported 200 Moors as well as 150 male and female West Africans left alongside Drake and may have wound up in North America, though at least one returned to England, then immediately fled for France, an escaping trend in coming centuries. One scholar argues that the Africans taken to Roanoke in 1586 may have been "the direct ancestors of those Machapunga"—indigenes—"so adept in war" who tormented settlers for years to come.[85] (They may have been even more obstreperous but for a tragedy that occurred in mid-June 1586 when a terrible storm hit Drake's fleet while anchored in Roanoke, decimating the hundreds of Africans who had fled with him from Spanish settlements.)[86]

In Cartagena, Drake was said to have torched monasteries and not only released the enslaved but captured Moorish, Turkish, and Indian slaves.[87] It is possible that they too were taken to Roanoke, and it is possible that they merged with indigenes there, along with Huguenot and Jewish religious castaways, to result in today's "Melungeons," a hearty ethnic group in North America.[88]

Drake's peregrinations and the crassly opportunistic basis of his success continued to thrill Englishmen years after he expired. Just as Perfidious Albion deigned to ally with Morocco and Ottomans to climb the greasy pole of hegemony, celebrated too was the wiliness of a major slave-trading nation allying with Africans in Panama to outfox Spaniards. "The Negroes," he was reported to have said on 22 July 1572, "gave us some particular understanding of the present state of the towne," speaking of the site of an impending pillaging. They "told us . . . they had heard a report, that certain soldiers should come hither shortly . . . to defend their town against the Symerons [.] a black

people, which about eightie years past fled from the Spanish their masters, by reason of their crueltie and are since growne to a . . . nation,
under two Kings of their owne." Thus, the latest invaders were "willing to use those Negroes well," including building a fort since these
maroons "hated the Spaniards."[89]

A self-fulfilling opinion that generations of Englishmen continued
to share, a prejudice that continues to haunt Spanish progeny—and
victims too—in North America to this very day, was heightened with
the arrival of the swashbuckling Drake, bent on looting Spain on
behalf of England. (By the mid-nineteenth century, this anti-Span-
iard complex, engineered in the first instance by London, served to
rationalize seizing vast lands from Mexico.)[90] "The Spaniard," Drake
was reported to have said, "is a strange individual and self deception
with him has grown to be so much a part of national character that it
can be reckoned upon a surety," a throwback to the admonitions of
Las Casas decades earlier. He convinced himself that the maroons felt
similarly, not unlikely in retrospect. One—Diego—a "Negro" who
"spoke English" was a "noble fellow in more ways than one; he had
a carriage to his head and shoulders I have never seen the equal of at
court" and was "never obsequious or fawning." In fact, said Drake's
reputed "friend and follower," that is, Matthew Maunsell, his reli-
ability was shown since "from Drake alone did he take orders" as he
became a "companion, confidant and counsellor to our leader." This
African was allocated the preeminent compliment of the era, since,
said Manusell, "I doubt not that it was true that he had the blood of
some royal line in him as he claimed," solidifying "our alliance with
the Maroons."[91]

Drake had become a constant presence in waters claimed by Spain.
Before the reduction of Santo Domingo, he had made it to what came
to be called northern California, disreputably laying the groundwork
of what was to become the epicenter of English-speaking hegemony
in the future.[92] He landed reportedly[93] where Rodriguez Cabrillo had
landed in 1542, illustrating again how Iberians paved the way for
Englishmen.[94] Arguably, "Nova Albion" in this now populous region
was the first flag implanted by Englishmen on claimed territory[95] and

the founding site for the overseas British Empire (the voyage of Martin Frobisher to Baffin Island in 1576 where he made a claim for London is a contestant for this criminal crown).[96] This occurred six years before Roanoke, though both were incipient signs of slowly declining Spanish hegemony and the steady rise of England.[97] Drake's Pacific overture included arriving in the Marianas, a venture Madrid viewed suspiciously.[98]

Again, when Drake skirted the shores of New Spain, the authorities there diverted troops from fighting in today's U.S. Southwest to confront him, illustrating once again how the path was smoothed for English speakers.[99] There was a related fear in 1582 expressed to the man diplomatically referred to as "His Sacred Catholic Royal Majesty, the King, Our Lord, Don Felipe." Referring to what is now New Mexico and the region due south, Diego de Ibarra asserted: "Your Majesty orders me not to allow the Negroes in the said province to hold any communication with the native Indians, because of the many difficulties that result from it." Because "the Negroes in said province are separate and apart from the settlements of the natives," it was thought this important goal could be attained and, in any case, "great care will be taken to carry out Your Majesty's order."[100]

In short, these religious foes—or at least those whose conquest could be rationalized on religious grounds—extended to today's New Mexico, Florida's companion as a founder of the United States, well before Virginia and New England. Moving steadily northward in 1583, conquistadors arrived, eyeballing hungrily the unavoidable reality that the indigenes had "much victual" worthy of plunder and a "great store of game both of foot and wing . . . with plentie of fish, by reason of their great rivers running from the northward" and "many lakes of salt water." Unfortunately, it was added disconsolately, "they are a warlike people" in that "for the first night that our people pitched their camp . . . they shot & killed"; then, "afterward" when "demanded of whom they had learned that knowledge of God, they [spoke] of three Christians & one *Negro*"—notice the continuing distinction despite the latter's presumed religious bona fides—"had passed that way & [stayed] a while," a reference to an earlier Spanish incursion.[101] Notice as well that as late as 1869, when New Mexico was under the jurisdiction of republicans, the latter continued to look back with resentment at the rambunctiousness that indigenes had displayed centuries earlier against Spanish invaders.[102]

BY STICKING STUBBORNLY TO religiosity in an age of colonialism moving steadily toward the Pan-European "whiteness" that became London's specialty, Spain was determined to fall behind, though even when Madrid emulated London, they flubbed. Even after Alcazar, the local elite in Havana sought to expel the free Negro population but was blocked by higher powers.[103]

Religious intensity sat alongside colonialism uneasily, a system that tended to advantage racist intensity. This contradiction was not simply a product of the demographics and history of New Mexico and points immediately southward. By 1582, in what was to become Colombia, there were real fears of fraternizing between super-exploited African and indigenous laborers. The former especially were critical to the success of the wildly profitable emerald mines. Intriguingly, this kind of gem trading was executed in an organized and routine manner by a few dozen Sephardic merchant families, who had good reason to be skeptical of the presumed virtues of Madrid. Some were part of a far-flung Luso-Hispanic sphere, and those with ties to Portugal may have had even more reason to be wary of Madrid. Still, they were part of a transnational merchant community of a sort that capitalism delivered almost effortlessly in coming decades, and their being wooed successfully by London in the mid-seventeenth century was yet another step in Madrid's downwardness. For many, even most, emeralds sent outward from Cartagena moved across the Atlantic and Indian oceans through Sephardic and so-called New Christian family webs, then shifting to Oliver Cromwell's London by 1655. Even before then, these precious stones were handled by Sephardim living in Fez, Marrakesh, and Tangier—all within London's sphere of influence—along with Algiers and Tunis, all understandably suspicious of their Mediterranean neighbor in Madrid. Predictably, a Cartagena Inquisition was established by 1610, though premonitions were in place even earlier. Several jewel merchants were charged with "practicing Judaism," which could easily be interpreted as a simple way to seize wealth on religious grounds. Some of these merchants invested in the African Slave Trade, a bulwark of Cartagena, which meant dealings with Luanda and Portuguese, also being courted aggressively by London. Others had ties to Holland and Belgium, with Flemings too being interrogated as a result. Other geographic nodes included South Asia, where emeralds were savored by Sikh and Hindu alike, facilitated by Goa's seizure by Lisbon by 1510. But, again, with Portugal falling under the sway of Spain, moving Lisbon closer to London, this wound up depositing more chits in England's pot, even from a Cartagena within Madrid's sphere.[104]

Revealingly, the most famous Jewish trader to operate in early colonial Angola was Duarte Lopes. Born in 1550, he arrived in Luanda in 1578 and by 1583—curiously—he was Congo's representative to the Vatican. Jewish planters had been in nearby São Tomé since 1470.[105] Given Lisbon's entente with London, this was destined to redound positively for the latter in what was to become a primary haven for slave trading. Similarly, it was Walsingham who hired Joachim Gans, identified as a "Jew from Prague" and billed as the "first acknowledged Jew to set foot in America,"[106] during the ill-fated Roanoke venture. As was generally the case, this decision by London can be viewed as a step toward a synthetic "whiteness," a step toward religious tolerance and an undermining blow against the anti-Judaic pretensions of Madrid. And in this context Madrid could not be assured of seizing Lisbon's interests in south Asia. Tellingly, beginning in the 1580s Londoners turned aggressively toward south Asia, which was to become the jewel in the crown of what became the British Empire.[107] The first English audience with the potent Akbar of India took place in 1585.[108]

The ampler point is that the merger of the thrones of Spain and Portugal stimulated the African Slave Trade to Peru, producing more wealth for Madrid,[109] and more opportunities for seizing same by the likes of Sir Francis Drake. Moreover, though London had its own anti-Semitic problem—witness the expulsion of the Jewish community centuries before Spain did the same—England's subsequent underdog status did not admit many options beyond an entente with the Jewish diaspora, accelerated by the mid-seventeenth century pact with the anti-royalist Oliver Cromwell. Madrid's failure to move in a similar direction was just one more factor that thrust London to the forefront.[110]

For by 1700, Spanish armed forces were no more than 63,000; France's about 342,000; and, said one source, "Britain was not far behind."[111] The immediate future was to belong to the United States, which, sharpening the effective tool that was "whiteness," developed a population base that made these cited figures seem puny by comparison.

CHAPTER 7

Origins of the U.S.A.: Indigenous Floridians Liquidated | Ditto for New Mexico

A s Spain was stumbling in 1588 in the waters off England, it was encountering similar difficulties in Florida where settlement was affixed more firmly than in territories due north, but things remained rocky nonetheless. By 1580, officials on this North American peninsula were pleased to observe that the soil was fertile but there were not enough settlers to take advantage, an outgrowth of Madrid's shortsighted religious prerequisites. Officialdom demanded that more of the enslaved be sent from Havana, but this would simultaneously weaken Cuba while placing on Florida's shores disgruntled workers who had proven themselves quite willing to heed the insistent calls of militant indigenes and French corsairs alike.[1]

After all, by the 1590s an uptick in importation of enslaved Africans to Cuba meant more marronage (escaping from slavery), in a manner that could portend another Panama where runaway Africans (maroons) had collaborated with Drake, or the disruption provided by Miguel in Venezuela or their peers in Santo Domingo, which had been in a chronic state of conflict with these rebels since the 1520s when they established a foothold in the Baoruco region of the island. It required a major offensive to reduce their strength by the 1590s, which left the colonizer with hardly the stomach or forces to press further regionally. The maroon community of Orizaba in Venezuela was not taken by the settlers until 1609.[2] In nearby Brazil, ostensibly Portuguese and inferentially Spanish in light of Madrid's takeover of the Iberian neighbor, Africans had formed the now fabled Palmares in the late sixteenth century—and maintained it well into the following century—a de facto African state with the potential to destabilize the entire continent.[3]

In short, the overall strategic situation for Madrid in the Americas, even Florida, was not as strong as it may have appeared at first blush. This was no minor matter since by 1580 news had arrived that corsairs were bonding with indigenes, who were now in the process of organizing rebellion on the peninsula.[4] Puerto Rico too was menaced by corsairs, who also were flocking to St. Augustine, which appeared to be a chicken awaiting plucking; due north in Santa Elena indigenes attacked, but like hydraulic engineers, as reinforcements were rushed to bolster the Caribbean, corsairs simply headed north to pressure Florida.[5]

Settlement leaders were doubtlessly aware of the risks, but they desperately needed someone to build fortifications to blunt the offensive of corsairs and there were not many options. So, Havana was ordered to send thirty enslaved Africans to Florida forthwith,[6] with even more pledged.[7] St. Augustine was poorly armed, barely fortified, and perpetually in need of more troops, especially after the restive Guale revolted and passed the word that their French allies too were amassing.[8] Worryingly for settlers was that the interpreter for the Guale was apparently a French lad.[9] A Frenchman was also a primary physician in St. Augustine, while another was the best interpreter of the language used by the Guale,[10] yet another indicator of the difficulty in using religion as a leading marker for settler colonialism, as it could be faked: "whiteness" was seemingly more reliable. Nerves remained frayed when reports arrived that two enslaved Africans were found aboard a captured French pirate ship; they were ordered to be returned to their Spanish "owners," which was probably the least bad of all options available.[11]

As time passed, the problem did not diminish. By early 1582, French corsairs were detected at Matanzas, Cuba, at a time when St. Augustine was clamoring for more enslaved Africans because indigenes again had skirmished at Santa Elena. The report that fifty indigenous combatants had fallen in battle did not assuage the overall concern.[12] The authorities signaled the hole in the dike they deemed to be most critical, when a few days later, thirty Africans—twenty-three men and seven women, all reportedly in good condition—were sent to Florida to buttress flagging efforts.[13] By the spring of 1583, even more enslaved Africans from Havana were to be found in Florida working on fortifications and clearing fields for cultivation.[14]

These tasks involved, inter alia, working in unhealthy lime and brick fortifications.[15] But by the end of the year, they had built a platform of durable wood suitable for artillery, a building for the forge, and made repairs on the fort, including building an all-important church. They repaired the fort at Santa Elena, virtually destroyed by indigenes, cut lumber for a bank—another all-important building—and constructed living quarters for themselves, finally. They also helped to make ammunition, cleared the forest for sowing, and eleven of the enslaved were rented to soldiers for purposes that remain unclear.[16]

Despite this busyness, by mid-1585 French corsairs again were on the march, robbing a ship en route to Spain, seizing much booty at a time when Sir Francis Drake was doing the same. Thus, the authorities wanted two armed galleys to protect Florida's coast and immediate environs;[17] still, differences between Asturians and other settlers and Africans and all of the latter continued to fester.[18] Yet even as French corsairs continued as an irritant, Drake continued to be a transcendently looming worry, even as the former assaulted Santiago de Cuba.[19]

Conniptions waxed in the regional headquarters that was Santo Domingo when word arrived that Drake and his minions had sacked and burned St. Augustine, causing this isolated city to request aid that was also needed desperately farther south in the Caribbean. For the clever Drake also had taken artillery and other martial items and munitions. Still, Havana exhaled and dispatched artillery northward, and sent a delegation to New Spain for a subsidy, which could only weaken that colony too, in a skein of falling dominoes.[20] Dangerously, Drake also had focused on seizing the labor supply—enslaved Africans—and carting them away, eroding the sinew and fiber of Spanish settlements, a point reported appropriately on 4 July 1586.[21] A few days earlier, the easily foreseeable had occurred: Spaniards had concluded that Londoners were about to implant a base north of St. Augustine.[22] Once more, aid was requested to blunt this potentially disastrous maneuver. But which Spanish settlement would be weakened to do so?[23]

Drake symbolized the decline of Madrid and the rise of London in more ways than one. He was second-in-command during the Armada's debacle of 1588, and even when he died in 1596 (appropriately enough in Panama, site of past triumphs) he was continuing to undermine Spain. The wealth he reaped mostly went to the swells of London; still, when he passed, his last will and testament included a bequest to the poor of Plymouth, launching pad for further colonial projects, again in one of his past haunts: the mainland of North America.[24]

Luckily for Madrid, Drake and his crew got sidetracked en route to Santa Elena, although Spain's problems remained on course. Soldiers were complaining, and supplies were needed immediately from Havana for St. Augustine, though dispatching same could have weakened the former. In any case, the fortifications built by enslaved Africans were sufficient, it was thought, to withstand an indigenous assault but not one by corsairs. Spaniards had reason to fear that Drake was impressed with Florida because of fertility of the soil and proximity to frequently plied routes by vessels groaning with riches, military materièl, and, at times, enslaved labor. The good news was that three enslaved Africans who had escaped from the piratical Englishmen were now toiling in St. Augustine on fortifications.[25] When it was reported that Drake not only had Africans aboard but Turks too, it was not clear if Spaniards recognized that they may have been freed slaves and not co-equal allies of Englishmen. In any case, the counsel offered from St. Augustine was to abandon Santa Elena—yet another step forward for emerging republicans—and focus on defense of the north Florida settlement.[26]

It augured well for the peninsular settlers that Africans defected to the Spaniards, for they needed all the help they could get. By 1583, the St. Augustine elite reported that these bonded laborers had "made a platform for the artillery of this Fort of an indestructible wood. . . . They have made a blacksmith shop and whatever repairs were needed on the Fort. . . . They have helped to build a church here, sawed lumber for the building of many dwellings and have cleared the woods to some extent for planting." Apparently having accepted Catholicism, "eleven of these Negroes were hired [as] soldiers of this Fort," albeit "without the knowledge of the Treasurer."[27]

St. Augustine may have seemed more problematic than valuable, strategic locale aside, for officialdom there continually begged for subsidies and more enslaved Africans from Havana, apparently oblivious of the downstream consequences. There was even disagreement over the disposition of Africans seized from Frenchmen.[28] Yet even Captain Vicente Gonzalez, freshly arrived from Spain, acknowledged the great neediness of St. Augustine after the Drake sacking—assuming it survived.[29] But Spanish colonialism was akin to an urban fire department besieged by a skillful crew of pyromaniacs and arsonists, since there were also demands to bolster settlements due south in the Straits of Magellan, along with beefing up defense in the Caribbean, and Panama as well.[30] Spain was overstretched and down the road would have to yield to others more prepared to build settler colonialism.

Thus, by early 1587, official Havana was told by Governor Menendez Marques in St. Augustine that an English settlement was being built due north. Supposedly, these settlers had passed by his huddled encampment two years previously en route from the Caribbean with livestock. Africans who had escaped from Drake were told, he said, that they were being taken to this new settlement.[31]

The bad news for Spain in 1588 was the failed Armada, but also worth considering in this context was the continued drain of enslaved Africans from the Caribbean to Florida.[32] Trading Africans duty-free in the region in the aftermath may have deprived coffers of revenue needed to guard against their seditiousness.[33] Sedition was a term that could have been applied to discontented soldiers in St. Augustine, complaining by spring 1593 that they had not been paid in five years, leading to the inevitable, namely a rebellion, leading to imprisonment, all this after the governor-elect had somehow drowned.[34] Mutinous soldiers with unresolved grievances were not new in St. Augustine.[35]

Rebelliousness on all sides, along with reduced revenue, meant that by the summer of 1593 the governor in St. Augustine was instructed to keep a detailed record of the income delivered by the presence of enslaved Africans in order to determine if the return on this investment was greater than their expense.[36] What to do with Africans soaked up considerable staff time in the St. Augustine administration. By late 1593, the decision was made to send eight enslaved Africans to Florida from the Caribbean—six sawyers and two carpenters— though like pieces on a chessboard, four or five others were sent away from the peninsula because they were deemed too old to be of use there.[37] Another important demographic shift took place when about a dozen women, described as unmarried and respectable, were brought to Florida for potential marriages to military officers, a move that could make these men less likely to rebel.[38] If such were the case, the principle did not seem to be working, for soon nine soldiers were caught plotting an escape, two were hanged and the rest somehow tranquilized.[39] One Captain Salazar of Florida was shipped to Cuba as a result of this revolt, along with the most culpable officers, but they may have contributed to the swirling unrest there.[40]

Perhaps in response, consideration was given to hiring indigenes as seafarers and even contemplation of paying them adequately, a decision that clashed with the prevalent idea of plundering them, which was bound to have short-lived results.[41] For by the spring of 1594, English seafarers were spotted in the waters off Cuba and supposedly were contacting locals. Problems persisted in coercing soldiers to volunteer for duty in Florida, not to mention finding enslaved Africans to build the perpetually assaulted fortifications.[42] Tempers flared again when by late 1595 rumors were floated about an alleged and impending English attack on Santo Domingo, Puerto Rico, and Florida, the latter two to be claimed by victorious North American republicans subsequently.[43] In a possible countermeasure, soon there was an Irishman serving as a parish priest—Father Richard Artur—arriving directly from Spain.[44] Thus, by August 1595 there were "preparations" in Spain that, London was told, "are greater than those in 1588 and it is not to be doubted but that they intend to invade England and Ireland next summer."[45] Spain attacked Ireland on 17 March 1596 and Wales in November of the next year and threatened to do so repeatedly thereafter.[46]

But this religiously speckled Irish-Spanish solidarity did not suppress an insurrection of soldiers in Florida that was repressed, and again culprits were shipped to Cuba, as if that did not just simply shift the problem to an already stressed settlement.[47]

This was occurring at an unpropitious moment for peninsula settlers. In 1597, the Guale finally had had enough and engineered a blitzing revolt. They murdered five Franciscan friars and razed their mission, basically terminating missionizing by force. Reportedly, 400 warriors attacked. Settlers should not have been surprised; in 1576 they had rebelled similarly. The conflict dragged on until in 1600–1601 bloody retribution was visited upon indigenes as the surviving women and children were ordered to scalp their deceased kin, except for their leader who was subjected to decapitation.[48] Unrepentant, a Spaniard in St. Augustine bewailed the presence of "Indians, who so horribly killed six [sic] priests of the San Franciscan Order."[49] Yet the Spaniards were stuck, because by 1597 more Africans were arriving in Florida, though they had proven themselves to be cut from the same cloth as indigenes when it came to rebelliousness.[50]

Indigenes were disrupting the grand plan held in Madrid for Florida. Of course, early on "Florida" could mean the vast territory stretching to today's Hudson Bay, and this was more an indicator of the grandness of the vision for the peninsula. As so often happened, and still happens, on 22 September 1599 a monumental hurricane smacked St. Augustine, further mortifying settlers on edge from indigenous attacks. Frequent shipwrecks in the Keys and Bahama

Channel continued to afflict the land farther south, with the survivors starving or falling into the hands of merciless indigenes when they wandered ashore. By 1600, piously and hypocritically, confirmation was made of that which was obvious: indigenes were highly resistant to the theology of Catholicism, which was a rationale for either abandoning the peninsula altogether, or ridding the peninsula of unbelievers and their purported treacheries.[51] Making it plain, one twentieth-century historian spat out angrily that the "Indian revolt of the Guale was a desperate attempt to wipe out the Christian culture that had just taken root." In response, the attempt was made to wipe out the Guale populace and—minimally—their culture.[52]

A SIMILAR PROCESS WAS UNFOLDING across the continent in what was to become the U.S. state of New Mexico. In 1582 a Spanish leader was complaining that more soldiers were needed since unwelcoming indigenes had chased away and otherwise throttled his co-religionists. Still, this leader was so dreamily contemplating the uncovering of silver, gold, and other precious metals he thought he was closer to China than he actually was. Yet he did concede that settlers might be needed to hold territory and to block French, English, and Lutherans—not necessarily in that order. Possibly, 300 men on horses would suffice for the time being, but the religious test to be imposed upon arrivals inherently compromised the Madrid project.[53]

Undeterred, an adventurous Spaniard was heading north from Mexico City in 1584 with 400 men—100 of whom were married—all expert in war, though the idea was to pander to indigenes so they would not rebel. Tens of thousands of ducats had been spent on this expedition, but worry still reigned in that there was recognition that their relatively small number would not be sufficiently intimidating, indicating the need for more men that religious testing could hardly provide.[54] As with Drake pillaging the Spanish to boost his own nation, London was also translating—pillaging, literally—Spanish documents about China, with an eye planted firmly on the future.[55]

The reference to China was indicative of where Spanish dreams resided. By 1590, one Spaniard had just returned from there and arrived in Acapulco babbling about gold, silver, pearls, cotton, silk and other valuable commodities. The cloud on this rainbow of grandiosity was the presence of English pirates, a gift of foresight on the part of this subject in that in the long run these buccaneers' cousins would inherit the territory due north.[56]

Back in northern New Spain (today's New Mexico) in 1598 the invaders put on "trial" the "Indians of Acoma" for "having wantonly killed," among others, "Don Juan de Zaldivar, two captains, eight soldiers, and two servants." This "treachery," it was said fumingly, was an "outrage" as the accused "intercepted the soldiers on their way" and "shouted insults," and "called them scoundrels" in a parting shot.[57] Captain Geronimo Marquez recalled that "when the Spaniards reached the . . . pueblo, the Indians rose in large numbers" with unremitting fury and unleashed a fusillade of "arrows, stones, clubs and sticks . . . hurled them down the cliff."[58] The Spaniards may have perceived that the ferocious indigenes were not only fighting for their lives but for their way of life. Captain Gaspar Lopez Tabora observed: "They pursued the Spaniards in large groups and began to hurl countless stones, arrows and clubs" with "both men and women, participating in the attacks. . . . This was done treacherously and with premeditation. . . . The Indians were so numerous, threw so many stones and shot so many arrows" that they "forced the Spaniards to a high cliff." As if their experience was similar or their testimony rehearsed, he too found that the "treachery of the Indians was premeditated."[59]

On the other hand, it could be that common and startling images were frozen in common memory. "All of a sudden," said Alonso Gonzalez, "the Indians attacked the Spaniards from every direction with arrows, stones, sticks and war clubs" while wielding "swords and harquebuses,"[60] the latter precursors of rifles.

"Indians including the women attacked from both the terraces and ground with arrows, stones and war clubs" and "this witness," chimed in Antonio de Sarinana, "escaped by sliding down the cliffs." But he gathered his thoughts sufficiently to add venomously, "Unless this pueblo is destroyed and the Indians punished no one could live in the land in security," a cry that would be echoed in North America in coming centuries.[61]

Despite the setbacks, Spaniards kept arriving because of what one mouthwateringly depicted as the "wealth of the land," which mandated "war against these savages," and, in return, the assaulted "attacked with great fury."[62]

As republicans inched toward their takeover of this territory in the nineteenth century, this conflicted land continued to be termed by one historian as the "land of war."[63] According to contemporary scholar John Kessell, in 1599 there was an estimated "Pueblo Indian population" of 60,000, while by the year 2000, the U.S. Census put their numbers at 59,621,[64] a remarkable flat-line.

Another Spanish observer—who happened to notice a "mulatto" in the entourage—was struck when "Indians kept shouting that they wanted to fight" and "hurled many insulting words." By 22 January 1599, the confrontation continued, as the indigenes "spent all that night in huge dances and carousals, shouting, hissing and making merry, challenging the army to fight." Somehow, "the natives would not listen to reason."[65] An indigene who "appeared to be about fifty" was asked why the indigenes were so upset: "He said that the Spaniards had wounded an Acoma" and "his people became angry and killed them."[66]

Interestingly, it was reported subsequently, when certain indigenes sensed the presence of settlers they "hide their wives, daughters and provisions and build great smoky fires," which amounted to "signals of war," as if they expected their foes to be adept at human trafficking.[67]

But with all their bravado, even considering their devastation of indigenes, Madrid faced far-reaching problems, including overreach, that were to compromise their entire enterprise. At this moment of invasion, the Spanish interlopers included those described as "Africans" and "Mulattos." "Fifty-two percent," said contemporary genealogist David H. Snow, gave "Spain, Portugal, Canaries, Azores as places of origin," while "one person each gave Belgium, Greece and Italy," and "36 percent" were from Cuba and Mexico. A key interpreter was a "personal servant, identified as a Negro, named Juanillo, who apparently understood some of the Pueblo languages."[68] According to Captain Luis Velasco, speaking in 1597, the original expedition included "slaves—Negroes and Chichimecas, male and female."[69] Yet, despite these questionable allies, Spain had the audacity—or lack of good strategic sense—to question the bona fides of English Catholics who sought to migrate to Florida.[70]

Thus, in 1598 when a vessel arrived in Florida with seven non-Spaniards aboard, including an Englishman from London accompanied by "Germans," the authorities were keen to ensure that passengers aboard would be religiously correct. Six were artillerymen and one was a fifer, and if history is any guide, the authorities would be swift to admit the latter if he were Catholic and reject the others if they were not, irrespective of military need.[71]

Yet while Dutch and Turkish competitors especially were benefiting from the energy of Sephardim, they were still being sanctioned in New Spain. In the early stages of the Inquisition—in 1519, for example—the accused were shipped to Spain to be interrogated and punished, but (as noted) by 1569, they could be hounded in settlements, a policy that lasted until about 1813 and was virtually guaranteed to chase the persecuted into the arms of Madrid's antagonists, including republicans.[72]

Presuming that the Africans were religiously correct, it was no less striking that in New Spain the warning was given "not to allow the Negroes in the said province" to "hold any communication with the native Indians because of the many difficulties that result from it."[73] Bringing more Europeans on board in the name of "whiteness" broadened the base of the settler project in a way that religion could not, unless one assumed that Catholicism was to sweep the globe like a firestorm, destroying opponents in the process. The hyper-religious cry of "Kill, kill or else be Catholic" was dysfunctional at a time when contemporaneously the felt desire to cleanse the landscape of Native Americans was rising.[74]

What has been described as the first attempt to set up a colony in present New Mexico, unfolding in 1590, illuminates the contradictions that inhered in the Spanish model in this capacious territory.

Gaspar Castano de Sosa, spearhead of the venture, was Portuguese by birth, implying religious correctness, but his puny band of "37 Spaniards" was no match for "500 warriors." And, according to subsequent historians, they were greeted not unlike the "reception prepared for Coronado at Zuni in 1540, the Pecos Indians brought stones to the roof to throw down on the Spaniards" as the invaders' "gifts proved useless in winning the Indians' friendship."[75] Put bluntly, the invaders needed more soldiers in numbers that "whiteness" could provide more reliably.

That is not all. Castano de Sosa's putatively illegal move northward was, according to a recent scholar, driven by fear of the Inquisition (his Christianity was implied but apparently not actual—he was thought to be Jewish) and many of those who accompanied him were also thought to be "conversos" or "New Christians" or "Crypto-Jews." After the massive revolt of indigenes in 1680, accusations of religious incorrectness declined, possibly because the settlement itself was on the verge of liquidation, and, like their fellow European colonizers, the Spaniards recognized finally that they needed every settler they could round up. However, by then London was well on its way to elbowing aside Madrid.[76] Ironically, some of the most important founding fathers of New Mexico were Jewish, though they had to hide this identity, a factor that illustrates the frailty of judging the admissibility of settlers on religious grounds.[77]

Many of these "Jewish" families—the first families of what became the United States—were granted enormous land grants in northern New Spain. One extended as far as today's San Antonio, encompassing 360,000 square miles, bigger than today's Texas.[78] The father of Luis Carvajal, for example, arrived in New Spain in 1569 and attained notoriety as a conquistador and battler of indigenes, and by 1580 the family was governing what was called the "new kingdom of León."[79]

Yes, so-called Crypto-Jews or New Christians, that is, those passing as Christians though likely Sephardim, were part of the initial influx of settlers into what amounted to New Mexico. Since 1391, many from this community had been fleeing Spain for various locales. In other words, Gaspar Castano de Sosa, a founding father of this settlement in 1598, may have been a Crypto-Jew; shrouding his identity was a response no doubt to such inflammatory incidents as a Portuguese New Christian being burned at the stake in New Spain.[80]

His apprehensions about fellow Iberians notwithstanding, de Sosa also had to keep a wary eye on indigenes unhappy about invasions. He and his band encountered what was termed delicately "Indian troubles"; the pressure from these troubles combined with mutinous sentiments among fellow settlers that caused him to retreat southward —at least initially.[81]

While those who were Jewish were in hiding or posing as Christians, an Englishman visiting Constantinople and other sites under Turkish jurisdiction found that there "the Jews here have a synagogue . . . one having marryed [sic] an English woman and converted her to his religion." While Madrid was in virtual war with this capital, George Sandys found that "the foreign merchants here resident are for the most part English." But Sandys was already observing the color obsession that was to characterize settler colonialism when he observed that "Maltese are little [less] tawny than the Moors."[82] In short, Sandys was observing in microcosm why Spain was fated to decline: Turks, Sephardim, and English comprised a formidable bloc of antagonists who would not be denied.

Other Spaniards were more concerned about the immediacy of the perennial: the continuing revolt of those called "chichimecas"— rebellious indigenes—which was becoming increasingly costly at a time when Spain was leaking wealth to Drake.[83] By 1599, indigenes were using flint ammunition and bows in the manner of the Turks, it was said. Yet, since a contemporaneous report misjudged wildly the distance from Peru to China, knowledge about weaponry might have been askew too. One point was undeniably accurate: if Spain was to claim this territory and hold it in the face of various challenges, more settlers and soldiers would be needed.[84]

By 1600, indigenes were back on their heels, as the so-called Chichimeca Wars, which had been unfolding for decades began to turn in favor of the invaders, laying the groundwork for further expansion northward into what is now New Mexico, Arizona, and

Texas—that is, present republican strongholds.[85] But settlers were hardly faring better, as inhabitants were being reduced to eating charcoal and wild seeds. The two contenders were punching each other senseless, preparing the ground for the future republican conquest.[86]

Nevertheless, Madrid could escape internal contradictions to a degree by empowering minorities abroad—for example, Basques. Strikingly, those of this group without seemingly "Hispanic" surnames were able to soar to the highest level among republicans that inherited this territory.[87] Basques—and Andalusians too—were prominent among the sixteenth-century leaders of what became New Mexico.[88] Yet Basque unrest tended to soar as Spanish colonial pretensions receded, illustrating the value of colonialism in submerging internal contradictions.[89] Thus, Fracisco de Urinola, the governor of Nueva Vizcaya, was, says one scholar, "like so many other notable men active in Spanish-American discovery and colonization . . . a native of the Basque provinces." Unfortunately, like many invaders—Basque and others—he was caught up in atrocity, arrested on the charge of being implicated in the murder of no fewer than seven people: his wife, her paramour, and five Negro and native "servants" (or so they were described); that is, to hide an exploding love triangle, he did away with four indigenes and an African woman,[90] indicative of the cavalier attitude adopted at the highest level to the existence of the oppressed, which ensured their administration would be curtailed—eventually.

AT THE SAME TIME SPANIARDS were gnashing their teeth about events in northern New Spain, they were continually being pummeled by the Dutch, who with aid from London in particular were administering a mighty blow against Madrid.[91] Serving to undercut Madrid was gross mistreatment of indigenes, which had motivated Las Casas decades earlier. By 1595 the wise Dutch found an ally against Madrid in Chile in the combative Araucanians, who held legitimate grudges against Spain.[92] The Dutch had rebelled against the Habsburgs and Spanish, even before the Protestant Reformation, that is, in 1506, but this simmering picked up speed in 1568 with assistance from London: the Dutch Republic of 1580–81 was a landmark in the evolution of republican politics and capitalism too, then sped ahead for eight decades, withering Madrid, yet another reason for London's ascension.[93]

The Dutch Republic pioneered in becoming a conscientious objector in the religious wars, leaning toward religious tolerance that would become the stated hallmark of the new era of capitalism and republicanism. Of course, religious tolerance broadened the base for colonialism, as pioneered by London, which invited once despised Catholics to settle what was called "Maryland." Though not as close as lips and teeth, the Dutch still invited Queen Elizabeth to become "Queen of their Dominions."[94]

The Dutch surged at Portugal's expense—meaning Spain's expense—ousting Lisbon temporarily from Luanda, maintaining dozens of vessels off the Gold Coast by 1598,[95] and dispatching forty vessels to Asian ports by 1595.[96] Madrid also had to worry about dissident Portuguese, unreconciled to the Spanish takeover, and more than willing to collaborate with London. This irritant complicated a single-minded focus on England. Thus, when Francisco Villarreal, a Portuguese gentleman, was found on an English ship en route to London that was captured by a Spanish privateer, Juan de Escalante, valuable time was expended before it was ascertained that he was innocent of any wrongdoing.[97]

THUS, IN THE DECADE FLOWING from 1599, there were scores of Dutch vessels sailing to Africa.[98] By 1597, Dutchmen set sail for Java, via the Cape of Good Hope, and eventually established a settlement there that became a byword for a profoundly hateful contribution of capitalism to global culture: apartheid. But at that moment, these shrewd traders had broken the grip of Venice's hold on spices and pepper, leading to an Anglo-Dutch-Persian coalition that challenged not just Iberians but also Ottomans.[99] Further north, by 1599 Dutch forces were challenging their Spanish counterparts in the Canary Islands, an important site for Madrid.[100] By 1615, there were dozens of Dutch ships to be found in the vicinity of the Gold Coast.[101] As part of its anti-Spain offensive, the Dutch lengthened the battlefield, contesting Madrid's power worldwide; taking a page from Drake's playbook, they hindered Madrid tremendously, especially in such crucial sites as Chile, Mexico, and the Philippines. Dutch strength in ships and men on the Pacific Coast before 1621 was four times that of England, though the latter was the final beneficiary of this multifaceted offensive.[102]

During this decade, Madrid was preoccupied with the Dutch, worrying that Holland's ships were being disguised as merchant vessels, with double crews that included the armed version preparing to attack.[103] There was also anxiety in Madrid about the possibility that vessels of reputed Scottish allies were carrying forged documents, allowing them to penetrate Spanish waters, forcing an embargo on all Scottish vessels to the detriment of the Spanish and these allies.[104]

This was at a time when Madrid was concerned about deserters from their ranks in France and Flanders both,[105] especially since it appeared that Spain was in dire need of more seafarers,[106] a need that tended to grow over time.[107] This was delaying the embarkation of vessels, a potentially harmful blockage for a maritime empire.[108] Thus, to make an example to others considering desertion, Madrid instructed that those apprehended should be banished to the galleys.[109] This was a reflection of the fact that although the Americas and the Philippines were generating tremendous wealth, grain imports remained low for Spain, meaning problems in supplying seamen off the coast of Brittany with biscuits.[110] Brittany was a sore point for Madrid: by 1595 there was concern that ships from there could be used to war against Spain,[111] just as deserters from Spain's galleys were flocking there.[112]

Thus, by 1594, Madrid was preparing a privateering license for issue to Juan de Carasa, so that he could lead armed vessels against the enemies of His Catholic Majesty.[113] This was deemed to be a wise maneuver since Madrid had reason to believe that London was preparing an attack on northern Spain[114] at a time when a large quantity of lead, needed for ammunition, was being sought by them and by enemy privateers.[115]

But helping to make possible this Dutch resistance was England

and her allies,[116] which in turn benefited her neighbor, for espied in African waters by the early 1600s were more English vessels: in 1611 an English vessel was found off the coast of Angola with dozens of cannon and scores of men.[117] Plying the waters created opportunities for ransacking slave ships of other nations, as occurred during this time when a vessel from Guinea, bound for Cartagena, carrying hundreds of Africans, was captured on the high seas.[118]

The post-1588 economy created a supple service sector based in maritime, industrialization, and widespread urbanization—the seedlings of capitalism, in other words. The rising merchants and entrepreneurs also drove politics in their behalf. Between 1584 and 1597, about one-third of London's parliamentarians were members of overseas trading companies.[119]

Amsterdam's population soared from 50,000 in 1600 to 200,000 in 1650, at which point northwest Europe took yet another great surge forward.[120] The asset to Amsterdam provided by the expulsion of the Sephardim from Iberia is difficult to overestimate. Consider, for example, the man known as Menasseh ben Israel, whose father was tortured as a result of the Inquisition, which led to a hasty departure to Holland, where the son, according to his biographer, became the "most famous Jew in the world,"[121] and, in diverse circles, exceedingly influential in the bargain.

By 1580, there was an Ottoman-Habsburg truce, allowing Spain to focus more intently on Holland, as well as England and Persia.[122] But by the 1590s, the Ottomans and Habsburgs were in a familiar posture, at war, this time following the Sultan's invasion of Hungary, a conflict that dragged on for thirteen years. This complicated Spain's effort to combat other competitors, particularly the Dutch and English, as it was occupied with the Turks. Thus, by 1596 England attacked Cadiz successfully, depositing a large portion of Spain's Indies' flotilla at the bottom of the harbor. In response, 10,000 comrades departed Lisbon for Ireland, in conjunction with Spain seeking to land an army there, but, again, a storm wrecked this ambitious project. The Isles dodged disaster but still responded by arresting for treason Dr. Roderigo Lopez, Portuguese-born and

Jewish although a convert to Protestantism; accused of conspiring with the Iberians to poison Queen Elizabeth, he was executed.[123] In a manner that was quite harsh, London moved ruthlessly to suppress and liquidate real and imagined internal foes, so as to better confront the chief foe—Spain.[124]

A general crisis of the 1590s bent regimes of all sorts. The Ottomans were in a barely perceptible—to some—downward slide. Their crisis was climatic, economic, demographic, martial, and ancestral (palace intrigue, a staple of Constantinople). Drought compelled tens of thousands, even millions of peasants, off their land, which facilitated settler colonialism for Englishmen. Some of their Turkish peers had become soldiers in the 1593–1606 war against the Habsburgs and, as so often happens transnationally, they misdirected their fungible martial skills into the related trades of robbery, thievery, and gang-sterism, a prelude to piracy and, potentially, a destabilizing political factor. As historian Jane Hathaway put it, this "lay at the root of the infamous Jelali Rebellions which engulfed Anatolia in chaos during these years."[125]

Holland was not the only Protestant power that was advancing then though, retrospectively, this small nation can easily be seen as the mouse that roared and was bound to be squashed or trapped. In the 1590s, Sir Anthony Sherley sent aid to Henry IV in France, then sailed southward to the Portuguese settlement off the western coast of Africa, São Tomé Principe.

Exhibiting the nimbleness—perhaps dearth of principle—that was to characterize the British Empire at its height, he sought to entice Persians to unite with Christians against the Ottoman Turks (an erstwhile ally against Madrid); he also sought to establish firmer commercial intercourse between London and points farther east. Then it was on to Moscow. That he was to change his religion and soon work on behalf of Madrid only reinforces the lack of scruple that was growing like a weed in London and served to underlay settler colonialism and the concomitant seizing the land of others by means mostly repugnant. And the new era of commerce meant that the highest principle of all was accumulating capital by any means necessary.[126] Thus

Sherley received hosannas from his newest sponsors when in the late sixteenth century he received "praise" from a Jesuit in Madrid "for his conduct in liberating prisoners in Africa."[127]

More to the point, emerging was an Anglo-Dutch-Persian alliance that bid fair to establish a new global hegemony and certainly prepared the ground for the reduction in strength of Spaniards and Ottomans both. As early as 1589, London's diplomats and merchants were to be found in profusion in the Ottoman Empire, Tripoli, Persia, and Goa, prepping for future dominance.[128]

The island monarchy took advantage of the nearby ocean to sail far and wide. Thomas Cavendish became the second Englishman to circumnavigate the globe, by 29 November 1591 touching Brazil and avariciously capturing a Portuguese vessel carting enslaved Africans— yet another advantage of opportunistic nomadism made possible by increased wealth.[129] By 1594, Robert Dudley of England was to be found in Puerto Rico, under the noses of Spaniards. But the enhanced wealth flowing into Europe, based upon exploitation of the Americas and Africa, was buoying Western Europe generally. Florentines were prominent in sixteenth-century Brazil, for example, as, according to scholar Brian Brege, "Italian colonialism directly influenced Iberian colonialism," or put another way: settler colonialism was a Pan-European project containing the germ of "whiteness."[130]

By 1593, John Vincent had written what was termed his "third letter he has written since . . . arrival at barbarous Brazil"; he found sugar from there—and the West African land of São Tomé too—as "not so wholesome as Barbary sugars," which augured well for the ongoing alliance with Morocco.[131] Soon, more English vessels were to be found off the coast of Madagascar,[132] a future major depot for the horrid African Slave Trade. The same descriptor could be applied to Angola, where, at the end of the sixteenth century, at least four Englishmen were known to have visited[133]—the first of a tidal wave from due north. Just before this portentous arrival, Genoa began systematically rescuing enslaved Genoans from North Africa, the beginning of a systemic trend, which in a sense was accompanied by the ascendancy of the enslaved from farther south in Africa.[134]

This was hardly trivial in that it was one more sign of pushback against the once dominant Mediterranean Muslims. As noted, England and the Ottomans had united against their common foe in Madrid; the Vatican had forbidden military aid to the former, but the split in Christendom did not handcuff London, though it did undermine His Holiness's command. And since the Ottomans were as wicked in dealing with Christians as the latter were in manhandling Africans this heightened the wrath rising against London among the Catholics. The possibility of castration—or sparing same—was said to be one of the "inducements" in compelling captured Christians to convert to Islam. Tens of thousands of Christian prisoners were nested in North Africa, igniting an Easter collection in churches as a ritual to pay their ransom. Thus, on 19 October 1541, Spain embarked for Algiers with 500 ships and 12,000 sailors and soldiers—larger than the 1588 force designed for regime change in London—but, again, was flummoxed by a storm. So many men were captured that the slave economy of Algiers was said to collapse, and the price of captives plummeted to an onion per slave. This too was part of the strength of Ottoman Turkey, which was to descend significantly by 1699. This strength induced an underestimation of London, since the Ottomans dominated the immense region stretching from North Africa to Persia, including most of the vital coast. The territories from eastern Europe to Yemen likewise owed allegiance to the Sultan, as did a good deal of the land reaching the borders of India. Until 1683, the Ottomans were knocking on the door of Vienna repeatedly, perhaps because from about 900 until the eighteenth century their swords and spears were sharper and stronger than those of their opponents to the west; what was termed innocuously as "wootz" steel was far harder to damage. There were so many Slav Janissaries that they often spoke Serbo-Croatian among themselves. But an acute observer might have noticed that by 1599 the pinnacle of Ottoman strength had been reached and the time had come for the arrival at the summit of another power, which happened to be headquartered in London. Yet this observer would have to be acutely attuned to prevailing trends to ascertain this incipient trend.[135]

THERE WAS NO BETTER EXEMPLAR of the brutally bloody prag-
matism than what was then unfolding in Africa, as the slave trade was
given further impetus by the rise of the Dutch and the English, than
what was unfolding south of Morocco. Ironically, placing this odious
commerce in this stratosphere was England's old ally, Morocco. In
retrospect, the pounding of the Songhay Empire was the Rosetta
Stone serving to explicate Africa's precipitous decline. "Songhay
power was at its height" in 1590, says scholar John Hunwick, and
it fell thereafter with devastatingly malign consequences for a wide
swathe of the continent.[136]

Songhay had built a sophisticated military machine with a cavalry,
a flotilla of martial canoes, and brigades of smiths who made breast-
plates and weapons.[137] It should not be lost on readers that Christians
were not the only religionists shedding purported belief for ampler
profit, for when Morocco attacked southward this was a "Muslim-on-
Muslim" crime, facilitated by Englishmen.

The 1591 punishing defeat of the Songhay Empire sent seismic
tremors cascading throughout the continent, weakening polities of all
sorts, making West Africa notably more vulnerable to enslavement.[138]
This elephantine territory stretched as far south as today's Nigeria,
bringing more influence to Morocco, meaning more influence to its
European ally: England. But, above all, this provided propulsive
momentum to the slave trade. So emboldened, Morocco audaciously
proposed a joint campaign between the two partners to seize Spain's
colonies in the Americas and the Philippines. Then Africans, as a
direct result, began streaming into London itself, and the monarch,
like a republican homeowner in future centuries, began to complain
about all the Negroes moving into the neighborhood, ranting about
the "great number of Negroes and Blackamoors," her newest neighbors. Yes, England was in a state of famine due to poor harvests and the
punishing impact of enclosures, so like future republican politicians
she began to attack immigrants and "aliens." Paying attention, the
playwright William Shakespeare began incorporating these new real-
ities into his work. There was *Othello*, of course—the hero returned
from fighting "the enemy Ottoman on Cyprus,"[139] but *Twelfth Night*

too was haunted by images of Muslims, Turks, Egyptians, Africans. In the 1590s, in particular, these images were scattered throughout his work. His Aaron in *Titus Andronicus* was a malevolent, double-dealing "blackamoor," an irreligious Moor besides. The writer conflated him with Turks and Jews, along with Moors and atheists—that is, the "Other."[140]

Shakespeare was responding to real phenomena, as was the monarch, though she was complaining about what was a product of her own making. There was an arrival of more West Africans to her realm, an outgrowth of London's increased role in the slave trade. This led to increased anxiety about the African presence in London and ineffective attempts at deportation from about 1596 to 1601. Yet many of the most adept slave traders in London were the Portuguese New Christians or conversos welcomed as a counterweight to Madrid; though their population was in the scores, they punched above their weight in the financial arena.[141]

They were far from being alone, however. Thus, in 1599 the secretary of the Earl of Hertford was informed succinctly, "Pray enquire after and secure my Negress; she is certainly at the 'Swan,' a Dane's beer shop, Turnbull Street, Clerkenwell."[142]

Englishmen began scrambling to visit the site of future enrichment. A London traveler in 1597 provided requisite cartography, along with an exposition on the Congo River, an artery traversed repeatedly in coming decades with the aim of snatching and enslaving. He penned an exposition on the "weapons of the people of Angola," focused on "their daggers," a token of their "great skill and good order in matter of warre." The "Kingdom of Congo" was seen as "very populous," which could change easily by dint of slave trading. Moreover, this land was "very rich in mines of silver & most excellent copper."[143]

Africa was sieged, and polities sought shelter from the storm. Ethiopia, for example, began working more with Portugal, one of a number of deft maneuvers that spared Addis Ababa from a fate that swept much of the continent,[144] namely colonialism and enslavement. There had been a significant Ottoman penetration of the Indian Ocean coast of Africa stretching to today's Sri Lanka and to Siam, bringing a slipping Lisbon into conflict with Constantinople, with tensions rising, allowing for arbitrage by Ethiopian leaders.[145]

Topography—high altitude—and deft diplomacy may have spared Ethiopia from what befell much of the continent, but Congo-Angola was more typical of the fate of Africans. The heyday of what became known as the Atlantic Slave Trade smacked Luanda-Kinshasa with a category 5 body blow, and, it has been said that the catalyst for this devastation were the Portuguese slave traders of São Tomé, among whom were New Christians. Two thousand from this community were shipped, 600 surviving, and post-1492 this confluence of tragedy gave rise to even more human misery, as enslavement of Africans to grow sugar occurred. In 1512, arson erupted, and by January 1517 there was an uprising of the enslaved. At that juncture, non-Africans began fleeing to Brazil and were often replaced by *"degradados,"* the degraded or "lumpen" or gangsters. São Tomé was a catchment for regional trade and rapidly became involved in Congo, which it influenced negatively. The same was true for Angola and the "Angolars," likely Mbundu, who originated with a wreck of a slave ship in 1554 with the survivors swimming to São Tomé, where they became the vector for continuing unrest as they occupied a deserted portion of the island. By 1574, Africans torched most of the houses, mills, stores, and plantations. But it was in 1595 that a merger of events—rising slave powers in Holland and England; a declining power in Lisbon eager to wrest ever quicker profits through ever more brutal exploitation of a captive workforce; and Africans fed up with brutalization—that led to one of the more profound uprisings of Africans during the entire post-1492 era. The "Angolars" served as inspiration: though they may not have played a role in the revolt, they were able to provide sanctuary for rebels. Led by Amador, an African who should be seen as part of the pantheon that includes Nat Turner and Hatuey of Cuba, they slaughtered Europeans in churches, including priests and an army of thousands under his leadership destroyed virtually all of the despised sugar mills. It was estimated that there may have been as many as 5,000 in his contingent. Naturally, this escalated the flight to Brazil, pushing tensions across the Atlantic and sugar production too to a vaster land, making sugar and coffee production more feasible, not to mention settler colonialism as well.[146]

As for Amador, he was captured, hanged, drawn and quartered, after being accused of torching seventy sugar plantations. Coincidentally, as he was lynched, the power of neighboring Benin, Ilé-Ifè, Nupe, and small kingdoms such as Ijesa had begun to decline. As this was occurring, the rising Dutch were beginning to oust the Portuguese from their sinecures in West Africa and Brazil alike. London made the wise choice to finance Lisbon, which weakened Holland and made Portugal more dependent upon England, yet another reason for this kingdom's rise. This was all occurring as the incursion of Christianity was sowing division in West Africa, a condition made worse when Christian-backed factions prevailed: by the 1650s, the Jesuits in Luanda lolled in the most luxurious houses there and controlled dozens of plantations that contained more than 10,000 of the enslaved. By 1600, slave ships sailed regularly from Luanda to Buenos Aires and an umbilical cord of silver connected these two beleaguered continents. Understandably, by 1600 nobility on the Gold Coast were adorned with Dutch and Venetian beads.[147]

Thus, by 1600, although England was not a major power, an alert observer might have detected in the travails of Africa, the Americas, Spain, Ottoman Turkey—and even India,[148] where the monarchy was about to make a dramatic appearance—the impending arrival of a new force on the planet, headquartered in London.

CHAPTER 8

Apocalypse Dawning

The pioneers responsible for settling what was called Virginia in the early 1600s were reflective of the struggles of past decades. "The settlers landed," said a U.S. national marking the arrival of the invaders on "the 13th of May 1607," more than a century after the arrival of Cabot and more than two decades after Raleigh, marking yet another rung climbed by London and its progeny en route to global supremacy. Battle-hardened by internal and external conflicts, the invaders said the woman who called herself "Mrs. Roger Pryor" did well to observe that "the Indians were not friends," adding ironically that "but for the massacre of 1622," referring to an attempt to extirpate the settlement, "much might have been said in praise of the Indian."[1] In an exemplar of understatement, the late historian Carl Bridenbaugh opined that the initial invaders "failed completely to gauge the depth of the resentment of the English intrusion on the part of Powhatan . . . and their fellow [indigenous] kings."[2] Yet another salutation to the invaders marked their arrival on 24 April 1607—more than a decade before Plymouth Rock—welcoming John Smith, a leader, as "the real founder and preserver of the Anglo-Saxon in America." This battle-scarred freebooter previously had fought alongside the Dutch against the Spaniards and then, in a turnabout reflective of Perfidious Albion, fought against an erstwhile English ally, Ottoman Turks, who were to fade as London was rising.[3]   It was likely that Smith observed the mandate imposed on settlers, especially men, that they should be fitted with a suit of armor, a musket, a bandolier for deadly projectiles, twenty pounds of powder, and sixty pounds of shot.[4] Apparently, the invaders did not expect to be greeted with sweets and flowers by indigenes.

The native population had been battling Europeans for about a century along the Atlantic seaboard before this latest invasion, absorbing blows and dishing out a few, but in the long term, these bruising encounters made them more susceptible to conquest.[5] Even before the mass invasion of the North American mainland in 1607, Charles Leigh arrived on the northern coast of South America and sought to construct a "settlement among the Indians," who, in a self-serving fashion, he found to be "anxious for instruction," necessitating "able preachers to be sent to them" and, more martially, "the King's protection for emigrants to this colony," soon to be besieged.[6]

Of course, it was not all smooth sailing for the latest invaders: the first colony on the shores of New England, for example, was a French settlement in 1604 that faded into history, not least because of a stonily cold welcome by the original inhabitants.[7] "Hostile Indians" were the culprits, according to one study.[8]

Contributing to the seething cauldron of hostility was yet another group. "The first recorded Africans in British [sic] North America were brought to Virginia aboard a Dutch ship" in 1619 was the pronouncement that has become common wisdom, though readers may recall the Africans brought to the mainland as early as 1526 or even those who escaped the clutches of Sir Francis Drake decades later. No matter. Nevertheless, it is instructive to note that the 1619 Africans were taken from a Portuguese ship, which had sailed from Luanda bound for Vera Cruz,[9] all important sites of contestation before this important date.

In the years preceding 1619, it is true that more and more Europeans were descending upon Africa, seeking free labor for settlements. In 1603 Andreas J. Ulsheimer was met in West Africa, he said, "by

several thousand Blacks who intended to drive our people back and
defeat them." His startled band shouted the equivalent of a peace
offering at the feisty combatants, "but they paid as little attention," as
"the besieged Turks in Canisca [Kanisza] paid to the mass held by the
Capuchin monk who wanted thereby to exorcise and immobilize the
guns of the Turks, so that they could no longer shoot at the Christians
with them. For just as the Turks took the monk away from his altar,
which he had wanted to erect in front of the fortress, and shot him and
his altar to rubble, so these savage Moors seized our general, together
with the captain and the boy, ignoring their peace offer, and decapi-
tated them. They also hollowed out the heads and even before we had
marched away, drank out of them . . . after this the Blacks imagined
they had totally killed and defeated us and therefore ran towards us,
screaming atrociously and loudly."[10]

Quite appropriately, an account of the earthshaking founding of
Jamestown, rendered as the guns of war were blazing during the
First World War, pointed to similarly bloodcurdling predicates to
1607: the "revolt of the Protestants in Scotland, 1565," the same year
as St. Augustine was founded. The mutual "hatred" between Walter
Raleigh and Madrid, which drove his settlement in the 1580s; the
foundation of Quebec by French Catholics in 1605—all this and
more, said Conway Whittle Sams, motivated the "departure from
London, December 19, 1606." Still, this analyst was quick to stress a
point that was to yield under the necessities of forming a viable settler
colonialism in the name of "whiteness." Virginia, he said, "did not
tolerate the Catholics and was founded with the intention of prohibit-
ing them from coming to this country."[11]

Another analyst, looking back from the vantage point of 1933, found
that Spain was overstretched as early as the mid-sixteenth century,
creating an opening for England; besides, said Henry Wilkinson,
Madrid's "financing was from Lombardy, since, in their religious
frenzy, Spain had extruded not only the Moors but the Jews also,"
a policy inimical to a viable colonialism. Yet by the 1560s, he says,
Africans "greatly outnumbered the Spaniards" in the colonies, creating inherent instability and numerous arbitrage opportunities for the

enslaved to exploit.[12] London's ability to create Pan-Europeanism in settlements served to forestall what had debilitated Madrid.

Furthermore, and similarly important from its inception, London's settler project involved class collaboration, that is, the distinguishing feature of republicans who shouted bizarrely in the midst of mass enslavement and genocide that "All Men Are Created Equal." Jamestown was born with a mixture of the dispossessed and middle class that characterized Roanoke, with more financial heft marking those who invaded the land they called Virginia. One of the earliest pioneers, Sir Richard Grenville, born in 1540, gained military experience fighting in the Hungarian Army, but by 1571 he was a parliamentarian. He conducted the first colony to Virginia in 1585— which failed—then by 1588 he was embroiled in the battle against the Armada, but two years later fell in battle against the forces of Madrid. He was followed by those like Sir Thomas Smythe, born in 1558. In 1589 Walter Raleigh had assigned his interests in the settlement to him. He was also the first governor of the East India Company in 1600 and knighted in 1603, then was sent to Russia as an envoy. He was a member of the first Council of Virginia in 1606, continuing until 1609 and by 1614 was back in London lobbying self-interestedly for his North American settlement, as well as India. Henry Wriothesley, Third Earl of Southampton, was born in 1573 and was a friend and patron of Shakespeare. In 1601, he was tried and found guilty for the role he played in what was termed the Essex Revolt in Ireland, yet another attempt to erode London's hegemony there. By 1609, he too was part of His Majesty's Council for Virginia. George Sandys was born in 1577, and as had become the trait of those of his class, traveled widely in Europe, Asia, and Africa—the latter being the coming hunting ground for free labor. He joined the Virginia Company in 1621 and was treasurer of this presumed profit-making enterprise. Robert Rich, Second Earl of Warwick, was born in 1587, invested in commerce in West Africa and became a member of the Council for Virginia by the pivotal year of 1619. George Calvert, born in 1580, like many future residents of North America, was profoundly interested in London's colonial policy; he was a shareholder in the East

India Company and also the New England Company. By 1621, he was involved in an attempt to implant a colony in Newfoundland. By 1623, he was designated as Lord Baltimore, the same name as one of North America's leading cities. His rights were inherited by his son under whose direction Maryland was settled in the seventeenth century.[13]

In short, these settlers were uniting across class and even religious lines. Witness the settlement in what was called Maryland where Catholics were playing a leading role in this overall Protestant concern in one of the most profound rebrandings in global history, that is, the consolidation of "whiteness." This was a militarized "identity politics" that involved land, enslaved labor, and a passel of "rights" as combat pay for those willing to bludgeon indigenes and batter Africans. Thus, the land on which now sits the U.S. Capitol, the Library of Congress, and the surrounding streets, was controlled initially in 1670 by a prominent Catholic settler from Maryland. Unsurprisingly, two of the most venerable schools in the Republic's headquarters are of Catholic origin: Georgetown and Catholic universities.[14]

Once more, it would be an error to ascribe this conciliatory Protestant approach to Catholics—at odds with the St. Bartholomew's Day massacre in 1572—to the inherent progressivism of republicanism's antecedents. For this attitude would do little to explain the brutal ouster of indigenes from their land and the stocking of same with enslaved Africans. Instead, this attitude is best understood as a response to the brutal logic of settler colonialism in an alien land with inhabitants not necessarily polite to invaders. It was an essential part of the transition from religion as an animation of society to "race."

As the fortunes of some were rising, others were falling, and Raleigh was decidedly in the latter category. Despite the homage to him that continues in the land he helped to settle in the 1580s—including major cities named in his honor, along with poisonous cigarettes—his fall was swift following Queen Elizabeth's death in 1603. Soon he was back in the Tower, charged with treasonous conspiracy and, as 1619 approached, executed. Born into a Devon gentry family, he earned his spurs by overseeing the heinous massacre of surrendered enemies in Ireland in 1580, practice for his coming role in settler colonialism in North America. He was a beneficiary of the massive expropriation of land in Munster, again, a dry run for similar events he helped to unleash across the Atlantic.[15] Raleigh (and his half brother Sir Humphrey Gilbert) were motivated to form a settlement in the 1580s in North America in direct response to the massacre of Protestants in France—only to be executed himself.[16] The bloody end of a man who could be termed a true Founding Father of the United States was anomalous, given the ascension of some who surrounded him.

As Raleigh's collaborators were encroaching on the Atlantic seaboard, their presumed Spanish antagonists were marching on the future metropolis to be known as Los Angeles. On 27 November 1602 Father Antonio de las Ascension noticed a "multitude of Indians" in vessels who "looked like galley slaves," imbued "without the least fear"—which Spaniards then republicans would strive to instill in coming centuries.[17]

Farther west from today's Southern California, Londoners had extended their tentacles tentatively into south Asia, what would become the crown jewel of the British Empire: India.[18] When in July 1599 four Dutch vessels returned westward with spices, pepper, and cloves, circumventing overland routes and Arabs, the Levant Company was formed, and, opportunistically, within six weeks English merchants petitioned Queen Elizabeth and—true to the pattern of tailing after Rotterdam/Amsterdam—the East India Company was established,[19] an exemplar of what was to be called state monopoly capitalism, in that it could easily be described as "Exxon with guns."

London's policy of fighting Madrid to the last Dutchman was to generate a handsome payoff,[20] just as England sought to learn warfare from the then champion, Spain.[21] Finally, in 1604 another slap was administered to Holland when London and Madrid inked their portentous "Articles of Peace, [I]ntercourse and Commerce, Concluded in the Names of the Most High and Mighty Kings, and Princes James by the Grace of God, King of Great Britaine, France and Ireland, Defender of the Faith . . . and Philip the Third, King of Spaine. . . . Treatie at London the eighteenth day of August. . . ." The critical proviso compelled

London not to supply the Dutch with "artillerie, gunpowder, bullets, saltpeter or any other munition or assistance for warre, the Hollanders, or other enemies of the King of Spaine." There was to be no "conveying of any ships, merchandise, manufactures or any other things out of Holland and Zeeland into Spain." If this pact had been signed in, say, 1581, it could have changed the course of history, but even if observed by Londoners—not to be taken for granted—the Netherlands had gathered momentum insufficient for mere words to halt the nation's climb upward.[22]

Still, the invasion of North America was a kind of joint enterprise in that Puritans, some of whom had spent time in Holland, arrived on the eastern seaboard after an earlier move from the Isles. Apparently the descriptor—"Puritan"—was an epithet initially used during a crisis in 1556 when clergy were deprived of their living if they refused to wear clerical garb; supposedly, these zealots wanted the English Reformation to resemble more closely Swiss understandings of apostolic practice, a Pan-European approach that disposed them toward accepting the newer identity that was "whiteness." They also favored household Bible reading, prayer, psalm singing, catechizing and fasting. The Presbyterians who emerged from this petri dish of zealotry were positioned to impose their theocratic praxis, though (to be fair) their fervor was likely exceeded by fellow religionists, for example, Congregationalists and New England Separatists, even Baptists and Quakers, all of whom proved to be early beneficiaries of settler colonialism.[23]

As events evolved, London's formal withdrawal of aid to the Dutch contributed to Spain doing the same in Ireland, providing at least an opportunity for England to redirect funds from combating Irish dissidence to subduing North American indigenes.[24]

To complete the circuit, before 1620, just after Raleigh's execution, there were more Englishmen in North Africa than North America,[25] but this soon was to change, as Morocco was cast aside like a soiled tissue.

As the long sixteenth century was lurching to a close, London was at a crossroads: bright new horizons replete with colonial and enslaving booty beckoned, which required manpower that preexisting religious bigotry compromised. This was true for Madrid and London both. By 1596, the former headquarters was considering a mass conscription of all Christian men between the ages of eighteen and forty-four for a general militia[26]—at a time when the Moriscos were on the verge of mass expulsion and soldiers and settlers were being hammered in Florida and what was to become New Mexico. That same year, Madrid was uneasy about the large number of foreigners residing nearby and launched an inventory to detail their provenance, mandating that no more foreigners should be allowed to reside there and that visitors must stay at inns owned by natives.[27] This would have proved a wonderful opportunity to lay the foundation for "whiteness," the most reliable partner for the new age of colonialism, but the rousting of Europeans was occurring simultaneously with fear of a plague that would decimate the ranks.[28]

Even the Ottomans knew better: a 1477 census for Constantinople and Galata revealed that the proportion of Muslim households to non-Muslim ones was 59 percent to 41 percent, yet by 1600 as Madrid was shooing away non-Spaniards, especially non-Catholics, the population in Galata had shifted in favor of foreigners.[29]

This dilemma should have been easily inferred in London; thus, in 1593, Louis Tinoco informed the English monarch that he desired to serve London, thanking her for his release from North African captivity. He was Portuguese, presumably Catholic, and desired to inform Queen Elizabeth about the many plots and designs against her reign then being concocted on the Iberian Peninsula,[30] indicative of the value of transcending religious correctness. Yet during this same time, potential allies were being tormented on religious grounds: "Persecution of Catholics begins to be great," it was said in the early 1590s, "and is likely to increase; many gentlemen and gentlewomen and others expect imprisonment daily."[31] "A most religious persecution is practiced here upon Catholics," was the report from the Isles. "Old prisons will not hold them and new ones have to be built; that the torments they suffer are infinite and the manner of their deaths intolerable."[32] Essentially, London had the colonial wisdom to export

Catholics and other presumed dissidents to settlements, where they were relabeled as "white," with many soaring to fame, fortune and prosperous careers as ingenuous propagandists for the purported liberty delivered by republicanism.

Yet, militant Protestants could argue that they were overly suspicious with good reason, constantly in peril—as was said then—because of the "designs of Jesuits and traitors." These reprobates "draw men and women, by conscience into treasons and are so secretly entertained that without severe punishment they would remain, as a concealed infection in the entrails of the kingdom" for "these traitors have come in disguise as soldiers, mariners, merchants, or escaped prisoners."[33] The problem was not just Ireland either, for "the stirs are great in Scotland" too, the result of a "combination between a great part of the nobility to call persons out of Spain to change the State and religion established."[34] Catholics, it was thought, should have thanked their presumed Creator for the benevolence of Protestants who, rather than reenacting St. Bartholomew 1572, dispatched them to rough-hewn settlements instead.

THE OVERALL CLIMATE IN THE Isles was affected immeasurably and ineffably by a wider crisis of an already tempestuous era.[35] Famine, climate change, war, and calamity were the calling cards of the 1590s and the immediate period following.[36] This was not wholly new. A serious freeze in the fourteenth century had an overpowering impact on Europe.[37] By 1597, Morocco, London's partner, was hit with the plague, then became bogged down in a guerrilla conflict with those in the Songhay Empire who refused to accept the verdict of history and surrender.[38] North Africa as a whole may have benefited from Spain's expulsion of Moriscos in the early seventeenth century in that it provided skills, language proficiency, and the like, but the arrival of tens of thousands of refugees could also be destabilizing, stressing the overall environment.[39] Spain, which had expelled Sephardim, then Muslims, was a master of the self-inflicted wound but was convinced that the expulsion of the latter would remove a potential Ottoman and Moroccan ally,[40] not to mention a force that could ally with London.[41]

It is unclear if the "Gunpowder Plot" in London in 1605, which was thought to be one of the final credible attempts of Catholicism to unseat Protestants, was masterminded in Madrid. Certainly, there were those who thought so. The accused, Guy Fawkes, was said by detractors to be "no native Englishman" but Flemish (he was likely born in York), but he allegedly had left England in 1593 and enlisted as a soldier of fortune in the Spanish military in the Netherlands. Reputedly he was "present at the taking of Calais by the Archduke Albert in the year 1596." His alleged terrorism, seeking to assassinate the monarch and destroy the House of Lords, was thought to be of foreign origin. A chronicler in 1850, perhaps anticipating Sigmund Freud, noted that it was "his unhappy lot to be deprived of paternal care and guidance in the days of his boyhood," but, alas, only in his mid-thirties, he was caught and executed.[42]

Still, the specter of St. Bartholomew's continued to haunt London, for it was also in 1605 that a rumor was spread that the "Papists are arming a massacre like that of Paris intended and the houses marked," with "several Catholics implicated."[43] Yet, as the situation evolved, Protestants and Catholics rebranded as "white" united to massacre North American indigenes jointly, while enslaving Africans on an escalated basis.

In the prelude to the expansion of settler colonialism in North America in the early seventeenth century, the Edict of Nantes of 1598 granted—at least on paper—civil equality between Huguenots and Catholics, a kind of repudiation of 1572 and the St. Bartholomew's massacre. This could stanch the flow of Protestants across the Channel, which had been strengthening London which, in any case, had an advantage in not being compelled to maintain a large standing army to defend its sea-bound frontiers, allowing manpower to be exported overseas.[44] Yet, even as the republicans in the mid-nineteenth century were on the verge of seizing a grand swathe of Mexican territory, this religious cleavage still haunted. St. Bartholomew was revived, as noted specifically by a writer who suggested nervously that there was little to "fear" from Catholic Mexico, for at this point there was little reason to be concerned if Catholics were offended. Yet despite this official posturing, St. Bartholomew almost two hundred years later was called the "greatest bloodstain of the ensanguined sixteenth century," with the writer adding knowingly that "of all wars, religious wars are the worst, and of all religious wars of which we have any knowledge, those which were waged in France during the last half of the sixteenth century were the most atrocious." The writer did not acknowledge that the tactic reportedly used to entrap the Huguenots—employing "fraud and deception" to lure them to talks, then slaughtering them simultaneously in major cities—had been and would be a primary tactic deployed against North American indigenes, continuing confirmation that religious extremism had transmuted into colonial expropriation, soaked in racism.[45] Even a Cherokee writer, part of a group in the process of being subjected to a sweeping ethnic cleansing in North America in the 1830s, was stunned to find in Mexico that "bigoted Spaniards and priests once called all the heretic strangers, English and Americans, by the name of *Judeos* or Jews."[46] Meanwhile, despite bumpiness, this besieged grouping was adding sinew to the muscle of republicans about to be wielded decisively against that very same Mexico.

ON THE OTHER HAND, THE much smaller Netherlands showed that even a continental, non-island power, albeit with a formidable port—Rotterdam—could advance significantly. As the English were settling into Virginia, the Dutch had reached what is now New York City.[47] Like a number of Englishmen, Henry Hudson had cultivated ties with the Muscovy Company, which was followed by the Turkey Company in 1581, the Morocco Company in 1585, the Guinea Company in the instrumental year of 1588, then the East India Company after that. The ubiquitous Dutch were encroaching on Russia, which was yet another reason for England to turn to the Americas. In any case, Hudson did not live to witness how he was lionized in what became New York, including a leading transportation artery bearing his name.[48]

It was not only the celebrated Hudson who was seen as farsighted. As early as 1604, a "license" was allocated to Sir Edward Michelborne "and his associates to discover the passage into Cathay, China, Japan, Corea [Korea] and Cambaya and to trade there."[49] A few years later, yet another license was granted to Richard Penkevell "to discover the passage into China, Cathay, the Moluccas and other regions of the East Indies for 76 years."[50] (This obsession with China continued into the twentieth century, and quite possibly Beijing's current rise may complicate the continued hegemony of the North Atlantic–dominated world created in the sixteenth century.)[51] Frenchmen, scrambling to keep pace, staked their claim in what is now Canada,[52] but in the long run, Russia's expansion east and south may have been the most significant territorial advance of this complicated epoch.[53]

Eventually, gold and silver from what was called Guinea was transported to London, easing a currency shortage. Eventually, the enslaved Africans who were part of this commerce, along with the weapons that served to ensnare them, were part of a different kind of triangular trade: metals, arms, slaves. By 1609, new muskets were brought to Virginia and, along with religious proselytizing, served to subjugate indigenes.[54]

London was claiming more land too, spurred by a booming arms trade, albeit not in North America. Unsuccessful rebellions in what is now Ulster forfeited this factious province, in the wake of the failed revolt of the Earls of Tyrconnell and Tyrone, leading London to create a kind of settler colonialism there that was to ignite major problems for generations to come and mimic what was about to unwind on a massive scale across the Atlantic.[55] For it was in 1601 that official London was buzzing about the "traitor Tyrone who pretends to fight for the Pope's sovereignty" and who intended to "arrive in England with 8,000 men" ready to wreak havoc.[56]

Across the Atlantic, Spain continued to endure unsettling events that did not bode well for their version of colonialism. By 1598, the rebellious Guale continued to be punished in Florida; when a slave was allocated to a hospital, it was unclear if this was a response to how this facility needed bolstering in the face of revolt.[57] Reports continued to percolate about unrest among the Guale—and the not unrelated hardships experienced by settlers in St. Augustine,[58] suggesting more draconian exertion would be needed—but who could pass the religious test upon arrival and why go to underdeveloped Florida, as opposed to another settlement with more accoutrements? When twenty enslaved Africans arrived on the peninsula to stock a local hacienda in mid-1599, officialdom did not evince openly any concern about their loyalties, history notwithstanding.[59]

Settlers and their leaders should have been thinking more strategically. By early 1600, Spaniards were frantically seeking to enslave indigenes, as settlers reeled from a series of deaths—and fires--at the hands of furious Ais, Surruque, and other natives of the peninsula. This was occurring as anxieties arose about incursions by Englishmen.[60] Soon, about eight Africans escaped from St. Augustine and sought refuge among the Surruque in today's Cape Canaveral area, then headed farther south to the encampment of the Ais near today's Vero Beach, where they married women of this indigenous group as they engineered one of the earliest and most successful examples of self-liberating Africans—Africans freeing themselves—on the mainland.[61] Unsurprisingly, by 1601, there was yet another revolt of the indigenes to be confronted by settlers.[62]

By 1602 twenty more enslaved Africans arrived on the peninsula to bolster fortifications, which were certainly to be challenged.[63] A few months later, a group of enslaved were captured, snatched from invading Englishmen.[64] This group may have been part of a group that had been captured from an English pirate and whose presence was traced back to Drake years earlier when he and his crew sacked St. Augustine, bringing along Africans from Santo Domingo. Despite these Africans having witnessed turmoil of all sorts, perhaps unwisely a Spanish official begged permission to retain at least one of them.[65] Doubtlessly, Spaniards in the region would have desired to read an earlier English dispatch, which had heard "from Havannah that the Earl of Cumberland has left 300 men in garrison in Porto Rico," and besides, had "given liberty to the slaves who remain with the English and means to send more forces which puts these parts in fear of his return."[66]

Thus, by early 1603, a royal proclamation mandated improved treatment for the enslaved and putting them to good use, dueling dual directives.[67] But the walls were slowly closing in on Spaniards in Florida, which the more astute would have realized. For in addition to rebelling indigenes and sullen Africans, in the prelude to the hinge year that was 1607 and the arrival of Londoners due north, reports continued to arrive about Englishmen in Florida waters. In the late summer of 1603, yet another shipwreck of a Spanish vessel occurred in the Keys, just as two English ships arrived in the Bahama Channel and as two other non-Spanish vessels were spotted suspiciously near Havana.[68]

Admittedly, Madrid was distracted, seeking to contain a massive region stretching from Tierra del Fuego to the outer reaches of North America. By March 1603, Sebastian Vizcaino, a Spaniard, was in California and had detected a vein of metal, the likes of which would captivate republicans by 1849.[69]

By the spring of 1604, official St. Augustine cried out for more soldiers. The fort was in deplorable shape, and, dangerously, all the artillerymen were non-Spaniards. Havana had just exiled two soldiers there and they were sent back promptly, since they were viewed as yet another liability in a land replete with them. The enslaved continued to be a matter of concern too.[70] Matters had hardly improved in 1605 as the time arrived for a stiffer challenge: the mass arrival of Englishmen and their comrades due north. Settlers were aging and dying, yet there was a clamor for more enslaved Africans, which could provide a unique challenge all its own, especially since soldiers were—as ever—displeased with their plight.[71]

In a particular report, Governor Pedro de Ibarra neglected— unpredictably—to detail the most resolute challenge to settlement: unwelcoming indigenes. By 1606, one settler, Maria de Junco, was lamenting the death of her spouse, Juan Ramirez, captured by Ais, quartered and then, she claimed, roasted and eaten with his skull deployed as a gourd for sipping drinks.[72]

Though non-Spaniards in St. Augustine were presumably reli- giously correct, meaning Roman Catholic, the authorities went to some length to detail their nationalities, which by the summer of 1607 were referenced as Flemish, German, and Portuguese.[73] Intermarriage among Europeans, Africans, and Natives took place regularly,[74] which was not the case among the eventually victorious republicans, who were supposedly far more progressive than their royalist competitors. African children continued to be born in Florida, further calling into question the official date of African arrivals on the mainland in 1619.[75]

As late as 1837, when the annexation to the United States of the former Spanish and Mexican colony that was Texas was at issue, even opponents of this transformative maneuver were unsettled by the specter of religious conformity. As liberal republican William Channing put it, under Mexican rule "settlers were to adopt the Catholic faith . . . as the condition of settlement."[76] Yet, this religious sectarianism aside, Mexico enjoyed what has been described as a "Black Indian President" almost two hundred years ago,[77] whereas in the presumably more farsighted Republic, a similar occurrence did not arrive until the twenty-first century. Indeed, though natives like the Cherokees in the Republic sought vainly to "assimilate" to dominant norms, up to and including religious conversion and holding Africans in bondage, they were still ethnically cleansed, expelled, expropriated[78]—just as Mexico's "Black Indian President" was assuming office. And even though the Republic's vaunted Constitution promised freedom of religion—an essential aspect of reconciling Protestants and Catholics, thereby assisting settler colonialism and circumventing a replay of St. Bartholomew 1572—arguably the racist virus unleashed by genocide against indigenes and the enslaving of Africans created conditions that helped to compromise the rudimentary Republic pledge of religious liberty as well.[79]

Astonishingly, despite the arrival of English settlers north of Florida by 1607, Madrid, because of the proliferating problems in St. Augustine, was considering reducing the military garrison and the settlement as a whole,[80] which happened under duress more than two centuries later due to republican pressure. Frantically, Fray Alonso de Penaranda, a priest in good standing, reviewed the alleged accomplishments of St. Augustine, including religious conversions of indigenes—an ostensible basis for colonialism in the first place— but the very fact that abandonment of northern Florida was being contemplated just as Englishmen were arriving in the land they called Virginia was not a good sign for Madrid though good news for those who foresaw the eventual victory of London.[81] By November 1608, the mandate was given to Cuba to monitor the English settlement to the north, but this was much too little, much too late.[82]

Yet, contradictorily, the authorities continued to inspect arriving vessels in the name of the Inquisition, making sure that no religiously suspect settlers arrived, and this was occurring as the Guale continued on the warpath, indicating that plans for abandoning St. Augustine were not altogether induced voluntarily.[83] Thus, instructions from Madrid continued to detail how non-Spaniards should be handled, though flyspecking them was not necessarily an inducement for them to remain in the primitive settlement that was St. Augustine.[84] This questioning of non-Spaniards extended to Cuba, as if religious identity was insufficiently stable to encompass colonialism. By 1608, a Portuguese priest there, Vicente Ferreyra de Andrade, was sent back to Iberia and replaced.[85]

By 1609, the English settlement to the north was vulnerable and, possibly, could have been wiped out with adroit planning. But instead, of 120 soldiers due in St. Augustine, only sixty had arrived, though non-believing indigenes had just attacked recently converted natives; yet despite this ferment, the bright idea had arisen in Florida to launch an expedition targeting the alien settlement northward,[86] though if history were the guide, this planned expedition would be wildly insufficient to attain ambitious goals. This proposal could hardly be taken seriously, in any case, since weeks later yet another settler, Geronimo de Torres, was denouncing the horrible conditions in St. Augustine and expressed the fervent desire to depart.[87] It appeared that St. Augustine would be abandoned before Jamestown was wiped out by Spanish invaders, though orders continued to pour into Florida to keep a wary eye on the future Virginia.[88]

When the chief executive in St. Augustine began reporting on an increase in religious conversions of indigenes, it was unclear if this were just propaganda to ease calls for abandonment of the settlement or an indication of a breakthrough (or evidence of indigenous distress pointing to imminent surrender). Besides, Governor de Ibarra also pandered to Madrid by pledging to monitor what was happening northward, which may have simply been an attempt to evaluate upward his own faltering settlement as a counterweight to London.[89] Still, by 1611, Madrid continued to exert pressure on Cuba to aid in the reconnaissance mission targeting the English settlement, but by then this seemed to be an example of words substituting for action.[90]

ACCORDING TO SCHOLAR Herbert Eugene Bolton, the vanguard settler for the French was a fur trader interested in cutting deals with indigenes; for the Spanish, it was the conquistador and the mission; and for the English the "backwoods settler," with a rapacious interest in dislodging indigenes from the land, In retrospect, it is the latter that prevailed in North America. Madrid had laid claim to the bulk of two American continents, but its appetite exceeded its digestive ability in that Spain's population was too small and much of it could not be allocated overseas given European challenges. Moreover, Bolton suggests that London's bloodthirstiness exceeded that of Madrid, which also hindered the latter: "In the English colonies," he said, "the only good Indians were dead Indians. In the Spanish colonies it was thought worthwhile" to pursue a differing course,[91] Las Casas notwithstanding. I would say that religious sectarianism and Inquisition mandates hampered the ability of Madrid to pursue what turned out to be the winning course executed by London, which was Pan-Europeanism and "whiteness," broadening the base of settler colonialism—increasing the number of "backwoods settlers"—racializing and deeming inferior those not deemed to be "white" and moving aggressively on two fronts: seizing land and enslaving willy-nilly.

Nevertheless, a factor that served to place London on the path to preeminence—arms manufacturing—continued to assert itself muscularly in coming centuries. By the late eighteenth century, the gun trade was essential to the health of Birmingham, which paradoxically was dependent upon the African market, which absorbed defective weapons at a handsome profit. This facilitated war, instability, and prisoners of war, who then became enslaved to be shipped overseas for the enrichment of the British, then republicans. Those rousting Africans for enslavement also sold them for weapons that would be used to roust more Africans in a circle devoid of virtue. Gold too was part of London's bargain, and goldsmiths became private bankers as an entire system of cruel exploitation came to rest upon the shoulders of a beleaguered and exploited continent.

According to historian Priya Satia, this "war boom . . . insulated arms makers from the commercial costs of abolition" and had deep roots in that England organized the most significant ordnance complex in Europe. Founded in the 1400s, it had ramified ties with the emerging scientific establishment in London. By 1600, the leader of this entity was the Earl of Essex, comrade of Francis Bacon, a practitioner of empiricism and scientific praxis. This military complex, says Satia, fomented technological innovation, fueling the fabled Industrial Revolution, which catapulted Britain into global hegemony. War, she says, hastened the quest for methods to use coal to smelt metals, speeding innovation, contributing to the advent of the steam engine, puddling, copper sheathing, all ignited by war and produced by "contractor-industrialists."

Unlike Britain, which regulated the proliferation of weapons domestically from the fourteenth century forward, with restrictions increasing in the fraught sixteenth century as unrest spread throughout the Isles, republicans with a continent to conquer and Africans to keep in line were not as restrained. Homicide rates in England were relatively stable from the 1400s to the end of the eighteenth century. And, even then, over time offenses were perpetrated against property—as opposed to persons—as, says Satia, "feudal values of honor and status gave way to bourgeois values of money and market relationships."

Colonialism and slavery—modernity in sum—emerged from the barrel of a gun. And, as with so much of what catapulted London, no small debt was owed to the Ottomans, which made muskets equal to, if not better than, the best Western Europe had to offer and spread their handiwork especially to their partners in the sixteenth century, which included England. Actually, the Ottomans shipped weapons and military materièl in exchange for spices in Aceh and elsewhere, including shipping to Ethiopians, with whom they shared a star-crossed tie, which did in a sense serve to preserve Addis's sovereignty. Babur, the first Mughal emperor in South Asia, bought Turkish matchlocks as early as 1526, and Akbar, who followed him, was also interested in making these arms. But as events progressed, it was England—once the pupil, which became the teacher—that employed manufacturing techniques to make bicycles and automobiles, catapulting London further into the ionosphere. But then the cycle moved again, and the republicans took the lead, especially when Eliphalet Remington, of the eastern seaboard of North America, mass-produced the typewriter, after his arms business plummeted at the conclusion of the U.S. Civil War.[92]

Just as English elites parasitically allied with their Dutch peers, the same could be said—to a degree—about their relationship to other "allies," including Sephardim fleeing Iberia for London. Despite this community's assistance, England's propagandists were not above assailing this beset group, as late as 1661.[93] As the pieces on the chessboard were shuffled in the seventeenth century, Perfidious Albion was not the only nation reconsidering bedrock ties. By June 1631, pirates from Algiers and armed troops of Turks stormed ashore in West Cork and seized almost the entire village, dragging scores of mostly women and children to slavery in North Africa in a replay of what was then befalling West Africa. Indeed, seafarers sailing southward from England to raid Africa at times found themselves enslaved in North Africa in a repetitive pattern that was not to cease fully until London had been fortified by the plunder from its own slave trade and pillaging of the Americas.[94]

Some Londoners, given repeated attempts to invade England via Ireland, and Cork's uncertain allegiance to the monarch, may not have been altogether disappointed by this turn of events. Over the decades, Spain had sought alliance with Ireland against England in league with others of Dutch, French, Flemish, and Scottish ancestry. Hugh O'Donnell was among the Irishmen whose lifelong quest involved the Spanish liberation of his homeland, a deep-seated dissidence that may have impelled London to ship ever more Dubliners to faraway settlements.[95]

STILL, REPUBLICANS COULD BOAST about their retreat from the poison of St. Bartholomew 1572. In 2018, the U.S. president, Donald J. Trump, was perplexed to find that there were no Protestants on the highest court in the land: all were either Catholic or Jewish. "You had all Protestants," he remarked in a burst of bafflement, "and then in a few years none. Doesn't that seem strange . . . you should be able to have the main religion in this country represented on the Supreme Court."[96] Apparently, he did not fully comprehend the construction of "whiteness" and the success of this project in curbing religious hostility, a gigantic step toward building the Republic over which he presided. Yet the continuing persistence of racism continued to bear the seeds of a pernicious bigotry that in the longer term—like a loose thread on a well-sewn suit—could unravel the finely wrought "whiteness," leading to a recrudescence of, for example, anti-Jewish fervor, as suggested by a number of troubling incidents during the tumultuous tenure of the 45th president, including murderous attacks on synagogues and pro-Nazi marches.

Perversely, in the citadel of the victor of the world the sixteenth century created—Washington, D.C.—there are other catastrophic matters to consider beyond malignant racism. The question of climate must be contemplated when considering the profundity of the post-1492 era. Earlier centuries provide examples we ignore at our peril. As climate changed in Europe, a failure of local crops ensued, escalating the ongoing trend of long-distance trade. This was a risky course to pursue, leading to spreading the risk by securing investors and delivering more funding and increasing the possibility of profit or, alternatively, expanding the circle of the vindictively furious if a loss resulted. This fury at times was unleashed on the unsuspecting in the Americas and Africa.[97] That is, by the late 1500s, global temperatures dropped to new lows, and around 1600 they perhaps reached the coldest point in centuries or even millennia, though the period immediately preceding, beginning about 1300 was on average

cooler than what had come before. Coincidentally, it was then that
Spain endured an agricultural crisis that bled into finance, igniting a
general crisis of confidence, empire-wide. High rates of mortality in
Spain may have been restraining Madrid's ability to confront London
in North America. Colonized Florida did not benefit when the late
sixteenth century witnessed a spectacular increase in hurricane activity. In Europe generally, the height of European men fell at the same
time, yet another sign of crisis. In Russia, the continent's giant, crisis
meant a third of the population perished and the country lapsed into
murderous civil war, accompanied by famine. Simultaneously, in
England one freezing winter followed another, while exceedingly wet
summers meant the ruination of crops.[98]

Though the wealth generated by plunder and pillage continues
to advantage North American republicans, the racism that served to
produce the accumulation of this filthy lucre disadvantages the leaders in Washington, D.C., when it comes to confronting the climate
emergency we all must now confront.[99] Nevertheless, if humanity
is—somehow—to escape from this diabolical environmental scenario
that devilishly awaits, difficult questions must be posed and answered
about the maldistribution of resources, which, even without climate
collapse, continues to consign millions to an uncertain fate, while
generating untoward policies that place the planet in peril.

Notes

INTRODUCTION

1. *New York Times*, 8 April 1977.

2. Cf. Ivan Van Sertima, *They Came Before Columbus: The African Presence in Ancient America* (New York: Random House, 1976), 130: Here the scholar speaks broadly of the "unconscious racial reflex of British scholars."

3. Gerald Horne, *The Counter-Revolution of 1776: Slave Resistance and the Origins of the United States of America* (New York: New York University Press, 2014).

4. Gerald Horne, *The Apocalypse of Settler Colonialism: The Roots of Slavery, White Supremacy and Capitalism in Seventeenth Century North America and the Caribbean* (New York: Monthly Review Press, 2018). B.M.S. Campbell, *Transition: Climate, Disease and Society in the Late Medieval World* (New York: Cambridge University Press, 2016).

5. Cf. Frank Tannenbaum, *Slave and Citizen: The Negro in the Americas* (New York: Knopf, 1947): The point argued in these pages is not that Catholicism was more progressive than Protestantism in handling slavery but that the nation where the latter prevailed—that is, England—as an underdog felt compelled to move away from religious sectarianism to confront the primary foe in Madrid by allying with, for example, the Ottoman Turks and Morocco (predominantly Muslim nations); as an underdog moving away from religious sectarianism, London proved to be more flexible in forming settlements, for example, Maryland, where Catholics played a major role: likewise, Madrid was capable of embracing African conquistadors—Catholics certainly—whereas London, pressed to the wall, embraced a Pan-European project that generally was not able to make as much room for African conquerors in North America. This project continued for some time, for example, Stephen Conway,

Brittania's Auxiliaries: Continental Europeans and the British Empire, 1740–1800 (New York: Oxford University Press, 2017).

6. Donald Matthews, *At the Altar of Lynching: Burning Sam Hose in the American South* (New York: Cambridge University Press, 2017). Fortunately, some scholars of late have explored how religion helped to propel "race." See, for example, Terence Keel, *Divine Variations: How Christian Thought Became Racial Science* (Stanford: Stanford University Press, 2018); John Hayes, *Hard, Hard Religion: Interracial Faith in the Poor South* (Chapel Hill: University of North Carolina Press, 2017). Tisa Wenger, *Religious Freedom: The Contested History of an American Ideal* (Chapel Hill: University of North Carolina Press, 2017), 1, 3, 10–11: The author argues that religious liberty "helped define American whiteness and make the case for U.S. imperial rule." Thus, "religious freedom talk" became code for "white and Protestant," juxtaposed against "the supposed bondage of the pagan and the Catholic." This trope of religious liberty "served as an imperial mechanism of classification and control, helping to define not only what counted as religion . . . but also the contours of the racial." Yes, the victims of this entrapment—especially African-Americans—in a form of intellectual and theological judo, sought to deploy religion against the victimizer, but the halting nature of real progress today should suggest that this ideological grappling—turning the strength of the oppressor's tool back against him—may have reached the outer limits of its possibilities. See also Peter Kerry Powers, *Goodbye Christ? Christianity, Masculinity and the New Negro Renaissance* (Knoxville: University of Tennessee Press, 2017). Of course, the fifteenth century publication of the Gutenberg Bible and the technological innovation it represented marked a turning point in the rise of both literacy and dissidence within Christianity more generally. See Janet Ing, *Johann Gutenberg and His Bible: A Historical Study* (New York: Typophiles, 1990). See also Margaret Leslie Davis, *The Lost Gutenberg* (New York: TarcherPerigee, 2019) and Eric Marshall White, *Editio Princeps: A History of the Gutenberg Bible* (London: Miller, 2017).

7. Geraldine Heng, *England and the Jews: How Religious Violence Created the First Racial State in the West* (New York: Cambridge University Press, 2019), 11, 12, 14, 20, 48, 52, 70. Cf. David M. Whitford, *The Curse of Ham in the Early Modern Era: The Bible and the Justifications for Slavery* (Burlington, Vermont: Ashgate, 2009) and David M. Goldenberg, *Black and Slave: The Origins and History of the Curse of Ham* (Boston: de Gruyter, 2017).

8. Frederic J. Baumgartner, *France in the Sixteenth Century* (New York: St. Martin's, 1995), xi: "The long sixteenth century" is referenced here.

9. Marching forward in time, the white supremacist in 2019 who massacred Muslims in New Zealand earlier visited the Balkans to study the uprooting of Christians: *London Daily Mail*, 16 March 2019.

10. Taina Seijas, *Asian Slaves in Colonial Mexico: From Chinos to Indians* (New York: Cambridge University Press, 2014).

11. Larry Eugene Rivers, *Slavery in Florida: Territorial Days to Emancipation* (Tallahassee: University Press of Florida, 2000), 2.

12. Gerald Horne, *Race to Revolution: The U.S. and Cuba During Slavery and Jim Crow* (New York: Monthly Review Press, 2014); Gerald Horne, *White Supremacy Confronted: U.S. Imperialism and Anticommunism vs. the Liberation of Southern Africa, from Rhodes to Mandela* (New York: International Publishers, 2019).

13. Andrew C. Hess, *The Forgotten Frontier: A History of the Sixteenth Century Ibero-African Frontier* (Chicago: University of Chicago Press, 1978), 20.

14. One scholar has "estimated that the Spanish Crown's original investment in Columbus's first voyage provided a return of 1, 733, 000 per cent." See David Childs, *Invading America: The English Assault on the New World, 1497–1630* (Yorkshire: Seaforth, 2012), 278.

15. Andy Wood, *The 1549 Rebellion and the Making of Early Modern England* (New York: Cambridge University Press, 2007).

16. John Butman and Simon Target, *New World Inc.: The Making of America by England's Merchant Adventurers* (New York: Little Brown, 2018), 10, 16.

17. Gerald Horne, *The White Pacific: U.S. Imperialism and Black Slavery in the South Seas After the Civil War* (Honolulu: University of Hawaii Press, 2007).

18. Aline Helg, *Slave No More: Self-Liberation Before Abolition in the Americas* (Chapel Hill: University of North Carolina Press), 2019, 18, 19, 21, 22.

19. Eduardo Galeano, *Open Veins of Latin America: Five Centuries of The Pillage of a Continent* (New York: Monthly Review Press, 1973), 50. See also Peter J. Blackwell, *Miners of the Red Mountains: Indian Labor in Potosi, 1545–1650* (Albuquerque: University of New Mexico Press, 1984).

20. D. Michael Bottoms, *An Aristocracy of Color: Race and Reconstruction in California and the West, 1850–1890*, (Norman: University of Oklahoma Press, 2013), 27.

21. Benjamin Madley, *An American Genocide: The United States and the California Indian Catastrophe, 1846–1873* (New Haven: Yale University Press, 2016).

22. Susan Richburg Parker, "Slaves Flee St. Augustine—1603," *El Escribano*, 41(2004): 1–8, 1. For more on this revolt, see Paul E. Hoffman, *A New Andalucia and a Way to the Orient: The American Southeast During the Sixteenth Century* (Baton Rouge: Louisiana State University Press, 1990), 78. See also Jerald T. Milanich, *Florida Indians and the Invasion from Europe* (Gainesville: University Press of Florida, 1995), 115 and Kathleen Deagan and Darcie MacMahon, *Fort Mose: Colonial America's Black Fortress of Freedom* (Tallahassee: University Press of Florida, 1995), 13.

23. Casey Farnsworth, "The Revolt of the Agueybana II: Puerto Rico's Interisland Connections," in Ida Altman and David Wheat, eds., *The Spanish Caribbean and the Atlantic World in the Long Sixteenth Century* (Lincoln: University of Nebraska Press, 2019), 25–45, 25.

24. Andrew Lawler, *The Secret Token: Myth, Obsession and the Search for the Lost Colony of Roanoke* (New York: Doubleday, 2018), 19–20.

25. Robert Cushman Murphy, "The Earliest Spanish Advances Southward from Panama Along the West Coast of South America," *Hispanic American Historical Review*, 21 (Number 1, February 1941): 1–28, 16.

26. Lesley Byrd Simpson, *The Encomienda in New Spain: Forced Native Labor in the Spanish Colonies, 1492–1550* (Berkeley: University of California Press, 1929), 16.

27. Nick Hazlewood, *The Queen's Slave Trader: John Hawkyns [sic], Elizabeth I and the Trafficking in Human Souls* (New York: Morrow, 2004), 42, 43,

28. Kathleen Deagan and Darcie MacMahon, *Fort Mose: Colonial America's Black Fortress of Freedom* (Tallahassee: University Press of Florida, 1995), 13.

29. David Ewing Duncan, *Hernando de Soto: A Savage Quest in the Americas* (Norman: University of Oklahoma Press, 1996), xix.

30. Charles C. Mann, *1491: New Revelations of the Americas Before Columbus* (New York: Knopf, 2005), 99.

31. David J. Weber, "American Westward Expansion and the Breakdown of Relations Between Pobladores and 'Indios Barbaros' on Mexico's Far Northern Border," *New Mexico Historical Review*, 56 (Number 3, July 1981): 221–238.

32. Cf. Edward Westermann, *Hitler's Ostkrieg and the Indian Wars: Comparing Genocide and Conquest* (Norman: University of Oklahoma Press, 2016) and James Q. Whitman, *Hitler's American Model: The United States and the Making of Nazi Race Law* (Princeton: Princeton University Press, 2017).

33. "Address of A.B. Renehan of Santa Fe". . . at the Conference of the League of the Southwest, at Santa Barbara, California. June 9, 1923 on 'Laws and Equities Affecting the So-Called Settlers on Pueblo Indian Land Grants,' *Huntington Library-San Marino, California*. See also Geoffrey Parker, *Emperor: A New Life of Charles V* (New Haven: Yale University Press, 2019).

34. *New York Times*, 8 November 2019.

35. Robert C. Schwaller, "African Maroons and the Incomplete Conquest of Hispaniola," *The Americas*, 75(Number 4, October 2018): 609–638, 611, 637. See also Matthew Restall, "Black Conquistadors: Armed Africans in Early Spanish America," *The Americas*, 57(Number 2, 2000): 171–205; Ignacio Gallup-Diaz, "A Legacy of Strife: Rebellious Slaves in Sixteenth-Century Panama," *Colonial Latin America Review*, 19(Number 3, December 2010): 417–435, 417, 423, 429, 430, 433: These Africans "wrecked the Isthmus of Panama in 1555–1556" in what was termed the "War of Vallano," named after the "rebellious slave Vallano." These Africans, it was reported, "had an army numbering more than 1200 men and women." By 1574 it was said that there were about "3000" maroons in that vicinity. As late as the 1580s, the marauding of "uncontrollable rebel slaves" remained a major force. Sir Francis Drake of England "coordinated his activities with a band of free blacks," weakening Madrid and allowing London to advance.

36. Kay Wright Lewis, *A Curse Upon the Nation: Race, Freedom and Extermination in America and the Atlantic World* (Athens: University of Georgia Press, 2017), 31.

37. Matthew Restall, *When Montezuma Met Cortes: The True Story of the Meeting that Changed History* (New York: HarperCollins, 2018), 298.

38. Jerald T. Milanich and Susan Milbrath, eds., *First Encounters: Spanish*

Explorations in the Caribbean and the United States, 1492–1570 (Gainesville: University Press of Florida, 1989).

39. Nancy E. Van Deusen, *Global Indios: The Indigenous Struggle for Justice in Sixteenth Century Spain* (Durham: Duke University Press, 2015), 2, 247. See Matthews Restall, *When Montezuma Met Cortes*, 298: By the early sixteenth century there were more than 500,000 enslaved across the Caribbean, Mesoamerica, and Central America. Cf. Nabil Matar, *British Captives in the Mediterranean and the Atlantic: 1563–1760* (Leiden: Brill, 2014).

40. Karen Anderson Cordova, *Surviving Spanish Conquest: Indian Flight and Cultural Transformation in Hispaniola and Puerto Rico* (Tuscaloosa: University of Alabama Press, 2017), 108.

41. Matthew Restall, *When Montezuma Met Cortes*, 304.

42. Woodbury Lowery, *The Spanish Settlements Within the Present Limits of the United States: Florida, 1562–1574* (New York: Putnam's, 1905), 14.

43. Hugh Thomas, *World Without End: Spain, Philip II and the First Global Empire* (New York: Random House, 2014), 230, 232, 260, 267, 279, 282, 289. Readers should note that for the sake of convenience I will at times refer to certain regions by their modern names—for example, Italy, Germany, New Mexico, etc.—though aware that these entities were not necessarily cognizable in the sixteenth century.

44. Christopher Hollis, *The Jesuits; A History* (New York: Macmillan, 1968).

45. Dennis O. Flynn, et.al., eds., *China and the Birth of Globalization in the 16th Century* (Aldershot: Ashgate, 2010).

46. Kris Lane, *Potosi: The Silver City that Changed the World* (Oakland: University of California Press), 2019, 57, 69. See also Arturo Giraldez, *The Age of Trade: The Manila Galleons and the Dawn of the Global Economy* (Boulder: Rowman & Littlefield, 2015).

47. John Butman and Simon Target, *New World Inc.: The Making of America by England's Merchant Adventurers* (New York: Little Brown, 2018), 23.

48. *Washington Post*, 24 December 2018. See also John A. Stormer, *None Dare Call it Treason* (Florissant: Liberty Bell Press, 1964). That the sixteenth century continues to resonate today is reflected not only in the recent invocation of Harrington's evocative words but also in reference to the Pilgrimage of Grace, a revolt that threatened Henry VIII's England, until the conspirers' reach exceeded their grasp and they were crushed. "As in many Tudor risings," said the contemporary pundit, Robert Shrimsley, "public discontent over issues like food prices was [harnessed] until it morphed into a challenge to the Crown. By the time it was suppressed, few were fighting for the causes that initially drove them to action. It is a lesson Britain's Brexit hardliners should consider. . . ." *Financial Times*, 5 March 2019. See also Michael Questier, *Dynastic Politics and the British Reformations, 1558–1630* (New York: Oxford University Press, 2019).

49. Christopher Putchinski Beats, "African Religious Integration in Florida During the First Spanish Period," M.A. Thesis (University of Central Florida, 2007), iii, 3.

50. Gerald Horne, *Negro Comrades of the Crown: African Americans and the British Empire Fight the U.S. Before Emancipation* (New York: New York University Press, 2012), 3, 46.

51. On contestation between London and Madrid, particularly during the heralded revolt of the enslaved, encapsulated as "Stono's Revolt," see Gerald Horne, *The Counter-Revolution of 1776: Slave Resistance and the Origins of the United States of America* (New York: New York University Press, 2014). On the contestation between the slaveholders' republic and Florida before and after statehood, see Gerald Horne, *Negro Comrades of the Crown: African-Americans and the British Empire Fight the U.S. Before Emancipation* (New York: New York University Press, 2012).

52. Aline Helg, *Slave No More*, 77–78, 46–48.

53. Frank Tannenbaum, *Slave and Citizen: The Negro in America* (New York: Knopf, 1946).

54. Pedro Menendez de Aviles to King Philip II, February-March 1565, in Edward W. Lawson, editor and translator, *Letters of Pedro Menendez de Aviles and Other Documents Relative to His Career, 1555–1574* (St. Augustine Historical Society-Florida).

55. Herbert Bolton, "The Mission as a Frontier Institution in the Spanish American Colonization," *American Historical Review*, 23(Number 1, October 1917): 42–61, 61.

56. W. J. Eccles, *The French in North America, 1500–1783* (Markham, Ontario: Fitzhenry & Whiteside), 1998, 8. Cf. Suzannah Lipscomb, *The Voices of Nîmes: Women, Sex and Marriage in Reformation Languedoc* (New York: Oxford University Press, 2019).

57. D. Michael Bottoms, *An Aristocracy of Color: Race and Reconstruction in California and the West, 1850–1890* (Norman: University of Oklahoma Press, 2014), 107.

58. Alejandro de la Fuente, *Havana and the Atlantic in the Sixteenth Century* (Chapel Hill: University of North Carolina Press, 2008), 1,2.

59. Paul E. Hoffman, *A New Andalucia and a Way to the Orient: The American Southeast During the Sixteenth Century* (Baton Rouge: Louisiana State University Press, 1990), 225.

60. Tobias P. Graf, *The Sultan's Renegades: Christian-Europe Converts to Islam and the Making of the Ottoman Elite, 1575–1610* (New York: Oxford University Press, 2017). See also Joshua M. White, *Piracy and Law in the Ottoman Mediterranean* (Stanford: Stanford University Press, 2018).

61. Stefan Stantchev, "Venice and the Ottoman Threat, 1381–1453," in Norman Housley, ed., *Reconfiguring the Fifteenth Century Crusade* (New York: Palgrave, 2017), 161–205, 181. See also Maria Fusaro, *Political Economies of Empire in the Early Modern Mediterranean: The Decline of Venice and the Rise of England, 1450–1700* (New York: Cambridge University Press, 2015).

62. Maria Antonio Garces, ed., *An Early Modern Dialogue with Islam: Antonio de Sosa's Topography of Algiers (1612)* (South Bend: University of Notre Dame Press, 2011), 27.

63. Thomas D. Goodrich, *The Ottoman Turks and the New World: A Study of Tarih-I Hind-I Garbi and Sixteenth Century Ottoman Americana* (Wiesbaden: Harrassowitz, 1990), 5, 9. See also Thomas A. Carlson, *Christianity in Fifteenth Century Iraq* (New York: Cambridge University Press, 2018).

64. Christopher Ocker, *Luther, Conflict and Christendom: Europe and Christianity in the West* (New York: Cambridge University Press, 2018).

65. L.R. Bailey, *Indian Slave Trade in the Southwest A Study of Slave Taking and Traffic in Indian Captives* (Los Angeles: Western Lore, 1966), xii.

66. Cf. Steve Tibble, *The Crusader Armies, 1099–1187* (New Haven: Yale University Press, 2018). The author downplays the religious character of the Crusades.

67. Debra Blumenthal, *Enemies and Familiars: Slavery and Mastery in Fifteenth Century Valencia* (Ithaca: Cornell University Press, 2009), 41.

68. Cihan Yujse Muslu, *The Ottomans and the Mamluks: Imperial Diplomacy and Warfare in the Islamic World* (London: Tauris, 2014), 295.

69. Nancy Bisaha, "Reactions to the Fall of Constantinople and the Concept of Human Rights," in Norman Housley, ed., *Reconfiguring the Fifteenth Century Crusade* (New York: Palgrave, 2017), 285–331, 297–300, 305, 310.

70. Norman Housley, "Conclusion: The Future of Crusading in the Fifteenth Century," in ibid., Housely, editor, 325–331, 325.

71. Alessandro Stanziani, "Slavery and Bondage in Central Asia and Europe: Fourteenth Nineteenth Centuries," in Christopher Witzenrath, ed., *Eurasian Slavery, Ransom and Abolition in World History* (Burlington, Vermont: Ashgate, 2015), 81–104, 97–98.

72. Andrew C. Hess, *The Forgotten Frontier: A History of the Sixteenth Century Ibero-African Frontier* (Chicago: University of Chicago Press, 1978), 125, 175.

73. Bruno Macaes, *The Dawn of Eurasia: On the Trail of the New World Order* (New Haven: Yale University Press, 2018), 66.

74. Nancy Shields Kollman, *The Russian Empire, 1450–1801* (New York: Oxford University Press, 2017), 192. See also Parag Khanna, *The Future Is Asian: Commerce, Conflict and Culture in the 21st Century* (New York: Simon & Schuster, 2019).

75. Jane Hathaway, *The Chief Eunuch of the Ottoman Harem: From African Slave to Power Broker* (New York: Cambridge University Press), 29.

76. Leopold Ranke, *The Ottoman and the Spanish Empires in the Sixteenth and Seventeenth Centuries* (Philadelphia: Lea & Blanchard, 1845), 33.

77. Mauricio Tenorio-Trillo, *Latin America: The Allure and Power of an Idea* (Chicago: University of Chicago Press), 2017.

78. Robert H. Power, "Francis Drake & San Francisco Bay: A Beginning of the British Empire," Davis: Library Associates of the University of California-Davis, 1974, Vertical File, San Francisco Public Library.

79. See e.g. Gerald Horne *The Apocalypse of Settler Colonialism: The Roots of Slavery, White Supremacy and Capitalism in 17th Century North America and the Caribbean* (New York: Monthly Review Press, 2018), passim.

80. Michael A. Gomez, *African Dominions: A New History of Empire in Early and Medieval West Africa* (Princeton: Princeton University Press, 2018), 110.

81. François Xavier Fauvelle, *The Golden Rhinoceros: Histories of the African Middle Ages* (Princeton: Princeton University Press, 2018), 194.

82. Rebecca Zorach and Michael W. Phillips, Jr., *Gold* (London: Reaktion, 2016).

83. Andrew Lambert, *Seapower States: Maritime Culture, Continental Empires and the Conflict that Made the Modern World* (New Haven: Yale University Press, 2018), 269.

84. Thomas E. Watson, *The Massacre of St. Bartholomew in Paris, France: Overwhelming Proof that it was the Result of the Teachings, the Law and the Practice of Popery* (Thomson, Georgia: Jeffersonian, 1914). See also C. Vann Woodward, *Tom Watson: Agrarian Rebel* (New York: Oxford University Press, 1963).

85. Steven J. Gunn, *The English People at War in the Age of Henry VIII* (New York: Oxford University Press), 137, 284, 148, 150, 151.

86. Mauricio Drelichman and Hans-Joachim Voth, *Lending to the Borrower from Hell: Debt, Taxes and Default in the Age of Philip II* (Princeton: Princeton University Press, 2014), 19, 23, 26, 29. Of course, today's United States makes this earlier "borrower from hell" seem like a minnow or piker by way of comparison.

87. Parker quoted in John Lewis Gaddis, *On Grand Strategy* (New York: Penguin, 2018), 152.

88. Gustav Ungerer, *The Mediterranean Apprenticeship of a British Slaver* (Madrid: Editorial Verbum, 2008), 15, 29, 72–74, 164. See also Heather Dalton, *Merchants and Explorers: Roger Barlow, Sebastian Cabot and Networks of Atlantic Exchange, 1500–1560* (New York: Oxford University Press, 2016). See, for example, *New York Times*, 9 November 2016: "White women helped elect Donald Trump."

89. Stephen Charles Cory, *Reviving the Islamic Caliphate in Early Modern Morocco* (Burlington, Vermont: Ashgate, 2013), 199, 236. See also Jessica A. Coope, *The Most Noble of People: Religious, Ethnic and Gender Identity in Muslim Spain* (Ann Arbor: University of Michigan Press, 2017).

90. Jerry Brotton, *The Sultan and the Queen: The Untold Story of Elizabeth and Islam* (New York: Penguin, 2017), 171. Cf. Ruth Nisse, *Jacob's Shipwreck: Diaspora, Translation and Jewish-Christian Relations in Medieval England* (Ithaca: Cornell University Press, 2017), and Alan E. Bernstein, *Hell and Its Rivals: Death and Retribution Among Christians, Jews and Muslims in the Early Middle Ages* (Ithaca: Cornell University Press, 2017).

91. Miranda Kaufman, *Black Tudors: The Untold Story* (London: One World, 2017), 138.

92. Ibid., Stephen Charles Cory, 186. See also R. G. Howarth, "The Tragedy of Othello, the Moor of Venice," 20 April 1953, Huntington Library-San Marino, California.

93. David Herlihy, *The Black Death and the Transformation of the West* (Cambridge: Harvard University Press, 1997), 17.

94. Eva Alexandra Uchmany, "The Participation of New Christians and Crypto-Jews in the Conquest, Colonization and Trade of Spanish America,

1521–1660," in Peaolo Bernardini and Norman Fiering, eds., *The Jews and the Expansion of Europe to the West, 1450–1800* (New York: Berghahn, 2001), 186–202, 187 and in the same volume, Ernest Pijning, "New Christians and Sugar Cultivators and Traders in the Portuguese Atlantic, 1450–1800," 485–500, 486.

95. Toby Green, *The Rise of the Trans-Atlantic Slave Trade in Western Africa, 1300–1589* (New York: Cambridge University Press), 2012, 135.

96. Victoria Freeman, *Distant Relations: How My Ancestors Colonized North America* (Toronto: McClelland & Stewart, 2000), 13.

97. Geraldine Heng, *England and the Jews: How Religion and Violence Created the First Racial State in the West* (New York: Cambridge University Press, 2019) and Geraldine Heng, *The Invention of Race in the European Middle Ages* (New York: Cambridge University Press, 2019).

98. Gerald Horne, *Confronting Black Jacobins: The U.S., the Haitian Revolution and the Origins of the Dominican Republic* (New York: Monthly Review Press, 2015).

99. Gerald Horne, *Cold War in a Hot Zone: The U.S. Confronts Labor and Independence Struggles in the British West Indies* (Philadelphia: Temple University Press, 2007); Gerald Horne, *Class Struggle in Hollywood, 1930–1950: Moguls, Mobsters, Stars, Reds & Trade Unionists* (Austin: University of Texas Press, 2001).

1. APPROACHING 1492 | APPROACHING APOCALYPSE

1. James H. Sweet, "The Iberian Roots of American Racist Thought," *William and Mary Quarterly* 54, no. 1 (1997): 143–66, 145. Cf. Frank Snowden, *Before Color Prejudice: The Ancient View of Blacks* (Cambridge, MA: Harvard University Press, 1983) and Washington Irving, *The Life of Mahomet* (London: Bohn, 1850). Benjamin Isaac, *The Invention of Racism in Classical Antiquity* (Princeton, NJ: Princeton University Press, 2004); Rebecca F. Kennedy, et al., eds., *Race and Ethnicity in the Classical World: An Anthology of Primary Sources in Translation* (Indianapolis: Hackett, 2013). See also Anthony Pagden, *The Burdens of Empire*, 97: "Racism . . . is clearly the product of nineteenth century positivism" the author then cites fellow scholar Colin Kidd and asserts, "the absence of racialist doctrine did not mean that racist prejudice was similarly invisible. Racist attitudes existed but, significantly did not rest upon clearly articulated theories of racial difference. Race—like ethnicity and even national consciousness (as distinct, say, from allegiance to one's monarch)—was a matter of second order importance behind commitment to church and state." See also Brian Hamm, "Between Acceptance and Exclusion: Spanish Responses to Portuguese Immigrants in the Sixteenth Century Caribbean," in Ida Altman and David Wheat, eds., *The Spanish Caribbean and the Atlantic World in the Long 16th Century* (Lincoln: University of Nebraska Press, 2019), 113–135, 113, 132: Portuguese, though Catholic, were accused of being either Protestant or Jewish by their neighboring Iberians, while other European Catholics often referred to Spaniards as

Jewish. This religious mischaracterization then was leapfrogged—ultimately and not least by Londoners and their progeny—by the inherent mischaracterization that was "race," which proved to be a sturdier and more effective marker of difference.

2.   Anthony Julius, *Trials of the Diaspora: A History of Anti-Semitism in England* (New York: Oxford University Press, 2012).

3.   Gerald Horne, *The Apocalypse of Settler Colonialism* (New York: Monthly Review Press, 2018), passim.

4.   Debra Blumenthal, *Enemies and Familiars: Slavery and Mastery in Fifteenth Century Valencia* (Ithaca, NY: Cornell University Press, 2009), 277.

5.   Michael A. Hoffman II, *They Were White and They Were Slaves: The Untold History of the Enslavement of Whites in Early America* (Dresden, NY: Wiswell Ruffin House, 1991), 4, 5.

6.   B. H. Slicher Van Rath, *The Agrarian History of Western Europe, A.D. 500–1850* (New York: St. Martin's, 1963), 32, 30–31.

7.   At times, I will employ contemporary descriptors of regions, for example, "Newfoundland" or "Florida" or even "Dixie" in a context where those terms may not have been deployed but as a matter of convenience for readers.

8.   Peggy Pascoe, *What Comes Naturally: Miscegenation Law and the Making of Race in America* (New York: Oxford University Press, 2010).

9.   Robert Cruikshank, *The Spanish Hero; or, History of Alonzo the Brave, Containing an Authentic Account of the Wars Between the Spaniards and the Moors, in the Reign of Alphonso III* . . . (London: Bailey, 1820[?]), Huntington Library, San Marino, California. At the same site see also Washington Irving, *Legends of the Conquest of Spain* (Philadelphia: Carey and Lea, 1835) and Washington Irving, *The Alhambra: Of Tales and Sketches of the Moors and Spaniards* (Philadelphia: Carey and Lea, 1832).

10. Brian A. Catlos, *Kingdoms of Faith: A New History of Islamic Spain* (New York: Basic, 2018), 25.

11. See e.g. Norman Stillman, ed., *Encyclopedia of Jews in the Islamic World* (Leiden: Brill, 2010). Cf. Allan Harris Cutler and Helen Elmquist Cutler, *The Jew as Ally of the Muslim: Medieval Roots of Anti-Semitism* (South Bend: University of Notre Dame Press, 1986).

12. Catlos, *Kingdoms of Faith*, 81, 132. See also Antonio Feros, *Speaking of Spain: The Evolution of Race and Nation in the Hispanic World* (Cambridge, MA: Harvard University Press, 2017), 79: Beginning in the 8th century, it is said, there were those in the Jewish community who collaborated with Arabs invading the Peninsula.

13. Wendy Childs, *Anglo-Castilian Trade in the Later Middle Ages* (Manchester: Manchester University Press, 1979), 235.

14. Maryanne Kowaleski, *Local Markets and Regional Trade in Medieval Exeter* (New York: Cambridge University Press, 1995).

15. Van Rath, *The Agrarian History of Western Europe, A.D. 500–1850* (New York: St. Martin's, 1963), 30–32.

16. Pamela Nightingale, *A Medieval Mercantile Community: The Grocers'*

Company and the Politics and Trade of London, 1000–1485 (New Haven, CT: Yale University Press, 1995), 38–39, 78.

17. Norman Simms, "Troubled Souls: The Inner and Outer Life of Jews in England after the Expulsion of 1290," in Charles Meyers and Norman Simms, eds., *Troubled Souls: Conversos, Crypto-Jews and Other Confused Jewish Intellectuals from the Fourteenth through the Eighteenth Century* (Hamilton, NZ: Outrigger, 2001), 164–89.

18. David Nicolle, *The Portuguese in the Age of Discovery, c. 1340–1665* (Long Island City, NY: Osprey, 2012), 4, 11.

19. T. H. Lloyd, *England and the German Hanse, 1157–1611: A Study of Their Trade and Commercial Diplomacy* (New York: Cambridge University Press, 1991), 62–63, 111–13.

20. Kowaleski, *Local Markets and Regional Trade in Medieval Exeter* (New York: Cambridge University Press, 1995).

21. Catherine Fletcher, *The Black Prince of Florence: The Spectacular Life and Treacherous World of Alessandro de' Medici* (New York: Oxford University Press, 2016), 151.

22. Nicholas Morton, *Encountering Islam in the First Crusade* (New York: Cambridge University Press, 2016).

23. John Edwards, "Reconquista and Crusade in Fifteenth Century Spain," in Norman Housley, ed., *Crusading in the Fifteenth Century: Message and Impact* (New York: Palgrave, 2004), 163–81, 165. See also Norman Housley, *The Later Crusades, 1274–1580: From Lyons to Alcazar* (New York: Oxford University Press, 1992).

24. Ibid., David Nicolle, 4.

25. Philip W. Porter, *Benin to Bahia: A Chronicle of Portuguese Empire in the South Atlantic in the Fifteenth and Sixteenth Centuries, with Comments on a Chart of Jorge Reniel* (St. Paul, MN: North Central, 1959), 3.

26. Jonathan Phillips, *The Life and Legend of the Sultan Saladin* (New Haven, CT: Yale University Press, 2019).

27. Frank Welsh, *The Battle for Christendom: The Council of Constance, the East–West Conflict and the Dawn of Modern Europe* (Woodstock, NY: Overlook, 2008), xiv.

28. Kathleen Deegan and Darcie McMahon, *Fort Mose: Colonial America's Black Fortress of Freedom* (Tallahassee: University Press of Florida, 1995), 5.

29. John W. Toland, *Saracens: Islam in the Medieval European Imagination* (New York: Columbia University Press, 2002), 202. See also Thomas Newton, *Notable Historie of the Saracens . . .* (London: Veale, 1575).

30. M. L. Brown, *Firearms in Colonial America: The Impact on History and Technology, 1592–1792* (Washington, DC: Smithsonian, 1980), 6.

31. *Early Firearms of Great Britain and Ireland from the Collection of Clay P. Bedford* (New York: Metropolitan Museum of Art, 1971), Huntington Library. See also Kenneth Chase, *Firearms: A Global History to 1700* (New York: Cambridge University Press, 2003).

32. Donal Sasson, *The Anxious Triumph: A Global History of Capitalism, 1860–1914* (London: Allan Lane, 2019).

33. Priya Satia, *Empire of Guns: The Violent Making of the Industrial Revolution* (New York: Penguin, 2018), 8, 29, 36, 125.

34. Frederic J. Baumgartner, *France in the Sixteenth Century* (New York: St. Martin's, 1995), 57–58.

35. Iain MacInnes, *Scotland's Second War of Independence, 1332–1357* (Rochester, NY: Boydell, 2016).

36. Steven J. Gunn, *The English People at War in the Age of Henry VIII* (New York: Oxford University Press, 2018), 2.

37. Welsh, *The Battle for Christendom*, 69, 165.

38. Gideon Brough, *The Rise and Fall of Owain Glyn Owr: England, France and the Welsh Rebellion in the Late Middle Ages* (London: I. B. Tauris, 2017).

39. J. N. Hillgarth, *The Mirror of Spain, 1500–1700: The Formation of a Myth* (Ann Arbor: University of Michigan Press, 2000), 421–22. See also Geoffrey Parker, *Emperor: A New Life of Charles V* (New Haven, CT: Yale University Press, 2019).

40. *A Compleat History of the Piratical States of Barbary . . . by a Gentleman Who Resided There Many Years in a Public Character* (London: Griffiths, 1750), 60, Huntington Library.

41. Jacob Rader Marcus and Marc Saperstein, *The Jews in Christian Europe: A Source Book, 315–1791* (Pittsburgh: Hebrew Union College Press and University of Pittsburgh Press, 2015), 163. See also Ron D. Hart et al., *Fractured Faiths: Spanish Judaism, the Inquisition and New World Identities* (Albuquerque, NM: Fresco, 2016).

42. Pamela Nightingale, *A Medieval Mercantile Community*, 1995, 78.

43. Charles C. Mann, *1491: New Revelations of the Americas Before Columbus* (New York: Knopf, 2005), 131. J. M. Appel, "Is All Fair in Biological Warfare? The Controversy over Genetically Engineered Biological Weapons," *Journal of Medical Ethics* 35, no. (2009): 429–32.

44. Benjamin R. Gampel, *Anti-Jewish Riots in the Crown of Aragon and the Royal Response, 1391–1392* (New York: Cambridge University Press, 2016). See also Peter Mark and José da Silva Horta, *The Forgotten Diaspora: Jewish Communities in West Africa and the Making of the Atlantic World* (New York: Cambridge University Press, 2011).

45. Gerald Horne, *The Apocalypse of Settler Colonialism*, passim.

46. Peter Fritzsche, *An Iron Wind: Europe Under Hitler* (New York: Basic, 2016), 17.

47. Meyer Kaserling, *Christopher Columbus and the Participation of Jews in the Spanish and Portuguese Discoveries* (New York: Longmans, Green, 1894), x, 31.

48. J. N. Hillgarth, *The Mirror of Spain, 1500–1700: The Formation of a Myth* (Ann Arbor: University of Michigan Press, 2000), 194.

49. Jeremy Cohen, *A Historian in Exile: Solomon Ibn Verga, Shevet Shehudah and the Jewish-Christian Encounter* (Philadelphia: University of Pennsylvania Press, 2017).

50. Peter Edward Russell, *Prince Henry 'The Navigator': A Life* (New Haven, CT: Yale University Press, 2000), 252–53.

51. Toby Green, *The Rise of the Trans-Atlantic Slave Trade in Western Africa, 1300–1589* (New York: Cambridge University Press, 2012), 72, 3.

52. G. R. Crone, *The Voyages of Cadamasto and Other Documents on Western Africa In the Second Half of the Fifteenth Century* (London: Hakluyt Society, 1937), xii, xiii. See also J. F. P. Hopkins et al., eds., *Corpus of Early Arabic Sources for West African History* (Princeton, NJ: Markus Wiener, 2005).

53. Crone, *The Voyages of Cadamasto and Other Documents on Western Africa in the Second Half of the Fifteenth Century*, xii, xv.

54. Welsh, *The Battle for Christendom*, 165.

55. Cohen, *A Historian in Exile*, 8.

56. O. G. S. Crawford, ed., *Ethiopian Itineraries, circa 1400–1524, Including those Collected by Alessandro Zorzi at Venice in the Years 1519–1524* (Cambridge: Hakluyt Society, 1958), 3.

57. François Xavier Fauvelle, *The Golden Rhinoceros: Histories of the African Middle Ages* (Princeton, NJ: Princeton University Press, 2018), 228, 238, 223, 3, 193–94.

58. David Gitlitz, *Secrecy and Deceit: The Religion of the Crypto-Jews* (Albuquerque: University of New Mexico Press, 2002), xix, xx.

59. Stefan Stantchev, "Venice and the Ottoman Threat, 1381–1453," in Norman Housley, ed., *Reconfiguring the Fifteenth Century Crusade*, 161–205, 181.

60. O. G. S. Crawford, *Ethiopian Itineraries, circa 1400–1524*, 12.

61. Nicolle, *The Portuguese in the Age of Discovery*, 41.

62. Russell, *Prince Henry 'The Navigator,'* 249.

63. Glenn J. Ames, ed., *En Nome de Deus: The Journal of the First Voyage of Vasco de Gama to India, 1497–1499* (Leiden: Brill, 2009), 2.

64. Donnan, *Documents Illustrative of the History of the Slave Trade to America, Volume I*, 1.

65. Herman Bennett, *African Kings and Black Slaves: Sovereignty and Dispossession in the Early Modern Atlantic* (Philadelphia: University of Pennsylvania Press, 2019), 137.

66. Pamela Nightingale, *A Medieval Mercantile Community* (New Haven, CT: Yale University Press, 1995), 111, 545.

67. Jacques Heers, *The Barbary Corsairs: Pirates, Plunder and Warfare in the Mediterranean, 1480–1580* (New York: Skyhorse, 2018), 24.

68. T. J. Desch Obi, *Fighting for Honor: The History of African Martial Art Traditions in the Atlantic World* (Columbia: University of South Carolina Press, 2008), 69.

69. Miranda Kaufman, *Black Tudors: The Untold Story* (London: Oneworld, 2017), 13.

70. *Final Call* [Chicago], June 4, 2019.

71. Porter, *Benin to Bahia*, 4, 5, 11, 12. See also William D. Phillips, *Slavery in Medieval and Early Modern Iberia* (Philadelphia: University of Pennsylvania Press, 2014).

72. Hugh Thomas, *Rivers of Gold*, 48.

73. Pieter de Marees, ed., *Description and Historical Account of the Gold Kingdom*

of Guinea (1602) Translated from the Dutch and Edited by Albert Van Dantzig and Adam Jones (New York: Oxford University Press, 1987), xiii.

74. John Southern Burn, *The History of the French, Walloon, Dutch and Other Foreign Protestant Refugees Settled in England from the Reign of Henry VIII to the Revocation of the Edict of Nantes . . .* (London: Longman, 1846), v. See also James Anthony Froude, *English Seamen in the Sixteenth Century* (London: Longmans, 1895).

75. Ames, ed., *En Nome de Deus*, 2, 14.

76. Robin Law, *The Slave Coast of West Africa, 1550–1750: The Impact of the Atlantic Slave Trade on an African Society* (New York: Oxford University Press, 1991), 117.

77. Bennett, *African Kings and Black Slaves*, 122, 123.

78. Proviso, 1475, in Ernesto Schafer, ed., *Indice de la Coleccion de Documentos Ineditos de Indias* (Madrid: Consejo Superior de Investigaciones Cientificas, Instituto Gonzalo Fernandez de Oviedo, 1947), 3.

79. Crawford, ed., *Ethiopian Itineraries, circa 1400–1524*, 12, 22.

80. John Buchan, *Prester John* (London: Nelson, 1910).

81. Benjamin Weber, "Toward a Global Crusade? The Papacy and the Non-Latin World in the Fifteenth Century," in Norman Housley, ed., *Reconfiguring the Fifteenth Century Crusade* (New York: Palgrave, 2017), 11–44, 12, 25, 32.

82. Pavel Soukup, "Crusading Against Christians in the Fifteenth Century: Doubts and Debates," in Housley, ed., *Reconfiguring the Fifteenth Century Crusade*, 85–122, 98.

83. Jurgen Sarnowsky, "The Military Orders and Crusading in the Fifteenth Century: Perception and Influence," in Housley, ed., *Reconfiguring the Fifteenth Century Crusade*, 123–60, 133.

84. David Northrup, *Africa's Discovery of Europe, 1450–1850* (New York: Oxford University Press, 2002), 3, 4, 6.

85. Winthrop Jordan, *White over Black: American Attitudes toward the Negro, 1550–1812* (Chapel Hill: University of North Carolina Press, 2012).

86. Debra Blumenthal, *Enemies and Familiars: Slavery and Mastery in Fifteenth Century Valencia* (Ithaca, NY: Cornell University Press, 2009), 1, 4.

87. Hugh Thomas, *Rivers of Gold: The Rise of the Spanish Empire* (London: Weidenfeld and Nicolson, 2003), 29.

88. Deegan and MacMahon, *Fort Mose*, 6.

89. Christopher Witzenrath, ed., *Eurasian Slavery, Ransom and Abolition in World History* (Burlington, VT: Ashgate, 2015), 2, 8, 12–13.

90. Northrup, *Africa's Discovery of Europe, 1450–1850*, 6.

91. Alberto Vieira, "Sugar Islands: The Sugar Economy of Madeira and the Canaries, 1450–1650," in Stuart B. Schwartz, ed., *Tropical Islands: Sugar and the Making of the Atlantic World, 1450–1800* (Chapel Hill: University of North Carolina Press, 2004), 42–84, 68.

92. Thomas D. Goodrich, *The Ottoman Turks and the New World: A Study of Tarih-I Hind-I Garbi and Sixteenth Century Ottoman Americana* (Wiesbaden: Harrassowitz, 1990), 5, 9.

93. John F. Guilmartin, Jr., "Ideology and Conflict: The Wars of the Ottoman Empire, 1453–1606," in Douglas M. Peers, ed., *Warfare and Empires: Contact and Conflict Between European and Non-European Military and Maritime Forces and Cultures* (Brookfield, VT: Ashgate, 1997), 1–53, 1.

94. Gabor Agoston, *Guns for the Sultan: Military Power and the Weapons Industry in the Ottoman Empire* (New York: Cambridge University Press, 2005).

95. Gustav Ungerer, *The Mediterranean Apprenticeship of British Slavery* (Madrid: Editorial Verbum, 2008), 15, 41.

96. Elizabeth Donnan, ed., *Documents Illustrative of the History of the Slave Trade to America, Volume I* (New York: Octagon, 1969), 2.

97. Andrea Clarke, *Tudor Monarchs: Lives in Letters* (London: British Library, 2017), 26.

98. Andrew C. Hess, *The Forgotten Frontier: A History of the Sixteenth Century* (Chicago: University of Chicago Press, 1978), 30.

99. John Vogt, "Saint Barbara's Legion: Portuguese Artillery in the Struggle for Morocco, 1415–1578," in Douglas M. Peers, ed., *Warfare and Empires: Contact and Conflict between European and Non-European Military and Maritime Forces and Cultures* (Brookfield, VT: Ashgate, 1997), 73–79, 73. Cf. Trevor Hall, ed., *Before Middle Passage: Translated Portuguese Manuscripts of Atlantic Slave Trading from West Africa to Iberian Territories, 1513–26* (Burlington, VT: Ashgate, 2015).

100. Andrew Lambert, *Seapower States: Maritime Culture, Continental Empires and the Conflict that Made the Modern World* (New Haven, CT: Yale University Press, 2018), 222.

101. David Childs, *Invading America*, 108.

102. Edmund Abaka, *House of Slaves and 'Door of No Return': Gold Coast/Ghana Slave Forts, Castles and Dungeons in the Atlantic Slave Trade* (Trenton, NJ: Africa World, 2012), 78, 93.

103. Kris Lane, *Potosi: The Silver City That Changed the World* (Oakland: University of California Press, 2019), 6.

104. Charles H. Parker, *Global Interactions in the Early Modern Age, 1400–1800* (New York: Cambridge University Press, 2010), 27.

105. J. S. Cummins, ed., *Christianity and Missions, 1450–1800* (Brookfield, VT: Ashgate, 1997).

106. P. E. H. Hair, "Discovery and Discoveries: The Portuguese in Guinea, 1444–1650," in Ann Mackenzie and Dorothy S. Severin, "Spain and Portugal: The Discoveries and the Colonies, 1492–1898," in *Bulletin of Hispanic Studies* 69, no. 1 (January 1992): 11–28, 12, 15. See also Richard Kagan and Philip Morgan, *Atlantic Diasporas: Jews, Conversos and Crypto-Jews in the Age of Mercantilism, 1500–1800* (Baltimore: Johns Hopkins University Press, 2009).

107. Lambert, *Seapower States*, 268.

2. APOCALYPSE NEARER

1.   Entry, October 28, 1492, and November 12, 1492, in Oliver Dunn and James E. Kelley, Jr., eds., *The Diario of Christopher Columbus's First Voyage to*

America, 1492–1493 (Norman: University of Oklahoma Press, 1989), 117, 147, 253. See also Phillip Valentine, *The Landing of Columbus at San Salvador* (Worcester, MA: Hailton, 1892), and Jayme Sokolow, *The Great Encounter: Native Peoples and European Settlers in the Americas, 1492–1800* (Armonk, NY: M. E. Sharpe, 2003).

2.   Helen Nader, ed., *The Book of Privileges Issued to Christopher Columbus by King Fernando and Queen Isabel, 1492–1502* (Berkeley: University of California Press, 1996), 35. See also Christopher Columbus, "The Journal Account of the First Voyage and Discovery of the Indies," in Ministry of Cultural and Environmental Assets, *Nuova Raccolta Colombiana* (Rome: Instituto Poligrafico, 1988).

3.   John W. Blake, ed., *Europeans in West Africa, 1450–1560: Documents to Illustrate the Nature and Scope of Portuguese Enterprise in West Africa, the Abortive Attempt of Castilians to Create an Empire There and the Early English Voyages to Barbary and Guinea*, vol. 1 (London: Hakluyt Society, 1942), 198, 189, 196. See also Gerald Roe Crone, ed., *The Voyages of Cadamosto and Other Documents on Western Africa in the Second Half of the Fifteenth Century* (Nendeln, Leichtenstein: Kraus, 1967); Gomes Eannes de Azurara, *The Chronicle of the Discovery and Conquest of Guinea* (New York: Franklin, 1963).

4.   Jonathan Hart, *Representing the New World: The English and French Uses of the Example of Spain* (New York: Palgrave, 2001), 15.

5.   Brian A. Catlos, *Kingdoms of Faith*, 377, 392, 395.

6.   Wendy Childs, *Anglo-Castilian Trade in the Later Middle Ages* (Manchester: Manchester University Press, 1978), 155.

7.   Douglas Hunter, *The Race to the New World: Christopher Columbus, John Cabot and a Lost History of Discovery* (New York: Macmillan, 2011). See also Clements R. Markham, ed., *The Journal of Christopher Columbus . . . and Documents Relating to the Voyages of John Cabot and Gaspar Corte Real* (London: Hakluyt Society, 1893).

8.   Alfred Leslie Rowse, *The Elizabethans and America* (New York: Harper, 1959), 6, 7.

9.   Blake, *Europeans in West Africa*, 163.

10.   Jacques Heers, *The Barbary Corsairs: Pirates, Plunder and Warfare in the Mediterranean, 1480–1580* (New York: Skyhorse, 2018), 38.

11.   Imtiaz Habib, *Black Lives in the English Archives, 1500–1677: Imprints of the Invisible* (Burlington, VT: Ashgate, 2008), 52.

12.   See e.g. John Boyd Thacher, ed., *Christopher Columbus: His Life, His Work, His Remains as Revealed by Original Printed and Manuscript Sources . . .* (New York: Putnam's Sons, 1903). See also Markham, ed., *The Journal of Christopher Columbus*.

13.   Steven Epstein, *Speaking of Slavery: Color, Ethnicity and Human Bondage in Italy* (Ithaca, NY: Cornell University Press, 2001), xii, 189, 191. See also Patrick Manning, ed., *Slave Trades, 1500–1800: Globalization of Forced Labour* (Brookfield, VT: Ashgate, 1996).

14. M. L. Brown, *Firearms in Colonial America: The Impact on History and Technology, 1592–1792* (Washington, D.C.: Smithsonian, 1980), 36, 40.

15. Major H. B. C. Pollard, *A History of Firearms* (Boston: Houghton Mifflin, 1926), 29. See also Carl P. Russell, *Guns on the Early Frontiers: A History of Firearms from Colonial Times Through the Years of the Western Fur Trade* (Berkeley: University of California Press, 1957).

16. Helen Nader, ed., *The Book of Privileges to Christopher Columbus by King Fernando and Queen Isabel, 1492–1502* (Berkeley: University of California Press, 1996), 35. See also *Personal Narrative of the First Voyage of Columbus to America from a Manuscript Recently Discovered in Spain, Translated from Spanish* (Boston: Wait and Son, 1827), New-York Historical Society.

17. R. H. Major, ed., *Select Letters of Christopher Columbus . . .* (London: Hakluyt Society, 1870), 9, 13. See also John Cummins, ed., *The Voyage of Christopher Columbus: Columbus' Own Journal of Discovery* (New York: St. Martin's, 1992).

18. James Alexander Robertson, ed., *True Relation of the Hardships Suffered by Governor Hernando de Soto and Certain Portuguese Gentlemen During the Discovery of the Province of Florida: Now Newly Set Forth by a Gentleman of Elvas* (DeLand: Florida State Historical Society, 1932), 22–23. On indigenes fleeing and escaping from Spanish, see e.g., 35, 56, 61, 64, 66, 77, 83, 140–41, 188–89, 252–53; on indigenes attacking invaders see e.g. 59–60, 151–52, 203–04, 209–10, 239–40, 267–69, 389–90.

19. Heers, *The Barbary Corsairs*, 193.

20. Clarence Henry Haring, *Trade and Navigation between Spain and the Indies in the Time of the Habsburgs* (Cambridge: Harvard University Press, 1918), 135. See also Fray Diego Duran, *The History of the Indies of New Spain* (Norman: University of Oklahoma Press, 1994) [originally published in sixteenth century].

21. James H. Sweet, "The Iberian Roots of American Racist Thought," 147. See also Karen Racine and Beatriz G. Mamigonian, eds., *The Human Tradition in the Atlantic World, 1500–1850* (Lanham, MD: Rowman and Littlefield, 2010).

22. Karen Anderson Cordova, *Surviving Spanish Conquest: Indian Flight and Cultural Transformation in Hispaniola and Puerto Rico* (Tuscaloosa: University of Alabama Press, 2017), 51, 61, 45, 40.

23. Carl Ortwin Sauer, *Sixteenth Century North America: The Land, the Peoples as Seen by Europeans* (Berkeley: University of California Press, 1971). Cf. George R. Fairbanks, *The Spaniards in Florida Comprising the Notable Settlement of the Huguenots in 1564 . . .* (Jacksonville, FL: Columbus Drew, 1868), 12: Ponce de León landed April 3, 1512, "a few miles north of St. Augustine . . . found the natives fierce and implacable." See also Charles Bingham Reynolds, *The Landing of Ponce de León: A Historical Review* (Mountain Lakes, NJ: self-pub., 1934), Brown University.

24. Bernard Ship, *The History of Hernando de Soto and Florida: Or Records of the Events of Fifty-Six Years, from 1512 to 1568* (Philadelphia: Cotton, 1881), 71, 79.

25. Charles Hudson, *Knights of Spain, Warriors of the Sun: Hernando de Soto and the South's Ancient Chiefdoms* (Athens: University of Georgia Press, 1997), 32.

26. George Winship, ed., *Sailors' Narratives of Voyages Along the New England Coast, 1524–1624* (Boston: Houghton Mifflin, 1905), 2, 5.

27. Lesley Byrd Simpson, *The Encomienda in New Spain: Forced Labor in the Spanish Colonies, 1492–1550* (Berkeley: University of California Press, 1929), 16.

28. Woodbury Lowery, *The Spanish Settlements within the Present Limits of the United States: Florida, 1562–1574* (New York: Putnam's Sons, 1905), 14.

29. Herbert Priestley, ed., *The Luna Papers: Documents Relating to the Expedition of Don Tristan de Luna y Arrelano for the Conquest of La Florida in 1559–1561*, vol. 1 (DeLand, FL: Florida State Historical Society, 1928), xx.

30. Lawrence S. Rowland, *Window on the Atlantic: The Rise and Fall of St. Elena* (Columbia: South Carolina Department of Archives and History, no date), St. Augustine Historical Society. See also Ivan Van Sertima, *They Came Before Columbus*, 25: The Jamassi—or Yamasee—of the southeastern quadrant of North America were "black," according to the author.

31. Jane Landers, "Africans in the Land of Ayylon: The Exploration and Settlement of the Southeast," in Jeannine Cook, ed., *Columbus and the Land of Ayllon: The Exploration and Settlement of the Southeast* (Darien, GA: Darien Printer News, 1992), 105–24, 110. See also David G. Moore et.al., "Conflict, Violence and Warfare in La Florida," in Clay Mathers et.al., eds., *Native and Spanish New Worlds: Sixteenth Century Entradas in the American Southwest and Southeast* (Tucson: University of Arizona Press, 2014), 205–30.

32. Green, *The Rise of the Trans-Atlantic Trade in Western Africa, 1300–1589*, 91. See also Charles Hudson and Carmen Chaves Tesser, eds., *The Forgotten Centuries: Indians and Europeans in the American South, 1521–1704* (Athens: University of Georgia Press, 1994), 1.

33. Anthony Stevens-Acevedo, *The Santo Domingo Slave Revolt of 1521 and the Slave Laws of 1522: Black Slavery and Black Resistance in the Early Colonial Americas* (New York: Dominican Studies Institution, City University of New York, 2019).

34. Jane Landers, "African Presence in Early Spanish Colonization of the Caribbean and the Southeastern Borderlands," vertical file on "Blacks, Miscellaneous," St. Augustine Historical Society.

35. Douglas Hunter, *The Place of Stone: Dighton Rock and the Erasure of America's Indigenous Past* (Chapel Hill: University of North Carolina Press, 2017).

36. Donald E. Chipman, *Spanish Texas, 1519–1821* (Austin: University of Texas Press, 1992).

37. Norman Housley, "Introduction," in Housley, ed., *Crusading in the Fifteenth Century: Message and Impact* (New York: Palgrave, 2004), 1–12.

38. Claudius Sieber-Lehmann, "An Obscure but Powerful Pattern: Crusading, Nationalism and the Swiss Confederation in the Late Middle Ages," in Housley, ed., *Crusading in the Fifteenth Century*, 81–93, 85. Cf. J. C. Sharman, *Empires of the Weak: The Real Story of European Expansion and the Creation of the New World Order* (Princeton, NJ: Princeton University Press, 2019).

39. Charles H. Parker, *Global Interactions in the Early Modern Age, 1400–1800*, 28.

40. Jeremy Black, *European Warfare, 1494–1660* (London: Routledge, 2002). Cf. Michael Roberts, *The Military Revolution, 1560–1660* (Belfast: Bord, 1956).

41. David Herlihy, *The Black Death and the Transformation of the West* (Cambridge, MA: Harvard University Press, 1997).

42. Clarence Henry Haring, *Trade and Navigation Between Spain and the Indies in the Time of the Habsburgs* (Cambridge, MA: Harvard University Press, 1918), 104, 135.

43. Seymour B. Liebman, *The Inquisitions and the Jews in the New World: Summaries of Procesos, 1500–1810* ... (Coral Gables, FL: University of Miami Press, 1974), 18. See also Martin H. Sable, *Columbus, Marrano, Discoverer from Majorca* (Milwaukee: self-pub., 1992), Brown University: Here the explorer is depicted as Jewish—or possibly Moroccan or Icelandic or with roots in the British Isles. See also Jacob R. Marcus, *The Colonial American Jew, 1492–1776*, Volume I (Detroit: Wayne State University Press, 1970).

44. Seymour B. Liebman, *New World Jewry, 1493–1825: Requiem for the Forgotten* (New York: Ktav, 1982), 15. See also Martin A. Cohen and Abraham J. Peck, eds., *Sephardim in the Americas: Studies in Culture and History* (Tuscaloosa: University of Alabama Press, 1993).

45. Eva Alexandra Uchmany, "The Participation of New Christians and Crypto-Jews in the Conquest, Colonization and Trade of Spanish America, 1521–1660," in Peaolo Bernardini and Norman Fiering, eds., *The Jews and the Expansion of Europe to the West, 1450–1800* (New York: Berghahn, 2001), 186–202, 187.

46. Mordecai Arbell, *The Jewish Nation of the Caribbean: The Spanish-Portuguese Jewish Settlements in the Caribbean and the Guianas* (Jerusalem: Gefen, 2002), 11.

47. Ernst Pijning, "New Christians and Sugar Plantations and Traders in the Portuguese Atlantic, 1450–1800," in Bernardini and Fiering, eds., 485–500, 486, 487. A similar process occurred in Brazil. See Geraldo Pieroni, "Outcasts from the Kingdom: The Inquisition and the Banishment of New Christians to Brazil," in Bernardini and Fiering, *The Jews and the Expansion of Europe to the West, 1450–1800*, 242–51, 243.

48. Jacob Rader Marcus and Marc Saperstein, *Jews in Christian Europe: A Source Book, 315–1791* (Pittsburgh: Hebrew Union College Press and University of Pittsburgh Press, 2015), 193.

49. James C. Boyajian, "New Christians and Jews in the Sugar Trade, 1550–1750: Two Centuries of Development of the Atlantic Economy," in Bernardini and Fiering, eds., *The Jews and the Expansion of Europe to the West, 1450–1800*, 471–84, 471.

50. Mann, *1491: New Revelations of the Americas Before Columbus*, 43.

51. Alfred Leslie Rowse, *The Elizabethans and America* (New York: Harper, 1959), 6. See also Kathleen J. Bragdon, *Native Peoples of Southern New England, 1500–1650* (Norman: University of Oklahoma Press, 1996).

52. David Nicolle, *The Portuguese in the Age of Discovery, c. 1340–1665* (Long Island City, NY: Osprey, 2012), 14.

53. Ames, *En Nome de Deus*, 107, 41, 53, 56. See also Sanjay Subrahmanyam, *The*

Career and Legend of Vasco da Gama (New York: Cambridge University Press, 1997).

54. Timothy J. Coates, *Convicts and Orphans: Forced and State Sponsored Colonizers in the Portuguese Empire, 1550–1755* (Stanford, CA: Stanford University Press, 2001), 86.

55. T. Bentley Duncan, *Atlantic Islands: Madiera, the Azores and the Cape Verdes in Seventeenth Century Commerce and Navigation* (Chicago: University of Chicago Press, 1972), 198.

56. David Nicolle, *The Portuguese in the Age of Discovery*, 6. See also George Theal, *The Portuguese in South Africa* (New York: Negro Universities Press, 1969).

57. Heers, *The Barbary Corsairs*, 25, 191.

58. John Edwards, "Reconquista and Crusade in Fifteenth Century Spain," in Housley, ed., *Crusading in the Fifteenth Century*, 163–81, 167, 173, 178.

59. James H. Sweet, "The Iberian Roots of American Racist Thought," 156. See also Trevor Hall, ed., *Before Middle Passage: Translated Portuguese Manuscripts of Atlantic Slave Trading from West Africa to Iberian Territories, 1513–1526* (Burlington, VT: Ashgate, 2015).

60. Antonio Feros, *Speaking of Spain: The Evolution of Race and Nation in the Hispanic World* (Cambridge, MA: Harvard University Press, 2017), 79, 144.

61. Horne, *Negro Comrades of the Crown*.

62. Robinson A. Herrera, *Natives, Europeans and Africans in Sixteenth Century Santiago de Guatemala* (Austin: University of Texas Press, 2003), 5, 114–15, 215. See also David M. Davidson, "Negro Slave Control and Resistance in Colonial Mexico, 1519–1650," *Hispanic American Historical Review* 46, no. 3 (August 1966): 235–53.

63. Gerald Horne, *White Supremacy Confronted: U.S. Imperialism and Anticommunism vs. the Liberation of Southern Africa, from Rhodes to Mandela* (New York: International Publishers, 2019).

64. Luis Dominguez, ed., *The Conquest of the River Plate (1535–1555)* (London: Hakluyt Society, 1891), xiv.

65. Taliesin Trow, *Sir Martin Frobisher: Seaman, Soldier, Explorer* (Barnsley, UK: Pen and Sword, 2010), ix.

66. Markham, ed., *The Journal of Christopher Columbus*, xii, xiii, xxxvii.

67. Ungerer, *The Mediterranean Apprenticeship of British Slavery*, 54.

68. Thomas Kaufman, *Luther's Jews: A Journey into Anti-Semitism* (New York: Oxford University Press, 2017), 76. See also Craig Harline, *A World Ablaze: The Rise of Martin Luther and the Birth of the Reformation* (New York: Oxford University Press, 2017) and Richard Rex, *The Making of Martin Luther* (Princeton, NJ: Princeton University Press, 2017).

69. Thomas Albert Howard and Mark A. Noll, eds., *Protestantism after 500 Years* (New York: Oxford University Press, 2016), 70.

70. Alex Ryrie, *Protestants: The Faith that Made the Modern World* (New York: Viking, 2017), 266, 267.

71. W. Michael Mathes, ed., *The Conquistador in California: 1535: Voyage of*

Fernando Cortes to Baja California in Chronicles and Documents (Los Angeles: Dawson's Bookshop, 1973), Huntington Library.

72. Judith John, *Dark History of the Tudors: Murder, Adultery, Incest, Witchcraft, Wars, Religious Persecutions, Piracy* (London: Amber, 2014), 37.

73. Dan O'Sullivan, *The Reluctant Ambassador: The Life and Times of Sir Thomas Chaloner, Tudor Diplomat* (Gloucestershire, UK: Amberley, 2016), 17–18.

74. Frank Welsh, *The Battle for Christendom: The Council of Constance, the East-West Conflict and the Dawn of Modern Europe* (Woodstock, NY: Overlook, 2008), xiv, xvi, 16, 18.

75. Victoria Freeman, *Distant Relations: How My Ancestors Colonized North America* (Toronto: McClelland and Stewart, 2000), 12.

76. S. A. Skilliter, ed., *William Harborne and the Trade with Turkey, 1578–1582: A Documentary Study of the First Anglo-Ottoman Relations* (London: Oxford University Press, 1977), 23.

77. O'Sullivan, *The Reluctant Ambassador*, 17–18, 31.

78. A. F. Allison and D. M. Rogers, eds., *A Catalogue of Catholic Books in English Printed Abroad or Secretly in England, 1558–1640* (London: Arundel, 1964). Cf. David Wallace, *Europe: A Literary History, 1348–1418* (New York: Oxford University Press, 2016).

79. Freeman, *Distant Relations*, 13.

80. Alessandro Stanziani, "Slavery and Bondage in Central Asia and Russia: Fourteenth–Nineteenth Centuries," in Witzenrath, ed., *Eurasian Slavery*, 81–104, 97.

81. Brian A. Catlos, *Kingdoms of Faith: A New History of Islamic Spain* (New York: Basic, 2018), 396, 402, 403, 413.

82. Andrew Hess, *The Forgotten Frontier: A History of the Sixteenth Century Ibero-African Frontier* (Chicago: University of Chicago Press, 1978), 175.

83. Leonie Frieda, *Francis I: The Maker of Modern France* (New York: HarperCollins, 2018), 241, 243.

84. Introduction in Virginia H. Aksan and Daniel Goffman, eds., *The Early Modern Ottomans: Remapping the Empire*, 1–12, 7; Gábor Ágoston, "Information, Ideology and Limits of Imperial Policy: Ottoman Grand Strategy in the Context of Ottoman-Habsburg Rivalry," in Virginia H. Aksan and Daniel Goffman, eds., *The Early Modern Ottomans: Remapping the Empire* (Cambridge: Cambridge University Press, 2007), 75–103. See also H. Eredem Cipa, *The Making of Selim: Succession, Legitimacy and Memory in the Early Modern Ottoman World* (Bloomington: Indiana University Press, 2017), 3.

85. María Antonia Garcés, ed., *An Early Modern Dialogue with Islam: Antonio de Sosa's Topography of Algiers (1612)* (South Bend, IN: University of Notre Dame Press, 2011), 1, 27.

86. Cf. John G. Bourke, "Notes on the Language and Folk-Usage of the Rio Grande Valley (with Special Regard to Survivals of Arabic Customs)," *Journal of American Folklore* 9, no. 33 (April–June 1896), University of New Mexico, Albuquerque.

87. Mercedes Maroto Camino, *Exploring the Explorers: Spaniards in Oceania, 1519–1794* (Manchester: Manchester University Press, 2008), 3.

88. Roger Crowley, *Empires of the Sea: The Siege of Malta, the Battle of Lepanto and the Contest for the Center of the World* (New York: Random House, 2008), xviii.

89. O'Sullivan, *The Reluctant Ambassador*, 39–40, 54.

90. O'Sullivan, *The Reluctant Ambassador*, 32.

91. Giancarlo Casale, *The Ottoman Age of Exploration* (New York: Oxford University Press, 2010), 158, 59, 80.

92. Heers, *The Barbary Corsairs*, 209.

93. Jane Landers, "African Presence in Early Spanish Colonization of the Caribbean."

94. Hernando Cortes to Emperor, 1522, in George Folsom, ed., *The Despatches of Hernando Cortes . . . Addressed to the Emperor Charles V . . .* (New York: Wiley and Putnam, 1843), 145, 6, 49.

95. Folsom, ed., *The Despatches of Hernando Cortes . . . Addressed to the Emperor Charles V . . .* , 6, 7, 8.

96. E. A. Payne, ed., *Voyages of the Elizabethan Seamen to America* (London: De La Rue, 1880), vi. See also James Anthony Froude, *English Seamen in the Sixteenth Century* (New York: Scribner's, 1895).

97. Sarah Gristwood, *Game of Queens: The Women Who Made Sixteenth-Century Europe* (New York: Basic, 2016), 102, 109.

98. Clare Kellar, *Scotland, England and the Reformation, 1534–1561* (New York: Oxford University Press, 2004).

99. David Potter, ed., *A Knight of Malta at the Court of Elizabeth I: The Correspondence of Michel de Seure, French Ambassador at the Court of Elizabeth I* (New York: Cambridge University Press, 2014), 2.

100. Andrea Clarke, *Tudor Monarch: Lives in Letters* (London: British Library, 2017), 62.

101. Niall Fallon, *The Armada in Ireland* (Middletown, CT: Wesleyan University Press, 1978), 2, 4.

102. J. N. Hillgarth, *The Mirror of Spain, 1500–1700: The Formation of a Myth* (Ann Arbor: University of Michigan Press, 2000), 421–22, 425.

103. Merwyn Carey, *English, Irish and Scottish Firearms Makers: When, Where, and What They Made from the Sixteenth Century to the Nineteenth Century* (New York: Crowell, 1954).

104. M. L. Brown, *Firearms in Colonial America: The Impact on History and Technology, 1592–1792* (Washington, D.C.: Smithsonian, 1980), xiii, citing Charles Winthrop Sawyer, *Firearms in American History* (Boston: self-pub., 1910), 1. See also Carl P. Russell, *Guns on the Early Frontiers: A History of Firearms from Colonial Times Through the Years of the Western Fur Trade* (Berkeley: University of California Press, 1957).

105. *Early Firearms of Great Britain and Ireland* (New York: Metropolitan Museum of Art, 1971), vii, Huntington Library.

106. Standish O'Grady, *Red Hugh's Captivity: A Picture of Ireland, Social and*

Political Life by the Reign of Queen Elizabeth I (London: Ward and Downey, 1889), 1.

107. Bolivar Christian, *The Scotch Irish Settlers in the Valley of Virginia: Alumni Address at Washington College, Lexington, Virginia* (Richmond, VA: Macfarlane and Ferguson, 1860), Huntington Library.

108. Ada Kathleen Longfield, *Anglo-Irish Trade in the Sixteenth Century* (London: Routledge, 1929). See also David Armitage, *Greater Britain, 1516–1576: Essays in Atlantic History* (Burlington, VT: Ashgate, 2004).

109. Freeman, *Distant Relations*, 6, 11, 12.

110. Catherine Fletcher, *The Black Prince of Florence: The Spectacular Life and Treacherous World of Alessandro de' Medici* (New York: Oxford University Press, 2016).

3. LIQUIDATION OF INDIGENES | RELIANCE ON AFRICANS |TENSIONS IN LONDON

1. Ida Walton, *The War for Mexico's West: Indians and Spaniards in New Galicia, 1524–1550* (Albuquerque: University of New Mexico Press, 2010), 278, 221, 299. See also Matthew Babcock, *Apache Adaptation to Hispanic Rule* (New York: Cambridge University Press, 2018). See also Henry J. Tobias. *A History of Jews in New Mexico* (Albuquerque: University of New Mexico Press, 1990); Cary Herz, *New Mexico's Crypto-Jews: Image and Memory)* Albuquerque: University of New Mexico Press, 2007).

2. Horne, *The Counter-Revolution of 1776*, passim.

3. John Kessell, *Kiva, Cross and Crown: The Pecos Indians and Mexico, 1540–1840* (Washington, D.C.: National Park Service, 1979), 32, 33.

4. Philip Wayne Powell, *Soldiers, Indians and Silver: North America's First Frontier War* (Berkeley: University of California Press, 1952), 62.

5. Undated Paper on sixteenth Century Africans, Box 4, France Scholes Papers, University of New Mexico, Albuquerque. On an uprising of indigenes in Cuba see Juan de Agramonte [Santiago de Cuba] to the Crown, September 3, 1539, Archivo General de Indias-Sevilla/AGI, 54-1-34/2, Stetson Collection, St. Augustine Historical Society. On the 1770s see Horne, *The Counter-Revolution of 1776*.

6. Henry Wilkinson, *The Adventures of Bermuda* (London: Oxford University Press, 1933), 5.

7. Deegan and MacMahon, *Fort Mose*, 12.

8. Thomas, *World Without End*, 121, 156. See also Matthew Restall, *The Black Middle: Africans, Mayas and Spaniards in Colonial Yucatan* (Stanford, CA: Stanford University Press, 2009).

9. Kaufman, *Black Tudors: The Untold Story* (London: Oneworld, 2017), 13, 16. Cf. Monica Azzolini and Isabella Lazzarini, eds., *Italian Renaissance Diplomacy: A Sourcebook* (Toronto: Pontifical Institute of Medieval Studies, 2017).

10. Gonzalo Fernandez de Oviedo, ed., *Writing from the Edge of the World: The Memoirs of Darien, 1514–1527* (Tuscaloosa: University of Alabama Press, 2006), 114, 154–55.

11.   Robert Goodwin, *Crossing the Continent, 1507–1540: The Story of the First African American Explorer of the American South* (New York: HarperCollins, 2008), 306, 308.

12.   Herbert Priestley, ed., *The Luna Papers: Documents Relating to the Expedition of Don Tristan de Luna y Arrellano for the Conquest of La Florida in 1559–1561*, vol. 1 (DeLand, Florida: Florida State Historical Society, 1928), xx. See also Jerald T. Milanich and Susan Milbrath, eds., *First Encounters: Spanish Explorations in the Caribbean and the United States, 1492–1570* (Gainesville: University Press of Florida, 1989).

13.   Karen Vieira Powers, *Women in the Crucible of Conquest: The Gendered Society of Spanish American Society, 1500–1600* (Albuquerque: University of New Mexico Press, 2005), 5; see also José Ignacio Avellaneda, *The Conquerors of the New Kingdom of Granada* (Albuquerque: University of New Mexico Press, 1995).

14.   Danna A. Levin Rojo, *Return to Aztlan: Indians, Spaniards and the Invention of Nuevo Mexico* (Norman: University of Oklahoma Press, 2014). See also Rose Marie Beebe and Robert M. Senkewicz, eds., *Lands of Promise and Despair: Chronicles of Early California, 1535–1846* (Berkeley, CA: Heyday, 2001). See also Carl Ortwin Sauer, *Sixteenth Century North America* (Berkeley, CA: University of California Press, 1971).

15.   Alejandro de la Fuente, *Havana and the Atlantic in the Sixteenth Century*, 36.

16.   Kaufman, *Black Tudors*, 119, 120.

17.   Alejandro de la Fuente, *Havana and the Atlantic in the Sixteenth Century*, 83. Cf. Frances Luttikhuizen, *Underground Protestants in Sixteenth Century Spain: A Much Ignored Side of Spanish History* (Bristol, CT: Vandenhoeck and Ruprecht, 2017).

18.   William B. Carter, *Indian Alliances and the Spanish in the Southwest, 750–1750* (Norman: University of Oklahoma Press, 2009).

19.   Las Casas, *An Historical and True Account of the Cruel Massacre and Slaughter of 20,000 of People in the West Indies by the Spaniards*, translated from the French edition, 1620, New-York Historical Society.

20.   Clements R. Markham, ed., *The Hawkins' Voyages During the Reign of Henry VIII, Queen Elizabeth and James I* (London: Hakluyt Society, 1878), iv.

21.   Lewis Hanke, *Bartolome de las Casas: An Interpretation of His Life and Writings* (The Hague: Nijhoff, 1951), 19.

22.   Alonso de Zorita, *Life and Labor in Ancient Mexico: The Brief Summary Relation of the Lords of Spain* (New Brunswick, NJ: Rutgers University Press, 1963), 11.

23.   William S. Maltby, *The Black Legend in England: The Development of Anti-Spanish Sentiment, 1558–1660* (Durham, NC: Duke University Press, 1971).

24.   Mark Meuwese, *Brothers in Arms, Partners in Trade: Dutch-Indigenous Alliances in the Atlantic World, 1595–1674* (Leiden: Brill, 2012).

25.   Kathleen Deegan and Darcie MacMahon, *Fort Mose*, 10.

26.   Brian R. Hamnett, *The End of Iberian Rule on the American Continent, 1770–1830* (New York: Cambridge University Press, 2017), 58–59.

27. Kris Lane, *Potosi: The Silver City That Changed the World* (Oakland: University of California Press, 2019), 34, 64. See also Kris Lane, *Quito 1599: City and Colony in Transition* (Albuquerque: University of New Mexico Press, 2002), and Jeffrey A. Cole, *The Potosi Mita, 1573–1700: Compulsory Indian Labor in the Andes* (Stanford, CA: Stanford University Press, 1985).

28. Merrill P. Freeman, "Coronado's Expedition in 1540: From the City of Mexico to the Seven Cities of Cibola," Tucson: Arizona Archaeological Society, March 19, 1917, Ephemera hal-4, Arizona State University, Tempe. At the same site, see also F. W. Hodge, "The First Discovered City of Cibola," 1895, Ephemera hal-10.

29. Robert Goodwin, *Crossing the Continent, 1507–1540: The Story of the First African American Explorer of the American South* (New York: HarperCollins, 2008), 222, 328.

30. Harold O. Weight, "Melhior Diaz . . . Captain with Coronado," 1953, Ephemera hal-7.

31. Richard Flint, ed., *Great Cruelties Have Been Reported: The 1544 Investigation of the Coronado Expedition* (Dallas: Southern Methodist University Press, 2002), 65, 171, 183, 195, 203, 522. See also Andrés Reséndez, *A Land So Strange: The Epic Journey of Cabeza de Vaca, the Extraordinary Tale of a Shipwrecked Spaniard who Walked across America in the Sixteenth Century* (New York: Perseus, 2007).

32. George Parker Winship, ed., *The Journey of Coronado, 1540–1542* (New York: Greenwood, 1922), vii. See also George Parker Winship, "Why Coronado Went to New Mexico in 1540," 1896, New-York Historical Society. See also Carina Johnson, *Cultural Hierarchy in Sixteenth-Century Europe: The Ottomans and Aztecs* (New York: Cambridge University Press, 2011): The Habsburgs tended to demonize and exoticize Ottomans and Aztecs and heterodox Christians too in legitimating its authority.

33. J. H. Simpson, "Coronado's March in Search of 'The Seven Cities of Cibola' and Discussion of their Probable Location," Ephemera hal-9.

34. Katharine Bartlett, "Notes Upon the Routes of Espejo and Farfan to the Mines in the Sixteenth Century," January 1942, Ephemera hal-5.

35. Leslie Pierce, *Empress of the East: How a European Slave Girl Became Queen of the Ottoman Empire* (New York: Basic, 2017), 145, 31, 23, 21, 16, 219, 237.

36. Gabor Agoston, *Guns for the Sultan: Military Power and the Weapons Industry in the Ottoman Empire* (New York: Cambridge University Press, 2005). See also Rhoads Murphey, *Ottoman Warfare, 1500–1700* (London: UCL Press, 1999) and Salih Ozbaran, *The Ottoman Response to European Expansion: Studies on Ottoman-Portuguese Relations in the Indian Ocean and Ottoman Administration in the Arab Lands During the Sixteenth Century* (Istanbul: Isisi, 1994).

37. Richard E. Greenleaf, *Zumarraga and the Mexican Inquisition, 1536–1543* (Washington, D.C.: Academy of American Franciscan History, 1961), 76, 77. See also Richard Greenleaf, *The Mexican Inquisition of the Sixteenth Century* (Albuquerque: University of New Mexico Press, 1969). See Brian R. Hamnett,

The End of Iberian Rule on the American Continent, 39: In Salvador, Bahia, in 1740 out of "150 merchants, most of them of Portuguese origin . . . out of a total population around 7000 . . . a large proportion (c. 45 percent) were converted Jews."

38. John F. Schwaller, ed., *The First Letter from New Spain: The Lost Petition of Cortes and His Company, June 20, 1519* (Austin: University of Texas Press, 2014), 119–20.

39. German Arciniegas, *Germans in the Conquest of America: A Sixteenth Century Venture* (New York: Macmillan, 1943), 3.

40. Leopold Ranke *The Ottoman and the Spanish Empires in the Sixteenth and Seventeenth Centuries* (Philadelphia: Lea and Blanchard, 1845), xi.

41. Nancy van Deusen, "Coming to Castile with Cortes: Indigenous 'Servitude' in the Sixteenth Century," *Ethnohistory* 62, no. 2 (April 2015): 285–308, 286. On New Spain in the early years, see *Documents and Narratives Concerning the Discovery and Conquest of Latin America* (Berkeley, CA: Cortes Society/Bancroft Library, 1942), Brown University. At the same site see also G. R. G. Conway, *The Last Will and Testament of Hernando Cortes . . .* (Mexico City: self-pub., 1939), Brown University.

42. G. R. G. Conway, *An Englishman and the Mexican Inquisition, 1556–1560* (Mexico City: self-pub., 1927), University of Virginia, Charlottesville. At the same site see also Juan Antonio Llorente, *The History of the Spanish Inquisition: From the Time of the Establishment of the Reign of Ferdinand VII, Composed from the Original Documents of the Archives of the Supreme Council and from those of Subordinate Tribunals of the Holy Office* (Philadelphia: Campbell, 1843).

43. Thomas, *World without End*, 53, 244.

44. Frank T. Proctor III, *'Damned Notions of Liberty: Slavery, Culture and Power in Colonial Mexico, 1640–1769* (Albuquerque: University of New Mexico Press, 2010), 3.

45. Schulamith C. Halevy, "Anusim in North America: The Ingathering," Box 8, Tomas Atencio Papers, University of New Mexico, Albuquerque.

46. See Lawrence A. Clayton, Vernon James Knight, Jr., and Edward C. Moore, eds., *The De Soto Chronicles: The Expedition of Hernando de Soto to North America in 1539–1543*, vol. 1 (Tuscaloosa: University of Alabama Press, 1993), 53, 63, 89, 289.

47. Caleb Curren, "In Search of de Soto's Trail (A Hypothesis of the Alabama Route)," *Bulletins of Discovery* 1 (October 1986): 2–3, Brown University.

48. Diary of Voyage of Juan Rodriguez Cabrillo, June 27, 1542, Carton 13, Herbert Bolton Papers, University of California, Berkeley. See also Herbert Eugene Bolton, *The Colonization of North America, 1492–1783* (New York: Macmillan, 1930); Harlan Hague, *The Road to California: The Search for a Southern Overland Route* (Glendale, CA: Clark, 1978).

49. Charles E. Chapman, *A History of California: The Spanish Period* (New York: Macmillan, 1921), 21, 22, 23, 24, 32.

50. Silke Strickrodt, *Afro European Trade in the Atlantic World: The Western Slave Coast c. 1500–1885* (Rochester, NY: Boydell and Brewer, 2017), 1.

51. Steven Gunn, *The English People at War in the Age of Henry VIII* (New York: Oxford University Press, 2018). See also Rory McEntegart, *Henry VIII, the League of Schmalkalden and the English Reformation* (Rocheste, NY: Boydell, 2002).

52. Andrea Clarke, *Tudor Monarchs: Lives in Letters* (London: British Library, 2017), 78, 90, 91, 110. See also Peter Marshall, *Heretics and Believers: A History of the English Reformation*, New Haven: Yale University Press, 2017. See also *A Declaration Conteyning the Just Causes and Consideration of this Present Warre with the [Scots] . . . 1542*, Huntington Library.

53. Sarah Gristwood, *Game of Queens: The Women Who Made Sixteenth-Century Europe* (New York: Basic, 2016), 187.

54. Clare Kellar, *Scotland, England and the Reformation, 1534–1561* (New York: Oxford University Press, 2004).

55. Imtiaz Habib, *Black Lives in the English Archives: Imprints of the Invisible* (Burlington, VT: Ashgate, 2008), 52, 64.

56. Clarke, *Tudor Monarchs*, 125, 136.

57. Jacob Rader Marcus and Marc Saperstein, *Jews in Christian Europe: A Source Book, 315–1791* (Pittsburgh: Hebrew Union College Press and University of Pittsburgh Press, 2015), 225.

58. Francis J. Bremer, *John Winthrop: America's Forgotten Founding Father* (New York: Oxford University Press, 2003), 312, 313.

59. Kaufman, *Black Tudors*, 35.

60. Gustav Ungerer, *The Mediterranean Apprenticeship of British Slavery* (Madrid: Editorial Verbum, 2008), 80.

61. Mordechai Arbell, *The Jewish Nation of the Caribbean: The Spanish-Portuguese Jewish Settlements in the Caribbean and the Guianas* (Jerusalem: Gefen, 2002), 11, 12, 226.

62. Edward Arber, ed., *The First English Three Books on America: [? 1511]–1555 A.D.* (Birmingham, UK: n.p., 1985).

63. Vivien Kogut Lessa de Sa, ed., *The Admirable Adventures and Strange Fortunes of Master Anthony Kivet: An English Pirate in Sixteenth Century Brazil* (New York: Cambridge University Press, 2015).

64. Lawrence Shaw Mayo, *The Winthrop Family in America* (Boston: Massachusetts Historical Society, 1948), 3, 11. See also Kathleen A. Bragdon, *Native Peoples of Southern New England, 1500–1650* (Norman: University of Oklahoma Press, 1996).

65. David Quinn and A. N. Ryan, *England's Sea Empire, 1550–1642* (London: Allen and Unwin, 1983), 21, 24, 28. Demobilized soldiers continue to be a major issue: See e.g. Kathleen Belew, *Bring the War Home: The White Power Movement and Paramilitary America* (Cambridge, MA: Harvard University Press, 2018).

66. John Guy, *Gresham's Law: The Life and World of Queen Elizabeth I's Banker* (London: Profile, 2019). See also George Soros, *George Soros on Globalization* (New York: PublicAffairs, 2002).

67. Agostino Mascardi, "An Historical Relation of the Conspiracy of John Lewis,

Count de Fieschi, Against the City and Republic of Genoa in the Year 1547,"
Edinburgh, 1885, University of Virginia, Charlottesville.

68.   John Butman and Simon Target, *New World, Inc.: The Making of America by England's Merchant Adventurers* (New York: Little, Brown, 2018), 87.

69.   Janet E. Hollinshead, *Liverpool in the Sixteenth Century: A Small Tudor Town* (Lancaster, UK: Carnegie, 2007).

70.   Kaufman, *Black Tudors*, 175.

71.   Taliesin Trow, *Sir Martin Frobisher: Seaman, Soldier, Explorer* (Barnsley, UK: Pen and Sword, 2010), 10–11.

72.   Frederic J. Baumgartner, *France in the Sixteenth Century* (New York: St. Martin's, 1995), 123.

73.   Heers, *The Barbary Corsairs: Pirates, Plunder and Warfare in the Mediterranean, 1480–1580* (New York: Skyhorse, 2018), 92.

74.   Trow, *Sir Martin Frobisher*, 22.

75.   Charles Winthrop Sawyer, *Firearms in American History* (Boston: Author, 1910), 1, 16.

76.   See E. Delmar Morgan and C. H. Coote, eds., *Early Voyages and Travels to Russia and Persia by Anthony Jenkinson and Other Englishmen*, vol. 1 (London: Hakluyt Society, 1876).

77.   Charles H. Parker, *Global Interactions in the Early Modern Age, 1400–1800* (New York: Cambridge University Press, 2010), 31. See also Pietro Martire d'Anghiera, *The Decades of the Newe Worlde or West India . . .* (London: Paules Churchyarde, 1555), Massachusetts Historical Society, Boston.

78.   Andrew C. Hess, *The Forgotten Frontier: A History of the Sixteenth Century Ibero-African Frontier* (Chicago: University of Chicago Press, 1978), 73.

79.   Frederic J. Baumgartner, *France in the Sixteenth Century* (New York: St. Martin's, 1995), 65, 79, 93, 117, 118, 119.

80.   *The History of the Campagnes 1548 and 1549 being an Exact Account of the Martial Expeditions Perform'd in Those Days by the Scots and French on One Side and the English and their Foreign Auxiliaries on the Other, Done in French under the Title of the Scots War . . .* (Paris, 1556), Huntington Library: The original observer writing in French was "eye-witness to what he relates." See also David Potter, *Henry VIII and Francis I: The Final Conflict, 1540–1547* (Leiden: Brill, 2011).

81.   Baumgartner, *France in the Sixteenth Century*, 206.

82.   Heers, *The Barbary Corsairs*, 74. Cf. Ezel Kural Shaw and C. J. Heywood, *English and Continental Views of the Ottoman Empire, 1500–1800* (Los Angeles: UCLA Library, 1972), University of Virginia, Charlottesville. Christine Isom-Verhaaren, *Allies with the Infidel: The Ottoman and French Alliance in the Sixteenth Century* (New York: Tauris, 2011).

83.   Lane, *Potosi*, 30.

84.   Sir William Stirling-Maxwell, *Don Juan or Passages from the History of the Sixteenth Century* (London: Longmans, Green, 1883), 95, 96, 100, 104, 118, 119, 120. See also Chouki el-Hamel, *Black Morocco: A History of Slavery, Race and Islam* (New York: Cambridge University Press, 2013).

85. Brian A. Catlos, *Kingdoms of Faith: A New History of Islamic Spain* (New York: Basic, 2018), 396, 402, 403.

86. Vincent Mignot and A. Hawkins, *The History of the Turkish or Ottoman Empire from its Foundation in 1300 . . . Volume II* (Exeter, UK: Stockdale, 1787), 23–24.

87. Stirling-Maxwell, *Don Juan of Austria or Passages from the History of the Sixteenth Century, 1547–1578*, 85.

88. Henry Stanley, *The Three Voyages of Vasco da Gama and his Viceroyalty . . .* (London: Hakluyt Society, 1869), xiv.

89. Alejandro de la Fuente, *Havana and the Atlantic World in the Sixteenth Century* (Chapel Hill: University of North Carolina Press, 2007), 1.

90. Paul E. Hoffman, *A New Andalucia and a Way to the Orient: The American Southeast During the Sixteenth Century* (Baton Rouge: Louisiana State University Press, 1990), 128.

4. FLORIDA INVADED

1. See also *A Brief History of the Life of Mary Queen of Scots and the Occasions that Brought her and Thomas Duke of Norfolk to their Tragical Ends, Shewing the Hopes the Papists then Had of a Popish Successor in England; and their Plots to Accomplish them with a Full Account of the Tryals of that Queen and of the Said Duke . . .* (London: Cockerill, 1681), Huntington Library. See also Marc Lesbarot, *History of New France* (Toronto: Champlain Society, 1907).

2. R. A. Brock, ed., *Documents Chiefly Unpublished Relating to the Huguenot Emigration to Virginia and to the Settlement at Manakin-Town* (Richmond: Virginia Historical Society, 1886). See also Henry Folmer, *Franco-Spanish Rivalry in North America, 1524–1763* (Glendale, CA: Clark, 1953).

3. W. J. Eccles, *The French in North America, 1500–1783* (Markham, ON: Fitzhenry and Whiteside, 1998), 2. See also Marc Lescarbot, *History of New France* (New York: Greenwood, 1968).

4. See e.g. Clements R. Markham, ed., *The Travels of Pedro de Sieza de Leon, A.D. 1532–1550 . . . Chronicle of Per* (London: Hakluyt, 1864).

5. Frederic J. Baumgartner, *France in the Sixteenth Century* (New York: St. Martin's, 1995), 147, 158, 159.

6. Memo from William Cecil, 1558–59, in Dan O'Sullivan, *The Reluctant Ambassador: The Life and Times of Sir Thomas Chaloner, Tudor Diplomat* (Gloucestershire, UK: Amberley, 2016), 109.

7. A. L. Beier, *Masterless Men: The Vagrancy Problem in England, 1560–1640* (London: Methuen, 1985), xix, xxi, 29.

8. David Quinn and A. N. Ryan, *England's Sea Empire, 1550–1642* (London: Allen and Unwin, 1983), 21, 24, 28. P. E. H. Hair, ed., *Hawkins in Guinea, 1567–1568* (Leipzig: University of Leipzig Press, 2000) and Harry Kelsey, *Sir John Hawkins: Queen Elizabeth's Slave Trader* (New Haven: Yale University Press, 2003) and Rayner Unwin, *The Defeat of John Hawkins: A Biography of His Third Slaving Voyage* (New York: Macmillan, 1960).

9. David M. Whitford, *The Curse of Ham in the Early Modern Era: The Bible and Justification for Slavery* (Aldershot, UK: Ashgate, 2009).

10. Miranda Kaufman, *Black Tudors: The Untold Story* (London: Oneworld, 2017), 244.

11. Frank Aydelotte, "Elizabethan Seamen in Mexico and the Ports of the Spanish Main," *American Historical Review* 43, no. 1 (October 1942): 1–19, 2.

12. John Barrow, *The Life, Voyages and Exploits of Admiral Sir Francis Drake . . .* (London: Murray, 1843), 9–10. See also *A True Declaration of the Troublesome Voyage of John Hawkins to the Parties of Guynea and the West Indies in the Year of Our Lord 1567 and 1568* (London: n.p., 1569), Huntington Library, San Marino.

13. Kaufman, *Black Tudors*, 77.

14. Report on John Hawkins in Henry Burrage, ed., *Early English and French Voyages, 1534–1608* (New York: Scribner's, 1906), 137–48. See also *The Voyages and Adventurers of Miles Philips, A West Country* Sailor . . . (London: Payne, 1724): At Cabo Verde there were "landed about 160 of our men to take Negroes," whereupon they were "set upon by a great number of Negroes who with their poison'd arrows hurt many of our men . . . they got but few Negroes." See also Wayne Franklin, *Discoverers, Explorers, Settlers: The Diligent Writers of Early America* (Chicago: University of Chicago Press, 1979).

15. John Butman and Simon Target, *New World Inc.: The Making of America by England's Merchant Adventurers* (New York: Little, Brown, 2018), 153,

16. "Hawkins-Third Voyage," in E. A. Payne, *Voyages of the Elizabethan Seamen to America* (London: De la Rue, 1880), 52–63, 53. See also Rayner Unwin, *The Defeat of John Hawkins: A Biography of His Third Slaving Voyage* (New York: Macmillan, 1960) and Harry Kelsey, *Sir John Hawkins: Queen Elizabeth's Slave Trader* (New Haven, CT: Yale University Press, 2003).

17. Kelsey, *Sir John Hawkins*, 18, 46, 65.

18. John Hawkins to Her Majesty, September 16, 1567, in Robert Lemon, ed., *Calendar of State Papers, Domestic Series, of the Reigns of Edward VI, Mary, Elizabeth, 1547–1580* (NL: Liechtenstein, 1967), 299.

19. Bishop Grindall to Lord Cecil, July 13, 1567 in Lemon, ed., *Calendar of* State Papers, 295.

20. Report, June 28, 1561 in Lemon, ed., *Calendar of State Papers*, 178.

21. Toby Green, *A Fistful of Shells: West Africa from the Rise of the Slave Trade to the Age of Revolution* (Chicago: University of Chicago Press, 2019), 117.

22. Green, *A Fistful of Shells*, 218.

23. Russell Lohse, *Africans into Creoles: Slavery, Ethnicity and Identity in Colonial Costa Rica* (Albuquerque: University of New Mexico Press, 2014), 10, 11. See also Cortez H. Williams, "The Black Experience: An Investigation of the Plight of Blacks in the United States and Latin America from the Fifteenth to the Nineteenth Century" (PhD diss., University of New Mexico, 1976). See also William B. Carter, *Indian Alliances and the Spanish in the Southwest, 750–1750* (Norman: University of Oklahoma, 2009). See also José Ignacio Avellaneda, *The Conquerors of the New Kingdom of Granada* (Albuquerque: University of New Mexico Press, 1995).

24. Danna A. Levin Rojo, *Return to Aztlan: Indians, Spaniards and the Invention of Nuevo Mexico* (Norman: University of Oklahoma Press, 2014).

25. Gustav Ungerer, *The Mediterranean Apprenticeship of British Slavery* (Madrid: Editorial Verbum, 2008), 92.

26. Peter Boyd Bowman, "Negro Slaves in Colonial Mexico," *The Americas* 36, no. 2 (October 1969): 134–51, 136.

27. "John Hawkins Investigates the Coast of Florida (1565)," in Louis B. Wright, ed., *The Elizabethans' America: A Collection of Early Reports by Englishmen on the New World* (Cambridge, MA: Harvard University Press, 1965), 36–45.

28. G. R. G. Conway, "Antonio de Espejo as a Familiar of the Mexican Inquisition," *New Mexico Historical Review*, 1931, HAI-14, Arizona State University, Tempe.

29. *Sailor Narratives of Voyages Along the New England Coast, 1524–1624, with Notes by George Parker Winship* (Boston: Houghton Mifflin, 1905), 26.

30. John W. Robertson, *Francis Drake & Other Early Explorers Along the Pacific Coast* (San Francisco: Grabhorn, 1927), 100, 38, 108.

31. Diego de Medrano to Don Juan de Cervantes Casaus, August 31, 1654, in Thomas Naylor and Charles W. Polzer, eds., *The Presidio and Militia on the Northern Frontier of New Spain: A Documentary History, Volume I, 1570–1700* (Tucson: University of Arizona Press, 1986), 411, 424.

32. Luis Weckmann, *The Medieval Heritage of Mexico* (New York: Fordham University Press, 1992), 86.

33. Robert Goodwin, *Crossing the Continent, 1507–1540: The Story of the First African American Explorer of the American South* (New York: HarperCollins, 2008, 53).

34. *A True Declaration of the Troublesome Voyage of John Hawkins to the Parties of . . . the West Indies in the Year of Our Lord 1567 and 1568.*

35. Conway Whittle Sams, *The Conquest of Virginia: The First Attempt* (Norfolk, VA: Keyser–Doherty, 1924), x.

36. J. P. D. Cooper, *The Queen's Agent: Sir Francis Walsingham and the Rise of Espionage in Elizabethan England* (New York: Pegasus, 2012), 99.

37. "The Bull of Excommunication Against Elizabeth (February 25, 1570)," in Donald Stump and Susan M. Felch, eds., *Elizabeth and Her Age* (New York: Norton, 2009), 156.

38. John Lewis Gaddis, *On Grand Strategy* (New York: Penguin, 2018), 139. See also Mary O'Dowd, ed., *Calendar of State Papers: Ireland, Tudor Period, 1571–1575* (Dublin: Irish Manuscripts Commission, 2000).

39. John Cooper, *The Queen's Agent: Sir Francis Walsingham and the Rise of Espionage in Elizabethan England* (New York: Pegasus, 2012), 150, 163. See also *A Brief History of the Life of Mary Queen of Scots . . . with a Full Account of the Tryals of that Queen . . . from the Papers of a Secretary of Sir Francis Walsingham* (London: Cockerill, 1681).

40. John Miller, *Early Modern Britain, 1450–1750* (New York: Cambridge University Press, 2017), 124.

41. C. R. Boxer, ed., *Further Selections from the Tragic History of the Sea, 1559–1565* (London: Hakluyt, 1967), 13. See also Clements R. Markham, ed., *The Travels*

NOTES TO PAGES 104–107

of Pedro de Cieza de Leon, A.D. 1532–1550 . . . Chronicle of Peru (London: Hakluyt Society, 1864).

42. John W. Blake, *Europeans in West Africa, 1450–1560: Documents to Illustrate the Nature and Scope of Portuguese Enterprise in West Africa, the Abortive Attempt of Castilians to Create an Empire there and the Early English Voyages to Barbary and Guinea, Volume II* (London: Hakluyt Society, 1942), 261.

43. Sarah Gristwood, *Game of Queens: The Women Who Made Sixteenth-Century Europe* (New York: Basic, 2016), 229, 246. See also David Grummit, *The Calais Garrison and Military Service in England, 1436–1558* (Woodbridge, UK: Boydell and Brewer, 2008),

44. Clare Kellar, *Scotland, England and the Reformation, 1534–1561* (New York: Oxford University Press, 2004).

45. Thomas Wright, *Queen Elizabeth and Her Times: A Series of Original Letters . . .* (London: Colburn, 1838), xxxiv–xxxvii, xlvii. See also Bernadette Cunningham, ed., *Calendar of State Papers: Ireland, Tudor Period, 1568–1571* (Dublin: Irish Manuscripts Commission, 2010).

46. O'Sullivan, *The Reluctant Ambassador*, 156.

47. Sir William Stirling-Maxwell, *Don Juan of Austria or Passages from the History of the Sixteenth Century, 1547–1578* (London: Longmans, Green, 1883), 118–20.

48. Jacques Heers, *The Barbary Corsairs: Pirates, Plunder and Warfare in the Mediterranean, 1480–1580* (New York: Skyhorse, 2018), 102.

49. Brian A. Catlos, *Kingdoms of Faith: A New History of Islamic Spain* (New York: Basic, 2018), 407, 414.

50. Stirling-Maxwell, *Don Juan of Austria*, 120, 121.

51. Stirling-Maxwell, *Don Juan of Austria*, 172, 286.

52. Catlos, *Kingdoms of Faith*, 420, 422.

53. María Antonia Garcés, ed., *An Early Modern Dialogue with Islam: Antonio de Sosa's 'Topography of Algiers (1612)* (South Bend, IN: University of Notre Dame Press, 2011), 27.

54. Leslie Pierce, *Empress of the East: How a European Slave Girl Became Queen of the Ottoman Empire* (New York: Basic, 2017), 269, 285.

55. Royal Cedula, Madrid, to House of Trade, June 5, 1566, AGI 148-2-8, Tomo 16, John Stetson Collection, St. Augustine Historical Society.

56. Roger Crowley, *Empires of the Sea: The Siege of Malta, the Battle of Lepanto and the Contest for the Center of the World* (New York: Random House, 2008).

57. Philip Wayne Powell, "Presidios and Towns of the Silver Frontier of New Spain, 1550–1580," *Hispanic American Historical Review* 24, no. 2 (May 1944): 179–200, 187. See also Robert Davidsson, *Indian River: A History of the Ais Indians in Spanish Florida* (West Palm Beach, FL: Ais Indian Project, 2004).

58. Butman and Target, *New World Inc.*, 125. See also David G. Moore, et.al., "Conflict, Violence and Warfare in La Florida," in Clay Mathers, Jeffrey M. Mitchem, and Charles M. Haecker, eds., *Native and Spanish New Worlds: Sixteenth Century Entradas in the American Southwest and Southeast* (Tucson:

University of Arizona Press, 2014), 231–50, and in the same volume see Clay
Mathers, "Contest and Violence on the Northern Borderlands Frontier:
Patterns of Native-European Conflict in the Sixteenth Century Southwest,"
205–30.

59. Butman and Target, *New World Inc.*, 125.

60. Clarence Henry Haring, *Trade and Navigation Between Spain and the Indies:
In Time of the Habsburgs* (Cambridge, MA: Harvard University Press, 1918),
228.

61. Pedro Menendez de Aviles to Madrid, no date, in *The Unwritten History of
Old St. Augustine Copied from the Spanish Archives in Seville, Spain*, trans.
Annie Averette (St. Augustine, FL: The Record, circa 1909), 5–10, University
of Virginia, Charlottesville.

62. Larry Eugene Rivers, *Slavery in Florida* (Gainesville: University Press of
Florida, 2000), 3.

63. Anna Brickhouse, *The Unsettlement of America: Translation, Interpretation
and the Story of Don Luis Velasco, 1560–1945* (New York: Oxford University
Press, 2015), 1, 27. See also Charles Hudson et.al., eds., *The Transformation of
the Southeastern Indians, 1540–1760* (Jackson: University Press of Mississippi,
2002).

64. R. R. Otis, compiler, *French Intrusion into Spain's La Florida*, 1953, Brown
University. See also Nicolas Le Challeux, *A True and Perfect Description of the
Last Voyage . . . Attempted by Captaine John Rybault and General of the French
Men into Terra Florida, This Yeare Past 1565 . . .* Massachusetts Historical
Society, Boston, and Le Challeux, *Last Voyage of Ribaut* (London: n.p., 1566
[from the original in the British Museum, April 1920], Brown University. See
also Paul E. Hoffman, *Florida's Frontiers* (Bloomington: Indiana University
Press, 2002). See also transcription about Dominique de Gourgue, 1530–1593,
Box 1, Buckingham Smith Papers, New-York Historical Society.

65. Woodbury Lowery, *The Spanish Settlements within the Present Limits of the
United States, 1562–1574* (New York: Putnam, 1911), 95–96.

66. Luys de Padilla, Santo Domingo to D. Francisco de Vera, Official Judge
of Affairs of the Indies, 27 July 1565AGI 53-6-5 T.1/294 bis, John Stetson
Collection.

67. Reverend John Harrington, "The First Home of the Huguenots in North
America," Edwards Huguenot Society of America, 1896, New-York Historical
Society.

68. "Original Warrant of Philip II to General . . . Menendez de Avile," February 3,
1562, Volume 2, Woodbury Lowery Papers, Library of Congress, Washington,
D.C.

69. Emma Rochelle Williams, "The Huguenot Colonization at Fort Caroline near
the Mouth of St. John's River, Florida, 1562–1565," 1923, New-York Historical
Society. See also George Andrews Moriarty, *The New England Huguenots*
(London: Spottiswoode, 1929).

70. Preface in Jeanette Thurber Connor, ed., Jean Ribaut, *The Whole & True
Discouerye of Terra Florida . . .* [edition of 1563] (DeLand: Florida State

Historical Society, 1927), x, 9, 12. See also *The Famous Hystorye of the Life and Death of Captain Thomas Stukeley*, 1605, Huntington Library. See also Mickaël Augeron, John de Bry, and Annick Notter, eds., *Floride, Un Rêve Français (1562–1565)* (La Rochelle: Musée du Nouveau Monde, 2012).

71. Reverend Thomas Lathbury, *Guy Fawkes or a Complete History of the Gunpowder Treason, 1605* (London: Parker, 1839), 4.

72. Juan E. Tazon, *The Life and Times of Thomas Stukeley, (c. 1525–1578)* (Aldershot, UK: Ashgate, 2003).

73. O'Sullivan, *The Reluctant Ambassador*, 232.

74. Judith John, *Dark History of the Tudors: Murder, Adultery, Incest, Witchcraft, Wars, Religious Persecution, Piracy* (London: Amber, 2014), 154. See also John Foxe, *Foxe's Book of Martyrs: The Acts and Monuments of the Church* (London: Virtue, 1844).

75. David Arbesu, ed., *Pedro Menendez de Aviles and the Conquest of Florida: A New Manuscript* (Gainesville: University Press of Florida, 2017), 206. See also Gonzalo Solis de Meras, *Pedro Menendez de Aviles and the Conquest of Florida* (Gainesville: University Press of Florida, 2017). See also Gonzalo Solis de Meras, *Pedro Menendez de Aviles, Adelanto, Governor and Captain General* . . . (DeLand: Florida Historical Society, 1923).

76. Charles W. Baird, *History of the Huguenot Emigration to America* (New York: Dodd, Mead, 1885), 74.

77. Paul E. Hoffman, *A New Andalucia and a Way to the Orient: The American Southeast During the Sixteenth Century* (Baton Rouge: Louisiana State University Press, 1990), 140. See also Garcilaso de la Vega, *The Florida of the Inca: A History of Adelanto Hernando de Soto* . . . (Austin: University of Texas Press, 1951).

78. Rene Laudonniere, *A Notable History Containing Four Voyages Made by Certain French Captains Unto Florida*, ed. Martin Basanier and trans. Richard Hakluyt (Larchmont, NY: Stevens, Son and Stiles, [London, 1587] 1964), vii, Brown University.

79. Andrew Lawler, *The Secret Token: Myth, Obsession, and the Search for the Lost Colony of Roanoke* (New York: Doubleday, 2018), 21.

80. Jane Hawkes Liddell, "Colonization Failures in Brazil, Florida and North Carolina," in Peter Steven Gannon, ed., *Huguenot Refugees in the Settling of Colonial America* (New York: Huguenot Society of America, 1987), 63–74, 68.

81. See e.g. Anonymous, *"The Discovery of Florida: Being a True Relation of the Vicissitudes that Attended the Governor Don Hernando de Soto and Some Notables of Portugal in the Discovery of Florida* . . . , trans. Buckingham Smith (San Francisco: Grabhorn Press for the Book Club of California, 1946).

82. David Arbesu, ed., *Pedro Menendez de Aviles and the Conquest of Florida: A New Manuscript* (Gainesville: University Press of Florida, 2017), 206.

83. Lowery, *The Spanish Settlements Within the Present Limits of the United States, Florida, 1562–1574*, 143, 96, 160. See also Gonzalo Solis de Meras, *Pedro Menendez de Aviles: Adelanto, Governor and Captain General of Florida* (DeLand: Florida State Historical Society, 1923).

84. Alejandro de la Fuente, *Havana and the Atlantic in the Sixteenth Century* (Chapel Hill: University of North Carolina Press, 2011), 45.
85. Hernan Perez, Santo Domingo to Madrid, November 28, 1567, AGI 53-6-5 T.1/363, John Stetson Collection.
86. Luis R. Arana, translator, Contract in Name of Crown for Pedro Menendez on Expedition to Florida, *El Escribano* 2, no. 1 (January 1965): 18–26, 18.
87. Governor Francisco Bahamon, Puerto Rico to Madrid, February 10, 1566, AGI 54-3-6, John Stetson Collection.
88. Juan Ponce de León, Puerto Rico to Madrid, April 20, 1566, AGI 53-6-5 T.1, John Stetson Collection.
89. Pedro Menendez to Princess Juana, May 13, 1557, in *Letters of Pedro Menendez de Aviles and Other Documents Relative to his Career, 1555–1574*, vol. no. 1 ed. and trans. Edward W. Lawson, St. Augustine Historical Society.
90. Instructions given by Philip II to Captain General Menendez, January 23, 1562, in Lawson, ed., *Letters of Pedro Menendez de Aviles*.
91. Pedro Menendez de Aviles to King Philip II, February–March 1565, in Lawson, ed., *Letters of Pedro Menendez de Aviles*.
92. Herbert Ingram Priestley, *Tristan de Luna: Conquistador of the Old South: A Study of Spanish Imperial Strategy* (Glendale, CA: Clark, 1936), 91. See also Charles Hudson, *The Juan Pardo Expeditions: Explorations of the Carolinas and Tennessee, 1566–1568* (Washington, D.C.: Smithsonian, 1990). See also Herbert Ingram Priestley, ed., *The Luna Papers: Documents Relating to the Expedition of Don Tristan de Luna y Arrelano for the Conquest of La Florida in 1559–1561*, vol. 1 (DeLand: Florida Historical Society, 1928).
93. Lewis Hanke, *Bartolomé de las Casas: An Interpretation of His Life and Writings* (The Hague: Nijhoff, 1951), 7.
94. Pedro Menendez to His Catholic Majesty, October 15, 1565, in Lawson, ed., *Letters of Pedro Menendez de Aviles*, vol. 2.
95. Interrogatory of Pedro Menendez de Aviles, May 16, 1558, in Lawson, ed., *Letters of Pedro Menendez de Aviles*
96. Brochure from St. Augustine Jewish Historical Society, circa 2012, vertical file, St. Augustine Historical Society.
97. Seymour B. Liebman, *The Inquisitions and the Jews in the New World: Summaries of Procesos, 1500–1810* (Coral Gables, FL: University of Miami Press, 1974), 13. See also Joseph M. Corcos, *A Synopsis of the Jews of Curacao* (Curaçao: Imprenta de La Libreria, 1897), Brown University.
98. Seymour B. Liebman, *A Guide to Jewish References in the Mexican Colonial Era, 1521–1821* (Philadelphia: University of Pennsylvania Press, 1964), 8, 9.
99. Robert J. McCue, "The Holy Office of the Inquisition: Its Role in New Mexico," uncertain provenance and date, University of New Mexico, Albuquerque. On the Mexican Inquisition of 1571 see Ron D. Hart et al., *Fractured Faiths: Spanish Judaism, The Inquisition and New World Identities* (Albuquerque: University of New Mexico Press, 2016), 18.
100. Jane Landers, "Africans in the Land of Ayllon," no date, vertical file on "Blacks Miscellaneous," St. Augustine Historical Society. See also

Memorandum to Eugene Lyon, October 26, 1993, vertical file, St. Augustine Historical Society.

101.   Jerald T. Milanich, *Florida Indians and the Invasion from Europe* (Gainesville: University Press of Florida, 1995), 111.

102.   Pedro Menendez to King Philip II, February–March 1565 in Lawson, ed., *Letters of Pedro Menendez de Aviles*.

103.   Pedro Menendez to King Philip II, December 5, 1565, in Lawson, ed., *Letters of Pedro Menendez de Aviles*, vol. 2. See also Katherine Swan Lawson, *Martin de Arguelles: The First Spaniard Born in St. Augustine and the First European Child born on the Atlantic Coast of the United States in a Permanent European Settlement* (St. Augustine: St. Augustine Historical Society, 1941), Brown University.

104.   Pedro Menendez de Aviles to Madrid, December 5, 1565, AGI 54-1-31/143, John Stetson Collection.

105.   Pedro Menendez to His Catholic Majesty, December 4, 1569, in ibid., Lawson, ed. *Letters of Pedro Menendez de Aviles*, vol. 2. See also James Anthony Froude, *English Seamen in the Sixteenth Century* (London: Longmans, 1895) and Gonzalo Solis de Meras, *Pedro Menendez de Aviles and the Conquest of Florida* (Gainesville: University Press of Florida, 2017).

106.   Pedro Menendez to Madrid, September 10, 1565, AGI 143-3-12, John Stetson Collection, St. Augustine Historical Society.

107.   Report by Pedro Menendez Aviles, March 28, 1568, AGI MF WL MSS v 2 BM, MSS 33, 983, fol. 324, John Stetson Collection. See also Eugene Lyon, *The Enterprise of Florida: Pedro Menendez de Aviles and the Spanish Conquest of 1565–1568* (Gainesville: University Press of Florida, 1983).

108.   Royal Audencia de Santo Domingo to Madrid, October 18, 1569, AGI 53-6-5 T.1/357, John Stetson Collection.

109.   Royal Audencia de Santo Domingo to Madrid, October 18, 1569, AGI 53-6-5 T.1/357, John Stetson Collection.

110.   Report, circa 1570, AGI 145-1-11.

111.   Hugh Thomas, *World without End: Spain, Philip II, and the First Global Empire* (New York: Random House, 2015), 309: The number grew to 16 by 1586, then 19 in 1588, 18 in 1591, and 38 in 1595.

112.   De la Fuente, *Havana and the Atlantic in the Sixteenth Century*, 174.

113.   Jerry Brotton, *The Sultan and the Queen: The Untold Story of Elizabeth and Islam* (New York: Viking, 2016), 61. See also *A True Discourse Historicall of the Succeeding Governors in the Netherlands and the Civill Warres There Begun in the Yeere 1565 . . .* (London: Lownes, 1602), New-York Historical Society.

114.   Conway Whittle Sams, *The Conquest of Virginia: The Forest Primeval . . .* (New York: Putnam, 1916), 5.

115.   Thomas Wright, *Queen Elizabeth and Her Times: A Series of Original Letters . . .*, vol. 1 (London: Colburn, 1838), xxxiv–xxxv, xxxvii, xlvii. See also William Stevens Perry, *The Connection of the Church of England with Early American Discovery and Colonization* (Whitefish, Montana: Kessinger, 2007, originally published 1863), Massachusetts Historical Society, Boston.

116. Mary Ann Lyons, *Franco–Irish Relations, 150–1610: Politics, Migration and Trade* (London: Royal Historical Society, 2003).

117. Victoria Freeman, *Distant Relations: How My Ancestors Colonized North America* (Toronto: McClelland and Stewart, 2000), 29.

118. David Childs, *Invading America*, 214.

119. Jonathan Hart, *Representing the New World: The English and French Uses of the Example of Spain* (New York: Palgrave, 2000), 97.

120. Council of the Indies to Madrid, October 13, 1565, AGI 140-7-32, John Stetson Collection.

5. TURNING POINT

1. Taliesin Trow, *Sir Martin Frobisher: Seamen, Soldier, Explorer* (Barnsley, UK: Pen and Sword, 2010), 110, 113. See also Norman Thrower, ed., *Sir Francis Drake and the Famous Voyage, 1577–1580* (Berkeley: University of California Press, 1984).

2. Jerry Brotton, *The Sultan and the Queen: The Untold Story of Elizabeth and Islam* (New York: Viking, 2016), 45.

3. See for example, Thomas Churchyard, *A True Discourse Historical of the Succeeding Governors in the Netherlands and the Civil Warres There Begun in the Yeere 1565 . . .* (London: Lownes, 1602).

4. Andrea Clarke, *Tudor Monarchs: Lives in Letters* (London: British Library, 2017), 136, 161, 171, 185, 188.

5. Alison Games, *The Web of Empire: English Cosmopolitans in an Age of Expansion 1560–1660* (Oxford: Oxford University Press, 2008), 50.

6. Brotton, *The Sultan and the Queen*, 63. See also Bruce Ware Allen, *The Great Siege of Malta: The Epic Battle between the Ottoman Empire and the Knights of St. John* (Lebanon, NH: University Press of New England, 2015).

7. Sir William Stirling-Maxwell, *Don Juan of Austria, or Passages from the History of the Sixteenth Century, 1547–1578*, Volume I (London: Longmans, Green, 1883), 85.

8. Ibid., 290, 291.

9. Report to House of Trade, June 5, 1566, AGI 148-2-8, Tomo 16, Indiferente General 1967, John Stetson Collection.

10. Memorandum to Pedro Menendez, January 26, 1573, AGI 86-5-19, Santo Domingo, Royal Cedula-Madrid, John Stetson Collection.

11. Report, March 5, 1570, AGI 140-7-32, Indiferente General, John Stetson Collection.

12. See for example, Olivia Remie Constable, *To Live Like a Moor: Christian Perceptions of Muslim Identity in Medieval and Early Modern Spain* (Philadelphia: University of Pennsylvania Press, 2018).

13. Ibid., 286, 340.

14. John Butman and Simon Target, *New World Inc.: The Making of America by England's Merchant Adventurers* (New York: Little, Brown, 2018), 97.

15. David Childs, *Invading America*, 108.

16. Roger Crowley, *Empires of the Sea: The Siege of Malta, the Battle of Lepanto*

and the Contest for the Center of the World (New York: Random House, 2008), 279, 277, xviii, 66, 74, 198, 201.

17.   Jacques Heers, *The Barbary Corsairs: Pirates, Plunder, and Warfare in the Mediterranean, 1480–1580* (New York: Skyhorse, 2018), 103, 106, 109, 112, 113, 202.

18.   Stirling-Maxwell, *Don Juan of Austria*, vol. 2, 1, 22.

19.   Cf. Report, 1503, Volume 2, Woodbury Lowery Papers, Library of Congress: Thirty galleys arrive in Marseilles, bringing the Turkish envoy to France, slated to meet with the monarch (from Archives Nationales, Paris).

20.   John J. Guilmartin, Jr., "Ideology and Conflict: The Wars of the Ottoman Empire, 1453–1606," in Douglas M. Peers, ed., *Warfare and Empires: Contact and Conflict Between European and Non-European Military and Maritime Forces and Cultures* (Brookfield, VT: Ashgate, 1997), 1–53; in the same volume see also John Vogt, "Saint Barbara's Legion: Portuguese Artillery in the Struggle for Morocco, 1415–1578," *Military Affairs* 41, no. 4 (1977): 73–79, 73.

21.   Ellis Christian Lenz, *Muzzle Flashes: Five Centuries of Firearms and Men* (Huntington, WV: Standard, 1944), 18, 24: On the latter page, see the following: "The supposed origin of the snap-chance (snap-cock) firearm would indicate that chicken-thievery was a proclivity of certain Hollanders long before the American Negro, a henhouse and a moonless night became a regulation formula for humor."

22.   Baltasar Fra-Molinero, "Juan Latino and His Racial Difference," in T. F. Earle and K. J. P. Lowe, eds., *Black Africans in Renaissance Europe* (New York: Cambridge University Press, 2007). In the same volume see Sergio Tognetti, "The Trade in Black African Slaves in Fifteenth Century Florence," 213–24, and Martin Casares, "Free and Freed Black Africans in Granada in the Time of the Spanish Renaissance," 247–60.

23.   Thomas Newton, *Notable Histories of the Saracens . . .* (London: Veale, 1575).

24.   Report, February 1574, in Robert Lemon, ed., *Calendar of State Papers, Domestic Series, of the Reigns of Edward VI, Mary, Elizabeth, 1547–1580* (Nendeln, Liechtenstein: Kraus, 1967), 490.

25.   Report, September 1579 in Ibid., Robert Lemon, ed., *Calendar of State Papers, Domestic Series, of the Reigns of Edward VI, Mary, Elizabeth, 1547–1580*, 633.

26.   John K. Thornton and Linda Heywood, "The Treason of Dom Pedro Nkanga a Mvemba Against Dom Diogo, King of Kongo, 1550," in Kathryn Joy McKnight and Leo J. Garofalo, eds., *Afro-Latino Voices: Narratives from the Early Modern Ibero-Atlantic World, 1550–1812* (Indianapolis: Hackett, 2009), 2–37, 3.

27.   Mark Meuwese, *Brothers in Arms, Partners in Trade*, 81–82. See also Koen Bostoen and Inge Brinkman, eds., *The Kongo Kingdom: The Origins, Dynamics and Cosmopolitan Culture of an African Polity* (New York: Cambridge University Press, 2018).

28.   Frederic J. Baumgartner, *France in the Sixteenth Century*, 256, 217. See also Ernest Varamynd, *A True and Plaine Report of the Furious Outrages of Fraunce & the Horrible and Shameful Slaughter . . . without any Respect* (Striveling:

n.p., 1573), Huntington Library: There was reportedly "butcherly murthering . . . in all the towns of Fraunce."

29.   Trow, *Sir Martin Frobisher*, 23, 28. See also *The History of the Bloody Massacres of the Protestants in France in the Year of Our Lord, 1572 . . . written in Latin by the Famous Historian . . .* (London: Leigh, 1674), Huntington Library. At the latter site, see also "Sir Francis Walsingham's Letter Book Whilst Ambassador in France, 1570–1572."

30.   Sarah Gristwood, *Game of Queens: The Women Who Made Sixteenth-Century Europe* (New York: Basic, 2018), 303.

31.   Gerald Horne, *The Apocalypse of Settler Colonialism: The Roots of Slavery, White Supremacy, and Capitalism in Seventeenth Century North America and the Caribbean* (New York: Monthly Review Press, 2018), 22.

32.   Sarah Gristwood, 292.

33.   Report, October 25, 1582, in Robert Lemon, ed., *Calendar of State Papers, Domestic Series of the Reign of Elizabeth, 1581–1590 . . .* (Nendeln, Liechtenstein: Kraus, 1967), 73.

34.   James Eels, *Address before the Cleveland Presbytery on the Tercentenary Anniversary of the Death of John Knox, the Formation of the First Presbytery in England and the Massacre of St. Bartholomew's Day* (Cleveland: Leader, 1872). See also Jacques-Auguste de Thou, *The History of the Bloody Massacres of the Protestants in France in the Year of our Lord, 1572, Written in Latin by the Famous Historian. . . .* (London: Leigh, 1674).

35.   Amias Paulet to William Cecil, October 13, 1568, in Mary Anne Everett Green, ed., *Calendar of State Papers, Domestic Series, of the Reign of Elizabeth, Addenda, 1566–1579* (Nendeln, Liechtenstein: Kraus, 1967), 42

36.   Amias Paulet to Sir Hugh Paulet, December 13, 1568, in Green, ed., *Calendar of State Papers, Domestic Series, of the Reign of Elizabeth, Addenda, 1566–1579*, 67.

37.   Louis B. Wright, *Religion and Empire: The Alliance Between Piety and Commerce in English Expansion, 1558–1625* (Berkeley: University of California Press, 1943), vi, 33, 42.

38.   Butman and Target, *New World, Inc.*, 137, 138. See also Ruth Whelan and Carol Baxter, eds., *Toleration and Religious Identity: The Edict of Nantes and Its Implications in France, Britain and Ireland* (Portland, OR: Four Courts, 2003), 16.

39.   Ralph Norris, *A Warning to London by the Fall of Antwerp* (London: Long Shop, 1577).

40.   Mark Meuwese, *Brothers in Arms, Partners in Trade: Dutch-Indigenous Alliances in the Atlantic World, 1595–1674* (Leiden: Brill, 2012), 19.

41.   Taliesin Trow, *Sir Martin* Frobisher, 72.

42.   Butman and Target, *New World Inc.*, 77, 81.

43.   J. N. Hillgarth, *The Mirror of Spain, 1500–1700: The Formation of a Myth* (Ann Arbor: University of Michigan Press, 2000), 421–22, 425.

44.   Enrique Garcia Hernan, *Ireland and Spain in the Reign of Philip II* (Dublin: Four Courts, 2009).

45. Mr. Bodenham to Lord Burghley, circa 1570s, in Green, ed., *Calendar of State Papers . . . Addenda, 1566–1579*, 555.

46. Report to Lord Wharton, May 19, 1557 in Green, ed., *Calendar of State Papers . . . Addenda, 1566–1579*, 449–50.

47. "The King and Queen to the Earl of Shrewsbury," circa 1557, in Green, ed., *Calendar of State Papers...Addenda, 1566–1579*, 450.

48. Pedro Menendez to His Catholic Majesty, August 5, 1574 in *Letters of Pedro Menendez de Aviles and Other Documents Relative to his Career, 1555–1574*, ed. and trans. Edward W. Lawson, St. Augustine Historical Society.

49. Brotton, *The Sultan and the Queen*, 47, 76.

50. John Chamberlain to Dud. Carleton, January 17, 1599, in Mary Anne Everett Green, ed., *Calendar of State Papers. Domestic Series, of the Reign of Elizabeth, 1598–1601* (Nendeln, Liechtenstein: Kraus, 1967), 152.

51. George Peele, *The Battell of Alcazar, Fought in Barbarie, Between Sebastian King of Portugall and Abdemelee King of Morocco, with the Death of Captain Stukeley* (London: Bandworth, 1594), Huntington Library. At the same site see Girolamo Franchi di Conestaggio, *Historie of the Uniting of the Kingdom of Portugall to the Crowne of Castill: Containing the Last Warres of the Portugalls Against the Moores of Africke, the End of the House of Portugall . . .* (London: Hatfield, 1600). At the same site see also *The Strangest Adventure that Ever Happened Either in the Ages Passed or Present Containing a Discourse Concerning the Success of the King of Portugall Dom Sebastian From the Time of His Voyage to Affricke, When He Was Lost in the Battell Against the Infidels, in the Year 1578, Unto the Sixth of January . . . 1601* (London: Henson, 1601).

52. Report to Sir William Cecil, circa 1570s, in Green, ed., *Calendar of State Papers . . . Addenda, 1566–1579*, 248.

53. John Butman and Simon Target, *New World Inc.*, 140, 143.

54. Mark Meuwese, *Brothers in Arms, Partners in Trade*, 23.

55. Robert Aleksander Markys, *The Jesuit Order as a Synagogue of Jews* (Leiden: Brill, 2010).

56. Juan E. Tazon, *The Life and Times of Thomas Stukeley (c. 1525–1578)* (Aldershot, UK: Ashgate, 2005). See also John Izon, *Sir Thomas Stucley: Traitor Extraordinary* (London: Melrose, 1956). (Not atypically, this adventurer's name was spelled variously.)

57. Walter Raleigh, *The English Voyages of the Sixteenth Century* (Glasgow: Maclehose, 1910), 166, 167. See also *The Famous Historye of the Life and Death of Captaine Thomas Stukeley* (1605), Huntington Library.

58. Harry Potter, *Edinburgh Under Siege, 1571–1573* (Stroud, UK: Tempus, 2003). See also Clare Kellar, *Scotland, England and the Reformation, 1534–1561* (New York: Oxford University Press, 2004).

59. Richard Copley Christie, ed., *Letters of Sir Thomas Copley . . . Queen Elizabeth and Her Ministers* (London: Chiswick, 1897), xxviii, xxxv: Sir Thomas was among those who fought alongside the forces of Madrid, though it is unclear if he might have been a double—or even a triple—agent.

60. Mary Ann Lyons, *Franco–Irish Relations, 1500–1610: Politics, Migration and Trade* (London: Royal Historical Society, 2003).

61. Eugene Lyon, "St. Augustine, 1580: The Living Community," in Kathleen A. Deegan, ed., *America's Ancient City: Spanish St. Augustine, 1565–1763* (New York: Garland, 1991), 194–207, 198.

62. Excerpt of Narrative of Francisco Lopez de Mendoza, September 12–29, 1565, in Lawson, ed., *Letters of Pedro Menendez de Aviles and Other Documents Relative to his Career, 1555–1574.*

63. Narrative of a Voyage made by Captain Gonzalo of Pensacola, September 28, 1566, in Lawson, ed., *Letters of Pedro Menendez de Aviles and Other Documents Relative to his Career, 1555–1574.*

64. Pedro Menendez de Aviles to Madrid, September 23, 1567, in Lawson, ed., *Letters of Pedro Menendez de Aviles and Other Documents Relative to his Career, 1555–1574,* and in the same volume Pedro Menendez to His Catholic Majesty, November 27, 1569.

65. Pedro Menendez to His Catholic Majesty, December 31, 1559 in Lawson, ed., *Letters of Pedro Menendez de Aviles and Other Documents Relative to his Career, 1555–1574.*

66. Petition of Alonso Ordonez, Captain Diego Flores de Robles and Vicente Manrique, February 20, 1577, AGI 54—5-16/13, Santo Domingo 231 and Report from the Council of Indies, February 28, 1577, AGI 140-7-33, Indiferente General 739, John Stetson Collection.

67. Report, circa 1570, AGI 145-1-11, Indiferente General 1383, John Stetson Collection.

68. Governor Francisco Carreno to His Catholic Majesty, February 12, 1578, AGI 54-1-15, Santo Domingo 99, John Stetson Collection.

69. Investigation into Esteban de las Alas, November 10–24, 1570, in Lawson, ed., *Letters of Pedro Menendez de Aviles and Other Documents Relative to his Career, 1555–1574.*

70. Paul E. Hoffman, *A New Andalucia and a Way to the Orient* (Baton Rouge: Louisiana State University Press, 2004), 140, 141, 225.

71. Charles E. Bennett, ed., *Three Voyages: Rene Laudonniere* (Gainesville: University Press of Florida, 1975), xiii, 9, 13: There were complaints of hermaphrodites or what in the twenty-first century could be termed "intersex people" and "sodomites" among the indigenes. See also Jean Ribaut, *The Whole and True Discoverie of Terra Florida, a Facsimile Reprint of the London Edition of 1563,* ed. Jeannette Thurber Connor (DeLand: Florida Historical Society, 1927) and Annick Notter et al., eds., *Floride, Un Rêve Français (1562–1565)* (La Rochelle: Musée du Nouveau Monde, 2012).

72. Luys de Padilla to D. Francisco de Vera, Official Judge of Affairs of the Indies, July 27, 1565, AGI 53-6-5 T.1/294 bis., John Stetson Collection.

73. Pedro Menendez to His Catholic Majesty, September 10, 1565, AGI 143-3-12, John Stetson Collection.

74. Council of the Indies to His Catholic Majesty, October 13, 1565, AGI 140-7-32, Indiferente General 738, John Stetson Collection.

75. Pedro Menendez Marquez to His Catholic Majesty, July 22, 1571, AGI 41-6-1/36, John Stetson Collection.

76. Report, November 12, 1572, AGI 79-4-2, Tomo V, Santo Domingo 1122, Royal Cedula, El Pardo to Yucatan, John Stetson Collection.

77. Juan Ponce de León to His Catholic Majesty, April 20, 1566, AGI 53-6-5, T.1, John Stetson Collection.

78. Report from Pedro Menendez, March 28, 1568, AGI MF WL MSS v2 BM add MSS 33, 983, fol. 324, John Stetson Collection.

79. Royal Audencia de Santo Domingo to His Catholic Majesty, October 18, 1569, AGI 53-6-5 T.1/357, John Stetson Collection.

80. Herman Perez to His Catholic Majesty, November 28, 1567, AGI 53-6-5 T.1/363, John Stetson Collection.

81. Garcia Osorio of Havana to His Catholic Majesty, 1571, AGI 54-3-31, Santo Domingo, John Stetson Collection.

82. Pedro Menendez to His Catholic Majesty, January 30, 1566, in Lawson, ed., *Letters of Pedro Menendez de Aviles and Other Documents Relative to his Career, 1555–1574*.

83. Pedro Menendez to His Catholic Majesty, December 5, 1565, AGI 54-1-31/143, Santo Domingo 115, John Stetson Collection.

84. Governor Francisco Bahamon to Madrid, February 10, 1565, AGI 54-3-6, John Stetson Collection.

85. Pedro Menendez to His Catholic Majesty, December 3, 1570, in Lawson, ed., *Letters of Pedro Menendez de Aviles and Other Documents Relative to his Career, 1555–1574*.

86. Report, March 20, 1571, AGI 139-1-13, Tomo 13 Indiferente General 427, John Stetson Collection.

87. Pedro Menendez to His Catholic Majesty, January 1570, in Lawson, ed., *Letters of Pedro Menendez de Aviles and Other Documents Relative to his Career, 1555–1574*.

88. Jane Landers, "Africans in the Land of Ayllon: The Exploration and Settlement of the Southeast," in Jeannine Cook, ed., *Columbus and the Land of Ayllon: The Exploration and Settlement of the Southeast* (Darien, GA: Darien Printer News, 1992), 105–24, 114. See also Eloy Gallegos, *Santa Elena: The Spanish Pioneers in United States History; Spanish Settlements on the Spanish Seaboard from Florida to Virginia, 1513 to 1607* (Knoxville, TN: Villagra, 1998) and Eugene Lyon, *Saint Elena: A Brief History of the Colony, 1566–1587* (Columbia: Institute of Archaeology and Anthropology, University of South Carolina, 1984), St. Augustine Historical Society.

89. His Catholic Majesty to Pedro Menendez, May 12, 1566, in Lawson, ed., *Letters of Pedro Menendez de Aviles and Other Documents Relative to his Career, 1555–1574*.

90. Charles H. Reynolds, *Old Saint Augustine: A Story of Three Centuries* (St. Augustine, FL: self-pub., 1885), 20.

91. Susan Richburg Parker, "Slaves Flee St. Augustine—1603," *El Escribano* 41 (2004): 1–8, 2.

92. Report, 1561–1562, vol. 2, Woodbury Lowery Papers.

93. Pedro Menendez to His Catholic Majesty, July 22, 1571, in Lawson, ed., *Letters of Pedro Menendez de Aviles and Other Documents Relative to his Career, 1555–1574*.

94. Royal License, March 3, 1573, in Lawson, ed., *Letters of Pedro Menendez de Aviles and Other Documents Relative to his Career, 1555–1574*. See also Report, March 3, 1573, ARG Archive de Conde Revilla-Gigedo ARG 2-5 A.6 Num. 15, John Stetson Collection.

95. Royal Cedula, San Lorenzo El Real to House of Trade, Sevilla, July 3, 1573, AGI 86-5-19, Santo Domingo, John Stetson Collection.

96. Pedro Menendez to His Catholic Majesty, March 18, 1574, in Lawson, ed., *Letters of Pedro Menendez de Aviles and Other Documents Relative to his Career, 1555–1574*.

97. Pedro Menendez to Pedro Menendez Marques, September 8, 1574, in Lawson, ed., *Letters of Pedro Menendez de Aviles and Other Documents Relative to his Career, 1555–1574*.

98. Amy Turner Bushnell, "Situado and Sabana: Spain's Support System for the Presidio and Mission Provinces of Florida," *Anthropological Papers of the American Museum of Natural History* 74 (September 1994): 1–249, 62. See also Paul E. Hoffman, *Florida's Frontiers* (Bloomington: Indiana University Press, 2002). See also Herbert Eugene Bolton and Mary Ross, *The Debatable Land: A Sketch of the Anglo-Spanish Conquest for the Georgia Country* (Berkeley: University of California Press, 1925).

99. Report, Circa 1570s, AGI 2-5-4/12/ 3–20, Patronato 257, John Stetson Collection.

100. Report from Havana to Madrid, January 14, 1577, AGI 54-1-34-1, Santo Domingo 118, John Stetson Collection.

101. Report, June 20, 1577, vol. 3, Woodbury Lowery Papers (From Archivos General de Sevilla).

102. Lawrence S. Rowland, *Window on the Atlantic: The Rise and Fall of Saint Elena* (Columbia: South Carolina Department of Archives and History, n.d.) St. Augustine Historical Society.

103. Consulta from Council of Indies-Madrid, March 20, 1577, AGI 140-7-33, Indiferente General 739, John Stetson Collection.

104. Governor Francisco Carreno-Havana to His Catholic Majesty, April 2, 1577, AGI 85-5-9, Santo Domingo 99, John Stetson Collection.

105. Royal Cedula-San Lorenzo El Real, June 10, 1577, AGI 86-5-19, Santo Domingo 2528, John Stetson Collection.

106. Juan Bautista Roman-Havana to His Catholic Majesty, July 6, 1578, AGI 54-1-34/4 Santo Domingo 118, John Stetson Collection.

107. Governor Francisco Carreno to His Catholic Majesty, July 8, 1578, AGI 54-1-15, Santo Domingo 99, John Stetson Collection.

108. Karen Lynn Paar, " 'To Settle to Conquest': Spaniards, Native Americans and the Colonization of Saint Elena in Sixteenth Century Florida" (PhD diss., University of North Carolina, Chapel Hill, 1999), 76, 187.

109. Pedro Menendez to His Catholic Majesty, July 22, 1571, AGI 54-5-16/8, Santo Domingo 231, John Stetson Collection.

110. John E. Worth, *Discovering Florida: First Contact Narratives from Spanish Expeditions along the Lower Gulf Coast* (Tallahassee: University Press of Florida, 2014), 20, 41.

111. Eugene Lyon, "St. Augustine 1580: The Living Community," *El Escribano* 14 (1977): 20–33, 20

112. Ignacio Gallup-Diaz, "A Legacy of Strife: Rebellious Slaves in Sixteenth-Century Panama," *Colonial Latin America Review* 19, no. 3 (December 2010): 417–35, 419, 423, 429, 433.

113. R. B., "The English Heroe or Sir Francis Drake Revived. . . . His Voyage in 1572 to Nombre de Dios . . ." (London: Nath, 1687), Huntington Library.

114. Hugh Thomas, *World without End: Spain, Philip II, and the First Global Empire* (New York: Random House, 2015), 227.

115. Pedro Menendez Marques, Havana, to His Catholic Majesty, July 1, 1574, AGI 54-2-2, Santo Domingo 124, John Stetson Collection.

116. Royal Cedula-El Pardo to Governor of Cuba, August 10, 1574, AGI 86-5-19, Santo Domingo, John Stetson Papers.

117. Philip Wayne Powell, "Presidios and Towns on the Silver Frontier of New Spain, 1550–1580," *Hispanic American Historical Review* 24, no. 2 (May 1944): 179–200, 188. See also Herbert Eugene Bolton, *The Hasainais: Southern Caddoans as Seen by the Earliest Europeans* (Norman: University of Oklahoma Press, 1987).

118. Clements R. Markham, ed. and trans., *Narratives of the Voyages of Pedro Sarmiento de Gamboa to the Straits of Magellan* (London: Hakluyt Society, 1895), xviii.

6. 1588: ORIGINS OF THE U.S.A.?

1. See, for example, David Howarth, *The Voyage of the Armada: The Spanish Story* (New York: Viking, 1981).

2. John Lewis Gaddis, *On Grand Strategy* (New York: Penguin, 2018), 152, 142, 143. See also N. A. M. Rodger, *The Armada in the Public Records* (London: Her Majesty's Stationery Office, 1988). See also Augustine Ubaldini [Petruccio], *A Discourse Concerning the Spanishe Fleete Invading Englande in the Yeare 1588* (London: Hatfield, 1590) and Julian S. Corbett, ed., *Papers Relating to the Navy During the Spanish War, 1585–1587* (Brookfield, VT: Navy Records Society, 1987).

3. Thomas Long, *A Compendious History of All the Popish and Fanatical Plots and Conspiracies Against the Established Government in Church and State in England, Scotland and Ireland from the Year of Queen Elizabeth['s] Reign to this Present Year 1684 . . .* (London: Black Swan, 1684). See also "The Act of Parliament of the 27th of Queen Elizabeth to Preserve the Queen's Person and Protestant Religion and Government, from the Attempts of the Papists, Then Big with Hopes of a Popish Successor . . ."1679. Both can be found at the Huntington Library.

4.   Sir George Carey to Sir Francis Walsingham, July 20, 1985, in Robert Lemon, ed., *Calendar of State Papers, Domestic Series of the Reign of Elizabeth, 1581–1590* (Nendeln, Liechtenstein: Kraus, 1967), 253. See also W. Noel Sainsbury, ed., *Calendar of State Papers, Colonial Series, 1574–1660* (London: Longman Green, 1860).

5.   Ada Kathleen Longfield, *Anglo-Irish Trade in the Sixteenth Century* (London: Routledge, 1929).

6.   Victoria Freeman, *Distant Relations: How My Ancestors Colonized North America* (South Royalton, VT: Steerforth, 2000), 29.

7.   Nate Probasco, "Queen Elizabeth's Reaction to the St. Bartholomew's Day Massacre," in Charles Beem, ed., *The Foreign Relations of Elizabeth I* (New York: Palgrave, 2011), 77–100, 87.

8.   John Butman and Simon Target, *New World Inc.: The Making of America by England's Merchant Adventurers* (New York: Little, Brown, 2018), 168, 172.

9.   Katherine Swan Lawson, *Martin de Arguelles: The First Spaniard Born in St. Augustine and the First European Child born on the Atlantic Coast of the United States in a Permanent European Settlement* (St. Augustine, FL: St. Augustine Historical Society, 1941).

10.   R. D. W. Connor, *The Beginnings of English America: Sir Walter Raleigh . . . Settlements on Roanoke Island, 1584–1587* (Raleigh: North Carolina Historical Commission, 1907). See also Franklin McCann, *English Discovery of America in 1585* (New York: King's Crown/Columbia University Press, 1952). See also *A True Reporte of the Late Discourses and Possession Taken in the Right of Crown of England, of the New Found Land: By that Valiant And Worthye Gentleman, Sir Humphrey Gilbert . . .* (London: Hinde, 1583). See also Charles Baird, *History of the Huguenot Emigration to America* (New York: Dodd, Mead, 1885), 74.

11.   Edward Ingle, "Roanoke: A Tale of Raleigh's Colony," *Overland Monthly,* November 1886, Huntington Library.

12.   Thomas Hariot, *A Briefe and True Report of the New Found Land of Virginia of the Commodities. . . . Direction of the Honourable Sir Walter Raleigh . . .* (London: Robinson, 1588), Huntington Library.

13.   Report, May 17, 1587, in Lemon, ed., *Calendar of State Papers, Domestic Series of the Reign of Elizabeth, 1581–1590*, 411–412.

14.   Katy Gibbons, *English Catholic Exiles in Late Sixteenth-Century Paris* (Woodbridge, UK: Boydell and Brewer, 2011). See also *A Short Declaration of the Ende of Traytors and False Conspirators Against the State . . . Published by Richard Crompton . . .* (London: Charlewood, 1587), Huntington Library.

15.   Reverend Thomas Lathbury, *Guy Fawkes or a Complete History of the Gunpowder Treason, A.D. 1605* (London: Parker, 1839), 2, 4, 11, 30, 108. See Arlette Jouanna, *The Saint Bartholomew's Day Massacre: The Mysteries of a Crime of State* (Manchester: Manchester University Press, 2013) and *A Briefe Discoverse Dialogue Shewing How False & Dangerous Their Reports are, Which Affirme the Spaniards Intended. . . . Re-establishment of the Romish Religion...* (London: Field, 1590), Huntington Library.

16.   J. P. D. Cooper, *The Queen's Agent: Sir Francis Walsingham and the Rise of Espionage in Elizabethan England* (New York: Pegasus, 2012), 78, 99, 143.

17.   Peter Padfield, *Armada: A Celebration of the Four Hundredth Anniversary of the Defeat of the Spanish Armada, 1588–1988* (Annapolis: Naval Institute Press, 1988), 20, 23. 28. See also Carla Rahn Phillips, ed., *The Struggle for the South Atlantic: The Armada of the Strait, 1581–1584* (London: Hakluyt Society, 2016).

18.   Graham Robb, *The Debatable Land: The Lost World between Scotland and England* (New York: Norton, 2018), 36, 62, 77, 117, 129, 132, 134, 144, 145, 158. It is noteworthy that the mother of the 45th U. S. President, Donald J. Trump, was descended from the turmoil engendered by an earlier land grab, the "Highlands Clearance," which swept families out of Scotland, igniting yet another migration. See *New York Times*, June 4, 2019. See also "The Irish Conquest of America," *Economist*, March 16, 2019: "Besides Mr. [Michael] Pence," U.S. Vice President, "two of whose grandparents were born in Ireland—the Republican House leader, Kevin McCarthy, is Irish-American, as was his predecessor, Paul Ryan, and their Senate counterpart, Mitch McConnell. Among the many other Irish-Americans who have served Mr. Trump are his sometimes advisers Steve Bannon and Kellyanne Conway and his current and former chiefs of staff, Mick Mulvaney and John Kelly."

19.   Des Ekin, *The Last Armada: Queen Elizabeth, Juan del Aguila and Hugh O'Neill: The Story of the 100 Day Spanish Invasion* (New York: Pegasus, 2015), 216.

20.   Andrew Lawler, *The Secret Token: Myth, Obsession, and the Search for the Lost Colony of Roanoke* (New York: Doubleday, 2018), 84.

21.   Standish O'Grady, *Red Hugh's Captivity: A Picture of Ireland, Social and Political by the Reign of Queen Elizabeth* (London: Ward and Downey, 1889), 1, 66.

22.   Clifford M. Lewis and Albert J. Loomie, *The Spanish Jesuit Mission in Virginia, 1570–1572* (Chapel Hill: University of North Carolina Press, 1953), 51.

23.   Charlotte M. Gradie, "The Powhatans in the Context of the Spanish Empire," in Helen C. Rountree, ed.,*Powhatan Foreign Relations: 1500–1722* (Charlottesville: University Press of Virginia, 1993), 154–72.

24.   Anna Brickhouse, *The Unsettlement of America: Translation, Interpretation and the Story of Don Luis Velasco, 1560–1945* (New York: Oxford University Press, 2015), 1, 27, 28, 47. See also Robbie Ethridge and Charles Hudson, eds., *The Transformation of the Southeastern Indians, 1540–1760* (Jackson: University Press of Mississippi, 2002). Evidently, Martin Frobisher executed a variation of this theme when he seized an Eskimo who he brought to Europe and passed off as Asian: Padfield, *Armada*, 38.

25.   James Barnes, *Drake and His Yeomen: A True Accounting of the Character and Adventures of Sir Francis Drake as told to Matthew Maunsell, His Friend and Follower . . .* (New York: Macmillan, 1899), 396, 397.

26.   Hamilton McMilland, *Sir Walter Raleigh's Lost Colony . . . Historical Sketch . . . the Fate of the Colony of Englishmen Left on Roanoke Island in 1587*

(Wilson, NC: Advance, 1888). See also *The Armada Tercentary, Deputation of the Lord Mayor of London*, reprinted from the *Western Monthly News*, April 18, 1888, Huntington Library.

27. Reverend Thomas Lathbury, *The Spanish Armada, A.D. 1588 or the Attempt of Philip II and Pope Sixtus V to Re-Establish Popery in England* (London: Parker, 1840). See also Robert Cecil, "Earl of Salisbury, Letter to . . . Earle of Leycester," 1586, and William Burghley, *The State of England in 1588; A Letter from a Priest to the Spanish Ambassador at Paris* (London: Milland and Cooper, 1746), both sited at Massachusetts Historical Society. At the same site, see also William Burghley, *The Execution of Justice in England for Maintenance of Publique and Christian Peace Against Certaine Stirrers of Sedition and Adherents to the Traytors and Enemies of the Realme, without any Persecution of them For Questions of Religion, as Is Falsely Reported . . .* (London: Barker, 1583).

28. Sean O'Faolain, *The Great O'Neill: A Biography of Hugh O'Neill, Earl of Tyrone, 1550–1616* (New York: Longmans, 1942), 64, 78, 83, 102.

29. Caroline McCullagh, "When a Briton was King of California," *Christian Science Monitor*, October 3, 1942, Huntington Library.

30. Lawler, *The Secret Token*, 71.

31. Miranda Kaufman, *Black Tudors: The Untold Story* (London: Oneworld, 2017), 144.

32. Harry Kelsey, *Sir John Hawkins: Queen Elizabeth's Slave Trade* (New Haven, CT: Yale University Press, 2003), 18, 46, 65.

33. Daniel Boorstin, "Remarks at Dinner in Celebration of Library of Congress' 'The World Encompassed,'" March 19, 1981, San Francisco Public Library.

34. John Lothrop Motley, *History of the United Netherlands: From the Death of William the Silent to the Synod of Dort . . .* vol. 2 (New York: Harper, 1861), 100, 101.

35. Helen Wallis, *The Voyage of Sir Francis Drake Mapped in Silver and Gold* (Berkeley: Friends of Bancroft Library, 1979), San Francisco Public Library.

36. William Cornelison Schouten, *The World Encompassed by Sir Francis Drake . . . and the Relation of a Wonderful Vo[y]age* (Cleveland: World, 1966).

37. Henry B. Wagner, *Sir Francis Drake's Voyage Around the World: Its Aims and Achievements* (San Francisco: Howell, 1926), 2.

38. John Lothrop Motley, *History of the United Netherlands*, Volume II, 365, 373. Cf. Francisco Vasquez de Coronado, *Letter to Mendoza, August 3, 1540* (Boston: Old South, 1896), Massachusetts Historical Society. Cf. *The Deposition of Don Diego Piementelli . . . Master of One Regiment of the Campe of King of Spayne . . . in Holland* (London: Woolfe, 1588). See also *A Spaniard in Elizabethan England: The Correspondence of Antonio Perez's Exile* (London: Tamesis, 1974).

39. Edward Palmer to F. Walsingham, September 19, 1588, in Mary Anne Everett Green, ed., *Calendar of State Papers, Domestic Series, of the Reigns of Elizabeth and James I, Addenda, 1580–1625* (Nendeln, Liechtenstein: Kraus, 1967), 254–56, 255, 256.

40. J. P. D. Cooper, *The Queen's Agent*, 172, 237.

41. Stephen Alford, *The Watchers: A Secret History of The Reign of Elizabeth I* (New York: Bloomsbury, 2012), 19.

42. Gaddis, *On Grand Strategy*, 139, 142.

43. Nicholas [Niccolò] Machiavelli, *The Arte of Warre, Written in Italian by Nicholas Machiavelli and Set Forth in English*, trans. Peter Withorne (London: East/Wight, 1588), Huntington Library.

44. His Catholic Majesty to Diego de Orellana de Chaves, August 7, 1596, Letters of King Philip II, Brigham Young University.

45. Niall Fallon, *The Armada in Ireland* (Middletown, CT: Wesleyan University Press, 1978), 2, 4.

46. Laurence Flanagan, *Ireland's Armada Legacy* (Dublin: Gill and Macmillan, 1988), 7.

47. Zelia Nutall, ed., *New Light on Drake: A Collection of Documents Relating to His Voyage of Circumnavigation, 1577–1580* (London: Hakluyt Society, 1914), xxxi, lvi.

48. Antonio de Moura, *Philippine Islands, Moluccas, Siam, Cambodia, Japan and China at the Close of the Sixteenth Century* (London: Hakluyt Society), 1868. See also Pieter M. Judson, *The Habsburg Empire: A New History* (Cambridge, MA: Harvard University Press, 2016).

49. Peter Gerhard, *Pirates on the West Coast of New Spain, 1575–1742* (Glendale, CA: Clark, 1960), 38.

50. Thomas Rundall, ed., *Memorials of the Empire of Japan in the XVI and XVII Centuries* (London: Hakluyt Society, 1850), x. See also Fray Diego Duran, *The History of the Indies of New Spain* (Norman: University of Oklahoma Press, 1994 [originally published in the 16th century]).

51. Charles E. Chapman, *A History of California: The Spanish Period* (San Francisco: Holmes, 1921), 21–24, 32, 39. See also Rose Marie Beebe and Robert M. Sekewicz, eds., *Lands of Promise and Despair: Chronicles of Early California, 1535–1846* (Berkeley: Heyday, 2001) and Gerald Horne, *Facing the Rising Sun: African-Americans, Japan and the Rise of Afro-Asian Solidarity* (New York: New York University Press, 2018). See also Letters from Jesuits in Japan, 1606, Carton 23, Herbert Bolton Papers.

52. Major H. B. C. Pollard, *A History of Firearms* (Boston: Houghton Mifflin, 1926), 31.

53. David Nicolle, *The Portuguese in the Age of Discovery c. 1340–1665* (Oxford: Osprey, 2012), 40.

54. Luis G. Santos, *The English Armada: The Greatest Naval Disaster in English History* (London: Bloomsbury, 2018), 1.

55. *A Letter Written on October 4, 1589 by Captain Cuellar of the Spanish Armada to His Majesty King Philip II . . . translated from the Original Spanish by Henry Dwight Sedgwick, Jr.* (New York: Richmond, 1895), New-York Historical Society.

56. Sir Roger Williams to Sir Francis Walshingham, June 1, 1589 in Lemon, ed., *Calendar of State Papers, Domestic Series of the Reign of Elizabeth, 1581–1590*, 603.

57. Jerry Brotton, *The Sultan and the Queen: The Untold Story of Elizabeth and Islam* (New York: Penguin, 2016), 154.

58. See, for example, Stanley Lane Poole, *The Story of the Moors in Spain* (Baltimore: Black Classic, 1990).

59. R. B. Wernham, *Before the Armada: The Emergence of the English Nation, 1485–1588* (New York: Harcourt Brace, 1966), 369–72, 204.

60. Seymour B. Liebman, *The Inquisitions and Jews in the New World: Summaries and Procesos, 1500–1810* (Coral Gables, FL: University of Miami Press, 1974), 19.

61. "Commission to William Hawkyns," 1580, in Lemon, ed., *Calendar of State Papers, Domestic Series of the Reigns of Edward VI, Mary, Elizabeth, 1547–1580,* 678.

62. Reverend Alexander Dyce, ed., *The Works of George Peele: Collected and Edited with Some Account of His Life and Writings . . .* (London: Pickering, 1829), vol. 1, xvi and vol. 2, 81: Peele authored a crowd-pleasing play about Alcazar. See also R. B. Wernham, *The Expedition of Sir John Norris and Sir Francis Drake to Spain and Portugal, 1589* (Brookfield, VT: Gower, 1988).

63. Hugh Thomas, *World without End: Spain, Philip II, and the First Global Empire* (New York: Doubleday, 2018), 195. See also G. F. di Conestaggio, *The Historie of the Uniting of the Kingdom of Portugall to the Crowne of Castill: Containing the Last Warres of the Portugals Against the Moores of Africke, the End of the House of Portugall and Change of that Government . . .* (London: Hatfield for Blount, 1600) and *The Battell of Alcazar, Fought in Barbarie, Between Sebastian King of Portugall and Abdelmelee King of Morocco, with the Death of Captain Stukeley* (London: Bandworth, 1594).

64. E. W. Bovill, *The Battle of Alcazar: An Account of the Defeat of Don Sebastian of Portugal at Ekl-Ksar El-Kebir* (London: Batchworth, 1952), 177, 182, 82, 43, 44. For more on Anglo-Moroccan relations, see, for example, C. R. Boxer, *Further Selections from the Tragic History of the Sea, 1559–1565* (London: Hakluyt, 1967), 15.

65. Kaufman, *Black Tudors,* 142.

66. Karen Ordahl Kupperman, *The Jamestown Project* (Cambridge, MA: Harvard University Press, 2007), 24, 30. See also *The Strangest Adventure that Ever Happened Either in the Ages Passed or Present . . . Concerning the Success of the King of Portugall Dom Sebastian, from the Time of His Voyage into Affricke, When He was Lost in Battle Against the Infidels in the Year 1578 . . .* (London: Henson, 1601), New-York Historical Society.

67. Jacques Heers, *The Barbary Corsairs: Pirates, Plunder, and Warfare in the Mediterranean, 1480–1580* (New York: Skyhorse, 2018), 229, 216, 223. See also J. F. P. Hopkins, ed., *Letters from Barbary, 1576–1774, Arabic Documents in the Public Records Office* (London: Oxford University Press, 1982).

68. Gerald Horne, *Blows against the Empire: U.S. Imperialism in Crisis* (New York: International Publishers, 2008), passim.

69. Nahil Matar, "Elizabeth Through Moroccan Eyes," in Beem, ed., *The Foreign Relations of Elizabeth I,* 145–67, 147, 152, 154.

70. Gerald Horne, *Race War! White Supremacy and the Japanese Attack on the British Empire* (New York: New York University Press, 2003).

71. Heather Miyano Kopelson, *Faithful Bodies: Performing Religion and Race in the Puritan Atlantic* (New York: New York University Press, 2014), 280.

72. *The Navigations, Peregrinations and Voyages, Made into Turkie by Nicholas Nicholay Daulphinois, Lord* . . . (London: Dawson, 1588), 8.

73. Report, circa 1582, in Lemon, ed., *Calendar of State Papers, Domestic Series of the Reign of Elizabeth 1581–1590*, 88. See also S. A. Skilliter, ed., *William Harborne and the Trade with Turkey, 1578–1582, A Documentary Study of the First Anglo-Ottoman Relations* (London: Oxford University Press, 1977).

74. Alejandro de la Fuente, *Havana and the Atlantic in the Sixteenth Century*, 178.

75. *The Suma Oriental of Tome Pires: An Account of the East from the Red Sea to Japan . . . 1512–1515 . . . and the Book of Francisco Rodrigues. . .* vol. 2 (London: Hakluyt Society, 1944), 268. Cf. Sir William Foster, ed., *The Red Sea and Adjacent Countries at the Close of the 17th Century* (London: Hakluyt Society, 1949) and Charles Fraser Beckingham, ed., *Some Records of Ethiopia, 1593–1646* (London: Hakluyt Society, 1954). See also Father Francisco Alvarez, *Narrative of the Portuguese Embassy to Abyssinia During the Years, 1520–1527* (London: Hakluyt, 1881). Part of what drove this Western European fascination with Ethiopia was the search for Prester John, that is, backup for the struggle against Islam. See John Buchan, *Prester John* (London: Nelson, 1910). On Mozambique during this contested era, see, for example, C. R. Boxer, *The Tragic History of the Sea, 1589–1622* (London: Hakluyt Society, 1959).

76. Toby Green, *A Fistful of Shells: West Africa from the Rise of the Slave Trade to the Age of Revolution* (Chicago: University of Chicago Press, 2019), 116, 134.

77. See, for example, Thomas Goodrich, *Ottoman Americana: The Search for the Sources of the Sixteenth Century Tarih-Hind-I garb* (New York: New York Public Library, 1982).

78. Brotton, *The Sultan and the Queen*, 172, 91, 116.

79. Philip S. Palmer, "'All Such . . . Matters as Passed on this Voyage': Early English Travel Anthologies and the Case of John Sarracoll's Maritime Journal (1586–1587)," *Huntington Library Quarterly* 76, no. 3 (Autumn 2013): 325–44, 325, 326, 333. See also "Red Dragon Logbook," 1586–1587, Huntington Library. See also Archibald Dalzel, *The History of Dahomey, an Inland Kingdom of Africa* . . . (London: Spilsbury and Son, 1793).

80. Edmund Bunny, *The Scepter of Judah* (London: Wight, 1584).

81. See, for example, Machiavelli, *The Arte of Warre, Written in Italian by Nicholas Machiavelli and Set Forth in English*.

82. Butman and Target, *New World Inc.*, 153, 159, 195, and David Beers Quinn, ed., *The Roanoke Voyages, 1584–1590*, vol. 1 (London: Hakluyt Society, 1955). On Drake in Florida, see George R. Fairbanks, *The Spaniards in Florida: Comprising the Notable Settlement of the Huguenots in 1564 and the History and Antiquities of St. Augustine* . . . (Jacksonville, FL: Columbus Drew, 1868), 65. See also *A Summarie and True Discoverie of Sir Francis Drake's West Indian Voyages Wherein Were Taken the Townes of Saint*

· *Jago, Santo Domingo, Cartagena & Saint Augustine* (London: Field, 1589), Huntington Library.

83.   Lawler, *The Secret Token*, 84. Mary Johnson, *Croatan* (Boston: Little, Brown, 1929).

84.   Mary Frear Keller, *Sir Francis Drake's West Indian Voyage, 1585–1586* (London: Hakluyt Society, 1981), 244, 32

85.   Lawler, *The Secret Token*, 72, 335–36.

86.   Kaufman, *Black Tudors*, 98.

87.   Brotton, *The Sultan and the Queen*, 133.

88.   Elizabeth Caldwell Hirschman, *Melungeons: The Last Lost Tribe in America* (Macon, GA: Mercer University Press, 2005), 10, 11. N. Brent Kennedy, *The Melungeons: The Resurrection of a Proud People: An Untold Story of Ethnic Cleansing in America* (Macon, GA: Mercer University Press, 1970), xviii, 120–21: The term "Melungeon" itself may be a term of Turkish origin.

89.   Philip Nichols Preacher, *Sir Francis Drake Revived: Calling Upon this Dull or Effiminate Age to Follow His Noble Steps for Gold and Silver . . . Reviewed by Sir Francis Drake Himself Before His Death* (London: Bourne, 1628).

90.   See, for example, Robert Anderson Wilson, *A New History of the Conquest of Mexico . . .* (Philadelphia: Challen and Son, 1859).

91.   James Barnes, *Drake and His Yeomen: A True Accounting of the Character and Adventures of Sir Francis Drake as told to Matthew Maunsell, His Friend and Follower . . .* (New York: Macmillan, 1899), 124, 142, 143.

92.   Henry Wagner, *Drake on the Pacific Coast* (Los Angeles: Zamorano Club, 1970). See also David Beers Quinn, *Sir Francis Drake as Seen by His Contemporaries* (Providence, RI: John Carter Brown Library, 1996) and Robert H. Power, *Francis Drake and San Francisco Bay: A Beginning of the British Empire* (Davis: University of California, Davis Library, 1974) and *Publication of the Evidence of Sir Francis Drake's Visit to California in 1579 . . .* (San Francisco: California Historical Society, 1937), Huntington Library. See also Document on Drake in San Francisco Bay, November 1, 1956, MS 3831, California Historical Society.

93.   Cf. Melissa Darby, *Thunder Go North: The Hunt for Drake's Fair and Good Bay* (Salt Lake City: University of Utah Press, 2019): The author argues that actually Sir Francis landed not in California but further north in today's Oregon.

94.   Caroline McCullagh, "When a Briton was King of California," 1942. Cf. Wagner, *Drake on the Pacific Coast*. At the same site see also Quinn, *Sir Francis Drake as Seen by His Contemporaries*.

95.   Adolph S. Oko, "Francis Drake and Nova Albion," *California Historical Society Quarterly* 43, no. 2 (June 1964): 1–24. See also Brian T. Kelleher, *Drake's Bay: Unravelling California's Great Maritime Mystery* (Cupertino, CA: self-pub., 1997) and *San Francisco Chronicle*, September 12, 2009, as well as *San Francisco Examiner*, July 1, 1979.

96.   Power, *Francis Drake and San Francisco Bay*.

97.   Robert H. Power, "Drake's Landing in California: A Case for San Francisco

Bay," *California Historical Quarterly* 52, no. 2 (Summer 1973): 101–30, San Francisco Public Library.

98. William A. Lessa, "Drake in the Marianas," *Micronesia* 10, no. 1 (1974): 1, Brown University.

99. Philip Wayne Powell, *Mexico's Miguel Caldera: The Taming of America's First Frontier (1548–1597)* (Tucson: University of Arizona Press, 1977), 64, 4. For more on an earlier "Chichimeca" uprising, see, for example, Luis Weckmann, *The Medieval Heritage of Mexico* (New York: Fordham University Press, 1992), 86. See also Anne I. Wosley and John C. Ravesloot, *Culture and Contact: Charles C. Di Peso's Gran Chichimeca* (Albuquerque: University of New Mexico Press, 1993) and Cynthia J. Van Zandt, *Brothers among Nations: The Pursuit of Intercultural Alliances in Early America, 1580–1660* (New York: Oxford University Press, 2008).

100. Letter from Diego de Ibarra, 1582, in Charles Wilson Hackett, ed., *Historical Documents Relating to New Mexico, Nueva Vizcaya and Approaches Thereto to 1773*, vol. 1 (Washington, D.C.: Carnegie, 1923), 109, 111. See also Morgan Veraluz, "Deserts of Plenty, Rivers of Want: Apaches and the Inversion of the Colonial Encounter in the Chihuahuan Borderlands, 1581–1788" (PhD diss., University of Michigan, 2014).

101. *New Mexico Otherwise the Voyage of Espeio, who in the Yeare 1583, with his Company, Discovered a Lande of 15 Provinces, Replenished with Townes and Villages . . .* (London: Cadman, 1928). See also Antonio Espeio, *New Mexico, Otherwise the Voyage of Anthony of Espeio, who in the Yeare 1583 with His Company . . .* (London: Cadman, 1586).

102. W. W. H. Davis, *The Spanish Conquest of New Mexico* (Doylestown, PA: self-pub., 1869), Huntington Library. See also Andrés Reséndez, *A Land So Strange: The Epic Journey of Cabeza de Vaca, the Extraordinary Tale of a Shipwrecked Spaniard who Walked Across America in the Sixteenth Century* (New York: Perseus, 2007).

103. Alejandro de la Fuente, *Havana and the Atlantic in the Sixteenth Century* (Chapel Hill: University of North Carolina Press, 2008), 181.

104. Kris Lane, *Colour of Paradise: The Emerald in the Age of Gunpowder Empires* (New Haven, CT: Yale University Press, 2010), 78, 83, 95, 98, 108, 111, 135, 202.

105. David Birmingham, "The Jewish Factor in Angolan History," *Portuguese Studies Review* 24, no. 1 (2016): 31–50, 33, 34, 35. See also Filipa Ribeiro da Silva, "Crossing Empires: Portuguese, Sephardic and Dutch Business Networks in the Atlantic Slave Trade, 1580–1657," *The Americas* 68, no. 1 (2011): 7–32.

106. Lawler, *The Secret Token*, 46.

107. William Foster, *Early Travels in India, 1583–1619* (London: Oxford University Press, 1921). See also Richard Eden, *The History of [Travel] in the West and East Indies, . . . Egypte, Ethiopia, Guinea . . .* (London: Iuggge, 1577).

108. Brotton, *The Sultan and the Queen*, 119.

109. David Northrup, "The Gulf of Guinea and the Atlantic World," in Peter

Mancall, ed., *The Atlantic World and Virginia, 1550–1624* (Chapel Hill: University of North Carolina Press, 2007), 170–93.

110. See, for example, Ron D. Hart et al., *Fractured Faiths: Spanish Judaism, the Inquisition and New World Identities* (Albuquerque: New History Museum, 2016). See also Vicki Blanchard, "The Indians and the Inquisition in New Mexico, 1536–1563" (honors thesis, Tulane University, 1969). Nancy Vogeley and Raquel Chang-Rodriguez, eds., *Account of the Martyrs in the Provinces of La Florida* (Albuquerque: University of New Mexico Press, 2017).

111. Mauricio Drelichman and Hans-Joachim Voth, *Lending to the Borrower from Hell: Debt, Taxes, and Default in the Age of Philip II* (Princeton, NJ: Princeton University Press, 2014), 243.

7. ORIGINS OF THE U.S.A.: INDIGENOUS FLORIDIANS LIQUIDATED | DITTO FOR NEW MEXICO

1. Consulta of the Council of Indies to the Crown, June 4, 1580, AGI 140-7-33, Indiferente General 739, and Report, 6 March 1580, AGI 86-5-19, Santo Domingo 229, John Stetson Collection

2. Alenjandro de la Fuente, *Havana and the Atlantic in the Sixteenth Century* (Chapel Hill: University of North Carolina Press, 2008), 183, 184.

3. Raymond K. Kent, "Palmares: An African State in Brazil," *Journal of African History*, 6(Number 2, 1965): 161–175; Robert N. Anderson, "The Quilombo of Palmares: A New Overview of a Maroon State in Seventeenth Century Brazil," *Journal of Latin American Studies*, 28(1996): 553–562.

4. Rodrigo de Junco, St. Augustine to House of Trade, October 3, 1580, AGI 42-1-6/1, Contractacion 5106, John Stetson Collection.

5. Rodrigo de Junco to Crown, October 12, 1580, AGI 54-5-16/25, Santo Domingo 231, John Stetson Collection.

6. Royal Cedula-Badajoz to St. Augustine, September 30, 1580, AGI 86-5-19, Santo Domingo 2528, John Stetson Collection.

7. Governor Gabriel de Luxan, Havana to Crown, November 1, 1581, AGI 54-1-15, Santo Domingo 99, John Stetson Collection.

8. Gutierre de Miranda, St. Augustine to Crown, October 14, 1580, AGI 54-1-16/26, Santo Domingo 231, John Stetson Collection.

9. Governor Pedro Menendez Marques to His Catholic Majesty, August 1, 1583, AGI 54-5-1, John Stetson Collection.

10. Report, August 1, 1583, Volume 4, Woodbury Lowery Papers, Library of Congress.

11. Royal Cedula, Elvas, to Pedro Menendez Marques, February 18, 1581, AGI 86-5-19, Santo Domingo 2528, John Stetson Collection.

12. Governor Gabriel de Luxan, Havana to Crown, January 1582, AGI 54-21-23, Santo Domingo 146, John Stetson Collection.

13. Report from Juan Cevadilla, Treasurer, Real Hacienda, Florida, January 22, 1582, AGI 54-5-14, Santo Domingo 229, John Stetson Collection.

14. Royal Cedula-Madrid to Governor Pedro Menendez Marques, April 19, 1583, AGI 86-5-19, Santo Domingo 2528, John Stetson Collection.

15. Royal Cedula-Madrid to Governor Menendez Marques, August 1, 1583, AGI 86-5-19, Santo Domingo 2528, John Stetson Collection.

16. Officialdom-St. Augustine to the Crown, December 20, 1583, AGI 54-5-16, Santo Domingo 231, John Stetson Collection.

17. Governor Gabriel Lujan-Havana to Crown, June 5, 1585, AGI 54-2-23, Santo Domingo 124, John Stetson Collection.

18. Report, 1584, AGI 53-1-14, Santo Domingo 14, John Stetson Collection.

19. Gabriel Lujan and Diego Fernandez-Havana to Crown, June 26, 1586, AGI 54-2-4, Santo Domingo 126, John Stetson Collection. Mary F. Keele, ed., *Sir Francis Drake's West Indian Voyage, 1585–1586* (London: Hakluyt Society, 1981), 12, 32, 39, 169.

20. Juan Baptista de Rojas, Treasurer-Havana to Crown, July 1, 1586, AGI 54-1-34/11, John Stetson Collection.

21. Officialdom-Havana to Crown, July 4, 1586, AGI 54-1-34/15, Santo Domingo 118, John Stetson Collection.

22. Governor Gabriel Lujan to Crown, July 1, 1586, AGI 54-2-4, Santo Domingo 126, John Stetson Collection.

23. Governor Menendez Marques to House of Trade, August 30, 1586, AGI 72-5-18, Contratacion 5108, John Stetson Collection.

24. Last will and testament of Sir Francis Drake, circa 1596, MS 612, California Historical Society-San Francisco. See also *A Libell of Spanish Lies . . . Fight in the West Indies . . . Death of Francis Drake* (London: Keyes, 1596), Huntington Library.

25. Governor Menendez Marques to Crown, July 17, 1586, AGI 147-6-5/4, Indiferente General 1887, John Stetson Collection.

26. Captain Juan de Posada, St. Augustine to Crown, September 2, 1586, AGI 72-5-18, Santa Fe 89, John Stetson Collection. Cf. Carina Johnson, *Cultural Hierarchy in Sixteenth Century Europe: The Ottomans and Mexicans* (New York: Cambridge University Press, 2011).

27. Letter from Fernando Miranda, et.al., August 20, 1583, in *The Unwritten History of Old St. Augustine, Copied from the Spanish Archives in Seville by Miss A. M. Brooks*, Annie Averette, trans. (St. Augustine: The Record, [circa 1909]), 27–29, 28.

28. Treasurer and Accountant, St. Augustine to Crown, October 12, 1586, AGI 54-5-14/7, Santo Domingo 229, John Stetson Collection.

29. Report from Captain Vicente Gonzalez, 1586, AGI 145-1-1, John Stetson Collection.

30. Report from Cristobal de Erasso, circa 1586, AGI 2-5-2/10, John Stetson Collection.

31. Report from Fernando Quinones, Havana, March 22, 1587, AGI 42-1-8/3, Contratactacion 5108, John Stetson Collection.

32. Royal Cedula-San Lorenzo, October 19, 1588, AGI 86-5-19, John Stetson Collection.

33. Royal Cedula-Madrid, April 17, 1592, AGI 86-5-19, John Stetson Collection.

34. Juan de Texada-Havana to Crown, March 22, 1593, AGI 54-1-15, Contratacion 5108, John Stetson Collection.

35. Report, October 13, 1584, Volume 4, Woodbury Lowery Papers, Library of Congress.

36. Royal Cedula-San Lorenzo to Governor, August 11, 1593, AGI 86-5-19, Santo Domingo 2528, John Stetson Collection.

37. Royal Cedula-San Lorenzo to Governor, October 2, 1593, AGI 86-5-19, SD 2528, John Stetson Collection.

38. Royal Cedula-San Lorenzo to Governor, October 2, 1593, AGI 86-5—19, Santo Domingo 2528, John Stetson Collection.

39. Juan Maldonado Barnuevo-Havana to Crown, November 2, 1593, AGI 54-3-5, John Stetson Collection.

40. Juan Maldonado Barnuevo-Havana to Crown, January 22, 1594, AGI 54-1—15, Santo Domingo 99, John Stetson Collection.

41. Royal Cedula-San Lorenzo, August 18, 1593, AGI 86-5-19, Santo Domingo 2528, John Stetson Collection.

42. Domingo Martinez de Avendano-Havana to Crown, May 9, 1594, AGI 54-2-5, Santo Domingo 127, John Stetson Collection. In 1591, a confident London was considering yet another assault on Spain. See *A Report of the Truth of the Fight About the Lies of A[z]ores, This Last Summer . . . and an Armada of the King of Spaine* (London: Windet, 1591), Huntington Library.

43. Juan Maldonado to Crown, December 18, 1595, AGI 54-2-6, Santo Domingo 128, John Stetson Collection.

44. Report, August 2, 1598, AGI 54-5-9/27, Santo Domingo 224, John Stetson Collection.

45. Report, August 9, 1595, in Mary Anne Everett Green, ed., *Calendar of State Papers, Domestic Series, of the Reign of Elizabeth, 1595–1597* (Nendeln, Liechtenstein: Kraus, 1967), 89.

46. Jonathan Gathorne-Hardy, *The Epic Voyage of Thomas Dallam and His Extraordinary Musical Instrument to Constantinople in 1599 and His Time in the Palace and Harem of the Ottoman Sultan* (Norwich, UK: Propolis, 2017), 52.

47. Juan Maldonado-Havana to Crown, March 1, 1595, AGI 54-2-5, Santo Domingo 128, John Stetson Collection.

48. David Hurst Thomas et al., "Murder and Martyrdom in Spanish Florida: Don Juan and the Guale Uprising of 1597," *Anthropological Papers of the American Museum of Natural History* 95 (August 2011): 1–154, 23, 42, 137.

49. Pedro Pertene to Crown, February 20, 1598, in Annie Averette, trans., *The Unwritten History of Old St. Augustine*, 31–32.

50. Report, June 1, 1599, Volume 5, Woodbury Lowery Papers: noted is the arrival of 20 Africans on May 16, 1597. In the same collection on the Guale revolt, see Report, May 18, 1599, Volume 5.

51. Charles Arnade, *Florida on Trial, 1593–1602* (Coral Gables, FL: University of Miami Press, 1959), iii, 16, 19, 27. On the importance of frequent storms and resultant shipwrecks and their role in shaping settler colonialism in Florida, see, for example, Frank Marotti, "'Storm Winds that Fulfill His Word': Tempests, the Jesuits and the Evangelization of Florida, 1566–1572," Box 1,

Folder 15, MC 63, Chronological History, St. Augustine Historical Society. Cf. Noel Malcolm, *Agents of Empire: Knights, Corsairs, Jesuits and Spies in the 16th Century Mediterranean World* (London: Allen Lane, 2015).

52.   Reverend Maynard Geiger, "The Franciscan Conquest of Florida (1573–1618)" (PhD diss., Catholic University, 1937), 88.

53.   Rodrigo de Rio de Losa to Viceroy, 1582, Carton 32, Herbert Bolton Papers, University of California, Berkeley.

54.   Report, 1584, Carton 32, Herbert Bolton Papers.

55.   *The Historie of the Great and Mightie Kingdom of China and the Situation Thereof: Together with the Great Riches, Huge Cities . . . Rare Inventions . . .* Translated out of Spanish . . . trans. R. Parke (London: Wolfem, 1598).

56.   Sebastian Vizcaino to the Crown, June 20, 1590, Carton 33, Herbert Bolton Papers.

57.   Report, 1598, in George P. Hammond, ed., *Don Juan de Oñate, Colonizer of New Mexico, 1595–1628* (Albuquerque: University of New Mexico Press, 1953), 428–79, 428, 430. See also James Lockhart, ed., *We People Here: Nahuatl Accounts of the Conquest of Mexico* (Berkeley: University of California Press, 1993).

58.   Testimony of Captain Geronimo Marquez, 1598, in ibid., George P. Hammond, 430–33, 432.

59.   Testimony of Captain Gaspar Lopez Tabora, 1598, in ibid., George P. Hammond, 433–36, 435.

60.   Testimony of Alonso Gonzalez, 1598, in Hammond, ed., *Don Juan de Oñate, Colonizer of New Mexico, 1595–1628*, 447–449, 448. See also Maurice Crandall, *The People Have Always Been a Republic: Indigenous Electorates in the U.S.-Mexico Borderlands, 1598–1912* (Chapel Hill: University of North Carolina Press, 2019).

61.   Testimony of Antonio de Sarinana, 1598, in Hammond, ed., *Don Juan de Oñate, Colonizer of New Mexico, 1595–1628*, 449–51, 450.

62.   Alonso Sanchez to Rodrigo del Rio, March 28, 1599, in George P. Hammond and Agapito Rey, eds., *Don Juan de Oñate: Colonizer of New Mexico, 1595–1628* (Albuquerque: University of New Mexico Press, 1953), 426–27.

63.   David J. Weber, "American Westward Expansion and the Breakdown of Relations Between Pobladores and 'Indios Barbaros' on Mexico's Far Northern Frontier, 1821–1846," *New Mexico Historical Review* 56 (July 1981): 221–38, 221.

64.   John Kessell, *Pueblos, Spaniards, and the Kingdom of New Mexico* (Norman: University of Oklahoma Press, 2008), 5, 6.

65.   Proceedings at Acoma, 1599, in Hammond, ed., *Don Juan de Oñate, Colonizer of New Mexico, 1595–1628*, 460–63, 461.

66.   Testimony of Caucachi, 1599, in Hammond, ed., *Don Juan de Oñate, Colonizer of New Mexico, 1595–1628*, 467–69, 467.

67.   George P. Hammond and Agapito Rey, eds., *Obregon's History of 16th Century Explorations in Western America* (Los Angeles: Wetzel, 1928), 237.

68.   David H. Snow, ed., *New Mexico's First Colonists: The 1597–1600 Enlistments*

for New Mexico under Juan de Oñate, Adelante & Gobernador (Albuquerque: Hispanic Genealogical Research Center of New Mexico, 1998), 2, 5, 12.

69. Testimony of Captain Luis de Velasco, 1597, in Charles Wilson Hackett, ed., *Historical Documents Relating to New Mexico, Nueva Vizcaya, and Approaches Thereto to 1773*, vol. 1 (Washington, D.C.: Carnegie, 1923), 423.

70. Jonathan Hart, *Representing the New World: The English and French Uses of the Example of Spain* (New York: Palgrave, 2000), 97.

71. Report, August 3, 1598, Volume 5, Woodbury Lowery Papers.

72. Robert McCue, "The Holy Office of the Inquisition: Its Role in New Mexico," unclear provenance, University of New Mexico, Albuquerque.

73. Diego de Ibarra to "His Sacred Catholic Royal Majesty, the King," circa 1600, in Hackett, ed., *Historical Documents Relating to New Mexico, Nueva Vizcaya, and Approaches Thereto to 1773*, vol. 1, 111. See also George P. Hammond and Agapito Rey, eds., *The Rediscovery of New Mexico, 1580–1594* (Albuquerque: University of New Mexico Press, 1966).

74. *An Account of the Persecutions and Oppressions of the Protestants in France* (London: Norris, 1686), Huntington Library.

75. Albert H. Schroeder and Dan S. Matson, eds., *A Colony on the Move: Gaspar Castano de Sosa's Journal, 1590–1591* (Santa Fe: School of American Research, 1965), 4, 85, 87.

76. Seth Kunin, *Juggling Identities: Identity and Authenticity Among the Crypto Jews* (New York: Columbia University Press, 2009), 7, 9.

77. Stanley Hordes, *To the End of the Earth: A History of the Crypto-Jews of New Mexico* (New York: Columbia University Press, 2005), 107. See also Martin A. Cohen, *The Martyr: Luis de Carvajal, a Secret Jew in Sixteenth Century New Mexico* (Albuquerque: University of New Mexico Press, 1973). Cf. Angela Ballone, *The 1624 Tumult of Mexico in Perspective (c. 1620–1650): Authority and Conflict Resolution in the Iberian Atlantic* (Leiden: Brill, 2018).

78. J. T. Canals, "The Tragic Quadrangle: . . . Account of an Attempted Settlement by Jewish Families from New Spain and Portugal in North America During the 16th Century and of an Enormous Land Grant in Northern Mexico Made by King Pilip II of Spain to Don Luis Carbajal [Carvajal] de la Cueva on June 14, 1589, which Had a Very Tragic Ending," May 1955, University of Texas, Austin.

79. Martin Cohen, "The Autobiography of Luis de Carvajal, the Younger," *American Jewish Historical Quarterly* 55, no. 3 (March 1966): 277–318. See also Herbert Eugene Bolton, ed., *Spanish Exploration in the Southwest, 1542–1706* (New York: Barnes and Noble, 1963).

80. Tomas Atencio and Stanley M. Hordes, *The Sephardic Legacy in New Mexico: A Prospectus* (Albuquerque: Southwest Hispanic Research Institute, University of New Mexico, 1987). See also Tomas Atencio, *Crypto-Judaism: Towards Understanding the Manitos of New Mexico* (Albuquerque: Rio Grande Institute, 1991), University of New Mexico.

81. Tom Lea, *Calendar of Twelve Travellers Through the Pass of the North* (El Paso: Hertzog, 1946), Huntington Library.

82. George Sandys, *Sandys Travailes: Containing a History of the Original and Present State of the Turkish Empire: Their Laws, Government, Policy, Military Force, Courts of Justice and Commerce. The Mahometan Religion and Ceremonies. A Decription of Constantinople . . . of Egypt . . . Grand Cairo . . . Alexandria . . .* (London: Leybourn, 1658), 7, 38, 39, 183.

83. Petition, September 2, 1595, Carton 33, Herbert Bolton Papers. See, for example, Anne I. Wosley and John C. Ravesloot, *Culture and Contact: Charles C. di Peso's Gran Chichimeca* (Albuquerque: University of New Mexico Press, 1993).

84. Report, October 4, 1599, Carton 33, Herbert Bolton Papers.

85. Philip Wayne Powell, *Soldiers, Indians and Silver: The Northward Advance of New Spain, 1550–1600* (Berkeley: University of California Press, 1952), 3.

86. Report by Fray Juan de Escalona, October 1, 1601, Carton 33, Herbert Bolton Papers.

87. Paul Laxalt, *Nevada's Paul Laxalt: A Memoir* (Reno, NV: Bacon, 2000).

88. Harry Fulsome, "Juan de Oñate and the Foundation of New Mexico," 2006, University of New Mexico, Albuquerque.

89. Milton Manuel da Silva, "The Basque Nationalist Movement: A Case Study of Modernization and Ethnic Conflict" (PhD diss., University of Massachusetts, Amherst, 1972).

90. J. Lloyd Meacham, "Francisco de Urinola, Governor of Nueva Vizcaya," in Charles W. Hackett et al., eds., *New Spain and the Anglo-American West: Historical Contributions Presented to Herbert Eugene Bolton,* vol. 1 (Los Angeles: Lancaster Press, 1932), 39–48, 42–43.

91. Lloyd E. Berry, ed., *The English Works of Giles Fletcher, the Elder* (Madison: University of Wisconsin Press, 1964), 28, 40. See also *The Situation of the Lands of Cleue and Munster Where the Spanish Forces Now Are* (London: Wolfe, 1599), Huntington Library, and at the same site, *A Briefe Relation, of What is Happened Since the Last of August 1598 by Coming of the Spanish Campe into the Dukedome of Cleue; and the Bordering Free Countries, which with Most Odious and Barbarous Crueltie they Take as Enemies . . . and the King of Spaine . . . Faithfully Translated out of the Dutch . . .* (London: Wolfe, 1599). See also *A True Copy of the Admonitions sent by the Subdued Provinces to the States of Holland: and the Hollanders Answere to the Same . . .* (London: Wolfe, 1598) and *An Admonition Published by the General States of the Netherlandish United Provinces . . . Touching His Now Intended Proceedings against the Spaniards and their Adherents* (London: Dight, 1602).

92. Peter Gerhard, *Pirates on the West Coast of New Spain, 1575–1742* (Glendale, CA: Clark, 1960), 123.

93. Miranda Kaufman, *Black Tudors: The Untold Story* (London: Oneworld, 2017), 119. Jacob Rader Marcus, *The Jews in Christian Europe,* 231.

94. John Butman and Simon Target, *New World Inc.: The Making of America by England's Merchant Adventurers* (New York: Little, Brown, 2018), 215.

95. Pieter de Marees, *Description and Historical Account of the Gold Kingdom of Guinea (1602) Translated from the Dutch,* trans. and ed. Albert van Dantzig and Adam Jones (New York: Oxford University Press, 1987), xiv.

96. Butman and Target, *New World Inc.*, 215.

97. His Catholic Majesty to Diego de Orellana de Chaves, August 14, 1593, Letters of King Philip II, King of Spain, Brigham Young University.

98. J. D. La Fleur, *Pieter van den Broecke's Journal of Voyages to Cape Verde, Guinea and Angola, 1605–1612* (London: Hakluyt Society, 2000), 4.

99. Jerry Brotton, *The Sultan and the Queen: The Untold Story of Elizabeth and Islam* (New York: Viking, 2017), 233. Sidney R. Welch, *Portuguese Rule and Spanish Crown in South Africa, 1581–1640* (Cape Town: Juta, 1950).

100. *A True Report of a Voyage to the Canary Islands*, 1599, [Dutch translation], Huntington Library.

101. Mark Meuwese, *Brothers in Arms, Partners in Trade: Dutch-Indigenous Alliances in the Atlantic World, 1595–1674* (Leiden: Brill, 2011), 71.

102. Engel Sluiter, "The Dutch on the Pacific Coast of America, 1598–1621" (PhD diss., University of California, Berkeley, 1937), 171, 233, 235.

103. His Catholic Majesty to Diego de Orellana de Chaves, February 9, 1593, Letters of King Philip II.

104. His Catholic Majesty to Diego de Orellana de Chaves, February 5, 1593, Letters of King Philip II.

105. His Catholic Majesty to Diego de Orellana de Chaves, September 4, 1593, Letters of King Philip II.

106. His Catholic Majesty to Diego de Orellana de Chaves, September 28, 1593, Letters of King Philip II.

107. His Catholic Majesty to Diego de Orellana de Chaves, March 18, 1596, Letters of King Philip II.

108. His Catholic Majesty to Diego de Orellana de Chaves, March 30, 1596, Letters of King Philip II.

109. His Catholic Majesty to Diego de Orellana de Chaves, December 2, 1594, Letters of King Philip II.

110. His Catholic Majesty to Diego de Orellana de Chaves, September 23, 1594, Letters of King Philip II.

111. His Catholic Majesty to Diego de Orellana de Chaves, March 16, 1595, Letters of King Philip II.

112. His Catholic Majesty to Diego de Orellana de Chaves, May 11, 1595, Letters of King Philip II.

113. Privateering License, July 1594, Letters of King Philip II.

114. His Catholic Majesty to Diego de Orellana de Chaves, February 23, 1594, Letters of King Philip II.

115. His Catholic Majesty to Diego de Orellana de Chaves, October 16, 1594, Letters of King Philip II.

116. Matthijs P. Rooseboom, *The Scottish State in the Netherlands: An Account of the Trade Relations Between Scotland and the Low Countries from 1292 till 1676 . . .* (The Hague: Nijhoff, 1910). See also G. D. Ramsay, ed., *The Politics of a Tudor Merchant Adventurer* (Manchester: Manchester University Press, 1979).

117. La Fleur, *Pieter van den Broecke's Journal of Voyages to Cape Verde, Guinea and Angola, 1605–1612*, 27, 62, 84.

118. Kenneth R. Andrews, ed., *English Privateering Voyages to the West Indies, 1588–1595* (New York: Cambridge University Press, 1959), 189, 31–34, 38–39.

119. Imtiaz Habib, *Black Lives in the English Archives: 1500–1677* (Burlington, VT: Ashgate, 2008), 66. See also Stephen Alford, *London's Triumph: Merchants, Adventurers and Money in Shakespeare's City* (New York: Bloomsbury, 2017).

120. Andrew Lambert, *Seapower States: Maritime Culture, Continental Empires and the Conflict that Made the Modern World* (New Haven: Yale University Press, 2018), 165.

121. Steven Nadler, *Menasseh ben Israel: Rabbi of Amsterdam* (New Haven: Yale University Press, 2018).

122. Andrew C. Hess, *The Forgotten Frontier: A History of the Sixteenth-Century Ibero-African Frontier* (Chicago: University of Chicago Press, 1978), 99.

123. Brotton, *The Sultan and the Queen*, 186.

124. *The Arraignment, Tryal and Condemnation of Robert Earl of Essex and Henry Earl of Southampton at Westminster, the 19th of February 1600 and in the 43 Year Reign of Queen Elizabeth: For Rebelliously Conspiring and Endeavouring the Subversion of the Government by Confederacy with Tyr-Owen, that Popish Traytor and His Complices . . .* (London: Basset, 1679), Huntington Library. At the same site, see also Ralph Byrchensha, *A Discourse Occasioned Upon the Latr Defeat, Given to the Arch-Rebels Tyrone and O'Donnell, by the Right Honourable Lord Mountijoy, Lord Deputie of Ireland, the 24th of December 1601* (London: Bradock, 1602), Huntington Library.

125. Jane Hathaway, *The Chief Eunuch of the Ottoman Harem*, 77.

126. *The Sherley Brothers, An Historical Memoir of the Lives of Sir Thomas Sherley, Sir Anthony Sherley and the Sir Robert Sherley, Knights by one of the Same House* (Chiswick, UK: Whittingham, 1848), 9, 15, 21, 34, 71. Simon Adams et al., eds., *England, Spain and the Grand Armada, 1585–1604: Essays from the Anglo-Spain Conferences* (Edinburgh: Donald, 1991).

127. Joseph Creswell, Jesuit-Madrid to Sir Anthony Sherley, circa 1599, in Green, ed., *Calendar of State Papers, Domestic Series, of the Reign of Elizabeth, 1598–1601* (Nendeln, Liechtenstein: Kraus, 1967), 372.

128. J. P. D. Cooper, *The Queen's Agent: Francis Walsingham at the Court of Elizabeth I* (New York: Pegasus, 2013), 285. Cf. Nadine Akkerman, *Invisible Agents: Women and Espionage in Seventeenth Century Britain* (New York: Oxford University Press, 2018).

129. Vivien Kogut Lessa De Sa, ed., *The Admirable Adventures and Strange Fortunes of Master Anthony Knivet: An English Pirate in Sixteenth Century Brazil* (New York: Cambridge University Press, 2015), 29.

130. Brian Brege, "Renaissance Florentines in the Tropics: Brazil, the Grand Duchy of Tuscany and the Limits of Empire," in Elizabeth Horodowich and Lia Markey, eds., *The New World in Early Modern Italy, 1492–1750* (New York: Cambridge University Press, 2017), 206–22, 208.

131. John Vincent to Sir Frasier Englefield, June 21, 1593, in Mary Anne Everett Green, ed., *Calendar of State Papers, Domestic Series, of the Reign of Elizabeth, 1591–1594* (Nendeln, Liechtenstein: Kraus, 1967), 355–56. See also *A True*

and Strange Discourse of the Travails of Two English Pilgrimes . . . Jerusalem, Gaza, Grand Cayro, Alexandria and Other Places . . . (London: Archer, 1611), Huntington Library.

132. Malyn Newitt, ed., *East Africa: Portuguese Encounters with the World in the Age of Discoveries* (Aldershot, UK: Ashgate, 2002), 159.

133. Andrew Battell, *The Strange Adventures of Andrew Battell of Leigh, in Angola and the Adjoining Regions* (London: Hakluyt Society, 1901), ix.

134. Steven Epstein, *Speaking of Slavery: Color, Ethnicity, and Human Bondage in Italy* (Ithaca, NY: Cornell University Press, 2001), 36.

135. Jonathan Gathorne-Hardy, *The Epic Voyage of Thomas Dallam*, 90, 91, 95

136. John O. Hunwick, ed., *Timbuktu and the Songhay Empire: Al-Sa'di's Ta'Rikh al-Sudan Down to 1613 and Other Contemporary Documents* (Leiden: Brill, 1999), xxix.

137. Toby Green, *A Fistful of Shells: West Africa from the Rise of the Slave Trade to the Age of Revolution* (Chicago: University of Chicago Press, 2019), 138.

138. Butman and Target, *New World Inc.*, 205.

139. Roger Crowley, *Empires of the Sea: The Siege of Malta, the Battle of Lepanto, and the Contest for the Center of the World* (New York: Random House, 2008), 280.

140. Brotton, *The Sultan and the Queen*, 258, 269, 270, 189, 190, 191.

141. Gustav Ungerer, *The Mediterranean Apprenticeship of British Slavery* (Madrid: Editorial Verbum, 2008), 89, 91.

142. Denis Edwards to Thomas Lankford, Secretary to the Earl of Hertford, May 28, 1599, in Mary Anne Everett Green, ed., *Calendar of State Papers, Domestic Series, of the Reign of Elizabeth, 1598–1601*, 199.

143. Philippo Pigafetia, *A Report of the Kingdome of Congo, a Region of Africa, and of the Countries that Border Rounde About the Same . . . that the Blacke Colour which is in the Skinnes of the Ethiopians & Negroes & I . . . Proceedeth not from Sunne . . . Drawne out of the Writings and Discourses of Odoardo Lopes a Portugall*, trans. Abraham Hartwell (London: Wolfe, 1597), 9, 14, 27, 52, 53, 55, 57, Huntington Library: "The language of the people of Angola is all one with the language of the people of Congo . . . they are both but one kingdome . . . the men are blacke & so are the women . . . their hayre is black & curled." See also William Lithgow, *The Totall Discourse of the Rare Adventures and Painefull Peregrinations of Long Nineteene Years Travailes fro Scotland to the Most Famous Kingdomes in Europe, Asia and Africa* (London: Okes, 1640). Huntington Library.

144. Christopher Witzenrath, ed., *Eurasian Slavery, Ransom and Abolition in World History* (Burlington, VT: Ashgate, 2015), 25.

145. Giancarlo Casale, *The Ottoman Age of Exploration* (Oxford: Oxford University Press, 2011), 111.

146. Robert Garfield, *A History of São Tomé Island, 1470–1655* (San Francisco: Mellen University Research Press, 1992), v, 30, 41, 51, 76, 77, 79, 121, 123, 131, 137, 140, 142, 147, 148, 170. Revealingly, "Palmares" or a huge maroon community developed in Brazil shortly after the Amador episode and flight across the

Atlantic. This community, which may have contained 20, 000 individuals, lasted for decades and raised searching questions as to whether slave based colonialism on the Iberian model was sustainable. The competing model of London which tended to rule out an "escape hatch" for non-slave Africans and—most important—rule out religiously correct tests for settlers, proved to be more viable in the long run. See Glenn Alan Cheney, *Quilombo dos Palmares: Brazil's Lost Nation of Fugitive Slaves* (Hanover, CT: New London Librarium, 2014) and Carl Degler, *Neither Black nor White: Slavery and Race Relations in Brazil and the United States* (New York: Macmillan, 1971). See also Marcelo D'Salete, *Angola Janga: Kingdom of Runaway Slaves* (Seattle: Fantagraphics, 2019). Yet, as Palmares was surging, due south on the continent, enslaved Africans continued to arrive. One scholar has sought to "drastically upwardly revise estimates of the early South Atlantic Slave Trade," a commerce underestimated in prevailing databases and analyses. Buenos Aires, for example, was an "active hub for the Atlantic Slave Trade from its 1580 foundation. . . ." By 1581, a "group of English merchants eager to pry open trade with Brazil docked" nearby. London was "aware that Iberian domination over the Americas south of the equator was far from secure and viewed the Rio de la Plata as a strategic access point to Brazil and Peru. English merchants were in Brazil during the early sixteenth century to participate in the Brazilwood trade and heard of Portuguese gains in sugar and silver in the River Plate during the 1550s–1560s"; then "Drake's famous 1577 voyage, during which he spent twelve days in the Rio de la Plata estuary" brought added intelligence about this region to London. Predictably, "these English traders participated in piracy [and] slave trading. . . ." As was the case elsewhere, anti-Jewish fervor in Iberia compelled Jewish migration to this region, which in a sense was a boon for London (and Amsterdam). "The Rio de la Plata was a particularly active place to settle" for them, "due to its distance from the nearest Tribunal of the Holy Office of the Inquisition. . . ." In Bahia a "clergyman wagered that as many as three quarters of the European residents were 'New Christians,'" that is, of Jewish origin. The "practice of sending convicts from Buenos Aires to Angola," a hunting ground for enslavers, contributed mightily to a bloodily dissolute climate. There was a "three to four month crossing from Angola to the Spanish Caribbean" versus a "two month voyage to the Rio de la Plata," favoring the latter as a port of disembarkation. Inexorably, "Buenos Aires' slave supplies depended upon expanding military incursions in West Central Africa," a policy in which convicts were quite useful. Their presumed opposite was also essential to this deadly process in that "as many as 1000 enslaved Africans labored on Jesuit properties near Cordoba"—in today's Argentina—"during this period." See Kara Danielle Schultz, "'The Kingdom of Angola is Not Very Far from Here': The Rio de la Plata, Brazil and Angola, 1580–1680," PhD dissertation, Vanderbilt University, 2016, 4, 15, 19, 20, 21, 27, 30, 34, 40, 51, 57, 70, 131.

147. Green, *A Fistful of Shells*, 137, 143.

148. William Dalrymple, *The Anarchy: The Relentless Rise of the East India Company* (New York: Bloomsbury), 2019.

8. APOCALYPSE DAWNING

1. Mrs. Roger Pryor, *The Birth of the Nation: Jamestown, 1607* (London: Macmillan, 1907), 10, 83.

2. Carl Bridenbaugh, *Jamestown, 1544–1609* (New York: Oxford University Press, 1980), 20. See also William Wallace Tooker, "The Mystery of the Name Pamunkey," Springfield, Massachusetts, 1895, Huntington Library. John Garland Pollard, *The Pamunkey Indians of Virginia* (Washington, D.C.: Government Printing Office, 1894), New-York Historical Society. At the latter site, see also Frank G. Speck, *The Nantichoke and Conoy Indians* (Wilmington: Historical Society of Delaware, 1927).

3. Mrs. A. A. Blow, "An Address Delivered before the Daughters of the American Revolution at their Congress Held in Washington, D.C., April 1905," Huntington Library. At the same site see also Robert Lee Taylor, "Some Notes on the First Recorded Visit of White Men to the Site of the Present city of Richmond, Virginia, Saturday and Sunday May 23 and 24, 1607, a Paper Read at a Meeting of the Association for the Preservation of Virginia Antiquities . . . June 10, 1899 . . ." Richmond, 1899.

4. David Childs, *Invading America*, 149.

5. James Axtell, *Imagining the Other: First Encounters in North America* (Washington, D.C.: American Historical Association, 1991), Massachusetts Historical Society.

6. Captain Charles Leigh to Council, July 2, 1604, in Mary Anne Everett Green, ed., *Calendar of State Papers, Domestic Series, of the Reign of James I, 1603–1610* (Nendeln, Liechtenstein: Kraus, 1967), 127.

7. *Tercentary of the Landing of the Popham Colony at the Mouth of the Kennebec River* (Portland: Maine Historical Society, 1907), Massachusetts Historical Society. At the same site, see also *Colonial Schemes of Popham and Gorges. Speech of John Wingate Thornton . . . at the Fort Popham Celebration . . . August 29, 1862* (Boston: Balch, 1863).

8. Alfred A. Cave, "Why Was the Sagadahoc Colony Abandoned? An Evaluation of the Evidence," *New England Quarterly* 68, no. 4 (December 1995): 625–40, 625. See also Michael J. Puglisi, "Reading Between the Lines: Early English Accounts of the New England Indians," *Historical Journal of Massachusetts* 24, no. 1 (Winter 1996): 1–18.

9. *The Angola to Virginia Connection: 1619–1999* (Williamsburg, VA: Jamestown-Yorktown Foundation, 1999), University of Virginia, Charlottesville. See also Virginia Bernard, *A Tale of Two Colonies: What Really Happened in Virginia and Bermuda?* (Columbia: University of Missouri Press, 2011), 169: Bermuda, says the author, was "the first English colony to import Africans as laborers. Virginia was the second."

10. Andreas Jonas Ulsheimer, "Voyage, 1603–1604," in Adam Jones, ed., *German Sources for West African History, 1599–1699* (Wiesbaden: Steiner, Verlag, 1983), 18–43, 21, 23.

11. Conway Whittle Sams, *The Conquest of Virginia: The Forest Primeval . . .* (New York: Putnam, 1916). Cf. William Stevens Perry, "The Connection of

the Church of England with Early American Discovery and Colonization,"
Portland, Maine, 1863, Massachusetts Historical Society.

12. Henry Wilkinson, *The Adventures of Bermuda* (London: Oxford University
Press, 1933), 3, 5.

13. Biographies in Thomas Fortune Ryan, *The London Company of Virginia: A
Brief Account of its Transactions in Colonizing Virginia* (New York: London,
1908), Huntington Library [no page numbers]. At the same site, see also "A
True Declaration of the Estate of the Colonie in Virginia . . . published [at the]
Direction of the Councell of Virginia," London, 1610 and *An Apologie of the
Earle of Essex, Against those Which Jealously and Maliciously Tax Him to be the
Hinderer of the Peace and Quiet of His Country* (London: Bradocke, 1603).

14. Margaret Brent Downing, "The Development of the Catholic Church in the
District of Columbia from Colonial Times Until the Present," *Records of the
Columbia Historical Society* 15 (1912): 23–53, 29.

15. Anna Beer, *Patriot or Traitor: The Life and Death of Sir Walter Raleigh* (New
York: Oneworld, 2019).

16. Edward Graham Daves, "Raleigh's New Fort in Virginia, 1585," 1893,
Huntington Library.

17. Report of Father Antonio de la Ascension, November 27, 1602, in David Kipen,
ed., *Dear Los Angeles: The City in Diaries and Letters, 1542 to 2018* (New York:
Modern Library), 425. See also Mark Rifkin, *Beyond Settler Time: Temporal
Sovereignty and Indigenous Self-Determination* (Durham: Duke University
Press, 2017).

18. William Golant, *The Long Afternoon: British India, 1601–1947* (New York:
St. Martin's, 1975). K. N. Chaudhuri, *The English East India Company: The
Study of an Early Joint-Stock Company, 1600–1640* (London: Routledge,
1999) and Femme Gaastra, *The Dutch East India Company: Expansion and
Decline* (Zutphen: Walburg, 2003).

19. Jonathan Gathorne-Hardy, *The Epic Voyage of Thomas Dallam and His
Extraordinary Musical Instrument to Constantinople in 1599 and His Time in the
Palace and Harem of the Ottoman Sultan* (Norwich, UK: Propolis, 2017), 167.
See also Rupali Mishra, *A Business of State: Commerce, Politics and the Birth of
the East India Company* (Cambridge: Harvard University Press, 2018).

20. *A Briefe Relation of What is Happened Since the Last of August 1598 by
Coming of the Spanish Campe into the Dukedome of Cleue: and the Bordering
Free Countries, which with Most Odious and Barbarous Crueltie they take as
Enemies . . . and the King of Spaine . . . Faithfully Translated out of the Dutch*
(London: Wolfe, 1599), Huntington Library.

21. Bernardino de Mendoza, *Theorique and Practise of Warre. Written to Don
Philip, Prince Castil, by Don Bernardino de Mendoza. Translated out of
the Castilian Tongue into Englishe*, trans. by Sir Edwarde Hoby Knight
(Middleburg: Schilders, 1597), Huntington Library. At the same site, see also
*An Admonition Published by the General States of the Netherlandish United
Provinces . . . Touching His Now Intended Proceedings Against the Spaniards
and Their Adherents* (London: Dight, 1602).

22. See "Articles of Peace, Entercourse and Commerce, Concluded in the Names of the Most High and Mighty Kings and Prines . . . by the Grace of God, King of Great Britaine, France and Ireland, Defender of the Faith & Philip the Third, King of Spain. . . . and Albertus and Isabella Clara Eugenia, Archdukes of Burgundie. . . . in a treatie at Lodon the 18th Day of August after the Old Stile in the Yeere of Our Lord God, 1604. Translated out of Latine into English," 1604, Huntington Library.

23. Michael P. Winship, *Hot Protestants: A History of Puritanism in England and America* (New Haven: Yale University Press, 2019).

24. David Finnegan, Éamonn Ó Ciardha, and Marie-Claire Peters, eds., *The Flight of the Earls: Imeacht na nIarlaí* (Derry: Guildhall, 2010). See also William Allen, *An Admonition to the Nobility and People of England and Ireland Concerning the Present Warres Made for the Execution of His Holiness . . . by the Highe and Mightie Kinge Catholike of Spain* (Antwerp: A. Coninncs, 1588), Huntington Library.

25. Daniel Vitkus, ed., *Piracy, Slavery and Redemption: Barbary Captive Narratives from Early Modern England* (New York: Columbia University Press, 2001), 2.

26. His Catholic Majesty to Diego de Orellana de Chaves, September 10, 1596, Letters of King Philip II, Brigham Young University.

27. Secretary Pedro Zapara to Diego de Orellana de Chaves, 24 October 1596, Letters of King Philip II.

28. Secretary Juan Gallo de Andrade to Diego de Orellana Chaves, 12 February 1597, Letters of King Philip II.

29. Jonathan Gathorne-Hardy, *The Epic Voyage of Thomas Dallam*, 83.

30. Louis Tinoco to Queen Elizabeth, December 1593, in Mary Anne Everett Green, ed., *Calendar of State Papers, Domestic Series, of the Reign of Elizabeth, 1591–1594* (Nendeln, Liechtenstein: Kraus, 1967), 395.

31. Report, May 1, 1591, in Green, ed., *Calendar of State Papers . . . 1591–1594*, 35.

32. Report, June 20, 1591, in Green, ed., *Calendar of State Papers . . . 1591–1594*, 60.

33. Report, October 18, 1591, in Green, ed., *Calendar of State Papers . . . 1591–1594*, 114.

34. Report, February 12, 1593, in Green, ed., *Calendar of State Papers . . . 1591–1594*, 314.

35. Susan D. Amussen and David E. Underdown, *Gender, Culture and Politics in England, 1560–1640: Turning the World Upside Down* (New York: Bloomsbury Academic, 2017).

36. Peter Clark, ed., *The European Crisis of the 1590s: Essays in Comparative History* (London: Allen and Unwin, 1985).

37. Frank Welsh, *The Battle for Christendom: The Council of Constance and the Dawn of Modern Europe* (New York: Overlook, 2008), 27.

38. Stephen Charles Cory, *Reviving the Islamic Caliphate in Early Modern Morocco* (Burlington, VT: Ashgate, 2013), 198.

39. Mercedes Garcia Arenal and Gerard Wiegers, eds., *The Expulsion of the Moriscos from Spain: A Mediterranean Diaspora* (Leiden: Brill, 2014). Cf. *Three Miseries of Barbary: Plague, Famine, Civill Wars, with a Relation of the*

Death of Mahamet the Late Emperor: And a Briefe Report of the Now Present Wars between the Three Brothers (London: Gosson, 1607), Huntington Library.

40.   *Newes from Spain, The King of Spaines Edict for the Expulsion & Banishment of More than Nine Hundred Thousand Moores out of His Kingdome, Which Conspired and Plotted to Bring the Kingdome of Spaine under the Cover . . . of the Turks and Saracens,* 1611, Huntington Library. At the same site, see also *The Ottoman of Lazaro Soranzo . . . Mahomet the Third, Great Emperour of the Turkes . . .* , trans. Abraham Hartwell (London: Windet, 1603).

41.   See e.g. Robert Ashley, *Almansor, the Learned and Victorious King that Conquered Spain, His Life and Death* (London: Parker, 1627) and *The Ottoman of Lazaro Soranzo.*

42.   *The Fawkes's of York in the Sixteenth Century Including Notices of the Early History of Guye Fawkes: The Gunpowder Plot Conspirator* (Westminster: Nichols, 1850), Huntington Library. At the same site, see also *A Brief History of the Life of Mary Queen of Scots and the Occasions that Brought Her and Thomas Duke of Norfolk to their Tragical Ends. Shewing the Hopes the Papists then Had of a Popish Successor in England; and their Plots to Accomplish them . . . From the Papers of a Secretary of Sir Francis Walsingham* (London: Cockerill, 1681).

         At the same site, see also *A True Narration of that Horrible Conspiracy Against King James and the Whole Parliament of England Commonly Called the Gun Powder Treason* (London: Leigh, 1674) and John Parker, *History of Remarkable Conspiracies Connected with European History During the Fifteenth, Sixteenth and Seventeenth Centuries* (Edinburgh: Constable, 1829) and *The Tryal and Execution of Father Henry Garnet, Superior Provincial of the Jesuits in England for the Powder Treason by Roger Widdrington a Roman Catholick; and by Him Addressed unto Pope Paul the Fifth; Printed in Latin in 1616 . . . .now Published to Make it Further Evident that it is no New Thing for Jesuits to Curse and Ban, to Justifie a Lie* (London: Robinson, 1679) and Samuel Clarke, *The Gunpowder Treason: Being a Remembrance to England of that Ancient Deliverance from that Horrid Plot, Hatched by the Bloody Papists, 1605 . . . that God May Have Glory and Papists Perpetual Infamy* (London: Maxey, 1657) and *A True Narration of that Horrible Conspiracy against King James and the Whole Parliament of England Commonly Called Gunpowder Treason . . .* (London: Leigh, 1674).

43.   John Lambe to Dr. Neile, February 26, 1605, in Green, ed., *Calendar of State Papers . . . 1603–1610,* 200.

44.   W. J. Eccles, *The French in North America, 1500–1783,* 13, 14. See also *The History of the Famous Edict of Nantes Containing an Account of all the Persecutions that Have Been Built in France . . .* (London, 1694), Huntington Library. See also "Quatercentenary Celebration of the Promulgation of the Edict of Nantes, April 13, 1598" (New York: Huguenot Society of America, 2002), Massachusetts Historical Society.

45.   C. C. H., *The Massacre at St. Bartholomew and the French Revolution* (Boston: Medium, 1848), Huntington Library. At the same site, see also William Gammell, *The Huguenots and the Edict of Nantes: A Paper Read Before the*

Rhode Island Historical Society (Providence, RI: Providence, 1886) and *The King's Edict and Declaration upon the Former Edicts of Pacification* (London: Man, 1599).

46. *Cherokee Phoenix & Indian Advocate*, 28 May 1831. (This richly valuable newspaper can be found at the Huntington Library.)

47. Barbara and Henri van der Zee, *A Sweet and Alien Land: The Story of Dutch New York* (New York: Viking, 1978). See also Peter Mancall, *Fatal Journey: The Final Expedition of Henry Hudson—A Tale of Mutiny and Murder in the Arctic* (New York: Basic, 2009). See also G. M. Asher, *Henry Hudson the Navigator: The Original Documents in Which His Career Is Recorded, Collected, Partly Translated and Annotated* (New York: Franklin, 1963).

48. John Meredith Read, Jr., *A Historical Inquiry Concerning Henry Hudson, His Friends, Relatives and Early Life, His Connection with the Muscovy Company and Discovery of Delaware Bay* (Albany, NY: Munsell, 1866), 9, 14, 58, 129, 130.

49. License, June 1604, in Green, ed., *Calendar of State Papers . . . 1603–1610*, 121.

50. License, January 9, 1607, in Green, ed., *Calendar of State Papers . . . 1603–1610*, 344.

51. Martin Jacques, *When China Rules the World: The Rise of the Middle Kingdom and the End of the Western World* (London: Allen Lane, 2009).

52. Alan Gordon, *The Hero and the Historians: Historiography and the Uses of Jacques Cartier* (Vancouver: University of British Columbia Press, 2010); Ramsay Cook, ed., *The Voyages of Jacques Cartier* (Toronto: University of Toronto Press, 1993). See also Declaration to the Queen, January 1598 in Green, ed., *Calendar of State Papers, Domestic Series, of the Reign of Elizabeth, 1601–1603* (Nendeln, Liechtenstein: Kraus, 1967), I, 16: On May 3, 1588, "we granted a patent to merchants of Exeter, London and Barnstaple for 10 years of the sole traffic to the river of Venaga, and all along the coast of Guinea to the River of Gambia, which term is now about to expire." Not unconnected was a report soon thereafter, encased in the same volume, 306: Report, August 24, 1599: "License to John Evelyn and others for 10 years, of the sole making of saltpeter and gunpowder."

53. Matthew P. Romaniello, *The Elusive Empire: Kazan and the Creation of Russia, 1552–1671* (Madison: University of Wisconsin Press, 2012).

54. Priya Satia, *Empire of Guns: The Violent Making of the Industrial Revolution* (New York: Penguin, 2018), 267–68.

55. Bolivar Christian, *The Scotch Irish Settlers in the Valley of Virginia: Alumni Address at Washington College, Lexington . . .* (Richmond: Macfarlane and Ferguson, 1860), Huntington Library. For more on the "arch-traytor Tyrone," see Sir Thomas Stafford, *Pacata Hibernia . . . Ireland Appeased and Reduced or an Historie of the Late Warres of Ireland Especially within the Province of Mounster, Under the Government of George Carew . . . the Siege of Kinsale, the Defeat of the Earle of Tyrone, and his Armie; the Expulsion and Sending Home of Don Juan de Aguila, the Spanish Generall, with his Forces . . .* (London: A.M., 1633).

56. Report, 1601, in Green, ed., *Calendar of State Papers . . . 1601–1603*, 566. See also *A Discoverie Occasioned Upon the Late Defeat, Given to the Arch-Rebels Tyronne and ODonell by the Right Honourable the Lord Mountjoy, Lord Deputie of Ireland, the 24 of December 1601, Being Christmas Eave . . . By Raph Byrchesha* (London: ML, 1602) and *The Arraignment, Tryal and Condemnation of Robert Earl of Essex and Henry Earl of Southampton at Westminster the 19th of February 1600 . . . for Rebelliously Conspiring and Endeavoring the Subversion of the Government by Confederacy with Try-Owen that Popish Traytor and His Complices . . .* (London: Basset, 1679), Huntington Library. At the latter site, see also *A Letter Written out of England to an English Gentleman Remaining at Padua, Containing a True Report of a Strange Conspiracie, Continued Between Edward Squire, Lately Executed for . . . Treason . . . Against the Person of the Queen . . .* (London: Barker, 1599).

57. Royal Cedula-Madrid to Governor Gonzalo Mendez de Canzo, November 9, 1598, AGI 86-5-19, Santo Domingo 2528, John Stetson Collection.

58. Report by Fray Francisco de Pareja, October 12, 1599, AGI 54-5-20, Santo Domingo 235, John Stetson Collection.

59. Report, June 1, 1599, AGI 54-5-14. Santo Domingo 229, John Stetson Collection.

60. Report by Gonzalo Mendez de Canzo, February 28, 1600, AGI 54-5-9/32, Santo Domingo 224, John Stetson Collection.

61. Article by Susan Parker, February 7, 1999, vertical file on "Africans, First Spanish Period," St. Augustine Historical Society-Florida.

62. Report, November 27, 1601, AGI 54-5-9, Santo Domingo 224, John Stetson Collection.

63. Report, January 23, 1602, AAGI 54-5-14, Santo Domingo 229, John Stetson Collection.

64. Report, May 22, 1602, AGI 54-5-9, Santo Domingo 224, John Stetson Collection.

65. Report, May 22, 1602, Volume 5, Woodbury Lowery Papers.

66. Giles Van Harwick to Peter Artson, November 19–20, 1598, in Green, ed., *Calendar of State Papers . . . 1598–1601*, 119.

67. Royal Cedula-Valladolid to Pedro de Ibarra, February 10, 1603, AGI 86-5-19, Santo Domingo 2528, John Stetson Collection.

68. Pedro de Valdes to Madrid, September 22, 1603, AGI 54-1-16, Santo Domingo 100, John Stetson Collection.

69. Report to His Catholic Majesty, March 26, 1603, Carton 33, Herbert Bolton Papers, University of California, Berkeley.

70. Governor Pedro de Ibarra to Madrid, April 12, 1604, AGI 54-5-9/49, Santo Domingo 224, John Stetson Collection.

71. Governor Pedro de Ibarra to Madrid, December 26, 1605, AGI 54-5-9/65, Santo Domingo 224, John Stetson Collection.

72. Report from Maria de Junco, 1606, AGI 53-2-9, John Stetson Collection.

73. Report, August 1, 1607, AGI 54-5-9, John Stetson Collection.

74. Proposal by Kathleen Deegan, "Indians and Blacks in Colonial St. Augustine,"

1985–1986, vertical file on ,"Africans-First Spanish Period," St. Augustine Historical Society.

75. Jacqueline Fretwell, St. Augustine Historical Society, to Isaiah Williams, April 14, 1989, vertical file on "Blacks-Miscellaneous," St. Augustine Historical Society: "The first Negro child born in St. Augustine was Agustin, legitimate son of Agustin and Francisca, slaves . . . baptized Sunday August 20, 1606": note that it is likely there were earlier Negro births on the peninsula before this date.

76. William Channing, *A Letter on the Annexation of Texas to the United States* (London: Green, 1837), Missouri Historical Society-St. Louis.

77. Theodore G. Vincent, *The Legacy of Vicente Guerrero: Mexico's First Indian President* (Gainesville: University Press of Florida, 2001).

78. Theda Perdue, *The Cherokee Removal: A Brief History with Documents* (Boston: St. Martin's, 2016) and Theda Perdue, *The Cherokee Nation and the Trail of Tears* (New York: Viking, 2007).

79. See e.g. Ray Allen Billington, *The Protestant Crusade, 1800–1860* (New York: Macmillan, 1938); Leonard Dinnerstein, *Antisemitism in America* (New York: Oxford University Press, 1994).

80. Report, November 6, 1607, AGI 54-5-9/79, John Stetson Collection.

81. Fray Alsonso de Penaranda to Madrid, January 1608, AGI 54-5-9/82, John Stetson Collection.

82. Royal Cedula to Bishop of Cuba, November 8, 1608, AGI 87-5-2, Tomo V, Mexico 1065, John Stetson Collection.

83. Governor Pedro de Ibarra, August 22, 1608, AGI 54-5-9/96, John Stetson Collection.

84. Royal Cedula to Governor de Ibarra, November 8, 1608, AGI 87-5-2, Tomo V, Mexico 1065, John Stetson Collection.

85. Royal Cedula to Bishop of Cuba, November 8, 1608, AGI 87-5-2, Tomo V, Mexico 1065, John Stetson Collection.

86. Governor de Ibarra to Madrid, January 6, 1609, AGI 54-5-9/98, John Stetson Collection.

87. Geronimo de Torres to Fray Geronimo Santiago, April 1609, AGI 53-2-10, John Stetson Collection.

88. Directives, June 19, 1609 and October 20, 1609, AGI 2-5-3/16, John Stetson Collection.

89. Report by Governor Pedro de Ibarra, November 28, 1609, AGI 54-3-6, John Stetson Collection.

90. Royal Cedula-Madrid to Governor of Cuba, Gaspar Ruiz de Pereda, March 30, 1611, John Stetson Collection.

91. Herbert Eugene Bolton, "The Mission as a Frontier Institution in the Spanish American Colonies," *American Historical Review* 23, no. 1 (October 1917): 42–61, 43, 45, 52, 61. See also Mary Ross, ed., *Writings and Cartography of Herbert Eugene Bolton Reprinted from New Spain and the West* (1932), Huntington Library.

92. Satia, *Empire of Arms*, 193, 213, 220, 229, 237, 254, 262, 285, 371, 379.

93. See e.g. *A Petition Against the Jewes Presented to the Kings Majestie and the Parliament Together with Several Reasons Proving the East India Trade, the Turkey Trade . . . May all be Driven Without Transporting Gold or Silver out of England . . .* (London: Violet, 1661): "The Jewes are so hated by the Turks . . . these Jewes are the greatest blasphemers of Christ of any people in the world, so that if they be permitted to continue amongst us they will bring the wrath of God upon us . . . [they] are either by birth, Portugals or Spaniards . . . the Jewes in all countries they come into are generally counterfeiters of money and adulterers of all manner of merchandise."

94. Des Ekin, *The Stolen Village: Baltimore and the Barbary Pirates* (Dublin: O'Brien, 2006).

95. Des Ekin, *The Last Armada: Queen Elizabeth, Juan del Aguila, and Hugh O'Neill: The Story of the 100 Day Spanish Invasion* (New York: Pegasus, 2015), 13, 38, 287, 336, 340. Brian Mac Cuarta, S.J., ed., *Reshaping Ireland, 1550–1700: Colonization and Its Consequences* (Dublin: Four Courts, 2011). See also *A Watch Worde for Warre . . . Rumors Amongst Us and the Suspected Coming of the Spanyard Against Us. Wherein We May Learned how to Prepare Ourselves to Repell the Enemie and to Behave Ourselves . . .* (Cambridge: Legal, 1596), Huntington Library. At the same site, see also Thomas Long, *A Compendious History of all the Popish & Fanatical Plots and Conspiracies Against the Established Government in Church & State in England, Scotland, and Ireland . . .* (London: Brown, 1684).

96. Michael Wolff, *Siege: Trump under Fire* (New York: Holt, 2019), 235. See also Abigail Pogrebin, *Stars of David: Prominent Jews Talk About Being Jewish* (New York: Broadway, 2005), 118, 220: The late U.S. diplomat Richard Holbrooke mentioned that the financier and former U.S. envoy to France, Felix Rohatyn, observed that "French articles about him always referred to him as Jewish, where American articles never mention it." My interpretation of this duality is that in the United States the construction of "whiteness" has subsumed being Jewish to a greater degree than in France. In a similar contrast between the "old continent" and the North American republic, William Kristol, a panjandrum of hardline conservatism in the United States, as a youth attended a Hebrew school in an Orthodox Spanish-Portuguese synagogue in Manhattan: "Shearith Israel is the grand Sephardic synagogue in New York," he recounted, That is, hundreds of years after the Sephardim were ousted from Iberia, some found a comfortable new home in the republic, where "whiteness" often trumped ethno-religious identity. Of course, there are those who insist that the words of Holbrooke and Kristol illustrate how progressive the republic is compared to the "old continent."

97. Dagomar Degroot, *The Frigid Golden Age: Climate Change, the Little Ice Age and the Dutch Republic, 1560–1720* (Cambridge: Cambridge University Press, 2018); Bruce M. S. Campbell, *The Great Transition: Climate, Disease and Society in the Late Medieval World* (Cambridge: Cambridge University Press, 2016).

98. Sam White, *A Cold Welcome: The Little Ice Age and Europe's Encounter with*

North America (Cambridge: Harvard University Press, 2018), 3, 21, 22, 23, 73, 75, 76, 79, 80, 82, 83, 132, 236.

99.   Robert Bullard, ed., *Confronting Environmental Racism: Voices from the Grassroots* (Boston: South End, 1993).

Index